LETTERS OF JEWS THROUGH THE AGES

FROM BIBLICAL TIMES TO THE MIDDLE OF THE EIGHTEENTH CENTURY

Edited, with an Introduction, Biographical Notes and Historical Comments

by

FRANZ KOBLER

VOLUME ONE

EAST AND WEST LIBRARY

First Edition 1952
Second Edition 1953
First Paperback Edition 1978

East and West Library,
a subsidiary of
Hebrew Publishing Company
80 Fifth Avenue
New York, N.Y. 10011

ISBN: 0-85222-212-2

Printed in the United States of America

WASSERSTROM

PART ONE

Letters from the times of the Kings, Prophets, Priests and Makers of the Talmud

FROM THE END OF THE EIGHTH CENTURY B.C.E.

TO THE FIFTH CENTURY C.E.

LETTERS OF JEWS THROUGH THE AGES

EDITED BY F. KOBLER

1. SEAL OF "SHEMA, SERVANT OF JEROBOAM", probably Jeroboam II, king of Israel (reigned 785–745 B.C.E.), cut into Jasper. Found at Megiddo in 1904.

TO MY WIFE
DORA

CONTENTS

VOLUME ONE

PART ONE

Letters from the times of the Kings, Prophets, Priests and Makers of the Talmud

FROM THE END OF THE EIGHTH CENTURY B.C.E. TO THE FIFTH CENTURY C.E.

PART TWO

Letters from the times of the Geonic and Spanish periods

FROM THE EIGHTH TO THE END OF THE FIFTEENTH CENTURY

VOLUME TWO

PART THREE

Letters from the times of the Mystics and Humanists

FROM THE BEGINNING OF THE SIXTEENTH TO THE MIDDLE OF THE EIGHTEENTH CENTURY

LIST OF ILLUSTRATIONS

Sincere thanks are due to all who have afforded facilities in the collection of the illustrations, especially to the Rev. M. Elton, Librarian, and to Miss Lehmann, of Jews' College, London.

PREFACE

Remember me by your letters, as is the custom among the Children of Israel, so that, when they are separated, writing brings them near again.

LEONE DA MODENA

MESSAGES have been exchanged between men since the beginning of civilization. For thousands of years they were conveyed to their destinations by the spoken words of messengers. But when readable signs replaced oral transmission a new and momentous phenomenon came into being: the letter. Whatever the material used for it – whether it was cut into clay, wood or wax, or written on bamboo, potsherds, parchment, papyrus or paper – the letter gave the first wings to man. It became the magic vehicle by which he himself – not a stranger – transmitted news, wishes, thoughts and feelings to other men in distant places. The written message extended the sphere of the individual and widened infinitely the range of human neighbourhood. It has multiplied the richness of our life, and from a merely utilitarian means of communication has become the most intimate link between men.

Letters have been written in almost all languages, and they have played an outstanding part in the development of all nations which have acquired the skill of writing. But the function of the letter in the life and history of *one* nation, the people of Israel, is peculiar and, indeed, unique. There are many reasons for this. One can certainly hardly conceive that letter-writing should anywhere have been put to better use or been more urgently necessary than among a people that from an early period continuously suffered the fate of exile and dispersion, and yet remained one family, striving incessantly to preserve its own unity and at the same time to maintain fruitful relations with the surrounding world. The combination of all these exceptional conditions led to a letter-writing activity the records of which extend – with rare intervals – over a period of nearly three thousand years – almost the whole of Jewish history itself.

A few traces only are left of Jewish letters written in antiquity –

they extend, nevertheless, over more than a millennium. But letters written in the language of ancient Israel did not disappear when the Hebrew tongue ceased to be the means of oral communication. It may even be said that the more the Diaspora spread in time and space, the more the Hebrew – and, in modern times, the Yiddish – letter became an instrument of holding the Jewish people together. Written by Jews in the language of their forefathers, of their prayers and studies, or in the plain vernacular of their daily life, these letters carried with them the atmosphere of the Jewish home and helped both to cement the family bond between the scattered Children of Israel and to preserve the values of Judaism. Through these letters Jews visited their distant brethren, fathers taught their sons, sages instructed their pupils, legal decisions were requested and given. It was through letters that the persecuted people raised their voices, and that they received consolation and help. In fact, all aspects of Jewish life were encompassed by this correspondence conducted over a great part of the globe through the ages.

But while Hebrew and Yiddish letters continued to serve the internal needs of the Jewish community, letters written in other languages became a channel through which Jews imbibed the spirit of their environment, and Jewish values began to influence the Gentile world. There is, within the orbit of Mediterranean and Western civilization, practically no language in which Jews have not maintained written intercourse, from the Persian, Greek, Latin and Arabic up to the modern languages. In the ability to carry on correspondence in foreign languages they have in fact excelled to such a degree that many Jews are counted among the greatest letter-writers of various nations.

The purpose of this work is to gather some leaves from all the branches of this huge correspondence, and to survey through such a selection the development of Jewish letter-writing from biblical to modern times. The present volumes cover this development from its beginning up to the dawn of the era of Emancipation, while a separate selection is planned for an analogous survey of the last two hundred years, a period of unprecedented upheaval in all spheres of Jewish life, including correspondence.

The widest possible definition of the letter has been adopted for this first general anthology of Jewish letters. 'Letters are experiences,' said Adolph Deissmann; and in accordance with this classical dictum any written communication to one or more persons which originated in an actual occasion has been regarded as a genuine letter. The sharp distinction, however, drawn by the eminent biblical scholar between 'letter' and 'epistle' did not seem suitable as a selective principle of this work. The intimate character that he rightly ascribes to the letter in its proper sense is often not lacking in learned Hebrew correspondence, while on the other hand the all-pervading element of learning transforms many personal Jewish letters into works of literature. While, therefore, fictitious letters have been, as a rule, excluded from the selection, open and learned letters of all kinds, including the Responsa, have been deemed admissible.

In general, the historical or intrinsic quality of a letter has served as the primary selective criterion. But alongside of important messages which influenced the life and thoughts of the whole people, plain letters carrying us – to use another of Deissmann's felicitous expressions – 'into the sacred solitude of simple, unaffected humanity' are also given a place. This work aspires indeed equally to be a treasury of famous historic documents and to revive the delicate charm of letters which belong to 'the gentler department of epistolary literature', as David Kaufmann, the great pioneer of Jewish epistolography, has called this rather neglected category of letters.

It was not regarded as the task of this work to unearth unknown documents, but rather to select from the letters scattered in biblical and post-biblical records a series of specimens illustrative of Jewish history, particularly on its spiritual side, and to present them in chronological order. Even so, the number of Jewish letters to be found in editions of single or collected letters over the long period surveyed here is so vast that to be really adequate any selection from this printed material would have to extend over a considerable series of volumes. Thus countless letters no less worthy of our attention than many which have been included in this book can be found in the available sources. I have tried, however, to do justice to some of the omitted gems by referring to them in the Introduction. There is particularly *one* species of letters which is not represented in the selection proper, although this category – the early Christian epistles – comprises the most influential and some of the most magnificent letters written by Jews. But any attempt to offer an instructive and impartial selection from these letters (which are easily accessible in numberless canonized and modern editions) within a special survey of Jewish letters would not only go beyond the scope of the present book but also impair the equilibrium of this survey because for reasons deeply rooted in the basic difference between Judaism and Christianity no corresponding letters of the great Rabbis from the same period are available. Nevertheless, the reader will find in the Introduction an appreciation of that special province of Jewish letter-writing which is the domain of Paul and the other early builders of the Church.

The work has, however, not been conceived merely as a selection of memorable single letters, but, at the same time, as a survey of Jewish *letter-writers.* With a few exceptions, for which there were special reasons, all correspondents represented within these pages were, at least originally, members of the House of Israel. They have been selected on the same principle as were the letters. Unknown men and women will, therefore, be found side by side with celebrated historical figures. On the other hand, particular selections from the letters of eminent letter-writers have been made with a view of bringing into relief their personalities and specific epistolary styles.

I have applied to the presentation of the letters the method adopted by me in previous publications. This method is to place each letter or group of letters in its proper setting by means of a brief historical or biographical introduction, in some cases also of a postscript recording the effect of the letter. In the present volume seventy-eight chapters, divided into three epochs, have been thus formed. Their sequence is sufficiently close to make the whole suitable for continuous reading. The quotation prefixed to each letter strikes, as it were, its keynote; in addition, the Introduction will enable the reader to fit each one into the general framework of the 'Story of Jewish Letter-writing'.

With the exception of the letters originally written in English, all the letters are presented in translations from the various languages – Hebrew, Aramaic, Arabic, Greek, Latin, Spanish, Portuguese, French, Italian, German and Yiddish. Wherever standard translations into English or adequate renderings into other modern languages were available, they have been reproduced or used as a basis for the present translation. Many of the letters have been translated specially for this book from the original languages (see Bibliography). Any textual criticism is, however, beyond the purpose of this work. For the reader who desires to penetrate more deeply into the texts, the Bibliography offers the necessary references. Economy of space and other reasons made in many cases abridgments of the letters indispensable. The omitted passages, whether long or short, have been indicated by three dots. The dates prefixed to the letters, within square brackets, are intended for the guidance of the reader and should not be taken as belonging to the original, although such dates sometimes occur.

The book is primarily designed for the general reader who will find himself introduced by it to the most reliable and most intimate sources of Jewish history and tradition. Another feature of the book may, however, appeal also to the trained student of Judaism to whom some parts of the selection will not be new: the synoptical treatment of Jewish letter-writing, designed to exhibit the world of Jewish letters in its totality, and to bring out its specific character, particularly its introspective note. If what Thomas Jefferson has said is correct, that 'the letters of a person form the only and genuine journal of his life', the amazing continuity and variety of Jewish letter-writing may justify us in saying that Israel's autobiography has been written in the letters of its children. In them, perhaps even more than in its literature, Israel has left the true record of its soul. The persistence of Jewish life through the millennia, the unbroken spiritual continuity of generations, the firm hold which the dispersed people, amidst a mostly hostile world, retained on the foundations of its religion, its yearning after the sacred homeland and its unshakable faith in a final redemption, all these genuine Jewish values, as also the results of the impact on the Jew by foreign influences are nowhere better traceable than within the corpus of Jewish correspondence.

There was never a time in Jewish history which called more emphatically for such an introspection than the present. In suffering and destruction, but equally in fulfilment of exalted hopes, the Jewish generation of these days has surpassed all previous experiences. Between the depth of the past and the heights in prospect for the future, the Jew of today may be ready for a dispassionate self-examination. This is indeed the hour to turn over the pages of ancient letters and to listen to the voices of the past.

This book is, however, also addressed particularly to non-Jewish readers who are eager to look behind the curtain drawn between them and the Jewish world by prejudice, hatred and ignorance. It is true they will rarely meet here love-letters or letters of a merely entertaining character such as many anthologies of letters offer in abundance. But the receptive minds among these readers will hardly fail to perceive the divine spark which illumines not only the messages of Israel's prophets and sages but even the utterances of many minor members of this perennial family of letter-writers.

★

The *Letters of Jews through the Ages*, originally planned as a single volume of 'Israel's Letters', was begun in London in the middle of World War II at the suggestion of Prof. Simon Rawidowicz, now at Brandeis University, Waltham, Massachusetts, Editorial Director of the 'Ararat' Publishing Society, London. I wish to record my indebtedness to Prof. Rawidowicz not only for this first impulse but also for the close interest he has taken in my work in its various stages. When after the completion of the projected final volume the first general survey of Jewish letters will become available, this will be due largely to the efforts of Prof. Rawidowicz.

The preparation of the book, although far advanced during my stay in England, was destined to be completed in the New World. In the vicissitudes of these years the loyal adherence of the publishers to the plan gave me constant encouragement. My special gratitude is due to Messrs. Alexander and Benzion Margulies, Directors of the 'Ararat' Publishing Society, for their generous co-operation in all steps necessary for the completion of this volume. Their exemplary devotion to the cause of the Jewish book, shown on this and other occasions, has contributed essentially to the publication of this work. I likewise wish to express my appreciation of the readiness of Dr. B. Horovitz, Director of the Phaidon Press and of the East and West Library, London, to join in this undertaking and to assist in the production of the book with his great experience and the resources of his distinguished publishing house. My special thanks are due to Dr. I .Grafe, Editorial Assistant of the East and West Library, and to Mr. William Margulies, Hon. Secretary of the 'Ararat' Publishing Society, for their untiring efforts in settling the countless technical details, and especially for their never-failing patience in maintaining for this purpose a long-drawn correspondence between London and San Francisco.

In my research work and in the framing of the book I was fortunate enough to enjoy the aid of numerous friendly helpers on this and the other side of the Atlantic. I extend to all of them my sincere gratitude. I must record my indebtedness particularly to Rabbi Dr. Arthur Loewenstamm, Assistant to the Principal of the Society for Jewish Study, London, whose loving and unselfish co-operation was for me a perennial source of encouragement, for extensive assistance in translations, advice on various matters, and free access to his library; to Mr. Maurice Simon, the noted scholar and translator of the Zohar, whose contribution to the final form of this book has been invaluable, for the indefatigable and erudite efforts he has bestowed on the revision and stylistic improvement of the manuscript, for helpful criticism and suggestions, and for careful assistance in proof-reading; to Dr. Solomon A. Birnbaum, University of London, for valuable counsel and for supplying important material; to Dr. Joseph L. Blau, Assistant Professor at the Columbia University, New York, for early editorial assistance and harmonious co-operation; to Mr. Shelomo Auerbach, London, Dr. J. Maitlis, London, Dr. William L. Markrich, Berkeley, California, Dr. Ernst Müller, London and Mr. A. Schischa, Letchworth, for their friendly collaboration, especially by assisting in translations; to Mr. Chaim Bloch, New York, Dr. David Diringer, Cambridge, Dr. Walter Eckstein, New York, Dr. Aaron Steinberg, London, and Dr. Max Weinreich, Research Director of the Yiddish Scientific Institute YIVO, New York, for references and useful suggestions, to Dr. Kurt Rathe, Rome, for a special research in the Vatican Library into the letters of Ansaldo Cebà; and to Prof. Walter J. Fischel, University of California, Berkeley, California, Mr. Max Markrich, San Francisco, Dr. Richard Teltscher, London, for the supply of material and loan of books.

I remember thankfully two dear friends and helpers who passed away during the preparation of this work: Rabbi Dr. S. Baron, formerly in London, subsequently in St. Louis, Missouri; and Mr. Ernst Foges, at that time in London, both of whom assisted in translations.

A grateful acknowledgment of all the kind permissions granted by authors, translators and publishers will be found on pp. xxvii–xxix. The appended Bibliography is also intended as a tribute to the hosts of scholars who by their research work furnished much essential material for this selection.

Finally, I cannot omit to record my gratitude to my wife, Dora Kobler, for the enthusiastic and active interest with which she accompanied this work from its very inception to its completion. No words of thanks can be adequate to her inspiring co-operation, her tireless assistance in research and many other ways, and above all for her unsparing labours in overcoming the difficulties encountered on the long road to the ultimate goal.

FRANZ KOBLER

San Francisco, California
September 1951

ACKNOWLEDGMENTS

Grateful acknowledgment is made and special thanks are due to the following authors, translators, holders of copyrights and publishers for permission to use their publications (indicated below and in the Bibliography) for the reproduction of letters and other material listed in the Bibliography:

William Foxwell Albright:

1. *The Oldest Hebrew Letters: the Lachish Ostraca*, in the *Bulletin of the American School of Oriental Research*, 1938.
2. *A re-examination of the Lachish Letters*, ibid., 1939.
3. *The Lachish Letters after five years*, ibid., 1941.

George Allen & Unwin, London: *The Correspondence of Spinoza*, translated and edited by A. Wolf.

Behrman House Inc., New York: *The Memoirs of Glückel of Hameln*, translated with Introduction and Notes by Marvin Lowenthal.

The Clarendon Press, Oxford:

1. *Aramaic Papyri of the Fifth Century B.C.*, edited with translation and notes by A. Cowley.
2. *The Jews in Egypt and Palestine under the Fatimid Caliphs*, by Jacob Mann.

Dropsie College for Hebrew and Cognate Learning, Philadelphia:

1. 'Jewish Quarterly Review':
   - (*a*) Hartwig Hirschfeld, *The Arabic Portion of the Cairo Genizah*, O.S. XVI, 1904.
   - (*b*) L. M. Simmons, *The Letter of Consolation of Maimun ben Joseph*, O.S. II, 1890.
   - (*c*) Moses Maimonides, *A Letter to the Jews of South Arabia, entitled* '*The Inspired Hope*,' translated by Sabato Morais, N.S. XXV, 1934–35.
   - (*d*) *Joseph Ezobi's Silver Bowl*, translated by J. Friedmann, O.S. VIII, 1895
   - (*e*) E. N. Adler, *A Letter of Menasseh ben Israel*, O.S. XVI, 1904.
   - (*f*) *Testament of Leb Norden*, O.S. IV, 1892.
   - (*g*) S. Schechter, *An unknown Khazar Document*, N.S. III.
2. *The Life and Works of Moses Hayyim Luzzatto*, by Simon Ginzburg.

Henry George Farmer: *Maimonides on Listening to Music*, from the Responsa of Moses ben Maimon, Medieval Jewish Tracts on Music, Bearsden, 1941.

William Heinemann Ltd., London: *The Works of Josephus*, translated by Henry St. John Thackeray, The Loeb Classical Library.

The Jewish Historical Society of England, London:

1. Lucien Wolf, *Jews in Elizabethan England*, Transactions J.H.S.E. Vol. XI.
2. Cecil Roth, *Leone da Modena and England*, Transactions J.H.S.E. Vol. XI.
3. E. N. Adler, *About Hebrew Manuscripts*, Transactions J.H.S.E. Vol. V.
4. Cecil Roth, *New Light on the Resettlement*, Transactions J.H.S.E. Vol. XI.
5. Lucien Wolf, *Crypto-Jews under the Commonwealth*, Transactions J.H.S.E. Vol. I.

The Jewish Publication Society of America, Philadelphia:

1. The Holy Scripture according to the Masoretic text: A New Translation.
2. *Saadia Gaon, His Life and Works*, by Henry Malter.
3. *Post-Biblical Hebrew Literature*, an Anthology, translated and edited by B. Halper.
4. *Hebrew Ethical Wills*, edited and translated by Israel Abrahams.
5. *Maimonides*, by David Yellin and Israel Abrahams.
6. *Studies in Judaism*, by S. Schechter.
7. *The Jews in Spain*, by Abraham A. Neuman.
8. *History of the Jews*, by H. Graetz, translated by Bella Lowy.
9. *The House of Nasi – Doña Gracia*, by Cecil Roth.
10. *The House of Nasi – The Duke of Naxos*, by Cecil Roth.
11. *A Life of Menasseh ben Israel*, by Cecil Roth.

Jews' College: The Jews' College Jubilee Volume, *R. Solomon Luria on the Prayer Book*, translated by B. Berliner.

John Lane The Bodley Head Ltd., London (The Viking Press, New York): *The Messiah of Ismir Sabbatai Zevi*, by Joseph Kastein, translated by Huntley Paterson.

Cecil Roth:

1. *Leone da Modena and the Christian Hebraists of his age*, Jewish Studies in Memory of Israel Abrahams, New York, 1927 (Jewish Theological Seminary).
2. *Quatre Lettres d'Elie da Montalto, Contribution à l'histoire des Marranes*, Revue des Études Juives.
3. *Early Aliyoth*, New Judaea, 1934.

(Other works by Cecil Roth, see under the headings: The Jewish Historical Society of England; The Jewish Publication Society of America; The Soncino Press, London.)

ACKNOWLEDGMENTS

Routledge & Kegan Paul, London:
1. *Moses Maimonides, The Guide of the Perplexed*, translated by Mr. Friedländer.
2. *Jewish Travellers*, edited by Elkan N. Adler.

Joseph Sarachek: *Don Isaac Abravanel*, Bloch Publishing Co., New York.

Society for Promoting Christian Knowledge, London: *The Letter of Aristeas*, translated by Henry St. J. Thackeray.

The Soncino Press, London: *Anglo-Jewish Letters*, edited by Cecil Roth.

The Wellcome Trust (The Wellcome-Marston Archæological Research Expedition to the Near East), London: *The Lachish Letters* (Lachish I), by Harry Torczyner, Lankester Harding, Alkin Lewis, J. L. Starkey.

Yiddish Scientific Institute – YIVO, New York: *Private Letters in Yiddish of* 1588, by Dr. B. Weinryb, in Historiše Šriftn fun YIVO II.

Solomon Zeitlin: *Maimonides, A Biography*, Bloch Publishing Co., New York.

Every endeavour has been made to give due acknowledgment to copyrighted material, but if nevertheless there has occurred any omission in this list, the Publishers offer their apologies. If informed, they will repair the omission in any subsequent edition.

INTRODUCTION

The Story of Jewish Letter-Writing

INTRODUCTION

The Story of Jewish Letter-Writing

I

THE PRELUDE: THE LETTERS OF THE BABYLONIANS, THE TELL EL-AMARNA LETTERS, AND THE ORAL MESSAGES OF THE HEBREWS

THE land from where Abraham came, ancient Mesopotamia, has to be regarded as the cradle of letter-writing. Thousands of preserved clay tablets inscribed with cuneiform writing provide an overwhelming evidence that long before the beginning of recorded Jewish history, in the first half of the second millennium B.C.E., at the time of Hammurabi, and earlier, royal, private and business letters were forwarded on the roads of the vast Babylonian empire. Also in Egypt, the other powerful neighbour of Palestine, with its predilection for written records, letter-writing flourished prior to the entry of Israel on the stage of history. Actually the earliest documents of Hebrew history are letters written by Egyptian vassals, some petty kings and governors of Syria, to the Pharaohs Amenophis III and his successor, Amenophis IV, the famous Akhnaton. These letters, composed in the Babylonian language, the diplomatic idiom of those days, and inscribed in cuneiform writing on hundreds of clay tablets, were discovered in 1888 in Egypt on the site of Akhnaton's residence, Tell el-Amarna. They confirm in an astonishing way the correctness of the biblical account. For the letters teem with references to the invasion of Canaan from across the Jordan by the Habiru and Sagaz, and there is now little doubt that these invaders have to be identified with the Hebrews. Particularly the letters addressed to Akhnaton by Abdi-Khiba, Governor of Jerusalem, about 1370 B.C.E., read like a dramatic supplement to the Book of Joshua. Abdi-Khiba's desperate appeals for help, such as is contained in the following letter, forecast indeed the impending conquest of Canaan by the Children of Israel:

Let the king care for his land, and be heedful of his land. The whole territory of my lord, the king, has fallen away. Ilimilku is destroying the entire land of the king. Let my lord, the king, care for his land. I say: 'I will go to my lord, the king, and see the countenance of my lord, the king.' But the enemy is powerful against me; therefore I am unable to come to my lord, the king. Hence may it seem right to my lord, the king, to send troops so that I may come and see the countenance of my lord, the king. As true as my lord, the king, lives, whenever an officer goes forth I say: 'The land of my lord is going to ruin.' If you do not listen to me all the princes will be lost, and my lord, the king, will have no more princes. Let the king think of the princes and let my lord, the king, send troops. The king has no longer any territory. The Habiri have devastated all the territory of the king. If troops come this year the territory will remain my lord, the king's, if no troops come the lands of my lord, the king, will be lost.

To the scribe of my lord, the king: Abdi-Khiba, thy servant. Bring these words, unaltered, before the lord, the king: 'The whole territory of my lord, the king, is going to ruin.'

In striking contrast to the abundant documentation of the development shown by Babylonian, Egyptian and even Canaanite letter-writing of the second millennium B.C.E., we are confronted with a complete lack of any surviving Hebrew letters from that period, whether in original or in record. To be sure, the scarcity of early Hebrew inscriptions is a general phenomenon, and many reasons which have been advanced for the loss of ancient Hebrew documents apply especially to letters. The possibility that already the early Hebrews exchanged written messages cannot, therefore, be excluded. The most momentous invention made by the Palestinian Semites, if not by the Hebrews themselves, probably in the second quarter of the second millennium B.C.E., the purely alphabetic writing, provided certainly an ideal instrument for that purpose. Moreover, the practice of letter-writing would have been in conformity with the widespread literacy of the Israelites which is repeatedly confirmed by the Bible. The 'Booktown' Kiriath Sepher, and the young man who, according to Judges VIII. 14, after having been captured and questioned by Gideon, wrote down the names of the seventy-seven Elders and Princes of Succoth, are telling witnesses in this repect. And the ordinance to write the divine commandments upon the posts of the house and on the gates could only be given to a people well and generally versed in the technique of writing.

And yet there is no reference made to any letter – neither in the Pentateuch, nor in the Books of Joshua, the Judges and, with only one exception, even in the two Books of Samuel. Apart from this single, relatively late, specimen (see below, p. xxxvi), not one of the many messages quoted in these books is a written document. They form, it is true, with their admirably accurate wording, with their profound psychological understanding and differentiation, a magnificent sequence of human communications. There are private messages of a subtle intimacy among them, like Abraham's courting message to his kin delivered by his servant (Gen. XXIV. 34–49), Jacob's offer to his brother Esau (Gen. XXXII. 5–6), or Joseph's invitation to Jacob, one of the most pathetic messages ever sent by a son to his father (Gen. XLV. 9–11). There are the majestic diplomatic addresses despatched by Moses from Kadesh to Edom (Num. XX. 14–17) and from the wilderness of Kedemoth to Sihon, King of Heshbon (Deut. II. 26–27), asking free passage with the most precise safeguards against any abuse. And there are finally the colourful messages of David recorded in the Books of Samuel, as the offer of friendship extended to the churlish Nabal (1 Sam. XXV. 6–8), the welcome to the men of Jabesh-Gilead, and the exciting message sent by the King after his tragic victory over his son Absalom to the priests Zadok and Abiathar (2 Sam. XIX. 12–13):

> Why are ye the last to bring the king back to his house? For the speech of all Israel is come to the king, to bring him to his house. Ye are my brethren, ye are my bones and flesh: wherefore then should ye be the last to bring back the king?

Whether the precise records of all these and other messages were based on transmitted reports or are to be regarded as inventions of the biblical narrators, they seem to provide a sufficient proof that the Hebrews, up to the beginning of David's reign (1013–973), decidedly preferred oral to written communications. We may assume that various factors were working in this direction: the reverence of the wandering tribes for the ancient customs, their predilection for the word spoken from mouth to mouth, and perhaps an innate shyness to use writing for other purposes than the preservation of the divine law.

2

THE MOST ANCIENT BIBLICAL LETTERS: FROM DAVID TO HEZEKIAH

About four centuries had to elapse after the period of the Tell el-Amarna letters before the first known Hebrew letter was written. This letter is inserted in the graphic story of David's passion for Bathsheba, the beautiful wife of Uriah the Hittite. We are nearing the climax of this thrilling biblical drama of crime and punishment, when we read in 2 Sam. XI. 14–15:

> And it came to pass in the morning that David wrote a letter to Joab and sent it by the hand of Uriah. And he wrote in the letter saying:
>
> Set ye Uriah in the forefront of the hottest battle, and retire ye from him, that he may be smitten, and die.

The biblical narrative links this first-included specimen of letter-writing – the ill-famed Uriah-Letter – with a series of tragic events: the execution of the King's order by the submissive Joab, Uriah's death in battle announced to David by Joab in a shrewd oral message, the curse pronounced by the prophet Nathan against the house of the King, David's repentance, and the death of the child born to him by Bathsheba. A deep religious meaning is hidden behind this episode. Actually the vain secrecy of men's wicked deeds, symbolized by David's treacherous letter, is contrasted with God's omniscience.

It is significant that the next biblical instance of letter-writing is also concerned with an analogous motive. As David was seized with the desire for the wife of Uriah, so Ahab, King of Samaria (876–843) and his wife Jezebel coveted the vineyard of Naboth the Jezreelite. Moreover, the letter which Jezebel, according to 1 Kings XXI. 9–10, wrote in several copies in Ahab's name to the nobles of the city of Naboth and sealed with the King's seal, seemed to be modelled on David's letter to Joab:

> Proclaim a fast, and set Naboth at the head of the people. And set two men, bad fellows, before him, and let them bear witness against him, saying, Thou didst curse God and the king. And then carry him out, and stone him that he die.

The analogy applies also to the ultimate consequence of Jezebel's successful treachery: the divine punishment pronounced against the King, the Queen, and Ahab's posterity. Jehu, Jehoram's general and anointed king, proceeds against Ahab's descendants in the same way as Jezebel acted against Naboth: with treacherous letters, composed with even a greater refinement and cruelty (2 Kings x. 2, 3, 6).

The history of Israel's letters thus starts with an emphatic warning against the temptation inherent in the letter as a secret instrument of man. Homer's Iliad, too, contains in the sixth book, v. 160 ff., the story of a treacherous letter, the only letter mentioned in the Greek epic. But this Homeric tale is devoid of the religious and moral implications which lend a special colour to the biblical treatment of the motive. Significantly, all the other messages connected with the fate of Uriah, Naboth and the sons of Ahab are oral messages. The ghastly letters appear indeed as anomalies, and not as normal means of communication. Written in a poignant style, 'sharp and short like an arrow', as Joel Müller, the classical historian of early Hebrew letters, has said of them, devoid of greetings and any concluding formula, they resemble secret weapons of kings rather than letters.

According to the Antiquities of Flavius Josephus, the next biblical example of early Hebrew letters is not Jezebel's deadly order but a very edifying document: the message of King Solomon to Hiram, King of Tyre, containing the request for assistance in the building of the Temple in Jerusalem. Josephus quotes the alleged epistle of Solomon, deviating somewhat from the texts given in 1 Kings v. 17–20 and 2 Chron. II. 2–9, as follows:

> Know thou that my father would have built a temple of God, but was hindered by wars, and continued expeditions; for he did not leave to overthrow his enemies till he made them all subject to tribute: but I give thanks to God for peace I at present enjoy and on that account I am at leisure, and design to build a house of God, foretold to my father that such an house should be built by me; wherefore I desire thee to send some of thy subjects with mine to cut down timber, for the Sidonians are more skilful than our people in cutting wood. As for wages to the hewers of wood, I will pay whatsoever price thou shalt determine.

Josephus asserts emphatically that Solomon's message as well as Hiram's answer, declaring his readiness to have many large cedar trees cut down and sailed as floats to any desired destination, were letters, and that authentic copies of them were still preserved in his days in the state archives of Tyre. The biblical sources, however, give the impression that Solomon's communication was oral (1 Kings v. 16; 2 Chron. II. 2). Tempting as it may be, therefore, to believe that the text of a letter written by David's great son was transmitted to posterity, the statement of Josephus can hardly be accepted.

Nevertheless, the period of David's and Solomon's reigns marks the beginning of Hebrew letter-writing. A special guild of scribes (sopherim), confined to particular families, is attested in Scripture (1 Chron. II. 55). They were in charge of the royal records and correspondence. Although no original letters are extant from the first four hundred years of the Hebrew kingdoms, the great number of preserved stone seals indicates the frequency of documentation and correspondence in the early centuries of the first millennium B.C.E. The first written royal message occurring in the Bible after the letters of David, Jezebel and Jehu belongs, however, to the memorable age of King Hezekiah (720–692). It is to be found in the Second Book of Chronicles (XXX. 1–9) and is ascribed to King Hezekiah himself (see Chapter 1). Although it is highly probable that this letter – an invitation to the Temple in Jerusalem – was composed by the Chronicler, it remains the only example of this kind in Scripture. It is incidentally the first letter called 'Iggereth', an expression which was to replace the original designation of the written message, 'Sepher' (a generic name for all kinds of writing), and was bound to become the commonly accepted designation of the letter.

3

THE ADDRESSES OF THE PROPHETS AND JEREMIAH'S LETTER TO THE EXILES

Not more than one instance of a letter written by a prophet in the early times to which the first royal letters belong is to be found in Scripture. This missive ('Mikhtav') was, according to 2 Chron. XXI. 12–15, addressed by the prophet Elijah – as must be supposed, shortly before his death – to Jehoram, King of Judah (851–844) and contained the prophecy of the king's doom. This isolated specimen of an early prophetic letter, probably a composition of the Chronicler, does not contradict but rather confirms the assumption that the spoken rather than the written word was originally the specific medium of prophetic inspiration.

This picture did not change substantially even after the appearance of the 'writing prophets' whose rise begins with Amos in the middle of the eighth century B.C.E. Now, too, the voice of the prophet remained the main instrument of his activity. At the gate of the Temple, in the streets and on the crossroads, in the palace of the kings, everywhere were heard the addresses of the inspired men who felt themselves 'under special commission from Jahweh to preach to his people' (W. F. Albright).

So great was the magic of these oral addresses that they still retained their arresting power when the prophets wrote them down, or their scribes, such as Jeremiah's Baruch, recorded them on dictation. Thus a new literary type of a unique beauty and significance was created. Max Weber called it 'the earliest known pamphlet literature of immediate political actuality'. But although the addresses of the prophets defy this and any literary classification, especially also the inclusion into the category of letters, they are inseparably linked with the history of letter-writing by the profound influence they have exerted upon the epistolary expression of Israel and all nations. They were bound to become the great inspiration for all religious and moral manifestos, for every kind of impassioned 'J'accuse' raised by men throughout the ages, and in this way the forerunners and unsurpassed models of all the open letters and epistles which have contributed to the elevation of humanity.

As a mighty signpost pointing in this direction stands the momentous call sent by Jeremiah in the year 594 B.C.E. to the exiles in Babylonia (Jer. XXIX. 1–23; see Chapter 2) among his own and the other oral prophetic addresses. Its genuineness and epistolary character is established beyond any doubt. The emotional effect of this incomparable letter on those to whom it was addressed must have been overwhelming. Heinrich Graetz has suggested that it perhaps inspired the prophet Ezekiel to step to the forefront. Certainly the impression made by its message on the captives changed their entire attitude to the life in the exile. The impulse given by it to the Jewish people has even continued to work throughout the ages up to the present day. It may be regarded as the patriarch of Jewish letters, the first of the recorded specimens sent from the Land of Israel to Jews living in another country.

4

THE OLDEST HEBREW LETTERS PRESERVED IN THE ORIGINAL

That the age of Jeremiah was already a period of highly developed correspondence among Jews is shown by another letter sent from Babylonia to Jerusalem in response to Jeremiah's letter (see p. 7–8). References to letter-writing occur also in other prophetic books (cf. Is. XXIX. 11–12, Ezek. II. 8–10; III. 1–3, Zech. V. 1–3).

Only recently, however, an archæological discovery of the highest importance has shed a brilliant light on the state of letter-writing in the days of Jeremiah and in the biblical era in general. The potsherds found in 1934 by the Wellcome Exploration Commission under J. L. Starkey at Tell ed Duweir, in Palestine, at the site of the biblical fortress town Lachish, proved to be the first – and up to this moment the only – unearthed original letters written in biblical times. The decipherment of these inscribed ostraca, the so-called Lachish Letters, has revealed that they are the remnants of a correspondence between Ya'osh, probably the military commander of Lachish, and Hoshaiah, an officer of the Jewish army, and that they were written during the fateful campaign of Nebuchadnezzar against the kingdom of Judah (see Chapter 3). Apart from their immense value for the religious, political and cultural history of the Jews, they provide evidence of the high standard and intensity of Jewish letter-writing in the days before the destruction of Solomon's Temple.

5

LETTERS FROM PERSIA

Jeremiah's epistle and the Lachish Letters are, to our present knowledge, the last extant specimens of Hebrew letter-writing from the biblical epoch. To be sure, the final historical books of Scripture, those of Ezra and Nehemiah, contain more exact texts of letters than any other part of the Bible, but these are, without exception, letters written by Persian kings and officials (see Chapter 4). Even Nehemiah's answer to Sanballat's letter (Neh. VI. 8–9) is once again a verbal message, though he refers in VI. 17 to an exchange of of letters between the nobles of Judah and Tobiah, leader of the

Samaritans. The Book of Esther, too, does not contain an exact reproduction of the letters which Mordecai and Esther sent to the Jews in order to institute the festival of Purim (Esther IX. 20–31). According to the Midrash, however, the whole Book was composed as a letter to the Jewish people.

6

ARAMAIC AND GRAECO-JEWISH LETTERS

The discovery of a hoard of Aramaic papyri in Elephantine (Egypt) at the beginning of this century revealed the existence in the sixth and fifth century B.C.E. of a Jewish military colony in southern Egypt, and threw much light on the social and religious life of the Jews in that remote corner of the ancient world. A substantial part of these invaluable documents are state papers and private letters, which until the discovery of the Lachish Letters were the oldest extant original specimens of Jewish correspondence. They testify to a high standard and great intensity of letter-writing among the Jews outside Palestine during the restoration of the Jewish Commonwealth and shortly afterwards (see Chapter 5).

A gap of about three hundred years separates these documents from the next known Jewish letters. These are from the second century B.C.E., and were either written originally or recorded in the Greek language. They have been incorporated in the Books of the Maccabees and offer distinguished examples of the epistolary art developed by the Jews of the Hellenistic epoch (see Chapters 7 and 8). Another, though undoubtedly artificial, example of their skill in Greek letter-writing is the so-called 'Letter of Aristeas'. Its author was apparently an Alexandrinian Jew of the second century B.C.E., who told the fanciful story of the origin of the Septuagint in the guise of a letter addressed by an Alexandrinian Greek to his brother. He even included in his narrative the texts of the letters allegedly exchanged between Ptolemy Philadelphus, King of Egypt, and Eleazar the High Priest (see Chapter 6).

Perhaps the most memorable among the extant Græco-Jewish letters is the letter which King Agrippa I, the grandson of Herod and Mariamne, wrote to Caligula, the Roman emperor, to avert the exhibition of the megalomaniac despot's image in the sanctuary of the Temple (see Chapter 11). In spite of its predominantly political significance, the note of self-revelation permeating this historic document lends to it the emotional character of a personal letter. Whether Philo who inserted the letter in his report about his own mission to Rome on behalf of the Jews was the author of this admirable document can only be a matter of conjecture. If he indeed composed this letter or participated in its drafting, we should have in it the only example of a letter written by the great philosophical harmonizer of Judaism and the Hellenic spirit.

The other eminent Græco-Jewish writer of the first century C.E., Flavius Josephus, has, unfortunately, left but few and by no means characteristic traces of his letters in his works. It must be particularly regretted that out of his correspondence with Agrippa II, the last king of Judaea, only a few short letters of the king are to be found in the autobiography of Josephus (see Chapter 12).

7

THE LAST EXTANT HEBREW LETTERS WRITTEN BEFORE THE FALL OF THE SECOND TEMPLE

Even scarcer than the remnants of the Græco-Jewish correspondence from the last centuries of Judaea's existence are the surviving examples of Hebrew letter-writing from that period. With the exception of the moving call sent probably by Rabbi Simeon ben Shetah to Rabbi Judah ben Tabbai, urging the great teacher to return from his exile to Jerusalem (see Chapter 9), and of Rabban Gamaliel's letters addressed from Jerusalem to Jewish communities in order to fix the calendar and to announce the time for the delivery of tithes (Chapter 10), no letter of the great Tannaite masters of the first centuries before and after the beginning of the Christian era is recorded. If a conclusion can be drawn from these few specimens and some Talmudical fragments of the second century C.E. (four letters written by Rabban Simeon ben Gamaliel about Calendar matters), we may assume that the rabbinic letters of that era resembled rather the terse Sayings of the Fathers than the elaborate letters of contemporary Greek, Roman or later Jewish sages. It is also noteworthy that even in Hellenistic literature, apart from the 'Letter of Aristeas' and a likewise apocryphal letter of Jeremiah, no traces of Jewish epistolary writings are extant.

8

THE JEWISH-CHRISTIAN INTERLUDE

It happened, nevertheless, at this juncture that Jewish letter-writing was called to a task which was to become probably the greatest achievement ever accomplished by means of letters. Paradoxically this supreme effort involved a tragic conflict with Judaism because its purpose consisted in the promotion of the new creed which, although born within the people and fold of Israel, and destined to become the spiritual link between Judaism and the Gentile world, was bound to separate itself from the maternal soil and to bring about the most ominous schism ever experienced within Israel. For letters make up the largest and incidentally the oldest part of the collection of writings called the New Testament. They were composed in the Greek vernacular of those days, the so-called Koinē, and in the Greek epistolary style, but Jews were their authors, above all Saul of Tarsus who became Paul the Apostle and thus the chief architect of the Christian Church. He must be also considered as the chief promoter of the Christian Epistle.

While Jesus of Nazareth, like the prophets of old and the pharisaic Rabbis, had used the spoken word for his teaching, Paul, according to his own confession a feeble orator, used the letter besides preaching as a main instrument for the dissemination of the new faith. This practice was a new phenomenon, unknown to any other people or religion, and even to Judaism itself. Although, as we have seen, the later prophets inaugurated the custom of transmitting religious notions by recording their speeches, actual prophetic letters remained extremely rare. To be sure, these written addresses and the general example of the prophets undoubtedly inspired the most famous of Rabban Gamaliel's disciples, and without them the Epistles could not have been written. But Paul's letters differed radically from the recorded speeches through which the word of the Lord was conveyed to the multitude of a whole people. Although destined to be read by countless millions, they were real letters addressed on special occasions to particular recipients and permeated to the utmost by the singular personality of their writer.

The ten Epistles generally recognized as genuine among the thirteen letters ascribed to Paul are addressed to seven various early

Christian congregations, those of Thessalonica (Salonica), Galatia, Rome, Corinth, Colossae, Ephesus and Philippi. There is also a purely private letter to a single addressee to be found among Paul's canonized Epistles, the letter to Philemon. Not only this intimate letter containing a delicate plea for a fugitive servant, written like those to the Ephesians and Philippians at the end of Paul's life during his imprisonment in Rome, but practically all letters of Paul are concerned with specific needs, problems and affairs of the addressees. In addition, they contain numerous references to actual events, many personal remarks and abundant, carefully worded greetings. Above all, every line of Paul's letters is pervaded by his own powerful and exuberant spirit. He made the letter a fiery vessel of his visions, passions and ideas, preached and confessed, argued, attacked and persuaded with the written word, whether it was put down by himself or, as it happened mostly, dictated and signed by him.

There is a definite relation between this overwhelming subjectivity of epistolary expression and Paul's passionate desire of propagating his personal belief in the messiahship and divinity of Jesus, just as, on the other hand, the super-personal addresses of the prophets were congenial to their faith in the one and invisible Lord. The mystical views of the Hellenistic Jew who, after having lost his firm hold of the world of the Torah, looked for a transcendent redemption, manifested themselves perfectly within the compass of a private correspondence with new communities of believers linked with him by the same personal faith and by his superior will. Thus each of Paul's letters marks one of the irretrievable steps leading him out of the House of Israel. Very significantly, therefore, has one of them, the Epistle to the Galatians, been called the 'Christian Declaration of Independence'.

And yet Paul has styled himself most emphatically one 'of the stock of Israel, of the tribe of Benjamin, an Hebrew of the Hebrews; as touching the law, a Pharisee' (Phil. III. 5). Moreover, modern criticism has thrown much light on Paul's Jewish bias. A Christian theologian, Arthur D. Nock, declared that there is not a paragraph in Paul's writings which does not include subconscious recollections of the Greek Old Testament, while Joseph Klausner maintains that Paul was even well acquainted with the Hebrew Scripture. Klausner also demonstrated how Paul availed himself of the typical Talmudic method of Scriptural exegesis, after the manner of the Midrash. Others have pointed to the numerous Hebraisms in Paul's language. It is true, Paul used these Jewish elements mostly for his attempts to prove the truth of his personal belief and to depreciate the doctrine of Judaism. Nevertheless, even by this practice all strata of Israel's sacred literature and oral tradition were poured into the Epistles and were amalgamated with the intimacy of the private Greek letter. Moreover, Judaic notions, particularly the Jewish, indeed the Pharisaic, conception of ethics, again and again break through the assertions of the Apostle with their original vigour and colouring. Thus the most sublime among all passages of Paul's letters, the celebrated 'Hymn of Love' (I Cor. XIII) offers a striking analogy to Rabban Johanan ben Zaccai's likewise most famous saying, in which preference is given to the 'good heart' over all other values (Sayings of the Fathers, II. 3). But above all, in the great Epistle to the Romans, although it contains Paul's basic ideas on the 'abrogation of the Torah' and the charge of 'Israel's blindness . . . until the fullness of Gentiles come in' (XI. 25), Paul has formulated his ethical teaching almost entirely with the words of the Torah and the Rabbis, as the following passage and the references to biblical and Talmudic quotations may indicate:

> Recompense to no man evil for evil.[1] Provide things honest in the sight of men. If it is possible, as much as lieth in you, live peacefully with all men. Dearly beloved, avenge not yourselves,[2] but rather leave it to the wrath of God: for it is written, Vengeance is mine[3]; I will repay, saith the Lord. Therefore if thine enemy hunger, feed him; if he thirst, give him drink: for in so doing, thou shalt heap coals of fire on his head.[4] Be not overcome by evil, but overcome evil with good (Rom. XII. 17–21).
>
> Owe no man any thing, but to love one another: for he that loveth another, hath fulfilled the law. For this, Thou shalt not commit adultery, Thou shalt not kill, Thou shalt not steal, Thou shalt not bear false witness, Thou shalt not covet[5]; and if there be any other commandment, it is briefly comprehended in this saying, Thou shalt love thy neighbour as thyself.[6] Love worketh no ill to his neighbour; therefore love is the fulfilling of the Law.[7] (Rom. XIII. 8–10)

Thus while Paul broke away from both the Jewish faith and Hebrew epistolary tradition, he brought about a new synthesis of Judaic values with Greek thought and the Hellenic art of letter-writing. What constituted a painful separation from the corpus of

Israel's letters was destined to prove, on the other hand, one of the mightiest impulses Western letter-writing has ever received.

Besides the above-mentioned authentic letters of Paul, eleven other letters have been canonized by the Church. Some of these have been ascribed to Paul, while the remainder are believed to have been written by other founders of the new religion: Peter, James, John and Jude. The true authorship of these letters is still uncertain, their Jewish origin is, however, unquestionable.

Two of these letters deserve particular attention: the Epistle to the Hebrews (commonly ascribed to Paul, but not written by him) and the General Epistle of James. The author of the former – whether he was, as it is said, the Alexandrinian learned Jew Apollos, or the Jewish native of Cyprus, Barnabas, or another Hellenized Jew – elaborated in his eloquent appeal to the Hebrew adherents of the new creed a comparison of Moses and Jesus, and, in the highly emotional Chapter XI, a panegyric of Faith, calling the great characters of the Holy Writ, from Abel to David, as witnesses of his christological interpretations. Entirely different in character is the Epistle that traditionally is ascribed to James, the oldest among the brothers of Jesus. He was, on account of his righteousness, called 'the Just', and while being an adherent of the Nazarenes strictly observed the ceremonial law. The Epistle is unique among the Christian letters in many respects. Apart from two short references to Jesus, no mention is made of him in all the 108 verses of the letter. It refers, however, to Abraham, Isaac, Elijah and Job, and is addressed to 'the twelve tribes in the dispersion'. But above all, the ethical ideas that are expressed in the letter not only show a complete harmony with those of Hebrew Scripture and the Talmud, but they also, in contrast to Paul's and the other early Christian letters, form the *only* contents of the Epistle. Thus, instead of being a typical Christian epistle, the letter of James represents rather the type of a Jewish letter of Admonition (see below, pp. lxvi f.), as may be illustrated by the following short excerpt:

Know this, my beloved brethren, let every man be swift to hear,[8] slow to speak,[9] slow to wrath[10]: for the wrath of man worketh not the righteousness of God. Wherefore lay apart the filthiness and superfluity of naughtiness; and receive with meekness the engrafted word which is able to save your souls.[11] But be doers of the word, and not hearers only,[12] deceiving your own selves. . . . If any man among you seem to be religious, and bridleth not his tongue,[13] but deceiveth his own heart, this man's religion is vain. Pure religion and undefiled before God and the Father is this: to visit orphans and widows in their affliction[14] and to keep himself unspotted from the world (I. 19–22, 26–27).

Hearken, my beloved brethren, Hath not God chosen the poor of this world rich in faith, and heirs of the kingdom which he hath promised to them that love him?[15] But ye have despised the poor. Do not rich men oppress you, and draw you before the judgment seats? Do not they blaspheme the worthy name by which ye are called?

If ye fulfil the royal law according to the scripture,[16] Thou shalt love thy neighbour as thyself, ye do well; but if ye have respect to persons, ye commit sin, and are convinced of the law as transgressors. For whosoever shall keep the whole law, and yet offend it in one point, he is guilty of all[17] (II. 5–10).

The enigma presented by the predominantly Jewish character of this Epistle has been thoroughly discussed by Christian and Jewish scholars in recent times. To some of them the fierce attack made in the letter against the adherents of the belief in the 'justification of faith' has suggested that it was written by a Nazarene in direct opposition to the teaching of Paul. Arnold Meyer, however, who devoted to the Epistle a voluminous treatise, holds that the letter was originally an allegorizing address of Jacob the Patriarch, composed by a Jewish author of the first century C.E., and was only later, probably after Paul's death, reshaped by an early Christian.

9

LETTERS OF THE TALMUDIC PERIOD

While the creation of the Christian Epistle marks the rise of a new epistolary branch within the Gentile world of letters, it meant nothing else than a short interlude in the millennial history of Jewish letter-writing. We may assume that the Hellenized Jews who were susceptible to the preaching of the Gospel also assimilated their letters to the new religious style. Thus some of the letters preserved on the Oxyrhynchus papyri showing such an influence might have been written by Jewish Christians. But as far as the Hebrew letter-writing in Palestine and Babylonia is concerned, the effect of the Jewish-Christian Epistle was totally negative and even adverse to the development of epistolary communication, at least on religious subjects. There is not only no reference to be found to any of the Christian Epistles in the vast body of the Talmud, but the avoidance of a polemical correspondence and the general rejection of letter-writing on sacred matters was one of the weapons used by the makers of the Talmud in their struggle against the rising tide of Christianity. The Rabbis, referring to passages of Scripture (particularly Deut. XVII. 11), maintained that the Law was to be taught and interpreted by oral tradition only, which they, as Rabbi Akiba put it, considered as a 'fence to the Torah'. The warning of Kohelet (XII. 12) against the making of books also was understood as an approval of this attitude and especially cited in condemnation of the mystical and allegorical literature of the Hellenistic era. There seems therefore, to exist a kind of causal relation between the use of letters for the propagation of the Christian faith and the almost complete lack of Hebrew or other letters written by confessing Jews during the first centuries of the Christian era.

Besides these spiritual reasons, political motives too strengthened the reluctance to cultivate letter-writing on a large scale in this period. An unguarded expression in writing could easily lead to persecution in the restless days of a permanent rebellion against the foreign rule. This reason may also explain the silence of the Jews in the face of the momentous offer of the emperor Julian the Apostate to rebuild the Temple, while the issue of a letter from Galilee, expressing Messianic hopes in the most terse form, was prompted by over-optimistic rumours due to a favourable gesture made by the Empress Eudocia (see Chapter 13).

Even when, after the completion of the Mishnah, there was constant intercourse between the Palestinian and Babylonian schools, oral transmission remained the chief vehicle by means of which the Rabbis of the two lands communicated their ideas to one another. Nevertheless, with the beginning of the third century learned questions and answers in writing began to be exchanged rather frequently between Babylonia and Palestine. In the fourth century, learned correspondence became even more general. These early rabbinic letters, as we can judge from the traces left in the Talmud, excelled by their brevity and rigid restriction to their subject matter. The great Amoraim (commentators) and their successors, the Saboraim (thinkers), still anxious to avoid the transmission of human decisions by writing, phrased their answers in familiar verses of

Scripture; they paid great attention to calligraphy and used ruled lines in the manner of the Holy Writ. Thus began the practice of Scriptural quotation, which was to become a distinctive and dominant feature of later Hebrew letter-writing.

10

THE RESPONSA OF THE BABYLONIAN GEONIM

We can do no more than conjecture the frequency, contents and style of the correspondence which was maintained between Hebrew scholars during the period of about three hundred years from the fourth century onward, because no records of these letters have been preserved. The fact that learned correspondence became more and more frequent in the last centuries of the Talmudic era can be inferred from the Talmudical prescription that scholars should settle only in places where there were special letter-writers, called 'lablarim' (Lat. *libellarius;* Sanh. 17a). We know even of the correspondence of a prominent Jew with a distinguished non-Jew – the exchange of letters maintained in the fourth century for many years between the Patriarch Gamaliel ben Hillel and the Syrian Hellenist Libanius, a favourite of the Emperor Julian, on the affairs of the Jewish community, of which only those of the non-Jewish correspondent have been preserved. But it was not before the beginning of the eighth century that a mighty current of learned rabbinic correspondence emerged from Babylonia (see Chapter 14).

The Talmudic schools of Babylonia, especially those of Sura and Pumbedita, had acquired an undisputed authority over the Diaspora. Jews in all countries looked to the heads of these schools, the Geonim (Excellencies) for advice and guidance. It became customary to submit questions to them in writing and ask for a reply. Thus steady streams of enquiries (Sheelot) were sent to Babylonia from all corners of the Diaspora, and were answered in a return stream of Responsa (Teshubot, i.e. replies) of the Geonim. The Hebrew letter triumphed over all the objections entertained against its use and even began to dominate Jewish life. The Geonim felt themselves responsible for the moral behaviour of their brethren, for their ways of life and their obedience to God, and used letter-writing for this sublime task with supreme mastery, as is pointed out by Israel Abrahams: 'The

Geonim never waste a word; they are rarely overbearing in manner but mostly use a tone which is persuasive rather than disciplinary. The Geonim were, in this real sense, therefore, princes of letter-writing.'

From the beginning of the sixteenth century up to recent times collections of these Responsa have been published. Numerous manuscripts discovered in our own days have furnished new material which has revealed to us the vast range of subjects treated by the Geonim. In addition to strictly legal matters, religious problems are dealt with, ranging from the order of the prayers (see Chapter 15) to the treatment of dissidents (see pp. 69 f.). The Geonim also had to answer geographical and historical queries. Thus the Responsum of the Gaon Zemah ben Hayim of Sura to the inquiry of the community of Kairuan about the fanciful stories of the adventurous traveller Eldad the Danite concerning the Lost Tribes (end of the ninth century) constitutes one of the first geographical and ethnographical records in medieval Hebrew literature, while, a century later, another query sent from the same community to the great Gaon Sherira of Pumbedita produced in reply the famous 'Sherira-Letter', the chief source of our knowledge about the composition of the Talmud (see pp. 116 ff.). Nor was philosophy banned from the orbit of the Geonic Responsa. Gaon Hai, Sherira's illustrious son, was a thinker who gave profound answers to questions on mysticism and God's prescience (see pp. 123 ff.).

II

PALESTINE AND EGYPT AS CENTRES OF MEDIEVAL JEWISH CORRESPONDENCE AND THE APPEARANCE OF SAADIA GAON

In general the Palestinian scholars, who also styled themselves Geonim, tried to emulate their Babylonian colleagues of Sura and Pumbedita, for the most part without attaining their level. Gaon Solomon ben Yehuda, in the first half of the eleventh century, maintained a particularly extensive Hebrew correspondence (see Chapter 21). But once again Egypt was destined to play an even more prominent part in the history of Jewish letter-writing than its ancient homeland. The former Hellenistic centre remained, under the Arab rule of the Fatimids, the emporium of the Mediterranean. A rich and vigorous life continued to flourish there in the still great and influential Jewish community and gave birth to a network of correspondence which was carried on within the country itself, and also linked the communities on the Nile with the rest of the Jewish world.

Almost nothing was known of this rich material until the great discovery of the Genizah at Cairo by Dr. Solomon Schechter in 1897. Genizah means literally a storehouse, actually a storehouse of discarded books and manuscripts. But it would be much more appropriate to call this hoard of invaluable Hebrew writings and records, accumulated during centuries in its hiding place, a treasure house of Jewish history. Although scores of experts have worked for decades to exploit this literary California, many mines have still been left untouched. But the admirable achievements of Solomon Schechter himself, of the late Prof. Jacob Mann, Prof. Davidson and many other scholars have enriched Jewish literature, illuminated Jewish history, and corrected many received opinions. They have, above all, made a highly spectacular, and certainly the most extensive, contribution to the history of Jewish letter-writing.

Letters, originals and copies, written in Hebrew on countless papyri, constitute one of the most valuable parts of this material. A considerable number belong to the Geonic period. Among them are many personal letters of the Geonim which reveal the human side of the authors more fully than do the Responsa (see the letter of Hai Gaon, on pp. 127). In addition, there are numerous letters written by the dignitaries of the communities dealing with communal affairs, above all with the cause of ransoming the captives (see Chapter 24); letters written in prison with requests for intervention; letters of recommendation, either written in distant countries (see Chapters 25 and 27) or produced on the spot (see Chapter 23); the letter of a sick man who asks the Gaon in Jerusalem to include him in his prayers; letters of travellers just arrived in the country; and business letters from neighbouring lands and from as far away as India (see Chapter 32). And there are – for the first time in medieval Jewish history – letters of women, telling in a moving way the stories of their needs and desires (see Chapters 26 and 34). We have, indeed before us a splendid display of various Jewish letters which, written in a cultivated Hebrew style by people well versed in Scripture and later

Jewish literature, are worthy companions to the numerous Geonic Responsa found in the same spot.

Egypt also gave birth to Saadia of Fayum, the founder of medieval Jewish religious philosophy. Though only a few of Saadia's letters – apart from numerous Responsa – are extant, the superiority of the sage in letter-writing too is established by these examples (see Chapter 16). The doughty fighter who conducted with indomitable spirit his polemics with Ben Meir about the Calendar, with the Karaites (see a specimen of their letters in Chapter 17), and with the Prince of the Captivity (the Exilarch), showed himself very human in letters to his pupils (see pp. 79 ff.). The most important contribution made, to our present knowledge, by Saadia to letter-writing is, however, the great Epistle he addressed to a Jewish community on the occasion of his inauguration as Gaon of Sura (see pp. 84 ff.). With a deep understanding of the suggestive power of rhythmical repetition, Saadia, in this letter, transmits a summary of Jewish wisdom in thirty appeals to the Children of Israel.

12

THE COURSE OF THE RESPONSA THROUGH THE CENTURIES

The fundamental change in the conditions of the Jewish people, caused by the rise of flourishing new Jewish settlements and schools of learning in the west of the civilized world, from the tenth century onwards, had a profound influence on Jewish letter-writing. The monopoly claimed by the Eastern schools in respect of the issue of Responsa was broken by the authority accorded to the new Yeshibot (Talmudic schools) in Western Africa, Spain, France and Germany. Moreover, in the West the Responsa ceased to be the utterances of privileged bodies and became a general feature of Jewish learned correspondence. As time passed and the Dispersion spread, every Rabbi of distinction was called upon to answer queries in the manner of the typical Responsa. Thus this correspondence grew into an enormous network embracing the whole Diaspora.

To reach their destinations the letters containing the questions and the answers often had to travel hundreds of miles. Special provisions had to be made for the despatch of the inquiries and answers. Jewish merchants travelling to fairs or for other commercial reasons carried the letters to the Rabbis and brought their answers back, but special messengers (in later times regular letter-carriers under state control) were also engaged and paid for the purpose of forwarding these and other Jewish letters.

The task of answering the Sheelot was regarded as a sacred duty. No other exigencies, no dangers, no distress prevented the Rabbis from satisfying the distant and mostly unknown interrogators. Rashi (Rabbi Solomon ben Isaac), the unsurpassed interpreter of Scripture and Talmud, apologized in one of his Responsa for the brevity of his answer because he and his family were busy with the vintage. At the end of a Responsum composed by Rabbi Moses Minz, the following moving apology can be read: 'I am unable to enlarge upon this because we have to face expulsion and imprisonment. The time granted by the Archbishop [of Bamberg] has already expired, and he is not willing to extend it for a day or even an hour.' The most pathetic figure of all the respondents and, at the same time, one of the greatest masters among them, Rabbi Meir of Rothenburg, continued to answer inquiries even from the German fortress where he was imprisoned until his tragic end (see p. 244).

The Teshubot as well as the Sheelot became, in general, more and more permeated with the personalities of the writers, their needs, their fate, their opinions and emotions. The interrogators told their cases often with an astonishing precision and introduced references to events which had only indirect connection with the subject (see p. 73). On the other hand, the Rabbis took the opportunity to make comments revealing their attitude towards the addressees and their causes. Thus Rashi, in one of his Responsa, used passionate words against a man who tried to obtain a divorce by slandering his wife: 'He is unworthy,' Rashi wrote, 'to belong to the race of Abraham, whose descendants are always full of pity for the unfortunate; and all the more for a woman to whom one is bound in marriage.' An even more outspoken burst of indignation occurs in a Responsum of Rabbi Solomon ibn Adret. When the brothers David and Azriel asked this leading rabbinical authority of Spanish Jewry for a final decision about their genealogical purity which had been calumniously impugned, Ibn Adret did not mince his words: 'When your letter reached me and I opened it, I stood aghast. The author of this wicked rumour, whatever his motive, has sinned grievously and deserved more severe punishment than one who had slaughtered his victim in cold blood.'

The Responsa remained in the later stages of their development, as in the Geonic period, mainly judicial decisions. In addition, however, the inquiries submitted to the Rabbis were in a steadily increasing measure concerned with theological, philosophical, historical, literary and scientific matters. Thus the Sheelot u-Teshubot not only helped to interpret and supplement the Law, to improve education, to strengthen faith and to cultivate the Hebrew language, but also promoted the circulation of opinions, ideas and experiences between communities and individuals in the East and West.

To trace the development of the Responsa means to follow closely the phases of Jewish history. The rise of Spanish Jewry led to the ascendancy of the Responsa written in the great centres of the Iberian peninsula and in the neighbouring Africa: beginning with the Teshubot of Rabbi Moses ben Enoch – who was brought, according to a legendary report, as captive to the shores of the Mediterranean and founded the Academy of Cordova – and culminating in the lucid and masterly epistles of Moses Maimonides (see Chapter 31), and in the gigantic responsive activities of Rabbi Solomon ibn Adret (see Chapter 38), Rabbi Asher ben Yehiel (see Chapter 39), Rabbi Isaac ben Sheshet Barfat (1326–1408) and Rabbi Simon ben Zemah Duran (1361–1444). It was, however, still in the heyday of Spanish Jewry that the growth of the Franco-German Diaspora led the rabbinic scholars of this part of Jewry to compete with their Spanish colleagues in the production of Responsa. The glorious name of Rashi (1040–1105) illuminates the early days of the Franco-German Sheelot u-Teshubot. In the thirteenth century Rabbi Meir of Rothenburg (see Chapter 36) was rivalled in fame as a writer of Responsa only by Rabbi Solomon ibn Adret; in the fifteenth century the responsive activity of outstanding German Rabbis like Jacob ha-Levi Mölln, Israel Isserlein and Israel Bruna exercised a particularly deep influence on the life of the Jews in Central Europe. Nor did Italy lag behind. The authority of Rabbi Joseph Colon, first of Bologna and later of Mantua, was so firmly established in the fifteenth century that the Rabbis of Nuremberg asked him to address their own community in a time of false accusations against fellow-communities (see Chapter 44, 1). Even the Christian world turned, in an historic *cause célèbre*, to the Rabbis of

Italy for advice: when King Henry VIII sought the nullification of his marriage with Catharine of Aragon they had to answer inquiries of priests and ambassadors concerning the pertinent precept of the rabbinical law. Like these Rabbis, Leon of Modena, too, answered the inquiry of a Christian scholar in Hebrew (see pp. 414 f.). Yet, on the other hand, Italian Rabbis did not hesitate to use the Italian language sometimes for their answers to Jewish interrogators.

The expulsion of the Jews from the Iberian peninsula again shifted the balance in the Responsa towards the East. From Cairo, to which already in the days of Maimonides numerous queries had been directed from near and far, Rabbi David ibn Abi Zimra (1464–1574) gave directions in thousands of Responsa to Eastern Jewry in all its vital problems. In the same period the Holy Land regained its fame as a centre of learning and learned correspondence through the gathering of famous scholars in Safed and Jerusalem (see Chapter 51). A third current of Responsa which began to flow in the sixteenth century came from the Jewry of Poland, the most populous Jewish settlement of those days and of many days to follow. Rabbi Solomon Luria (see Chapter 57) and Rabbi Moses Isserles (1520–1572) were the founders of this Eastern European tradition of Responsa. The Responsa composed in those countries had as their main purpose to guard the continuity of Jewish religion, law and custom. Many prominent writers of Responsa in the West hailed from the eastern part of Europe, above all Rabbi Zebi Hirsch Ashkenazi, who sent his Responsa in all directions from his 'Klaus' at Altona and was even privileged to decide the quarrel of the London community about the alleged pantheistic views of Rabbi David Nieto. At the same time his distinguished contemporary, Rabbi Hayim Jair Bacharach, a son of German Jewry, excelled as a respondent in Worms, the famous site of Rashi (see Chapter 74: 2).

This short survey gives only what might be called a rough cross-section of the development of the Responsa. Numerous well-known writers of Responsa have had to remain unnamed. Likewise the few specimens which could find their place in this work cannot claim to be an adequate representation of the countless Teshubot gathered throughout the centuries in hundreds of volumes. Only a special comprehensive selection would be able to fulfil such a task.

13

LETTERS OF ADMONITION

Analogous to the development of the Responsa is that of another peculiar feature of Jewish letter-writing: Letters of Admonition or Advice. To be sure the Letters of Admonition are generally regarded as a special form of an independent literary phenomenon, the Ethical Will. But many of these Wills assume the character of letters not only in their form but also in their contents, which often refer to other subjects besides ethical precepts. They should not, therefore, be separated from the great family of Jewish letters.

The Epistle of James to the Twelve Tribes, in certain portions, and Saadia's letter to the Children of Israel, have already been noted as early and excellent examples of this type. The transplantation of the custom of composing Ethical Wills to the West gave a further impetus to the development of Letters of Admonition properly so called. The most famous of all Ethical Wills, that of Judah ibn Tibbon, may even be a chain of letters written in different periods of Judah's life to his son Samuel; it is studded with personal remarks and reminiscences (see Chapter 29). True and very fine Letters of Admonition are also the epistles of Rabbi Moses ben Nahman to his sons from the Holy Land (see Chapter 33). On the other hand, it was a prospective journey which induced Joseph ibn Caspi to address to his twelve-year-old son a long Letter of Admonition, and a gay occasion, very remote from thoughts of death, which led to the composition of the poem 'The Silver Bowl' by Joseph Ezobi (see Chapters 35 and 40).

It is true that many Letters of Admonition betray a conventional pattern rather than the individuality of their authors. But for this monotony we are richly compensated by numerous examples of perfect self-expression. Leon of Modena, a master of letter-writing, uses amazingly plain language for his admonitions in a letter addressed to his favourite son (see p. 411); the advice of a grandfather to his grandson inserted in a private Yiddish letter (see pp. 460 f.) is touchingly sincere. The affectionate dedication of her Memoirs by mother Glückel of Hameln to her children and her continual manner of addressing them give this masterpiece of Jewish autobiography a strong epistolary character (see Chapter 75). The firm hold which the custom of paternal admonition has retained in the Jewish people up to modern times may be illustrated by the almost simultaneous composition of two very different Letters of Admonition in the middle of the eighteenth century: Moses Hayim Luzzatto's moving call to his disciples (see p. 586); and the simple letter of an ordinary Jew, Leb Norden of London, to his son, written in 1741:

My dear son, I will not burden you with many injunctions, for it will suffice for thee to obey the laws contained in the Torah. Yet, think of me always, for you know my love and my care for you. Honour thy Maker, walk in the ways of the upright, avoid both what is evil and what may seem so. Never gamble, for gambling has slain many victims; it leads to loss of money and to the neglect of the Torah. Moreover, it is an attempt to acquire wealth against the will of God. Avoid ostentation and arrogance, whether in thought or deed: dress simply, live simply, and be sparing in your household expenditure. Extravagance is the cause of worry, so be careful with the legacy I leave you, for miracles do not happen every day. But in giving alms be open-handed. Avoid quarrels, seek not to dominate others, be slow to anger. Honour your mother, and strive to perfect your character.

14

POSTSCRIPT TO THE RESPONSA AND LETTERS OF ADMONITION

The Responsa and the Letters of Admonition accompany the Jewish people during the whole drama of its Diaspora like the chorus of the Greek tragedy: they guide, judge, warn, advise and comfort the striving and suffering hero. The simile gains added point from the fact that many Letters of Admonition and some of the Responsa, like the 'Letter to the South' of Maimonides (see pp. 182f.), were meant by their authors to be recited before the community. Some of the Letters of Admonition have even been included in the prayer book, and most of them contain an injunction to the addressees to read them aloud at regular intervals (see pp. 164, 232, 235).

The Responsa of the great masters have in recent times provided not only the key to the true understanding and interpretation of the Hebrew Law as administered in the Middle Ages (see, e.g., the work on Ibn Adret by Isidor Epstein and D. M. Shohet's 'The Jewish Court in the Middle Ages'), but also material for the fascinating history of the medieval Jews, as it has been told by Israel Abrahams,

Salo Baron, and – for Spanish Jewry – by Abraham A. Neuman. On the other hand, the Responsa and Letters of Admonition, even when they contain personal references, lack the breath of life and actual contact with deeds and events. Letters of both categories were written in many instances as works of literature and have survived through the ages because they have been treated as literature.

15

PRIVATE HEBREW LETTER-WRITING IN THE MIDDLE AGES

In comparison with the numerous Responsa and Letters of Admonition, genuine letters of all kinds, particularly private letters, are very rare phenomena among the medieval and later Jewish records. Nevertheless, we may reasonably assume that genuine Jewish correspondence too increased in all parts of the Diaspora during the centuries which witnessed the development of Responsa and Ethical Wills, and that carelessness and lack of interest in the preservation of merely secular communications are, to a great extent, responsible for the poverty of the material. Perhaps the clearest indication of the increase in correspondence is the ban pronounced by Rabbi Gershom ben Judah (960–1028), 'the Light of the Exile', against anybody who should open a letter addressed to another, even if it was not sealed. The ban of Rabbi Gershom remained a firm safeguard of the privacy of Jewish letters during the following centuries. The formula 'By the ban of Rabbi Gershom' became a standing part of the addresses on Jewish letters.

At any rate, the few remnants of private Hebrew letters justify the statement that the devotion of the medieval Jew to the perennial values of Judaism manifested itself nowhere more clearly than in his personal correspondence. While writing to his contemporaries, he lived at the same time in the past with his forefathers; through using the language of the holy writings for correspondence (even for business letters, see pp. 220 ff.) he continually shaped his thoughts and feelings on the biblical and Talmudic models. The Jewish epistolary style which thus was created is known as 'Melitzah', and its guiding principle may be defined as the tendency to limit self-expression to the forms and contents given by Jewish tradition. To be sure, this flowery style with its mosaic of biblical quotations and metaphors often had the effect of concealing the intention of the writer behind a curtain of verbiage. Similar and even greater dangers were inherent in the 'paitanic' (poetical) style with its rhymes, embellishments and high-flown eulogies modelled on the Arabic pattern (see Chapter 28).

With the traditional framework of the letter firmly established, a cultivated correspondent was obliged to obey the commonly accepted rules. A large number of standing formulas were ready for use in the exordium, the apostrophe and the addresses. Others were indispensable parts of the text, as for instance the expressions 'May he live' or 'May his light shine' usually added to the names of persons mentioned in the letter, or current phrases fixed for greetings which invariably, as in the days of the Lachish Letters, were greetings of peace. The date of the Jewish year was originally added at the end of the letter and sometimes expressed by the use of biblical quotations containing letters of appropriate numerical value, while the day was indicated by reference to the weekly portion of the Torah.

16

EARLY HEBREW LETTERS FROM SPAIN

The beginning of the Spanish era is marked by the composition of one of the most memorable letters in the history of Jewish letter-writing: the epistle of Hasdai ibn Shaprut, the first physician and adviser at the court of the Ommayad rulers, Abd el-Rahman III and his successor, to the king of the Khazars (see Chapter 19). Although the voices which deny the authenticity of this letter and of the king's answer have not been silenced, the genuineness of the correspondence is now generally accepted. It is likewise assumed that Hasdai's talented secretary, Menahem ibn Saruk, the eminent Hebrew grammarian and poet, is to be credited with the draft of this brilliant piece of writing. The epistle is a state paper and yet, at the same time, a private letter, reaching its climax in a passionate expression of Hasdai's desire to witness the existence of an independent Jewish kingdom. The answer of King Joseph of the Khazars may have been modelled on Hasdai's letter, although the fragment of an original Hebrew letter written in Khazaria at about the same time (see p. 114) bears witness to a genuine Hebrew epistolary activity in the kingdom of the proselyte nation on the shore of the Caspian Sea.

By comparison with this correspondence, two other famous private letters of the Spanish period, the letter of condolence written by Samuel ha-Nagid to Rabbi Hananel, the son of the deceased scholar Rabbi Hushiel ben Elhanan (see Chapter 22), and Judah Halevi's complimentary letter to Nathan ben Samuel (see Chapter 28) are rather examples of a true paitanic style through which, however, the profound feelings of the writers break forth sometimes with great vigour. Letters of this kind form a brand of poetic epistles, though differing sharply from the tersely epigrammatic and genuinely poetic letters actually exchanged between poets (see Chapters 18 and 28).

17

MOSES MAIMONIDES STRIKES OUT A NEW LINE IN JEWISH LETTER-WRITING

Moses Maimonides is practically the first Jewish letter-writer of whose letters a comprehensive and diversified collection has been preserved. Not only the life work of the sage, but also his whole personality is reflected in his correspondence (see Chapter 31). Although his ability in answering learned and legal questions was unsurpassed, his greatness as a letter-writer rests perhaps even more upon his faculty for finding the way to the mind and heart of every correspondent. Through him letter-writing became a source of inspiration for the Jewish people, of assistance in their spiritual need. Whether he assured a correspondent that, although unable to read the writings of the sage in Hebrew, he was nevertheless a serious student of wisdom, or whether he strengthened the self-respect of a proselyte by exalting him above the descendants of Jacob (see pp. 194 ff. and 198 ff.), his was the part of a wise and benevolent healer. An admirable example of a consolatory letter had been given to Moses Maimonides by his own father (see Chapter 30), and he himself in his 'Iggereth Hashemad' (see pp. 178 ff.) had found the right words with which to guide his brethren in a most critical situation. Surpassing these in originality is the 'Letter to the South' which, addressed to a community on the outer fringe of the Jewish world, has become a letter to the whole Jewish people, defining the task of the people and giving meaning to its suffering and destiny (see pp. 182 ff.).

Maimonides wrote his letters in Hebrew and Arabic, in a lucid and flexible style, not overloaded with quotations and flourishes, but full of references to his own experiences and actual situations. A new type of letter-writing thus came into being, vigorous and personal. Besides learning and wisdom, expressions of joy and despair, tenderness, rigour and irony are also to be found in the letters of Maimonides. His style was varied to suit the character of his correspondents, who ranged from simple folk to great scholars and dignitaries. On the other hand, when answering individual questions of general concern, he saw before his eyes the many ordinary people who shared the doubts, the anxieties and the hopes of the actual correspondents. In such cases the anonymous masses were the real addressees of his letters. Thus the Responsum in the hands of Maimonides changed into a personal letter working upon the minds of present and future generations.

18

THE LEARNED LETTER AFTER MAIMONIDES

Under the influence of Maimonides, the learned Hebrew letter, as distinct from the formal authoritative Responsum, became a frequent form of correspondence. It is not to be wondered at that the followers and admirers of Maimonides excelled in this species. Don Isaac Abrabanel, minister to Spanish and Portuguese kings, reminds us, as a letter-writer, of his venerated master Maimonides (see Chapter 47). More than a hundred years later Joseph Solomon del Medigo, philosopher, physician and pupil of Galileo, replying to the questions of the Karaite Zerah ben Nathan, made an attempt to guide an ardent student of wisdom in a Maimonidean manner (see Chapter 68). As late as 1648, Menasseh ben Israel, an eminent letter-writer himself, even seems to have imitated, in a learned letter written in Spanish, the way in which Maimonides described his daily work to Samuel ibn Tibbon (see pp. 504 ff.).

19

THE POLEMICAL LETTER

The work of Maimonides also had another far-reaching influence on Jewish letter-writing through the great feud which flared up within the Jewish world, in the master's lifetime, over his philosophical teaching, and which grew into a hundred years' war between Faith and Reason. The main weapon used in this campaign was the letter, and it was wielded with great skill by both parties during all the stages of this the most momentous learned controversy in Jewish history: from the first battle-cry uttered in the polemical letter of Rabbi Meir ben Todros ha-Levi Abulafia, Rabbi of Toledo, up to the final phase of the struggle in the first decade of the fourteenth century, culminating in Rabbi Solomon ben Adret's letter forbidding the study of Greek philosophy before the age of twenty-five, and the magnificent defence of secular studies by the poet and philosopher Yedaiah Bedersi (see pp. 255–8).

The polemical epistle, developed to perfection during this struggle, continued to be an outstanding feature of Jewish letter-writing in the last centuries of the Middle Ages and even beyond. One of its main tasks became the response to the frequent challenges reaching the Jews from Christian quarters. Thus the controversy between the baptized Jew Pablo Christiani and Nahmanides drew from Jacob ben Elia a comprehensive polemical epistle. The polemical letter also assumed in various instances the character of a private letter. A tragic reason for the strengthening of this personal element was the conflict between the faithful adherents of Judaism – professing Jews and Marranos – and the apostates. This internal dissension left numerous traces in the epistolary records of Jewish history. The most impressive example of them is the letter sent by Profiat Duran, the noted grammarian and philosopher, to his baptized friend, David Bonet Bongoron (ben Goron), when the latter declined to re-embrace the faith of his father. The ironic challenge, 'Be not like thy fathers', and a sarcastic eulogy of David's adopted faith became the cover under which Profiat Duran proclaimed his unshakable faith in the truth of Judaism (see Chapter 42).

From this time family divisions caused by conversion gave rise to ever-new expressions of this controversy. Thus in the middle of the sixteenth century (1552) a Jew who accepted Christian faith – Ludovicus Carretus – explained the reason for his conversion in a lengthy Hebrew letter to his son and tried to induce the latter to join him, while, about half a century later, Dr. Elia Montalto, a famous Portuguese physician, who re-embraced Judaism, wrote a series of letters in Portuguese in the effort to persuade a neo-Christian relative to return to the ancient religion of his father (see Chapter 64). The schism within the Marrano camp continued to produce in the seventeenth century heated polemics conducted often by means of epistles. The most tragic counterpart to Profiat Duran's self-searching epistle may be found in Uriel da Costa's burning confession 'Exemplar humanae vitae'. We may even discover an echo of the great medieval Jewish controversies in Spinoza's polemical letters to Henry Oldenburg (see pp. 551 ff.) and in his scornful rebuke of his former pupil Albert Burgh who, after having turned Catholic, challenged the master in a provocative letter.

Another conflict which furnished new material for the polemical letter was the quarrel caused by the cabbalistic activity of Moses Hayim Luzzatto. This brought forth, much against the will of the mystic, a vast exchange of letters which gave Luzzatto the opportunity for the most powerful exposition of his standpoint (see pp. 580 ff.).

20

LETTERS TO AND FROM COMMUNITIES

From the very beginning of Jewish letter-writing, messages addressed to the whole of Israel or to single communities occur with striking frequency (see in Part One the Chapters 1, 2, 5, 7, 10 and 13). This social quality and function of the Jewish letter is deeply rooted in the character of Israel and its destiny. The life of the Jews among the nations intensified this collective task of the letter for reasons predominantly tragic. Some of the most sublime emanations of the Jewish spirit were caused by persecutions and destined for the anonymous masses. Isaiah's call 'Comfort ye, comfort ye my people!' has never found a nobler response than in the consolatory epistles of Maimon ben Joseph (see Chapter 30) and his great son (see pp. 182 ff.). There was, moreover, in consequence of the mounting persecutions of the Jews, another difficult task for the letter-writers: to bring the sad news to their brethren, to ask for help and to warn against approaching danger. The writers of these news-letters were acute observers and precise reporters. Leading spirits of their epoch are to be found among them, like Rabbi Hasdai Crescas, the profound thinker (see Chapter 41), and the ingenious interpreter of Scripture and mystical poet, Sabbatai Cohen (see Chapter 69).

Compared with the gloomy pictures contained in such reports of the ever-recurrent martyrdom of the Jews, a slightly gay undertone is discernible in the news-letter written, in 1413, by Don Abu Astruc ha-Levi, a participant on the Disputation of Tortosa. The writer displays exceptional power of observation, combined with a dramatic style, and not without a refreshing dash of irony. These elements are also to be found in the urgent call sent by Isaac Zarphati to the Jews of Germany to persuade them to leave their country at once and settle in Turkey (see Chapter 43). A more emotional note pervades another invitation extended with moving words of brotherly love by the Provençal community of Salonica to their countrymen (see Chapter 52).

There is a fine evidence of the mutual respect of the Jews in the Ghettos in the fact that the letters exchanged between them were carefully composed whether a trivial purpose or a matter of great and general concern was involved. At the beginning of the sixteenth century the campaign against the Hebrew books gave rise to a brisk exchange of letters, conducted in a vigorous Hebrew, between the community which was in greatest danger, that of Frankfort-on-Main, and other communities in Germany (see Chapter 48). The letter of the community of Pesaro to Joseph Nasi, Duke of Naxos, is an eloquent plea for the expelled Marranos. Even more impressive is the circular letter written at about the same time (in the 'sixties of the sixteenth century) by the tiny community of Cori in a moment of great distress. In this letter the affliction of the Jew and his yearning for deliverance by restoration to the Land of Israel found classical expression (see Chapter 55). Two centuries later, the replies of the Italian communities to the call of the Jews of Prague, threatened with expulsion, offer a beautiful example of solidarity expressed in noble language (see Chapter 78, p. 599).

The unprecedented stream of letters which poured over the Diaspora with news of the Sabbatian movement brought new colour into the picture. These letters and manifestos, full of fantastic, most exciting news, bristling with exuberant promises and hopes (see Chapter 72), passed from hand to hand and read in the synagogues, were the very lifeblood of the pseudo-Messianic movement. Once again, the letter seemed to become the instrument of a new creed. Though this did not happen, the manifestos and news-letters which had served the lost cause of Sabbatai Zevi remained the truest record of the way in which Israel's pent-up longing for salvation found vent in those days.

21

LETTERS OF JEWISH TRAVELLERS

Hebrew descriptions of travels are not preserved from earlier days than the ninth century C.E. The first extant record, the so-called letter or book of Eldad the Danite, is, however, neither a letter written on the journey nor a report of a voyage, but a story told afterwards and undoubtedly mixed with products of Eldad's imagination. Also later Hebrew itineraries, the famous books composed by the great travellers, Benjamin of Tudela and Petahia of Ratisbon, both of the second half of the twelfth century, valuable as they are as geographical and historical sources, lacked the personal appeal of letters.

On the other hand, the rare instances of early travellers' letters from the Cairo Genizah contain no description of journey, landscape or people. The writers look in the foreign countries for their own world which they carry with themselves. Even the passionate letter of Nahmanides to his children, from Jerusalem (see p. 225), gives no account of the voyage undertaken in such tragic circumstances. Nevertheless, its pathetic description of desolate Jerusalem makes this letter the most moving prelude to the travellers' letters which before long began to pour from the Land of Israel.

The travellers from Italy were privileged to take the lead in this development. There is a new note in the letters of these Jews imbued with the love of the Holy Land but also with a profound affection for the beautiful country of their birth. Though yearning for Palestine, these enthusiastic students of Torah and Talmud have open eyes for the wonders of the surrounding world. They mention all stages of the voyage, and report on the Jewish communities with great accuracy, and with critical comment (see Chapter 46). These writers do not confine themselves exclusively to items of Jewish interest (see Chapter 54). In general it is, however, the arrival in the Promised Land upon which they dwell principally in their letters. Compared with the black report of Nahmanides, the letter of Rabbi Obadiah of Bertinoro, the great scholar and saint, reads like a message of promise, a forecast of Palestine's future revival (see pp. 297–311). When, a few decades afterwards, a Jewish merchant from Italy arrived in Palestine, he was already able to give an account of the flourishing Jewish settlement in Safed (see Chapter 50).

Amid the reports of Palestine, the great mystery of those days, the whereabouts of the Ten Tribes, recurs time and again, and is accorded much attention. The restraint with which Rabbi Obadiah of Bertinoro reports the gossip about the Tribes reflects much credit on his enlightened spirit. On the other hand, we are not surprised to find outspoken references to the Tribes without any critical comment in the merchant's letters written after the appearance of the Messianic pretenders David Reubeni and Solomon Molko (see Chapters 49 and 50).

If we owe to the letters of Italian Jews the first accounts of the revival in Palestine which followed the conquest of Constantinople and Jerusalem by the Turks, it is a Jew from Moravia who has the merit of having told in his letters the saga of Safed, the city of the mystics, reborn in the sixteenth century. The letters of Shlomel Dresnitz to his relatives and friends reflect not only the atmosphere of the saintly Safed but also the warmth of the writer's pious soul (see Chapter 62). The letters of another mystic, Rabbi Isaiah Hurwitz of Prague depict dramatically the arrival of the famous scholar in the Holy Land and his enthusiastic reception by the rival communities (see Chapter 67). The noble heart of Moses Hayim Luzzatto, however, even from the Land of Israel, had nothing else to offer to the distant friends than itself (see p. 587f.).

22

HEBREW LETTERS WRITTEN TO AND BY GENTILES

The era of Humanism in which Hebrew Scripture, rabbinic writings and the Cabbalah became a main subject of Christian studies witnessed also the discovery and cultivation of the Hebrew letter by the non-Jewish world. The prelude to the Renaissance, the reign of the enigmatic Frederick II, is marked by a memorable event: Judah ben Solomon Cohen (b. 1219), one of the emperor's Jewish protégés, corresponded with Frederick and with the emperor's philosopher, Theodorus, about philosophical themes. In the middle of the sixteenth century the knowledge of Hebrew among Christian scholars was so widespread that Obadiah of Sforno, teacher of Reuchlin, could dedicate his commentary on Ecclesiastes in Hebrew to Henry II, King of France, 'at whose court', as this dedication puts it, 'many scholars are engaged in Hebrew studies'.

The climax of the Hebrew epistolary activities within the Christian world falls, however, in the seventeenth century. Particularly in England the great interest taken in Hebrew studies led also to a Hebrew correspondence of English scholars. The extant Responsum of Leone da Modena to an inquiry of the English scholar William Boswell tells us a great deal about these Anglo-Jewish relations (see p. 414).

On the continent of Europe, Germany at that time made the most remarkable contributions to Hebrew letter-writing. Johannes Buxtorf the Elder, the noted Christian scholar, composed in Latin his 'Institutio Epistolaris Hebraica', a comprehensive guide for Hebrew letter-writing, chiefly based on the already published first Jewish model letter-writers. This work, containing also a collection of rabbinic letters, was published at Basle in 1610. Buxtorf the Younger entertained an extensive Hebrew correspondence with Jewish scholars. From the second half of that century other Hebrew correspondences between outstanding Rabbis and German theologians are extant, such as the letters exchanged between Rabbi Sabbatai Cohen and Valentini Widrich, dealing with the purchase of Hebrew books, and the polemic between Rabbi Henoch ha-Levi and Johann Christoph Wagenseil. Finally, the seventeenth century witnessed the appearance of that prodigy of learning, Anna Maria Schurmann, who, although by no means the first Christian woman known to have written Hebrew letters, was certainly the most able and prolific among them.

23

ITALY TAKES THE LEAD IN JEWISH LETTER-WRITING

In the realm of Jewish letter-writing proper, the centre of gravity, after the downfall of Spanish Jewry, shifted to Italy. It has been said of the Jews of Italy in general that, 'because of their peculiar political and economic conditions and of their closer social and intellectual relations with the Gentile world they had developed a somehow distinctive cultural life of their own – an interesting synthesis of medieval Jewish and classic-Italian Renaissance spirit' (Salo Baron). This description applies in a particularly high degree to Jewish letter-writing. To be sure, the Italian pattern was basically not opposed to the genuine Hebrew tradition of letter-writing. The special style cultivated by the Italian people in Latin and Italian was, rather, an elaborate and artistic counterpart of the Hebrew epistolary method. 'Every letter assumed the character and importance of a little work of art, formed after classical models with the intention of achieving the greatest possible elegance' (Umberto Cassuto). Thus the Jews, accommodating themselves to this epistolary practice, became even more letter-conscious than before, and the cultivation of Jewish letter-writing developed on an unprecedented scale.

As early as the first half of the fifteenth century, Jewish communities in Italy, in imitation of the example set by the Italian courts and republics, engaged eminent writers as secretaries. From this time onward letter-writing among the Jews of Italy assumed spectacular forms and dimensions. Writing, awaiting, receiving, keeping and exchanging letters became an essential part of daily life (see Chapter 45). At the beginning of the sixteenth century Shelomo ben Elia da Poggibonzi, a banker and scholar, cultivated letter-writing as a special art. According to Prof. Cassuto's report, Poggibonzi's letters (nearly a hundred of them, collected by himself, are preserved in the Bodleian Library in Oxford) range from the business letter to the learned epistle.

When the printing of Hebrew books commenced in Italy, collections of letters and model letter-writers soon began to appear there. The 'Mayan Gannim' (Fountain of Gardens) edited by the Venetian Rabbi, Samuel Archevolti, a teacher of Leone of Modena, in 1553 was preceded only by the first known printed letter-writer, published anonymously at Augsburg in 1534. Although the twenty-five letters and answers contained in Archevolti's booklet are only models, nevertheless we can form from them certain conclusions regarding the style and themes of contemporary letters. A more comprehensive collection of 113 specimens by an anonymous editor was published in Cremona in 1566.

The individualistic tendency of humanism, penetrating into the Jewish world, intensified the desire for an exchange of letters in all strata of the Jewish public. People of all professions, of all ages and of both sexes were as eager to correspond as were men of learning.

Above all, there was a strong desire felt by everybody in those days of exciting events and discoveries simply to give and to get news. For this, and other needs, the Jews had to find words in a language which, though the people clung to it with unabating love, was not used for conversation, the language of Scripture, the tongue of their daily prayers and studies.

Thus, more than ever, letter-writing became an art that had to be learned. The 'letter-writers' were the handbooks of this art, and decided the victory of the tradition over personal self-expression. The examples offered in them were compositions made up of biblical and Talmudical quotations, very often misused in a scurrilous way not only for extravagant headings and introductions, but also for the contents of the letter. Even the driest business affairs were treated in such a manner. No wonder that many preferred to use the services of professional letter-writers.

24

LEONE DA MODENA PERFECTS THE STYLE OF HIS TIME

One of these professional letter-writers – though this was only *one* of the twenty-six professions he followed during his lifetime – became the embodiment of all these contrasting ideals and the precursor of a new development: Leone da Modena, the famous Rabbi of Venice (see Chapter 63). The very fact that a considerable part of his correspondence was preserved through his own efforts, that he took care to save even the letters of his early youth, indicates his appreciation of the personal letter. Leone's letters are full of sidelights on his storm-tossed and tragic life and on intimate details of the life lived in the Italo-Jewish communities. They reflect the contradictions of his character, his nostalgia for the cultural atmosphere of Venice, his ambitions, passions and predilections. With his remarkable sense of humour and irony, he is a sharp critic of other people, but he is no less prepared to confess his own faults and to accuse himself.

Prof. Ludwig Blau, who discovered and edited Leone's letters, maintains that they were genuine letters, not academic exercises, and that they 'show the Hebrew private style of his time. They were in accordance with the taste of his contemporaries, otherwise he would not have been engaged from all sides . . . Educated and illiterate people, Jews and Christians asked Leone for introductions and dedications, laudatory poems, letters of recommendation, etc.' Leone fulfilled the requirements of all those people who were themselves unable to do so. While they struggled in vain for self-expression, he succeeded, by combining the traditional style with his personal note, in creating a style of his own.

25

THE HEBREW LETTER ON THE EVE OF THE EMANCIPATION ERA

The epistolary activity of another Italian Rabbi, Mahalalel Halelujah of Ancona, recently made known by Henry Bernstein, seems to be not unconnected with Leone's example. This younger contemporary and countryman of Leone, while so far removed from the latter's anti-cabbalistic views that he even sympathized with the Sabbatian movement, nevertheless shared his love and appreciation of letter-writing. The collection of his letters, although much smaller than the remnants of Leone's letter-book, is another indication of a rising epistolary culture. Rabbi Mahalalel clearly recognized the educational possibilities of letters, as a passage in the preface to his collection indicates. In this endeavour, in which he used not merely models but real letters transmitted to certain persons on actual occasions ('I wrote this to . . .' is the unvarying superscription of each specimen in the 'Sepher Mahalalel'), we may perhaps recognize one of the earliest attempts to revive the Hebrew language and spirit long before the rise of the Haskalah (Enlightenment). A similar realization of the inspiring effect which the reading of actual letters might be expected to produce on the Jews of the seventeenth century can be found in the testament of Rabbi Jona Landsdorfer of Prague. It contains the following provision: 'My letters are to be distributed among the students who are able to understand them, but the right of property shall be restricted to the letter itself; whoever wishes to take a copy at his own expense may be permitted to do so.'

It was again Italy which in the first half of the eighteenth century produced the greatest forerunner of modern Hebrew literature and, incidentally, of modern Hebrew letter-writing, Moses Hayim Luzzatto (see Chapter 77). While maintaining to the full the literary flavour of Hebrew correspondence, he gave it a certain conversational tone which transformed the character of the Hebrew language. 'It is very interesting,' says Simon Ginzburg, Luzzatto's biographer, 'to read Luzzatto's letters together with those of his contemporaries (within the same period). . . . At once we can see for ourselves the great mission fulfilled by Luzzatto in the province of Hebrew prose. This mission was to create an exact, concise and simple style as the medium of expression of the modern Jew. Thus he prepared the ground for the revival of Hebrew as a spoken language by Ben Yehuda at the end of the nineteenth century.'

26

THE RISE OF THE YIDDISH LETTER

While the new form of the Hebrew private letter was in the making in the south of the European Jewish world, another species of genuine Jewish letter-writing developed in northern and eastern Jewry: the letter written in the Yiddish (Judaeo-German) language. Like the origin of the Yiddish language itself and of Yiddish literature, the beginning of Yiddish letter-writing is still shrouded in darkness. The earliest Yiddish letter the date of which can be ascertained, according to a thorough study devoted by Solomon A. Birnbaum to this document, belongs to the end of the fifteenth century. It is a letter smuggled into a prison cell, an outcry of compassion for an unhappy woman, believed to have been subjected to torture (see Chapter 44: 2). Written in Hebrew script and studded with Hebrew words, the Yiddish letter betrays its relationship to the Hebrew letter, but the refreshing elements of local colour, personal adaptability and sly humour distinguish it sharply from its older brother. Like the Yiddish song and the Yiddish story, the Yiddish letter, too, became for the Jew an essential element of social life.

The writers of Yiddish letters used abundantly the accepted Hebrew formulas for the titles, eulogies, dates and closing phrases, including the ban of Rabbi Gershom. They were also fond of inserting quotations from the Bible and Talmud. But the Hebrew components constituted only the framework and ornamental accessories of the letter, while the whole substance was presented in the Yiddish vernacular. To be sure, the Yiddish letter developed its own conventional forms and a traditional style. Many of these elements were borrowed from contemporary German letters. Yet the curious mixture of ancient expressions with the language of daily life, of solemnity with simplicity, of sublime notions with trivial jottings, possesses an incomparable charm. In these letters, the humble sons and daughters of the Ghetto paid to their fathers and mothers, their brothers and friends, the living and the dead, that respect which was denied to them by the outside world. This reverence, expressed with Oriental flourish, was, however, linked with a completely matter-of-fact treatment of the subjects in hand. The Yiddish letters seem as if spoken rather than written (indeed, actually they were often dictated), without any pretence and affectation. With their lack of style and punctuation, with their long-drawn accounts and their endless repetitions they have all the qualities of lively talk, and may for this reason be considered as the most typical private letters in the great family of the Jewish letter. They are, in the words of Landau-Wachstein, 'the monologue of the pre-modern drama, the immediate means of expression of the unlearned man and the echo of the relation between the masses and the sum of notions which constitute the character of a people'.

It is much to be regretted that only a small number of the early Yiddish letters have escaped the ravages of time. Rare specimens from the sixteenth century (see two of them in Chapters 56 and 58) have been published recently, but, above all, the collection of private letters, most of them written on one single day of the year 1619 in Prague, which have been miraculously preserved through their confiscation in the Thirty Years' War, compensate in some measure by the diversity of their contents and writers for many apparently irretrievable losses. The ancient Jewish community of Prague, with its Rabbis and students, merchants and officials, women and children, has been brought back to life in these letters (see Chapter 66).

A striking counterpart of the letters from Prague of 1619 is provided by the Yiddish letters concerned with the same community, this time as an object of help, when, in the years 1744–48, the Jews of Prague and Bohemia were threatened with expulsion. These letters are official or semi-official documents written by prominent men, and they lack, therefore, the spontaneity and intimacy which distinguish the accidentally preserved private letters of the previous century. Yet they are not wanting in directness of expression and personal colour, and their humane quality is reminiscent of the classical Hebrew letters beseeching assistance.

27

LETTERS OF WOMEN

The most ancient letter recorded in the Bible after David's letter to Joab is the letter of a woman: the no less treacherous and no less ominous message of Jezebel, the Phoenician wife of Ahab, King of Israel (see above, p. xxxvi). A few specimens of letters written by women were found in the Cairo Genizah. They indicate that Jewish women during the Middle Ages used Hebrew with great skill for their correspondence (see Chapters 26 and 34). But with the Yiddish letter the Jewess steps into the forefront of letter-writers by virtue of her unrivalled freshness and the sincerity of her approach, the accuracy of her reports and her genuine sense of humour. Mother Rachel, the widow of Rabbi Eliezer Susman Ashkenazi, writing in Yiddish from Jerusalem to her son (see Chapter 56), the wife of Loeb Sarel Gutmans with her original manner of mixing tender care for her husband with news and biting reproaches (see pp. 464f.), and Glückel of Hameln, telling her children the tale of her life like a long-drawn letter (see Chapter 75), express themselves with a natural charm which has been surpassed by hardly any female letter-writer outside the Jewish world.

Apart from the Yiddish writers, there were a few outstanding Jewesses in the sixteenth and seventeenth centuries who heralded the time when some Jewish women were to take their place among the great letter-writers of the world. A letter of Esperanza Malchi, who was in charge of the Sultan's harem, to Queen Elizabeth shows an admirable ability to express tactfully a blend of devotion and self-respect (see Chapter 61). Moreover, Sara Copia Sullam, the Italo-Jewish poetess, would have gained the glory of having added to Israel's letters the first comprehensive correspondence of a woman, if her letters to the Italian poet, Ansaldo Cebà, had not been suppressed (see Chapter 65).

28

LOVE LETTERS

The disappearance of Sara Copia Sullam's letters to Ansaldo Cebà means at the same time the loss of the first known love letters of a Jewish woman, though her friendship with the Christian poet whom she never met was from beginning to end a purely spiritual affection. At any rate, it is to Italian soil that the first Jewish love letters can be traced in the sixteenth century. There are many reasons why few love letters written by Jews and Jewesses can be found with earlier dates. The relations of the sexes among the Jews were fixed by a rigid code: the custom of child-marriages and parental or professional match-making left no room for courtship and love-affairs. After betrothal, the partners met and saw each other infrequently until the day of the wedding. In a lengthy Hebrew epistle addressed by a bridegroom to his father-in-law, *one* passage only refers to the bride: an apology for not having sent a present because of war difficulties (see pp. 458 f.).

We may suppose that even if a handful of courageous individuals had broken through the walls of convention, they could hardly have overcome their entanglement with another venerated ancient tradition; the Song of Songs, according to Israel Abrahams 'the perhaps most popular of all Books of the Old Testament', had formalized the expression of erotic feelings by the Jew for many generations. When, therefore, in an extraordinary case, a love letter *had* to be written, it was bound to become a canto of quotations from the Song of Songs (see Chapter 71).

On the other hand, the growing infiltration of modern ideas and ways of life into the Jewish world found one of its earliest expressions in love letters. We are indebted to Cecil Roth for having brought to light some of the rare surviving specimens. In one of them, written in Judaeo-Italian, quotations from Scripture or any other Hebrew source are conspicuous by their absence (see Chapter 59). An even more free outlet to the expression of personal feelings without an admixture of Jewish traditional elements is to be found in love letters that were exchanged in London in the first half of the eighteenth century between Catherine Villareal and Jacob (Philip) Mendes da Costa. These letters, likewise published by Cecil Roth, were written in English, and belong, therefore, also to the next and final chapter of this survey.

29

JEWISH LETTERS IN NON-JEWISH LANGUAGES

From the beginning of the Diaspora, Jews have cultivated correspondence in the languages of their various new homelands. The expulsion of the Jews from the Iberian peninsula and the momentous changes in the outside world after the close of the Middle Ages stimulated Jewish correspondence in non-Jewish languages to an unprecedented degree. The exiles, many of whom were unable to correspond in Hebrew, could not help addressing each other in those languages in which they had thought and talked for a lifetime and continued to think and to speak.

Thus the double loyalty – to Spain or Portugal and to Judaism – resounds from their letters. In Samuel Usque's dedication of his classic Book of Consolation to Doña Gracia Nasi, there is a warm filial devotion which imbues the lucid Portuguese lines with religious fervour (see Chapter 53). In the long political letter written in Spanish by Alvaro Mendez, Duke of Mytilene, to Dr. Rodrigo Lopez, body physician to Queen Elizabeth, the tragic hero of the London Marranos, reflections on God's justice are woven into the dramatic story of Dom Antonio and his attempts to regain the crown of Portugal, searchlights are thrown on India and the Promised Land, and everywhere the unbending will to fight Philip the enemy of the Jewish people can be felt (see Chapter 60: 2). And no Hebrew polemical epistle could surpass the zeal and learning of Dr. Elia Montalto's vehement plea for the return of his fugitive relatives to Judaism, presented in a series of letters in elegant Portuguese (see Chapter 64).

Now more than ever the Jews developed their ability, shown in previous stages of Jewish history, to adapt their thoughts and ways of expression to those of other nations. At the end of the thirteenth century a famous physician, one of the last Jewish residents of medieval England, applied in polished Old French, the language of the upper classes, to the Chancellor of King Edward I for a safe-conduct (see Chapter 37). Judah Serfatim, the envoy of Alvaro

Mendez, used the same language for his desperate plea on behalf of the ill-fated Dr. Lopez (see Chapter 60: 3); the state documents of Joseph Nasi, Duke of Naxos, real models of stiff official formalism, are composed partly in Latin and partly in Italian; and Alvaro Mendez as well as Esperanza Malchi (see Chapters 60: 1 and 61) found in Spanish the right words for letters addressed to Queen Elizabeth, while the London Marranos entertained an extensive correspondence in English with the highest English circles. Nor were the Ashkenazim less efficient, although Yiddish continued to be the medium of their private correspondence. The Viennese 'Court Jew' Samuel Oppenheimer never tired of writing letters, full of instructions, requests and complaints, to the Imperial Court and high officials in Vienna. The absence of a submissive note is striking in this correspondence of a 'tolerated Jew'. His successor, the learned Samson Wertheimer, however, took great care to address the Emperor Joseph I in a very respectful as well as dignified way when, in a letter, he recapitulated his merits on the occasion of his retirement from the management of his enterprise. The adventurous Süss Oppenheimer – Jew Süss – again used a sarcastic tone in writing to the envoy Keller about the obstacle to his nobility (see Chapter 76).

In their correspondence with the authorities concerning their own public affairs the Jews had to develop a particular skill. In general, it was not an easy task to reconcile Jewish notions and demands with the attitude of the Christian environment. When in 1618 Dr. Solomon Hirscheider, a physician of German origin, drew up, in German, a lengthy petition to the Senate of the Free City of Bremen for permission to settle there with some members of his family, he not only quoted abundantly, besides Scripture and Talmud, Plato, the Gospels, Paul's Epistles, Augustine and other Fathers of the Church, but also used seriously an argument which ran literally as follows: 'How should or could people convert each other . . . if they avoid communication and community?' Nor had he any objection to promising that the admitted Jews would be free to listen to sermons in the Church and to repair 'ad christianissimum'. By contrast with such a document – which, by the way, met with complete failure – the statesmanship of Menasseh ben Israel's epistolary activity in his campaign for the readmission of the Jews to England appears in its proper light. Menasseh pays tribute to the Fathers of the Commonwealth, but without a trace of servility, reconciling the interest of the Commonwealth with the demands of the Jewish people (see Chapter 70). After less than a century, English Jews themselves were able to initiate, by an impressive petition to the King of England, a diplomatic intervention on behalf of the Jews in Prague, and thus to set an epoch-making precedent (see p. 594).

Finally, as had happened in the Hellenistic and Arabic eras, Jews began to disseminate Judaism, to expound its essence and to create new religious and philosophical thoughts in non-Jewish languages, particularly through the medium of letters. In the sixteenth century Lazarus de Viterbo corresponded on the Bible in Latin with Cardinal Sirleto, and Uriel da Costa used the language of the Romans for his Farewell. Leone of Modena exchanged Italian letters with Christian scholars (see pp. 421 ff.), and presented Jewish notions in them with great clearness, in an almost modern manner. Nevertheless, these letters form only an appendage to Leone's widespread Hebrew correspondence. In Menasseh ben Israel we meet for the first time a Jewish scholar who conducted an international correspondence first and foremost with Gentile scholars. The reputation Menasseh won in the Christian world rested upon these letters written in Latin, Spanish and English no less than on his literary and political activity. Although posterity has corrected the exaggerated appreciation Menasseh enjoyed in his lifetime as a scholar and philosopher, his attempt to popularize Judaism by his epistolary activity might be called as remarkable as his achievement in the field of diplomatic correspondence.

In Baruch Spinoza there comes on the scene a letter-writer of more universal significance than any of his predecessors in modern times. It has been said of his correspondence that 'it delineates in highly dramatic fashion the unfoldment of the modern spirit of enlightenment' (Abraham Wolfson). But despite the revolutionary contents of Spinoza's letters, and although they were written in Latin and Dutch to non-Jews and edited by his closest Gentile friends, they bear, when viewed in the perspective of the history of Jewish letter-writing, perhaps the truest witness to Spinoza's debt to his Jewish heritage. His never-failing readiness to answer the questions of perplexed souls, his uncompromising love of truth, his deep sense of responsibility for the improvement of man's thoughts and conduct, his passion for instruction and devotion to the task of guiding his correspondents on the path to the love of God – all these qualities constituting the personality of him who, in the words of Bertrand Russell, 'is the noblest and most lovable of the great philosophers' are shared by Spinoza with the ancient Jewish sages, particularly with Moses Maimonides. Through Spinoza, indeed, the ripest fruits of Jewish letter-writing were offered to the whole of mankind (see Chapter 73).

30

EPILOGUE AND PREVIEW

The Jewish letter at the threshold of the era of Emancipation (middle of the eighteenth century) displayed a variety unknown in any previous period. Not one of the forms developed by Hebrew letter-writers in the course of about three thousand years had ceased to be cultivated. Responsa, Letters of Admonition, learned and polemical letters were composed, private letters in Hebrew and Yiddish continued to be exchanged in the eastern and western countries of the Diaspora. At the same time, the writing of letters in modern languages was increasingly practised by Jews. The name of Moses Mendelssohn and those of other Jews and Jewesses soon appeared in the glorious list of great modern letter-writers. It was particularly this epistolary skill which enabled the Jews to establish a strong social link with their environment even before their legal emancipation, and to influence deeply the cultural life of the Western world. Moreover, in Germany and England, in France and Italy, the internal correspondence of the Jews in the languages of their respective countries became a normal occurrence, acting at once as a mighty vehicle of spiritual enrichment but also as one of the most powerful means of assimilation.

When this process continued in the nineteenth century, the rising flood of Jewish letters written in modern languages seemed to engulf the Hebrew and Yiddish letter. Yet the letter written in these genuine Jewish languages, rejuvenated this time by the Haskalah, survived, and its new vitality was one of the first signs of Jewish renaissance.

The written Hebrew conversation of the scholars, poets and writers preceded and accompanied the rebirth of spoken Hebrew. The Hebrew letter was ready to serve the fighters of the national movement as it had been the mouthpiece of the Messianic pretenders and their apostles. The letters which had been written by pious pilgrims through the ages were now succeeded by the enthusiastic reports of the 'Lovers of Zion', of the pioneers, the rebuilders of the Land, who came with the streams of the Aliyoth and waves of immigration set in motion by the mounting catastrophe of the Jewish people.

Thus another epic of Israel's Letters has yet to be told: the story of how, in the course of the past two hundred years, the various currents of letters written by Jews all over the world developed into mighty streams, and how they played their part in the history of mankind and in the regeneration of the people and land of Israel. There was no room for this narrative and for its documentation in the present work, if the preceding three thousand years of Jewish letter-writing were not to be reduced to a disproportionately short prelude by the vastness of the modern material. The task of gathering in this overflowing harvest must, therefore, be left for another auspicious hour.

NOTES

1. Prov. XX. 22.
2. Lev. XIX. 18; Prov. XXIV. 29.
3. Deut. XXXII. 35.
4. Exod. XXIII. 4–5; Prov. XXV. 21–22.
5. Exod. XX. 13–17.
6. Lev. XIX. 18.
7. Cf. Hillel's answer to a heathen in Shabb. 31a.
8. Eccles. V. 1.
9. Prov. XVII. 27; Eccles. V. 2.
10. Prov. XIV. 29; XVI. 32; Eccles. VII. 9; Sayings of the Fathers V. 10, 14, 15.
11. Sayings of the Fathers VI. 1.
12. Sayings of the Fathers I. 17; Shabb. 88a.
13. Ps. XXXIV. 13; XXXIX. 1.
14. Is. I. 17.
15. Exod. XX. 6; Prov. VIII. 17.
16. Lev. XIX. 18.
17. Deut. XXVII. 26.

II. LACHISH LETTER IV. Obverse and reverse of an Ostracon, being the letter of Hoshaiah, officer of the Jewish army, to his superior Ya'osh, written probably in 587 B.C.E. (See p. 12.)

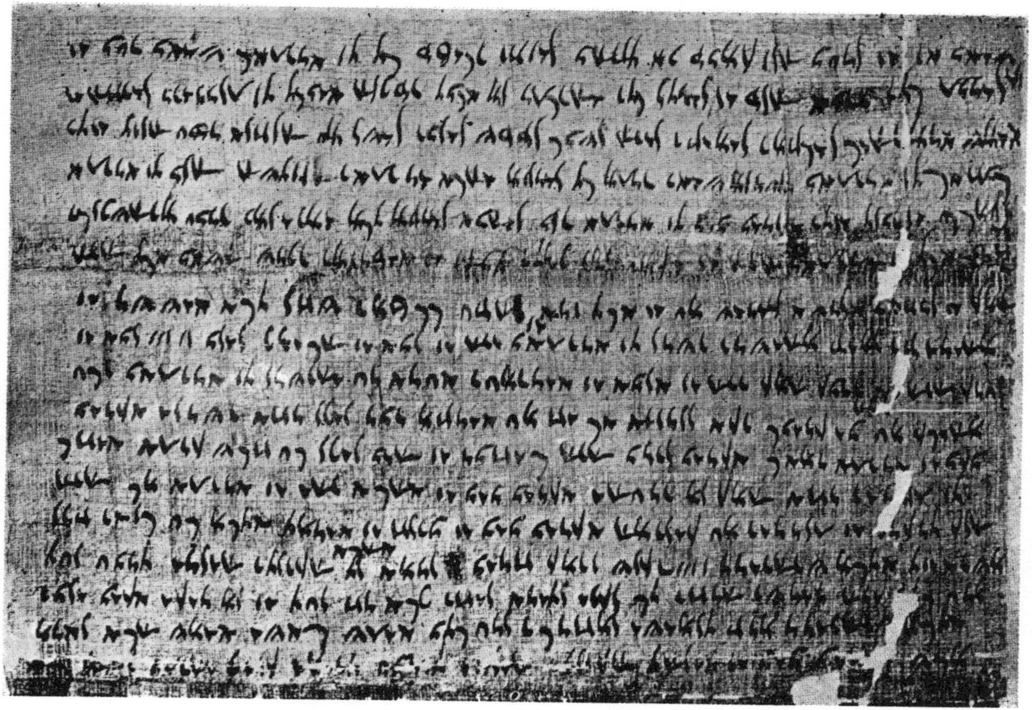

III. ELEPHANTINE PAPYRUS, being the beginning of the letter of Jedoniah, head of the Jewish garrison of Elephantine, to Bigvai (Bagohi), Persian governor of Judaea, written in 408 B.C.E. (See pp. 23–25.)

PART ONE

I

King Hezekiah invites the Children of Israel to a Solemn Passover at Jerusalem

SAMARIA had fallen. The northern Kingdom of Israel, with its own sanctuaries harbouring images of the Golden Calf in Dan and Bethel, had been overthrown by the Assyrians, and the country largely depopulated and annexed. But Jerusalem still stood. There the young king Hezekiah reigned (720–692 B.C.E.) and aspired to elevate the Kingdom of Judah to a newborn glory. Zealously devoted to the service of the God of Israel, he ordered the removal of the idolatrous altars in the mountains and groves, erected under Ahaz his father, and made a great effort to regain for Solomon's Temple, which the northern kingdom had abandoned ever since the days of Jeroboam centuries before, its position as the one and only sanctuary in all Israel.

The King, according to the account in 2 Chronicles xxx, after cleansing and rededicating the Temple, proclaimed a solemn Passover. He sent a circular letter to the Children of Israel, both in Judah and beyond its frontiers, inviting the people to come to Jerusalem to keep the feast. 'So the posts went with the letters from the hand of the King and his princes throughout all Israel and Judah, and according to the commandments of the King, saying':

HEZEKIAH, KING OF JUDAH, TO THE CHILDREN OF ISRAEL

'Yield yourselves unto the Lord, and enter into His sanctuary, which He has sanctified for ever'

[Jerusalem, end of the 8th century B.C.E.]

Ye Children of Israel, turn back unto the Lord, the God of Abraham, Isaac and Israel, that He may return to the remnant that are escaped of you out of the kings of Assyria. And be not ye like your fathers, and like your brethren, who acted treacherously against the Lord, the God of their fathers, so that He delivered them to be an astonishment, as ye see.

Now be ye not stiff-necked, as your fathers were; but yield yourselves unto the Lord, and enter into His sanctuary, which He hath sanctified for ever, and serve the Lord your God, that His fierce anger may turn away from you. For if ye turn back unto the Lord, your brethren and your children shall find compassion before them that led them captive, and shall come back into this land; for the Lord your God is gracious and merciful, and will not turn away His face from you, if ye return unto Him.

The Chronicler reports dramatically on the reception of the letters by the people: how many laughed the messengers to scorn and mocked them, while others, especially of Asher, Zebulun and Judah, humbled themselves, and how finally a large multitude assembled in Jerusalem and celebrated the solemn Passover with great joy. 'For since the time of Solomon, the son of David, King of Israel, there was not the like in Jerusalem.'

This episode as narrated by the Chronicler fits very well the character and the other deeds of Hezekiah, the reformer and warrior, who dared to resist Sennacherib's threats, and whose mind was full of bold plans like that of the water conduit commemorated in the famous Siloam inscription. Reformist and Messianic tendencies are closely interwoven both in the actual plan and in the wording of the document which announced it. The letter meant obviously far more than a mere invitation to a festival. Addressed to the inhabitants of Judah as well as to the Children of Israel who escaped the deportation into the Assyrian captivity, the message presents itself, apart from its hortatory significance, as an attempt to re-establish the unity of worship of the Judaeans and perhaps to bring Israel back into the fold.

There are, it must be admitted, serious reasons for questioning the authenticity of the letter and even of the whole narrative. The second book of the Kings is entirely silent about this event, while it reports, in Ch. XXIII, 21–23, the story told also by the Chronicler (2 Chron. XXXV. 1–19) of a solemn Passover held about a century later by King Josiah in order to celebrate the discovery of the Book of the Covenant. If, as is more plausible, preference should be given to the older, more reliable source, we should have to assume that the Chronicler, usually assigned to the period of 300–250 B.C.E., has invented the story of Hezekiah's solemn Passover out of his desire to glorify the Temple and its priesthood. But even if Hezekiah's letter to the people of Judah and Israel has to be considered as an artificial product of a much later period, it certainly constitutes the only and most ancient example of a manifesto ascribed by Scripture to a Jewish king.

2

The Prophet Jeremiah opens a New Epoch in Jewish History by his Epistle to the Exiles in Babylon

AT the beginning of the sixth century B.C.E. the kingdom of Judah, squeezed between the Babylonian and the Egyptian giants, was nearing its end. In 597 King Jehoiachin was carried away to Babylon, and a considerable part of the population went with him into captivity. Nebuchadnezzar placed on the throne Zedekiah, the youngest son of King Josiah, who at first submitted to Babylon. But optimistic self-styled prophets predicted speedy deliverance from the Babylonian yoke with the help of Egypt. Moreover, unscrupulous agitators working from Babylon incited the people in Jerusalem to oppose a peaceful policy. Their onslaught was directed particularly against one man: the prophet Jeremiah, who endeavoured to avert the imminent catastrophe by advocating the acceptance of the foreign rule. While he wrestled with the people of Jerusalem, he was no less anxious to warn and to encourage the perplexed exiles. For with his prophetic eye he saw that, whereas the struggle with Babylon was hopeless, there was a future and a great hope for the people in exile.

In this spirit Jeremiah maintained a correspondence with the captives in Babylon. Only one letter of this interchange has been preserved, in the twenty-ninth chapter of the book which bears the prophet's name. It was brought to Babylon by the hand of a mission sent by Zedekiah to Nebuchadnezzar in 594 B.C.E. This letter is one of Jeremiah's most impressive utterances; he was never greater than when he composed the verses of this epistle (Jer. XXIX. 4–23).

THE PROPHET JEREMIAH TO THE JEWISH CAPTIVES IN BABYLON

'Seek the peace of the city whither I have caused you to be carried away captive, and pray unto the Lord for it'

[Jerusalem, 594 B.C.E.]

Thus saith the Lord of hosts, the God of Israel, unto all the captivity, whom I have caused to be carried away captive from Jerusalem unto Babylon:

Build ye houses, and dwell in them, and plant gardens, and eat the fruit of them; take ye wives, and beget sons and daughters; and take wives for your sons, and give your daughters to husbands, that they may bear sons and daughters; and multiply ye there, and be not diminished. And seek the peace of the city whither I have caused you to be carried away captive, and pray unto the Lord for it; for in the peace thereof shall ye have peace.

For thus saith the Lord of hosts, the God of Israel: Let not your prophets that are in the midst of you, and your diviners, beguile you, neither hearken ye to your dreams which ye cause to be dreamed. For they prophesy falsely unto you in My name; I have not sent them, saith the Lord.

For thus saith the Lord: After seventy years are accomplished for Babylon, I will remember you, and perform My good word toward you in causing you to return to this place. For I know the thoughts that I think toward you, saith the Lord, thoughts of peace, and not of evil, to give you a future and a hope. And ye shall call upon Me, and go, and pray unto Me, and I will hearken unto you. And ye shall seek Me, and find Me, when ye shall search for Me with all your heart. And I will be found of you, saith the Lord, and I will turn your captivity, and gather you from all the nations, and from all the places whither I have driven you, saith the Lord; and I will bring you back unto the place whence I caused you to be carried away captive. For ye have said: 'The Lord hath raised us up prophets in Babylon.' For thus saith the Lord concerning the King that sitteth upon the throne of David and concerning all the people that dwell in this city, your brethren that are not gone forth with you into captivity; thus saith the Lord of hosts: Behold, I will send upon them the sword, the famine, and the pestilence, and will make them like vile figs, that cannot be eaten, they are so bad. And I will pursue after them with the sword, with the famine and with the pestilence and will make them a horror unto all the kingdoms of the earth, a curse, and an astonishment, and a hissing, and a reproach, among all the nations whither I have driven them; because they have not hearkened to My words, saith the Lord, wherewith I sent unto them My servants the prophets, sending them betimes and often; but ye would not hear, saith the Lord. Hear ye therefore the word of the Lord, all ye of the captivity, whom I have sent away from Jerusalem to Babylon: Thus saith the Lord of hosts, the God of Israel, concerning Ahab the son of Kolaiah, and concerning Zedekiah the son of Maaseiah, who prophesy a lie unto you in My name: Behold, I will deliver them into the hand of Nebuchadnezzar, King of Babylon; and he shall slay them before your eyes; and of them shall be taken up a curse by all the captivity of Judah that are in Babylon, saying, 'The Lord make thee like Zedekiah and like Ahab, whom the King of Babylon roasted in the fire'; because they have wrought vile deeds in Israel, have committed adultery with their neighbours' wives, and have spoken words in My name falsely, which I commanded them not; but I am He that knoweth, and am witness, saith the Lord.

There has been much speculation about the original length of the letter. According to some scholars the verses 4–7 only, covering the first two paragraphs of the preceding text, constitute the whole letter, while the remainder is made up of speeches delivered by Jeremiah on other occasions. Others exclude mainly the passages containing the definite prophecies about the time of the return and those dealing with the punishment of the people. These uncertainties concerning the scope of the letter, however, do not affect the question of its authenticity. There can be no doubt that 'this message is a real letter which only became literature by its subsequent admission into the book of the Prophet. . . . [It] is not, of course, a letter such as anybody might dash off in an idle moment; nay, lightnings quiver between the lines, Yahweh speaks in wrath and blessings; still, although a Jeremiah wrote it, although it is a documentary fragment of the history and the religion of Israel, it is still a letter, neither less nor more' (G. A. Deissmann).

The actual effect of Jeremiah's letter was immense. This can be gathered from the reaction of the false prophets attacked in it. They found it necessary to strike back against Jeremiah immediately by denouncing him to the priesthood and the people of Jerusalem. This task was performed by Shemaiah the Nehelamite, who dispatched several letters from Babylon to Jerusalem with the explicit purpose of inciting the priests to prosecute Jeremiah. A fragment of one of these, addressed to Zephaniah, son of Maaseiah, has been preserved in Jeremiah XXIX. 26–28. It runs as follows:

> The Lord hath made thee priest in the stead of Jehoiada the priest, that there should be officers in the house of the Lord, for every man that is mad, and maketh himself a prophet, that thou shouldest put him in the stocks and in the collar. Now therefore, why hast thou not rebuked Jeremiah of Anathoth, who maketh himself a prophet to you, forasmuch as he hath sent unto us in Babylon, saying, 'The captivity is long: build ye houses and dwell in them; and plant gardens, and eat fruit of them'?

Shemaiah marks exactly, though unwittingly, the point at which Jeremiah's message to the exiles began a new epoch in Jewish history. An idea never uttered nor even conceived by any other prophet was born in Jeremiah's call. That Jews could live outside the Holy Land, separated from the Temple and the sacred worship, and yet remain faithful Jews, that they had to look upon life in the exile as upon a lot assigned to them by God's will, without losing the hope for a return to their homeland, that their stay in Babylonia should be transformed, by fruitful deeds, into a blessing for themselves and their posterity as well as for their environment, that their prayers should even aim at the peace of Babylon in harmony with God's own thoughts – these were indeed revolutionary notions. With the birth of this new universalism, life in the exile ceased to be a mere burden of senseless suffering, it gained a moral meaning and a new spiritual impulse. The deported Jews in Babylon became conscious of their particular task, and began to lay the foundations of that community which not only effected the restoration of the Jewish Commonwealth in Palestine but even, not long after the destruction of the second Temple, emerged as a new centre of the Jewish world.

The significance of Jeremiah's letter surpassed by far both its historical antecedents and its immediate consequences. Visualizing the connection of the Jewish national existence with the fate of the outer world, linking the hopes for Israel's redemption with the duties towards the living generations, Jeremiah revealed the very law of Jewish history. The mysterious interrelation of Zion and the Galuth became apparent. Lands of exile could turn into homelands, and a new return to Zion could emerge from a community of exiles, if the people should search for God with all their hearts. Henceforth there was no contradiction in Judaism between love for Zion and the attachment to other countries where Jews might dwell. The responsibility towards God linked both together.

Thus Jeremiah's letter contained a message to all later generations, a Great Charter for a wandering people which, after the loss of its homeland, started its life amongst the nations. It was understood in this sense, and ever and again throughout the ages made the subject of comment and re-interpretation. The text of the letter as recorded in the Book of Jeremiah already shows traces of such comments in the various additions which enlarged and changed the original wording. The popularity of the letter also gave birth to a lengthy letter falsely attributed to Jeremiah, and addressed to the Jewish prisoners who were destined for deportation to Babylon. It is a warning against idolatry, usually incorporated in the apocryphal book of Baruch, but probably a separate product of the first century B.C.E. Passing over such spurious works, we may recognize Jeremiah's original letter to the captives in Babylon as the true ancestor of the great family of genuine epistles which were to become an important feature of later Judaism and Christianity.

3

The Lachish Letters: An Original Correspondence from the Last Days of Solomon's Temple

ON January 29, 1935, J. L. Starkey, the leader of the Wellcome Archæological Expedition to the Near East, while excavating at Tell ed Duweir, supposed to be the site of the biblical fortress town Lachish, in southern Palestine, discovered a group of inscribed ostraca (potsherds) in a small room adjoining the outer gateway of the ancient city. They were lying in a burnt layer with charcoal and ashes among hundreds of other pottery fragments. Most of them did not show any readable traces of writing, but eighteen pieces contained Hebrew writing in pre-exilic Phœnician Hebrew script, some of it 'as clear as the day it was made'. The examination of these ostraca showed that nearly all of them were letters or fragments of letters belonging to the age of Jeremiah – the first Hebrew original documents written in the days of the prophets to come into our hands. It was, in the words of Prof. H. Torczyner, to whom we are indebted for the first attempt to decipher and interpret the texts, 'the most valuable discovery made in the biblical archæology of Palestine'.

The whole of the eighteen ostraca were first published in 1938, with photographs, with an English translation and a commentary by Prof. Torczyner, while three readable ostraca discovered later were dealt with separately by Prof. Torczyner, Prof. H. Ginsberg and Dr. D. Diringer in special articles. Since then the ostraca have been subjected to minute examination by a host of scholars. Various different readings have been suggested and new interpretations offered, ranging from theories put forward by Prof. René Dussaud, J. W. Jack, Sir Charles Marston, Prof. J. Reider, and Prof. D. Winton Thomas, to the acute palæographical and philological criticisms raised by Prof. W. F. Albright, Dr. S. A. Birnbaum, Prof. U. Cassuto and Prof. Ginsberg, to mention some of the main participants in this struggle for the clarification of the mystery which surrounds these ancient scripts. But while controversy still rages round a number of details connected with them, substantial agreement has been reached concerning their general meaning and character. There is no question that some of the ostraca – perhaps most or even all of them – were letters sent by a Jewish officer Hoshaiah, probably a military commander stationed at a place near Lachish, to his superior

Ya'osh or Ya'ush, who was perhaps governor of Lachish. The contents of the letters, which Hoshaiah apparently dictated to various scribes, refer to military problems caused by the Chaldean invasion, which was taking place at the time, as described in the Book of Jeremiah. In the opinion of Prof. Torczyner the letters were written between 597 and 588 B.C.E. Other scholars maintain that they are to be dated toward the end of Zedekiah's reign and that most of them were written in 587, shortly before the fall of Jerusalem (586).

The six letters which we reproduce here are those numbered II, III, IV, V, VI and IX in the Editio Princeps. The translation given is based on the so far most definitive reading of Prof. W. F. Albright (in the Bulletin of the American School of Oriental Research), which summarizes critically the interpretations of Prof. Torczyner and the other scholars. The Divine Name, the Tetragrammaton, which occurs literally in the letters, has been retained here also unaltered.

THE JEWISH OFFICER HOSHAIAH TO HIS SUPERIOR YA'OSH

'The heart of thy servant hath been sick since thou didst write to thy servant'

[At an unknown place in Judah, near Lachish, probably in the year 587 B.C.E.]

II

To my Lord Ya'osh: May YHWH cause my lord to hear tiding of peace this very day, this very day!

Who is thy servant but a dog that my lord hath remembered his servant? May YHWH afflict those who say what thou dost not know.

III

Thy servant Hoshaiah hath sent to inform my lord Ya'osh: May YHWH cause my lord to hear tidings of peace!

And now thou hast sent a letter but my lord hath not enlightened thy servant concerning the letter which thou didst send to thy servant yesterday evening, for the heart of thy servant hath been sick since thou didst write to thy servant.

And as for what my lord hath said, 'Thou dost not know it! – Read any letter,' as YHWH liveth no one hath undertaken to read me a letter at any time, nor have I read any letter that may have come to me nor would I give anything for it!

And it hath been reported to thy servant, saying, 'The commander of the host, Coniah son of Elnatan,[1] hath come down in order to go into Egypt and unto Hodaviah son of Ahijah, and his men hath he sent to obtain supplies from him.' – And as for the letter of Tobiah, servant of the King, which came to Shallum, son of Jaddua, through the instrumentality of the prophet, saying, 'Beware!', thy servant hath sent it to my lord.

IV

May YHWH cause my lord to hear this very day tidings of good!

And now, according to everything that my lord hath sent [written], thus hath thy servant done. I have written on the door[2] according to all that my lord hath sent to me. And with regard to what my lord hath sent about the matter of Beth-ha-rapîd,[3] there is nobody there. And as for Semachiah, Shemaiah hath taken him and hath brought him up to the City [Jerusalem]. And as for thy servant, O my lord, let him be sent thither – where is he – where is he [Semachiah] but in [the city's] vicinity? Investigate and my lord will know that we are watching for the signals[4] of Lachish to all the indications which my lord hath given, for we cannot see Azekah.[5]

V

May YHWH cause my lord to hear tidings of peace and good this very day!

Who is thy servant but a dog, that thou hast sent to thy servant the letters. . . . Now thy servant hath returned the letters to my lord. May YHWH cause thee to see . . . according to His desire. How can thy servant benefit or injure the king?

VI

To my lord Ya'osh: May YHWH cause my lord to see this season in good health!

Who is thy servant but a dog, that my lord hath sent the letter of the king and the letters of the princes saying, 'Pray, read them'? And, behold, the words of the princes are not good, but to weaken your hands and to slacken the hands of the men[6] who are informed about them. . . . And now, my lord, wilt thou not write to them saying, 'Why do ye do thus even in Jerusalem? Behold, unto the king and unto his house are ye doing this thing!' And as YHWH thy God liveth it is true that since thy servant read the letters there hath been no peace for thy servant.

IX

May YHWH cause my lord to hear tidings of peace!

. . . hath sent 115. . . . Return word to thy servant by the hand of Shelemiah telling us what we shall do tomorrow . . .

Whatever the precise issue of these mysterious letters might have been, there is no doubt that they are related to the military agony of Judah and to the internal struggle raging within the invaded country. At the time of the correspondence the hope that besieged Jerusalem could still be saved was vanishing. Nevertheless, the King, his advisers and a part of the population clung, even at this critical stage of the war, to the alliance with Egypt, and rejected vehemently the idea of submission to Babylonia as advocated by Jeremiah and his followers. The divisions among the people seem to have affected the army and to have bred mutual suspicions among the commanding officers. In most of the letters Hoshaiah is apparently concerned to refute charges that he had, without permission, read and spoken about some important confidential letters. The prophet mentioned in III was identified by Prof. Torczyner with Uriah, who was put to death by King Jehoiakim, according to Jeremiah XXVI. 20–23, because he had opposed the policy of the King like Jeremiah. Other scholars, who are reluctant to adopt Prof. Torczyner's hypothesis that Uriah was slain by King Zedekiah, suppose that the prophet in question was Jeremiah himself.

Thus the letters throw a vivid sidelight on the dissensions of the people in the face of the great Babylonian invasion, and both in this way and in their allusions to current events provide an invaluable supplement to the picture drawn by Jeremiah. We see a military mission on the way to Egypt, the evacuation of a place is mentioned the name of which occurs in the Chronicles, and important orders given to Hoshaiah are reported to have been posted by him on the door like the commandments of the Torah. The fortified cities of Judah, Lachish and Azekah, expressly referred to by Jeremiah as the kingdom's last bastions, emerge before our eyes. The fall of Azekah is imminent, if it had not actually happened. But the brave fighters at another outpost look out for the signals of Lachish where Ya'osh carries on his hopeless task with unshakable persistence. The astonishing confirmations of the biblical account, accumulated within the narrow space of a handful of legible lines, make, indeed, to use the words of Sir Charles Marston, 'the Bible come alive'.

And yet this amazing experience brought about by the reading of the Lachish Letters is due, perhaps even more than to their contents, to what may be called their biblical tone. What Prof. J. Reider has said of the Letter III, that it 'reads smoothly and flowingly like a chapter of Samuel or Kings', may well be applied to the Letters in general. Greetings with wishes for peace open the messages, and the formula which is used to express devotion ('Who is thy servant but a dog') occurs also with slight variations in the Book of Samuel (1 Sam. XVII. 43) and Kings (2 Kings VIII. 13). But above all, a firm trust in God and resignation to His will pervades all the letters. No sign of idolatry can be discovered in any of the texts. The sacred name signifying the unity of God is invoked in the greetings and in the formula of the oath. Moreover, the name of Hoshaiah and most of the names occurring in the letters are biblical names compounded with the name YHWH. In addition, one of the ostraca (No. 1) is nothing more than a list of names which, with only two exceptions, show the same characteristic composition:

Gamariah son of Hissiliah
Jaazaniah son of Tobshillem
Hagab son of Jaazaniah
Mibtahiah son of Jeremiah
Mattaniah son of Neriah

There is not sufficient reason to identify Jeremiah and Neriah mentionep in this list with Jeremiah the prophet and Neriah, the father of his scribe, though such a possibility cannot be absolutely excluded. But unquestionably this ostracon without any intelligible text speaks to posterity no less eloquently than the other true Lachish Letters. The eight various names ending with the Holy Name are the most emphatic confession of the faith which was destined to survive the fortresses of Judah and even the Temple.

NOTES

1. Cf. Jer. xxvi. 22, 23, where we are told that Elnathan, son of Achbor, in the time of King Jehoiakim headed an expedition to Egypt in order to bring back the fugitive prophet Uriah.
2. Cf. Deut. vi. 9; xi. 20.
3. Cf. 1 Chron. iv. 12, where the name Beth-Rapha, the son of Eshton, occurs.
4. In an article in the *Jewish Quarterly Review*, April 1949, Prof. Torczyner has suggested that the word אותות in the original text means 'miraculous signs' and that this letter was addressed to the prophet Uriah. The letter belongs, as Prof. Torczyner now maintains, to the reign of Jehoiakim (608–598) or Jehoiachin (577).
5. Cf. Jer. xxxiv. 7.
6. Cf. Jer. xxxviii. 4.

4

Persian State Papers which changed the Course of Jewish History

THE letters inserted in the Book of Ezra are exclusively written by Persian kings and officials. But the irresistibility of the forces which were bringing about the revival of Israel is nowhere more manifest than within these letters, particularly in the three following documents. Through their medium the voice of Jewish prophecy makes itself heard, they are instrumental in its fulfilment and serve the purpose of Israel's rebirth, although some of them, such as the second of the reproduced specimens, seem to be directed against it. These records, incorporated into the Bible and transmitted in the holy tongue, are, therefore, in spite of their foreign origin, inseparable from the history of Israel's letters.

1. *The Edict of Cyrus*

The overthrow of the Babylonian empire by the Persian king Cyrus in 539 B.C.E. was followed almost immediately by the edict which became the great charter of the restoration. Its author was welcomed by the exilic Isaiah as the Shepherd, the Anointed of the Lord, and his deeds were praised as works inspired by God. The proclamation of the edict was, indeed, in the Book of Ezra (I. 1) as well as in the Chronicles (2 Chron. XXXVI. 22), expressly related to the prophecy of Jeremiah: 'Now in the first year of Cyrus, king of Persia, that the word of the Lord by the mouth of Jeremiah might be accomplished, the Lord stirred up the spirit of Cyrus, king of Persia, that he made a proclamation throughout all his kingdom and put it also in writing saying':

CYRUS, KING OF PERSIA, TO THE JEWISH PEOPLE IN HIS KINGDOM

'Whosoever there is among you of all his people—his God be with him—let him go up to Jerusalem'

[Ekbatana, 539 B.C.E.]

Thus saith Cyrus, King of Persia: All kingdoms of the earth hath the Lord, the God of heaven, given me; and He hath charged me to build Him a house in Jerusalem, which is in Judah.

Whosoever there is among you of all His people – his God be with him – let him go up to Jerusalem, which is in Judah, and build the house of the Lord, the God of Israel, He is the God who is in Jerusalem. And whosoever is left, in any place where he sojourneth, let the men of his place help him with silver, and with gold, and with goods, and with beasts, beside the freewill-offering for the house of God which is in Jerusalem.

2. *The Satrap Tatnai asks Darius, King of Persia, for an inquiry about the forgotten Edict*

Hardly two decades after the publication of the edict, the leaders of the returned Jews, Zerubbabel and the prophets Haggai and Zechariah, had to struggle for the official acknowledgment of the permission to rebuild the Sanctuary at Jerusalem. The Persian satrap Tatnai, governor of the western provinces, although himself adverse to the building of the Temple and instigated by neighbouring tribes hostile to the Jews, became the intermediary for the transmission of the Jewish claims to the Persian court.

TATNAI, GOVERNOR OF THE WESTERN PROVINCES OF PERSIA, AND HIS COLLEAGUES, TO DARIUS, KING OF PERSIA

'And thus they returned us answer, saying, We are the servants of the God of heaven and earth, and build the house . . . which a great king of Israel builded and finished'

[Jerusalem, 519 B.C.E.]

Unto Darius the King, all peace.

Be it known unto the King that we went into the province of Judah, to the house of the Great God which is builded with great stones, and timber is laid in the walls, and this work goeth on with diligence and prospereth in their hands. Then asked we those elders, and said unto them thus: 'Who gave you a decree to build this house, and finish this wall?' We asked them their names also, to announce to thee, that we might write the names of the men that were at the head of them. And thus they returned us answer, saying: 'We are the servants of the God of heaven and earth, and build the house that was builded these many years ago which a great king of Israel builded and finished. But because that our fathers had provoked the God of heaven, He gave them into the hands of Nebuchadnezzar, King of Babylon, the Chaldean, who destroyed this house, and carried the people away into Babylon. But in the first year of Cyrus, King of Babylon, Cyrus the King made a decree to build this house of God. And the gold and silver vessels also of the house of God, which Nebuchadnezzar took out of the temple that was in Jerusalem, and brought them into the temple of Babylon, those did Cyrus the King take out of the temple of Babylon, and they were delivered unto one whose name was Sheshbazzar, whom he had made governor; and he said unto him: Take these vessels, go, put them in the temple that is in Jerusalem, and let the house of God be builded in its place. Then came the same Sheshbazzar, and laid the foundations of the house of God which is in Jerusalem; and since that time even until now hath it been in building, and yet it is not completed.'

Now therefore, if it seem good to the King, let search be made in the King's treasure-house there, which is at Babylon, whether it be so, that a decree was made of Cyrus the King to build this house of God at Jerusalem and let the King send his pleasure to us concerning this matter.

Obviously a record of the edict was found in the archives. The answer sent by Darius to Tatnai confirmed the charter of Cyrus and ordered him to give active assistance to the Jews in rebuilding the Temple, which actually was completed at the beginning of 515 B.C.E.

3. *The Mandate of Artaxerxes, King of Persia, to Ezra, the Priest*

Some seventy years later, in the reign of Artaxerxes, Ezra, the priest and scribe, led a new band of immigrants from Babylonia to Jerusalem, carrying with him a letter from the King no less decisive for the course of Jewish history than those of Cyrus and Darius mentioned above. As the former had given the initiative to the restoration, and the latter had enabled the exiles to rebuild the Temple, so this one laid the legal foundations of the new Jewish Commonwealth.

ARTAXERXES, KING OF PERSIA, TO EZRA, THE PRIEST

'And thou, Ezra, after the wisdom of thy God, . . . appiont magistrates and judges, which may judge all the people that are beyond the River'

[Susa, 458 B.C.E.]

Artaxerxes, King of Kings, unto Ezra the priest, the scribe of the Law of the God of heaven, and so forth.

And now I make a decree, that all they of the people of Israel and their priests and the Levites, in my realm, that are minded of their own free will to go with thee to Jerusalem, go. Forasmuch as thou art sent of the King and his seven counsellors, to inquire concerning Judah and Jerusalem, according to the law of thy God which is in thy hand; and to carry the silver and gold which the King and his counsellors have freely offered unto the God of Israel, whose habitation is in Jerusalem, and all the silver and gold that thou shalt find in all the province of Babylon, with the freewill offering of the people, and of the priests, offering willingly for the house of their God which is in Jerusalem; therefore thou shalt with all diligence buy with this money bullocks, rams, lambs, with their meal offerings and their drink offerings, and shalt offer them upon the altar of the house of your God which is in Jerusalem. And whatsoever shall seem good to thee and to thy brethren to do with the rest of the silver and the gold, that do ye after the will of your God. And the vessels that are given thee for the service of the house of thy God, deliver thou before the God of Jerusalem. And whatsoever more shall be needful for the house of thy God, which thou shalt have occasion to bestow, bestow it out of the King's treasure-house. And I, even I, Artaxerxes the King, do make a decree to all the treasurers that are beyond the River, that whatsoever Ezra the priest, the scribe of the Law of the God of heaven, shall require of you, it be done with all diligence, unto a hundred talents of silver, and to a hundred measures of wheat, and to a hundred baths of wine, and to a hundred baths of oil, and salt without prescribing how much. Whatsoever is commanded by the God of heaven, let it be done exactly for the house of the God of heaven; for why should there be wrath against the realm of the King and his sons? Also we announce to you, that touching any of the priests and Levites, the singers, porters, Nethinim, or servants of this house of God, it shall not be lawful to impose tribute, impost, or toll, upon them.

And thou, Ezra, after the wisdom of thy God that is in thy hand, appoint magistrates and judges, who may judge all the people that are beyond the River, all such as know the laws of thy God; and teach ye him that knoweth them not. And whosoever will not do the law of thy God, and the law of the King, let judgment be executed upon him with all diligence, whether it be unto death, or to banishment, or to confiscation of goods, or to imprisonment.

Ezra himself has added to this letter the most eloquent postscript: 'Blessed be the Lord, the God of our fathers, who hath put such a thing as this in the king's heart, to beautify the house of the Lord which is in Jerusalem, and hath extended mercy unto me before the king, and his counsellors, and before all the king's mighty princes. And I was strengthened according to the hand of the Lord my God upon me, and I gathered together out of Israel chief men to go up with me' (Ezra VII. 27, 28).

5

The Elephantine Letters: News of Egyptian Jews from the Close of the Biblical Era

WE are told in the Book of Jeremiah that, after the capture of Jerusalem by the Babylonians, a considerable number of Jews emigrated to Egypt and settled there. Jeremiah gives a gloomy picture of the religious and moral state of this new Jewish colony in the land of the Pharaohs. Nothing, however, was known about its later development and fate, until in 1905 the discovery of papyri at Jeb (Elephantine), on an island near Assuan, brought that hidden chapter of Jewish early history again to light. Through these records, written in Aramaic, the world became acquainted with the existence and life of a Jewish colony established in Elephantine probably between 585 and 570 B.C.E. It would seem that originally some of the Jews who escaped into Egypt after the destruction of Jerusalem were settled on the southern borders of Egypt and entrusted with the duty of guarding the frontier, but that subsequently the community lost its military character. It did not, however, become absorbed in its surroundings, and retained its Jewish faith. Probably in 568 a big temple was erected in Elephantine. Here sacrifices were offered to Ya'u, the 'God of Heaven', although the cult of secondary deities was not excluded. The Elephantine papyri consist mostly of legal deeds, contracts and literary works. They also include, however, a certain number of letters and fragments of letters. We owe to the preservation of this correspondence the disclosure of some of the most interesting facts concerning the Jews of Elephantine.

1. *An Exhortation to keep the Passover*

The following letter bears witness to the revivalist efforts which were made during Nehemiah's lifetime in the remote colony on the Nile, and to the influence exercised by the Jews recently returned from Babylon to the Holy Land, and even by the Persian kings themselves, upon the religious life of the Egyptian Jews. Hananiah, the writer of this letter, was possibly identical with Hananiah, the ruler of the palace, who, according to Nehemiah VII. 2, was in charge over the restored Jerusalem. The letter itself is a religious appeal worthy of a 'faithful man' who 'feared God above many'. Oddly enough, its formula of greeting contains the Aramaic expression for 'the gods', which, however, as A. Cowley assumes, perhaps had become stereotyped in use, and had ceased to be consciously regarded as plural, just as was the case with the Hebrew Elohim.

HANANIAH TO JEDONIAH, HEAD OF THE JEWISH COMMUNITY OF ELEPHANTINE

'Anything at all in which there is leaven do not eat'

[Elephantine, 419 B.C.E.]

To my Brethren, Jedoniah[1] and his colleagues the Jewish garrison, your brother Hananiah. The welfare of my brethren may the gods seek.

Now this year, the fifth year of the King Darius,[2] word was sent from the King to Arsames[3] saying: In the month of Tybi let there be a Passover for the Jewish garrison. Now do you accordingly count fourteen days of the month Nisan and keep the Passover, and from the 15th day to the 21st day of Nisan [shall be] seven days of unleavened bread. Be clean and take heed. Do not work on the 15th day and on the 21st day. Also drink no beer, and anything at all in which there is leaven do not eat from the 15th day from sunset till the 21st day of Nisan, seven days, let it not be seen among you; do not bring [it] into your dwelling, but seal [it] up during those days. Let this be done as Darius the King commanded.

[Address] To my brethren, Jedoniah and his colleagues the Jewish garrison, your brother Hananiah.

It is interesting to speculate on the reasons which might have induced a Persian king to order the deliverance of the Jewish people from the Egyptian bondage to be celebrated by the Jews in Egypt, some ten centuries after the original event. In any case this letter, one of the last we possess from biblical times, constitutes a significant parallel to another of the earliest examples of Jewish letter writing – the invitation of King Hezekiah to the solemn Passover at Jerusalem (see *supra*, p. 3f.).

2. *The Jews of Elephantine plead for the rebuilding of their destroyed temple*

With the Jews who were settled in Babylonia the Jewish colony in Egypt may be considered as the advance guard of the Diaspora, as the first dispersed

Jews who tried to maintain their national and religious character by their strength of will. They became also the victims of an attack sharing all the features of later anti-Jewish outbreaks in the Dispersion. The following letter tells with admirable clarity the story of this event – the destruction of the temple at Elephantine in the year 411 B.C.E. – one of the earliest persecutions recorded in the annals of the Diaspora, at a time close to happenings reported in the Book of Esther.

JEDONIAH, THE HEAD OF THE JEWISH GARRISON OF ELEPHANTINE, TO BIGVAI (BAGOHI), GOVERNOR OF JUDAEA

'They entered the temple, they destroyed it to the ground'

[Jeb (Elephantine), 408 B.C.E.]

To our Lord Bigvai, Governor of Judaea,[4] your servants Jedoniah and his colleagues, the priests who are in Jeb, the fortress. The health of your lordship may the God of Heaven seek after exceedingly at all times, and give you favour before Darius the King, and the princes of the palace, and more than now a thousand times, and may he grant you long life and may you be happy and prosperous at all times.

Now your servant Jedoniah and his colleagues depose as follows: In the month of Tammuz in the 14th year of Darius the King, when Arsames departed and went to the King, the priests of the God Khnub, who is in the fortress of Jeb, formed a league with Waidrang who was governor here, saying, The temple of Ya'u the God, which is in the fortress of Jeb, let them remove from there. Then that Waidrang, the reprobate, sent a letter to his son Nephayan, who was commander of the garrison in the fortress of Syene, saying, The temple which is in Jeb the fortress let them destroy. Then Nephayan led out the Egyptians with the other forces. They came to the fortress of Jeb with their weapons, they entered that temple, they destroyed it to the ground, and the pillars of stone which were there they broke. Also it came to pass that five gateways built with hewn blocks of stone which were in that temple they destroyed, and their doors they lifted off and the hinges of those doors which were of bronze, and the roof of cedar wood, all of it with the rest of the furniture and other things which were there, they burnt with fire, and the basins of gold and silver and everything that was in that temple, all of it they took and appropriated to themselves. Already in the days of the kings of Egypt our fathers had built that temple in the fortress of Jeb, and when Cambyses came into Egypt he found that temple built, and though the temples of the Gods of Egypt all of them they overthrew, no one did any harm to that temple.

When this took place, we, with our wives and our children, put on sackcloth and fasted and prayed to Ja'u the Lord of Heaven, who let us see [our desire] upon that Waidrang. The dogs tore off the anklet from his legs, and all the men who had sought to do evil to that temple, all of them, were killed, and we saw [our desire] upon them.

Also, before this, at the time when this evil was done to us, we sent a letter to your lordship and to Johanan the High Priest[5] and his colleagues, the priests, who are in Jerusalem, and to Ostanes, the brother of Anani, and nobles of the Jews, but they have not sent any letters to us. Also since the month of Tammuz, in the 14th year of Darius the King, till this day we have worn sackcloth and fasted; our wives are become like widows, we do not anoint ourselves with oil and we drink no wine. Also from that [time] till [the present] day in the 17th year of Darius the King, neither meal-offering, incense, nor sacrifice have they offered in that temple.

Now your servants Jedoniah and his colleagues, and the Jews, all of them inhabitants of Jeb, say as follows: If it seem good to your lordship, take thought for that temple to build it, since they do not allow us to build it. Look upon your well-wishers and friends who are here in Egypt, [and] let a letter be sent from you to them concerning the temple of the God Ya'u to build it in the fortress of Jeb as it was built before, and they shall offer the meal-offering and incense and sacrifice on the altar of the God Ya'u on your behalf and we will pray for you always, we, our wives, our children, and the Jews, all who are here, if they cause the temple to be rebuilt, and it shall be a merit to you before Ya'u the God of Heaven more than that of a man who offers to him sacrifice and burnt-offerings worth as much as a thousand talents. As to gold, about this we have sent [and given] instructions. Also the whole matter we have set forth in a letter in our name to Delaiah and Shelemiah,[6] the sons of Sanballat, Governor of Samaria.[7] And of all this which was done to us Arsames knew nothing.

On the 20th of Marheshwan, the 17th year of Darius the King.

This document has been preserved in two drafts, each with numerous corrections, a sign of the great care with which it was drawn up. It must have required no small diplomatic skill on the part of the framers to seek help from the Persian governor of Judaea after the failure of the petition they had submitted previously to the High Priest. As far as we are aware, no written reply was sent to their appeals from Jerusalem or Samaria. But a memorandum, drawn up by the messenger of the petition and miraculously preserved among the papyri, informs posterity about the contents of a not unfavourable verbal reply given by the Governor of Judaea and the authorities of Samaria:

Memorandum from Bigvai and Delaiah.

They said to me: Let it be an instruction to you in Egypt to say to Arsames about the altar-house of the God of Heaven which was built in the fortress of Jeb formerly, before Cambyses, which Waidrang, that reprobate, destroyed in the 14th year of Darius the King, to rebuild it in its place as it was before, and they may offer the meal-offering and incense upon that altar as formerly was done . . .

Thus it seems that a compromise was reached, granting restoration of the temple and the former worship with the important exception of animal sacrifices. Despite this agreement, the temple of Jeb remained in ruins. Moreover, four years after these negotiations about rebuilding the Jeb temple, Persian rule in Egypt was ended by a revolt and it is probable that the Jewish colony of Elephantine ceased to exist.

3. *Private News from Elephantine*

To these historical documents we may add the fragments of a few private letters which have been found among the papyri. The plain, un-artificial language of these writings is much like that of the Lachish letters. The correspondents call themselves 'brethren', and the abundance of greetings indicates the cordiality which prevailed among the members of the community. But one difference which stands out strikingly between the letters of Lachish and Elephantine is that in some of them the term 'gods' and not God is used in the invocation of the Deity, a fact which bears out the complaints of the prophet Jeremiah (Jer. XLIV) about the polytheistic leanings of the Jews in Egypt. (See, however, A. Cowley's special comment to Hananiah's letter, *supra*, p. 22.)

(A)

HOSHAIAH BEN NATHAN TO PILTAI BEN YEOSH

'The welfare of my brother may the God of Heaven seek at all times'

[Somewhere in Egypt, second half of the 5th century B.C.E.]

To my brother Piltai, your brother Hoshaiah. The welfare of my brother may the God of Heaven seek at all times.

Greeting to Sheva and his children. Greeting to Ab . . . I have heard of the trouble which you took when . . . I went. I and Zeho b. Peha spoke to Paisan . . . and he sent a letter about it to Zeho . . . concerning the children. About you my heart is distressed. Your matter you should send to . . .

To my brother Piltai b. Yeosh, your brother Hoshaiah b. Nathan.

(B)

AN UNKNOWN WRITER TO ZEHO BEN PEHA AND HIS SONS

'Look after my house as you would do for your own house'

[Somewhere in Egypt, second half of the 5th century B.C.E.]

To my brother Zeho and his sons, your brother . . .
The welfare of my brother may the gods all seek abundantly at all times . . .

Whenever a letter came to me with tidings of your welfare, I rejoiced abundantly and I always sent a greeting to you. Now . . . they did not tell me. Consequently I was full of wrath against you before Dallah . . . After I [came] from Syene you did not send a letter to me about your welfare. Look after the servants and my home as you would do for your own house. . . . News of yourself, and your wishes send to me . . . in peace.

To my brother Zeho b. Peha and his sons . . . b. H. your brother.

(c)

HOSHEA TO . . . BEN HAGGAI

'When this letter reaches you do not delay, come down to Memphis at once'

[Memphis(?), second half of the 5th century B.C.E.]

To my brother . . . your brother Hoshea, greeting and peace abundantly be . . . upon you at all times.

Now we in the presence of Paisan the judge and his servant have paid the sum of 10 kerashin and a kerash remains . . . in your hands, that he should give 5 kerashin pure silver. Now . . . with you, as to his giving you the sum of 5 kerashin; and write for them a deed concerning them; and if they will not give you all the money at interest and do not say to you 'Give security', buy the house of Zaccur and the house of A. Š. N. . . . If they will not sell them, seek out a man who will buy the big house of Hodav and give it to him for the money at which it is valued.

When the letter reaches you, do not delay, come down to Memphis at once. If you have obtained money, come down at once. And if you have not obtained it, still come down at once. Go to Bethel-ad-dan and he will give you a striped coat of WASA, a coat of wool . . . a cloak of . . . dyed, and 6 kerashin. An old coat. And when he gives them to you, send to me. And if he does not give them to you, send to me. Now, if you come down to Memphis, do not leave anything to A. Š. N. . . . When the Jews bring them before Arsames say . . . you renounce your claims on me . . . and after their words do not delay, come down at once and at once bring down to me a coat in your hands to Memphis . . . as he wrote to me about it.

On the 27th of Tybi; this is Nisan, year . . .

To my brother . . . b. Haggai, your brother Hoshea.

(D)

HOSHEA TO LADY SELAVA

'To my lady Selava, your servant Hoshea'

[Somewhere in Egypt, second half of the 5th century B.C.E.]

To my lady Selava, your servant Hoshea greeting. May the gods all seek your welfare at all times.

Greeting to my lord Menahem. Greeting to my lady Abihi. Greeting to her son and her daughter. Greeting to Tekhnum and Ya'yishma. Greeting to Meshullemeth. Greeting to Hazul. Greeting to . . . which are upon you. Greeting to all of them. And now you have ratified . . . Ye'osh said to me as follows: Pay in gold . . .

To my lady Selava, your servant Hoshea.

These and a few other similar fragments must be considered the earliest known remnants of a purely private Jewish correspondence, separated by centuries from the next specimens of this kind. Moreover, Hoshea's urgent request to ben Haggai to meet him at Memphis is one of the most ancient Jewish business letters known, and lady Selava was the first and remained for many hundred years the only woman of Jewish origin to whom was addressed a letter which has still survived.

NOTES

1. Jedoniah was the chief priest and head of the community.
2. Darius II, King of Persia (424–404 B.C.E.).
3. Arsames, Persian high official, Governor of Egypt.
4. Bigvai or Bagohi (also Bagoas) was the successor of Nehemiah as Governor of Judaea.
5. Johanan, High Priest, mentioned in Neh. XII. 22, 23.
6. Delaiah and Shelemiah, names which occur in Neh. VI. 10 and XIII. 13.
7. Sanballat, Governor of Samaria, mentioned by Nehemiah frequently as his opponent, especially Neh. III. 33–34; VI. 1, 2, 5, 12, 14.

6

From the 'Letter of Aristeas'

FOR some three centuries before the destruction of the Temple in 70 C.E. the Jews in Egypt, and especially in Alexandria, formed a highly cultured community which effected a remarkable synthesis between Jewish religious practice and Greek speculative thought. This synthesis was based on a Greek translation of the Pentateuch which was no less esteemed by them than the original Hebrew by the Jews in Palestine. The so-called 'Letter of Aristeas' is a highly embellished account of the circumstances in which the Jews of Egypt came into possession of this treasure, known to subsequent generations, for reasons given in the 'Letter' itself, as the Septuagint. The 'Letter' tells the story of the embassy sent by Ptolemy Philadelphus, King of Egypt (285–247 B.C.E.), to Jerusalem in order to obtain a copy of the Torah and the assistance of Jewish translators, and how the seventy-two Hebrew scholars were received by the king, and how they performed the great task in exactly seventy-two days. In spite of the form chosen by the author – that of a letter addressed by Aristeas to his brother Philocrates – this document is a fictitious literary product. The writer, who pretends to be a Greek by birth, and one of the two high officials who were sent by the king to Jerusalem, was probably an Alexandrian Jew of the first century B.C.E. The report given in the letter was accepted as historical by Philo, Josephus, the Talmud, and the Church Fathers, but modern scholars have thrown doubt on many, if not most, of its statements. The literary value of the colourful narrative remains, however, unaffected.

1. *Aristeas describes the Temple and the Service of the High Priest*

Some of the descriptions contained in the 'Letter' are given with the vividness of an eye-witness, such as that of the overwhelming impression caused by the first sight of the Temple and by the service of the High Priest.

ARISTEAS TO 'HIS BROTHER PHILOCRATES'

'The general aspect of these things produces awe and reverence, so much so that one thinks one has passed into another sphere outside the world'

[Supposed date: Alexandria, first half of the 3rd century B.C.E.]

The next portion of my letter contains an account of our journey to Eleazar; but first I will describe the situation of the whole country.

When we reached the district, we beheld the city set in the centre of the whole of Judaea upon a mountain which rose to great height. Upon its crest stood the Temple in splendour, with its three enclosing walls, more than seventy cubits high, and of a breadth and length matching the structure of the edifice. The whole of the Temple was built with a magnificence and prodigality beyond all precedent. It was obvious that no expense had been spared on the great doorway and the fastenings which held it to the door-posts and the stability of the lintel. And the curtain was made very closely to resemble the door[1]; the fabric was kept in perpetual motion by the draught of wind underneath which caused it to bulge out from bottom to top, and the effect was a beautiful spectacle, from which it was hard to tear oneself away.

The altar was built of a size in keeping with the place and with the sacrifices which were consumed on it by fire, and the ascent to it was on a like scale. The place was approached by a gradual slope which allowed a proper regard for decency,[2] and the ministering priests were clad in 'coats of fine linen'[3] reaching to the ankles . . .

The priests' ministration in its exhibition of physical power and in its orderly and silent procedure could in no way be surpassed. For they all of their own free will undergo labours requiring much endurance, and each has his appointed task. Their service is without intermission, some providing the wood, others oil, others fine wheat flour, others the spices; while others bring the pieces of flesh for the burnt-offering, which they handle with extraordinary strength. For they grip with both hands the legs of the calves, most of which weigh over two talents, and then with wonderful dexterity fling the beast to a considerable height, and never fail to plant it on the altar. . . . The deepest silence prevails so that one would suppose that there was not a single person in the place, although the ministers in attendance number some seven hundred, not to mention the large multitude of those who bring their sacrifices to be offered; everything is performed with reverence and in a manner worthy of the divine majesty.

And when we beheld Eleazar carrying out his ministration in his priestly robes[4] and the lustre shed on him by the 'coat', wherewith he is clad, and the precious stones about his person, we were struck with a great amazement. For there are 'bells of gold'[5] around the border of his 'long robe' giving out a peculiar musical sound, and on either side of these are 'pomegranates'[6] embroidered in gay colours of a marvellous hue. He was girt with a rich and magnificent 'girdle',[7] woven in the fairest colours. And on his breast he wears what is called the 'oracle',[8] wherein are set 'twelve stones' of divers kinds, fastened with gold, bearing the names of the heads of the tribes according to their original order, each of them flashing with indescribable splendour according to its own natural hue. On his head he has the 'tiara',[9] as it is called, and over this the inimitable 'turban', the consecrated diadem, bearing engraven upon 'a plate of gold' in holy letters the name of God, set between his eyebrows, full of glory. Such is the raiment of him who is judged worthy of these things in the public services. And the general aspect of these things produces awe and reverence, so much so that one thinks one has passed into another sphere outside the world; indeed I confidently affirm that any man who witnesses the spectacle which I have described will experience an amazement and wonder indescribable, and will be profoundly moved in his mind at the sanctity attaching to every detail. . . .

2. *The legendary Correspondence about the Translation of the Pentateuch into the Greek*

The letters quoted by the author as having been, in this wording, exchanged between Ptolemy Philadelphus and Eleazar (or Eliezer), the High Priest, who is stated by Josephus to have been 'not inferior to any other of that dignity', are not authentic records. Nevertheless, they are worthy to be reproduced here, not only because they throw much light on the relations between Judaea and Egypt in the days of the Ptolomies, but also as one of the earliest known models of a correspondence conducted between a non-Jew and a Jew.

(A)

PTOLEMY PHILADELPHUS, KING OF EGYPT, TO ELEAZAR, THE HIGH PRIEST

'We desire to confer a favour not on these only, but on all Jews throughout the world and on future generations'

[Supposed date: Alexandria, first half of the 3rd century B.C.E.]

King Ptolemaeus to Eleazar the High Priest greeting and health.

Forasmuch as there are many Jews settled in our realm who were forcibly removed from Jerusalem by the Persians at the time of their Power, and others who entered Egypt as captives in the train of our father – of these he enrolled many in the army, giving them higher than the ordinary pay, and in like manner, having proved the loyalty of those who were already in the country, he placed under their charge the fortress which he built, that the native Egyptians might be intimidated by them; and we too since ascending the throne meet all men, but chiefly thy countrymen, in a very friendly spirit – we, then, have given liberty to more than a hundred thousand captives, paying their owners at the proper market price, and making good any wrong which they may have suffered through the passions of the mob. Our intent in this was to do a pious action and to dedicate a thank-offering to the Most High God, who has preserved our Kingdom in peace and in the highest esteem throughout the whole world. Moreover, we have drafted into the army those who are in the prime of life, and to such as are fitted to be attached to our person and deserving of the confidence of court have we assigned offices of state.

Now since we desire to confer a favour not on these only, but on all Jews throughout the world and on future generations, it is our will that your Law be translated from the Hebrew tongue in use among you into Greek, and so these writings also may find a place in our library with the other royal volumes. Thou wilt therefore do well and wilt repay our zeal, if thou lookest out six elders from each tribe, men of high repute, well versed in the Law and able to translate, that we may discover wherein the more part agree; for the investigation concerns matters of more than ordinary import. We think to gain great renown by the fulfilment of this task.

We have sent on this business Andreas, the chief of the bodyguards, and Aristeas, who hold honoured places in our court, to confer with thee. They bring with them dedicatory offerings for the temple, and for sacrifices and other purposes a hundred talents of silver. And shouldest thou also write to us concerning my desires, thou wilt do a favour and a friendly service and be assured that thy wishes will receive instant fulfilment. Farewell.

(B)

ELEAZAR, THE HIGH PRIEST, TO PTOLEMY PHILADELPHUS, KING OF EGYPT

'We selected six elders from each tribe good men and true, with whom we are also sending a copy of the Law'

[Supposed date: Jerusalem, first half of the 3rd century B.C.E.]

Eleazar, the High Priest, to King Ptolemaeus, his sincere friend, greeting. Do thou fare well and the Queen Arsinoe,[10] thy sister, and the children, so will it be well and as we desire; we too are in good health.

On receiving thy letter we greatly rejoiced because of thy purpose and noble resolve, and we collected the whole people and read it to them, in order that they might know thy pious reverence for our God. We showed them also the vials which thou hast sent, twenty of gold and thirty of silver, the five bowls and the table as dedicatory offerings, and the hundred talents of silver for the offering of sacrifices and for such repairs as the temple may require. These gifts were brought by Andreas, one of thy honoured courtiers, and Aristeas, good men and true and of excellent learning, who in all ways worthily reflect thy high principles and righteousness.

They have also imparted to us thy message, and have heard from our lips a reply in accordance with thy letter. For in all things which are to thy profit, even though thy request is contrary to our natural impulses, will we do thy bidding; this indeed is a mark of friendship and affection. For thou too hast in divers manners done great services to our countrymen which can never pass out of mind. We therefore straightaway offered sacrifices on thy behalf and on behalf of thy sister and thy children and thy friends, and the whole people prayed that thy undertakings might ever prosper, and that Almighty God would preserve thy kingdom in peace with honour, and that the translation of the holy law might be to thy profit and carefully executed.

And in the presence of them all we selected six elders from each tribe, good men and true,[11] with whom we are also sending a copy of the Law. Thou wilt then do well, righteous King, to give orders that, as soon as the translation of the books be accomplished, the men be restored to us again in safety. Farewell.

Much of the 'Letter' is taken up with an account – clearly apocryphal – of the banquet given by Ptolemy to his Jewish guests and the impression which they made on him by their wisdom and scholarship. One of the final scenes shows the assembly of the Jewish population at Alexandria, at which the work was read aloud and acclaimed with a great ovation.

And after the reading of the rolls the priests and the elders of the translators and some members of the Jewish community and the rulers of the people stood up and said: 'Forasmuch as the translation has been well and piously executed and with perfect accuracy, it is right that it should remain in its present form and that no revision should take place.' And when all had assented to these words, they bade them, in accordance with their custom, pronounce an imprecation upon any who should revise the text by adding to, or in any way transposing, or omitting aught from, what had been written; and herein they did well, to the intent that the work might for ever be preserved imperishable and unchanged.

These words reveal apparently the very *raison d'être* of the Septuagint: the translation was produced not so much, if at all, in order to enrich the famous library of Alexandria by a perfect edition of the Jewish Law, but rather to meet the needs of the large Greek-speaking Jewish colony in Egypt.

NOTES

1. Comp. Exod. XXXVI. 37.
2. Exod. XX. 26.
3. Exod. XXVIII. 39
4. Exod. XXVIII. 4.
5. Exod. XXVIII. 34.
6. *ibidem.*
7. Exod. XXVIII. 39.
8. 'The Urim and the Thummim', objects connected with the breastplate of the High Priest and used as a kind of divine oracle (Exod. XXVIII. 15–21; Lev. VIII. 8).
9. Or 'mitre' (Exod. XXVIII. 36–39).
10. Arsinoe II, sister and wife of Ptolemy Philadelphus, is said to have adopted the children of Arsinoe I.
11. The names of the translators were enumerated in a special postscript.

7

Jerusalem invites Alexandria to celebrate Hanukah

IN the year 165 B.C.E., on the 25th Kislev, after the victory of Judas Maccabeus over the Syrian army, the Jews gathered in the delivered Jerusalem to celebrate for eight days the rededication of the Temple which had been defiled by Antiochus Epiphanes, the feast of Hanukah, with lighting of lamps, with sacrifices, processions, music and songs. The feast was instituted as an annual celebration for all Israel and for all time, to commemorate the event. The Maccabees attributed to the new festival also a revivalist power which might contribute to the Messianic redemption.

Two letters prefixed to the Second Book of the Maccabees tell of two attempts made by Jerusalem to bring about the participation of the Jews of Alexandria in the feast. There is a sharp difference of opinion among scholars about the authenticity of these letters. But many authorities and strong arguments justify the inclusion of these rare documents in the history of Jewish letter-writing. Among those who assert their genuineness, H. Graetz regards the Greek wording as a translation from Hebrew originals, while modern critics maintain that the originals were written in Greek or Aramaic.

1. *A Message from the Liberated Jerusalem*

The letter addressed, according to 2 Macc. I. 10–36; II. 1–18, by Judas Maccabeus and the whole people of Jerusalem to Aristobulus, the Jewish philosopher and poet, who stood high in favour of King Ptolemy Philometer, is believed to have been sent to Alexandria either on the occasion of the first Hanukah or before its first repetition. Strangely enough, the recent victory is mentioned only in brief words, while various legends about the preservation of the sacred fire and the news about the restored Jerusalem library are told in detail. The authors of the epistle were apparently more concerned to assert in this way their assumption that Jerusalem had become again the centre of the whole Jewish world, than to glorify the military achievements.

THE PEOPLE OF JERUSALEM TO THE JEWISH COMMUNITY OF ALEXANDRIA

'We are about to celebrate the purification . . . and ye shall do well, if ye keep the same days'

[Jerusalem, 165 B.C.E. (?)]

We the people of Jerusalem and of the whole Judaea, the Elders and Judah[1] are sending greeting and health unto Aristobulus, King Ptolemy's teacher, who is of the stock of the anointed priests, and to the Jews that are in Egypt.

Insomuch as God hath delivered us from great perils, we thank Him greatly, as having been in battle against a mighty king. For He cast them out that fought within the Holy City...

Therefore whereas we are now purposed to keep the purification of the Temple upon the five-and-twentieth day of the month Kislev, we thought it necessary to certify you thereof, that ye might also keep it as the Feast of Tabernacles, and of the fire, which was given us when Nehemiah offered sacrifices after that he had builded the Temple and the altar. For when our fathers were led into Persia, the priests that were then devout took the fire of the altar privily, and hid it in a hollow place of a pit without water where they kept it sure, so that the place was unknown to all men. Now, after many years, when it pleased God, Nehemiah, being sent from the King of Persia, did send some of the posterity of those priests that had hid it to the fire. But as they told us they found no fire, but thick water; then commanded he them to draw it up, and to bring it; and when the sacrifices were laid on, Nehemiah commanded the priests to sprinkle the wood and the things laid thereupon with the water. When this was done, and the time came that the sun shone, which afar was hid in the cloud, there was a great fire kindled, so that every man marvelled. And the priests made a prayer whilst the sacrifice was consuming, I say, both the priests, and all the rest, Jonathan[2] beginning, and the rest answering thereunto, as Nehemiah did. And the prayer was after this manner:

> O Lord, Lord God, Creator of all things,
> Who art fearful and strong and righteous, and merciful,
> And the only and gracious King,
> The only giver of all things, the only just,
> Almighty and everlasting,
> Thou that delivereth Israel from all trouble,
> Thou didst choose the fathers, and sanctify them;
> Receive the sacrifice for the whole people Israel
> And preserve Thine own portion, and sanctify it.
> Gather those together that are scattered from us,
> Deliver them that serve among the heathen,
> Look upon them that are despised and abhorred,
> And let the heathen know that Thou art our God.
> Punish them that oppress us,
> And with pride do us wrong.
> Plant Thy people again in Thy holy place,
> As Moses hath spoken.

And the priests sang psalms and thanksgiving. Now when the sacrifice was consumed, Nehemiah commanded the water that was left to be poured on the great stones. When this was done, there was kindled a flame: but it was consumed by the light that shined from the altar. So when this matter was known, it was told the King of Persia, that in the place where the priests that were led away had hid the fire, there appeared water, and that Nehemiah had purified the sacrifices therewith. Then the King, enclosing the place, made it holy, after he had tried the matter. And the King took many gifts, and bestowed thereof on those whom he would gratify. And Nehemiah called this thing Naphtar, which is as much as to say, a cleansing: but many men call it Nephthi.[3]

It is also found in the records, that Jeremiah the prophet commanded them that were carried away to take of the fire, as it hath been signified. And how that the prophet, having given them the law, charged them not to forget the commandments of the Lord. . . . It was also contained in the same writing that the prophet, being warned of God, commanded the tabernacle and the ark to go with him, as he went forth into the mountain where Moses climbed up and saw the heritage of God. And when Jeremiah came thither, he found an hollow cave, wherein he laid the tabernacle, and the ark, and the altar of incense, and so stopped the door. And some of those that followed him came to mark the way, but they could not find it. Which when Jeremiah perceived, he blamed them, saying, as for that place, it shall be unknown until the time that God gather His people again together, and receive them unto mercy. Then shall the Lord shew them these things, and the glory of the Lord shall appear . . .

The same things also were reported in the writings and commentaries of Nehemiah; and how he founding a library, gathered together the acts of the kings, and the prophets, and of David and the epistles of the kings concerning the holy gifts. In like manner also Judah gathered together all those things that were lost by reason of the war we had, and they remain with us. Wherefore if you have need thereof send some to fetch them unto you.

Whereas we then are about to celebrate the purification, we have written unto you, and ye shall do well, if ye keep the same days. We hope also, that the God that delivered all His people, and gave them all an heritage, and the kingdom, and the priesthood, and the sanctuary, as He promised in the law, will shortly have mercy upon us, and gather us together out of every land under heaven unto the holy place: for He hath delivered us out of great troubles, and hath purified the place.

2. *A Letter of Comfort and Exhortation*

The other Maccabean letter (2 Macc. I. 1–9) is a short epistle written in a plain language which seems to suggest that it was originally composed in Hebrew. Reference is made in it to the perils which the Jews of Palestine went through during the reign of Demetrius II of Syria in the 169th year of the Seleucid era (145 B.C.E.) when Jonathan, Judah's brother and successor, supported Alexander Balas, who pretended to be the son of Antiochus Epiphanes. The letter, written in 124 B.C.E., was probably meant no less as a letter of consolation than as a reminder of the Hanukah celebration.

THE JEWS OF JUDAEA TO THE JEWS OF EGYPT

'We be here praying for you'

[Jerusalem, 124 B.C.E.]

The brethren, the Jews that be at Jerusalem and in the land of Judaea, wish unto the brethren, the Jews that are throughout Egypt, health and peace:

God be gracious unto you, and remember His covenant that He made with Abraham, Isaac and Jacob, His faithful servants. And give you all a heart to serve Him, and do His will, with a good courage and a willing mind; and open your hearts, in His Law and commandments, and send you peace. And hear your prayers, and be at one with you, and never forsake you in time of trouble. And now we be here praying for you.

In the time when Demetrius reigned, in the hundred – three-score and ninth year,[4] we the Jews wrote unto you in the extremity of trouble that came upon us in those years, from the time that Jason and his company revolted from the holy land and kingdom, and burned the porch, and shed innocent blood: then we prayed unto the Lord, and were heard, we offered also sacrifices and fine flour, and lighted the lamp, and set forth the loaves.

And now see that ye keep the Feast of Tabernacles[5] in the month Kislev.

In the hundred-four-score and eighth year [of the Seleucid era].

There is a touch of prophecy in the use of these festive letters as a prologue to the Maccabean epic. For they forecast the perpetuation of Hanukah, the Feast of Lights, which was so well calculated to keep alive the Maccabean spirit in the people of Israel.

NOTES

1. Ch. C. Torrey maintains that the date 'In the 188th year' of the Seleucid era, that is the year 124 B.C.E., usually referred to the next letter, belongs to this epistle. This opinion implies that the letter was sent to Alexandria more than three decades after Judas Maccabeus's tragic death. Torrey suggests, therefore, that the words 'The Elders and Judas' have to be replaced by the reading 'The Elders of Judah'.
2. Priests of the name Jonathan are mentioned in Neh. XII. 11, 14, 18.
3. The word Nephtar or Nephthi occurs in Greek and Latin manuscripts. It is considered to be of Syriac, Bactric or Semitic origin, and refers to mineral oil, which, exposed to intense sunshine, might have been set on fire. It is said that the place where the well was found was situated south of Jerusalem.
4. Ch. C. Torrey suggests a different reading of the passage referring to the year 169 of the Seleucid era, that is 143 B.C.E., and considers this year as the date of the letter.
5. The Feast of Hanukah was modelled on the Feast of Tabernacles, which also lasted for eight days.

8

Jerusalem greets Sparta

JONATHAN, the youngest of the Hasmonean brothers, succeeded Judas Maccabeus as leader of the Jewish people. In 152 B.C.E. he assumed the dignity of High Priest. This ingenious statesman became the builder of the new Jewish Commonwealth. In order to strengthen its independence, he sent an embassy to Rome to establish friendly relations with the Republic and at the same time addressed letters with a similar purpose to various city states through which the envoys passed on their journey. Only one of these has been preserved, in the First Book of the Maccabees (XII. 5–23), the letter to the people of Sparta. This letter refers to an earlier correspondence between Areus, King of Sparta, and the High Priest, Onias, and even quotes literally from the letter of Areus. Whether this unique quotation and Jonathan's own letter are historical documents or inventions of the author is still an open question. Jonathan's diplomatic activity certainly gives some support to the assumption that either this or some similar letter – the first known to have been sent from the Land of Israel to Europe – was written by the High Priest.

JONATHAN, THE HIGH PRIEST, TO THE PEOPLE OF SPARTA

'*We at all times . . . remember you in the sacrifices, and in our prayers*'

[Jerusalem, about 150 B.C.E.]

Jonathan, the High Priest, and the Elders of the Nation, the priests, and the other people of the Jews, unto the Lacedemonians their brethren send greeting.

There were letters sent in times past unto Onias the High Priest from Areus,[1] who reigned then among you, to signify that ye are our brethren as the copy here underwritten doth specify. At which time Onias[2] entreated the ambassador that was sent honourably, and received the letter wherein declaration was made of the league and friendship.

Therefore, we also, albeit we need none of these things, for that we have the holy books of Scripture in our hands to comfort us, have nevertheless attempted to send unto you for the renewing of brotherhood and friendship, lest we should become strangers unto you altogether: for there is a long time passed since ye sent unto us. We therefore at all times without ceasing both in our feasts, and other convenient days, do remember you in the sacrifices which we offer, in our prayers, as reason is, and as it becometh us to think upon our brethren.

And now right glad of your honour as for ourselves, we have had great toils and troubles on every side, for as much as the kings that are round about us have fought against us. Howbeit we would not be troublesome unto you, nor to others of our confederates and friends in these wars. For we have help from heaven, so as we are delivered from our enemies, and our enemies are brought under foot.

For this cause we chose Numenius, the son of Antiochus, and Antipater, the son of Jason, and sent them unto the Romans, to renew the amity that we had with them, and the former league. We commanded them also to go unto you, and to salute you, and to deliver you our letter, concerning the renewing of our brotherhood. Wherefore now ye shall do well to give us an answer thereto.

And this is the copy of the letter which Areus sent: "Areus, King of the Lacedemonians, to Onias, the High Priest, greeting.

It is found in writing that the Lacedemonians and the Jews are brethren, and that they are of the stock of Abraham. Now, therefore, since this is come to our knowledge, ye shall do well to write unto us of your prosperity. We do write again to you, that your cattle and goods are ours, ours are yours. We command, therefore, our ambassadors to make report unto you in this wise."

NOTES

1. Areus, Spartan king, 309–265 B.C.E.
2. Onias I, son of Jaddua, is mentioned by Josephus, Ant. XI. 8, as having been High Priest in the days of Alexander the Great. Thus a discrepancy would exist between the dates given in the preceding note and the year of Alexander's death (323).

9

Jerusalem's Call to the exiled Teacher of the Pharisees

ALEXANDER JANNAI, the Hasmonean, became High Priest and King of Judaea in 103 B.C.E. He attached himself to the Sadducean or aristocratic party in the State, and soon became intensely hated by the Pharisees, the popular party formed by the faithful custodians of the sacred tradition. The tension between the High Priest and the Pharisees exploded during a service in the Temple on the feast of Tabernacles. The worshippers, most of whom were Pharisees, gathered in the Temple, the customary palms and citrons in their hands. As the ceremony of the water libation was about to be performed, all eyes were fixed on the High Priest. The crowd was thunderstruck when he poured the water on the ground, as the Sadducees prescribed, instead of against the altar, as ordained by the Pharisees. In a flash, hundreds of citrons whizzed through the enormous hall towards the spot where Alexander stood, though without causing him injury. Infuriated by this outrage, he at once ordered his mercenaries to attack the rebellious worshippers. It was said that six thousand people lost their lives on the spot.

The ruthless persecution which followed this incident caused a flight of the most prominent Pharisees from the Holy Land. Among them was the leading Pharisaic teacher, Judah ben Tabbai, who took refuge in Alexandria. There he remained until the end of Alexander Jannai's reign. The King, after having relented in his enmity towards the Pharisees, on his deathbed advised his wife, the Queen Salome Alexandra, who was to succeed him, to make peace with them. One of her first acts accordingly was to invite Judah ben Tabbai to return to Jerusalem. Thus, *c.* 76 B.C.E., a letter reached the sage, the shortest and the most subtle call ever sent to an exile:

JERUSALEM TO JUDAH BEN TABBAI

'How long will my bridegroom live among you?'

[Jerusalem, about 76 B.C.E.]

From Jerusalem the great to Alexandria the little.

How long will my bridegroom live among you, and I remain separated from him in distress?[1]

The author of these picturesque lines was another outstanding Pharisee, Simeon ben Shetah, the brother of the Queen. He also had fled to Egypt but had returned to Jerusalem. Now Judah ben Tabbai followed him, and was at once appointed to the dignity of Nasi of the Sanhedrin.

NOTE

1. This wording is given in the Palestinian Talmud, Hagigah II. 2, 77d. There it is stated that the reluctance of Judah ben Tabbai to accept the appointment to the office of Nasi of the Sanhedrin was the reason for his flight to Egypt. The Babylonian Talmud contains the following variant statement with a somewhat different wording of the letter: 'When Jannai, the King slaughtered the Rabbis, Joshua ben Perahiah and his pupil Judah ben Tabbai went to Alexandria in Egypt. After peace was re-established, Simon ben Shetah sent him the following message: "From me, Jerusalem, the Holy City, to thee, my sister, Alexandria in Egypt. My husband dwelleth with thee, and I remain desolate"' (Sotah 47a; Sanh. 107b). Nevertheless, the majority of the historians assume in accordance with the Palestinian Talmud that Judah ben Tabbai was the addressee of the letter, although they accept the motive of his flight given in the Babylonian Talmud.

10

Rabban Gamaliel sends Messages fixing the Calendar to the Jews far and near

THE fixing of the calendar, of the new moons, holidays, leap years, the times for the delivery of the tithes, and so forth, was of such importance to the religious and national life of ancient Israel that this task was entrusted to the highest legal and judicial authority, the Sanhedrin, with the Nasi or patriarch at its head. The calendar once fixed, letters had to be sent by messengers to all important Jewish centres in order to make known the decisions of the Sanhedrin to the Jewish world. The Talmud has preserved three specimens of such letters from the days preceding the destruction of the Temple. Their author was Rabban Gamaliel I, the grandson of Hillel and teacher of Saul of Tarsus. He became head of the Sanhedrin in the first half of the first century C.E. To this activity refers apparently also the passage of the Talmud where it is described how he dictated the letters to the scribe: 'Rabbi Judah said that he and Rabban Gamaliel sat together with the Elders on the terrace of the Temple mount, and Johanan the scribe sat before them and Rabban Gamaliel said to him: "Write to our brethren in [so-and-so] as follows."'

RABBAN GAMALIEL TO THE BRETHREN

'We let you know hereby'

[Jerusalem, first half of the 1st century C.E.]

(A)

Rabban Gamaliel to the brethren in the upper South and to the brethren in the flat South:

May your peace grow! We[1] let you know hereby that the time has come when all the tithes[2] have to be delivered.

(B)

The same to the brethren in Upper Galilee and in Lower Galilee:

May your peace grow! We let you know hereby that the time has come when the tithes of the olives[3] have to be delivered.

(c)

The same to the brethren in the Babylonian exile, to the brethren in the Median exile, to the brethren in the Greek exile, and to the brethren in the whole world:

May your peace grow! We let you know hereby that sheep are still small, the doves not yet full grown, and the time of the first harvest has not yet come. It pleased, therefore, me and my colleagues to declare this year as a leap year.

NOTES

1. Letters of this kind had to be signed also by the Vice-President of the Sanhedrin.
2. Tithes, i.e. the tenth parts of the seed of the land and of the fruit of the trees which had to be delivered to Jerusalem or to be saved at home (Deut. XIV. 22, 23).
3. According to the rabbinical interpretation of Deut. XIV. 22, each tithe was to be taken of every year's produce separately.

II

King Agrippa I defends the Sanctity of the Temple against the Emperor Caligula

IN the year 40 C.E. the Jews of Palestine passed through a grave crisis. The newly enthroned emperor of Rome, the megalomaniac Caligula, decreed that statues of himself should be placed in all temples within the Roman Empire – which included Judaea – and there receive divine honours. His command was obeyed everywhere save in Jerusalem. Here the Jews made energetic representations to the Roman procurator of Syria, Petronius, pointing out that their Law categorically forbade them to allow images to be placed in the Sanctuary, and declaring their determination to perish rather than suffer such a desecration. The impetuous pleading of the Jews induced Petronius to postpone the execution of Caligula's order and to send a request for new instructions. But there was an imminent danger that Caligula, whose obstinacy and cruelty matched his pathological self-adoration, would take the rebellious Jews at their word.

This national disaster was averted by a man whose early career gave little prospect that he would one day become the saviour of his people, and its last beloved king. This was Agrippa, the son of Aristobulus, a grandson of the Idumean tyrant, Herod the Great, by his Hasmonean wife Mariamne. Agrippa had been brought up in Rome, where he had led the dissolute life of a Roman man of fashion and had become the bosom friend of the young Gaius Cæsar Caligula. On becoming emperor, Caligula not only released Agrippa from the prison into which he had been cast by Tiberius, but made him also ruler of one of the Syrian tetrarchies with the title of king. From this moment, Agrippa underwent a remarkable transformation: he ceased to be Roman in outlook and identified himself completely in sentiment with his own people. Soon this moral regeneration was put to a crucial test.

Agrippa happened to be in Rome when the alarming news of the Jewish opposition against Caligula's order reached the capital. He at once tried to persuade the Emperor to withdraw the fateful command. His exciting but fruitless conversation with the raging Caligula ended with his complete breakdown. He was carried back to his lodgings in a state of unconsciousness. When he had been brought to himself with the help of friends and physicians, he realized that one choice only was left to him: to take the risk of possible martyrdom. With this prospect before him, he addressed the following remarkable letter to the Emperor:

KING AGRIPPA I TO THE EMPEROR CALIGULA

'I will give up everything; I look upon everything as of less importance than the one point of preserving the ancient customs and laws of my nation unaltered'

[Rome, 40 C.E.]

O master, fear and shame have taken from me all courage to come into your presence to address you; since fear teaches me to dread your threats; and shame, out of respect for the greatness of your power and dignity, keeps me silent. But a writing will show my request, which I now here offer to you as my earnest petition.

In all men, O Emperor! a love of their country is innate, and an eager fondness for their national customs and laws. And concerning these matters there is no need that I should give you information, since you have a heartfelt love for your own country, and a deeply-seated respect for your national customs. And what belongs to themselves appears beautiful to everyone, even if it is not so in reality; for they judge of these things not more by reason than by the feelings of affection.

I am, as you know, a Jew: and Jerusalem is my country, in which there is erected the holy temple of the most high God. And I have kings for my grandfathers and for my ancestors, the greater part of whom have been called High Priests, looking upon their royal power as inferior to their office as priests; and thinking that the high priesthood is as much superior to the power of a king, as God is superior to man; for that the one is occupied in rendering service to God, and the other has only the care of governing them . . .

For in all the particulars in which men are enjoined by the laws, and in which they have it in their power to show their piety and loyalty, my nation is inferior to none whatever in Asia or in Europe, whether it be in respect of prayers, or of the supply of sacred offerings, or in the abundance of its sacrifices, not merely of such as are offered on occasion of the public festivals, but in those which are continually offered day after day; by which means they show their loyalty and their fidelity more surely than by their mouth and tongue, proving it by the designs of their honest hearts, not indeed saying that they are friends to Cæsar, but being so in reality.

Concerning the Holy City I must now say what is necessary. This, as I have already stated, is my native country, and the metropolis not only of the one country of Judaea, but also of many by reason of the colonies which it has sent out from time to time into the bordering districts of Egypt, Phœnicia, Syria in general, and especially that part of it which is called Cœlo-Syria, and also into those more distant regions of Pamphylia, Cilicia, the greater part of Asia Minor as far as Bithynia, and the furthermost corners of Pontus. And in the same manner into Europe, into Thessaly, and Boeotia and Macedonia, and Aetolia, and Attica, and Argos, and Corinth, and all the most fertile and wealthiest districts of Peloponnesus. And not only are the continents full of Jewish colonies, but also all the most celebrated islands are so too; such as Euboea, and Cyprus and Crete.

I say nothing of the countries beyond the Euphrates, for all of them except a very small portion, and Babylon and all the satrapies around, which have any advantages whatever of soil or climate, have Jews settled in them. So that if my native land is, as it reasonably may be, looked upon as entitled to a share in your favour, it is not one city only that would then be benefited by you but ten thousand of them in every region of the habitable world, in Europe, in Asia, and in Africa, on the continent, in the islands, on the coasts, and in the inland parts. And it corresponds well to the greatness of your good fortune, that, by conferring benefits on one city, you should also benefit ten thousand others so that your renown may be celebrated in every part of the habitable world, and many praises of you may be combined with thanksgiving.

You have thought the native countries of some of your friends worthy of being admitted to share all the privileges of a Roman constitution; and those who but a little while ago were slaves, became the masters of others who also enjoyed your favour in a higher, or at all events, not in a lower degree, and they were delighted too at the causes of your beneficence. And I indeed am perfectly aware that I belong to the class which is in subjection to a lord and master, and also that I am admitted to the honour of being one of your companions, being inferior to you in respect of my birthright and natural rank, and inferior to no one whomsoever not to say the most eminent of all men, in goodwill and loyalty towards you, both because that is my natural disposition, and also in consequence of the number of benefits with which you have enriched me; so that if I in consequence had felt confidence to implore you myself on behalf of my country, if not to grant to it the Roman constitution, at least to confer freedom and remission of taxes on it, I should not have thought that I had any reason to fear your displeasure for preferring such a petition to you, and requesting that most desirable of all things, your favour, which it can do you no harm to grant, and which is the most advantageous of all things for my country to receive. For what can possibly be a more desirable blessing for a subject nation than the goodwill of its sovereign?

It was at Jerusalem, O Emperor! that your most desirable succession to the empire was first announced; and the news of your advancement spread from the Holy City all over the continent on each side, and was received with great gladness. And on this account that city deserves to meet with favour at your hands; for, as in families the eldest children receive the highest honours as their birthright, because they were the first to give the name of father and mother to their parents, so in a like manner, since this is first of all the cities in the east to salute you as Emperor, it ought to receive greater benefit from you than any other; or if not greater, at all events as great as any other city.

Having advanced these pleas on the ground of justice and made these petitions on behalf of my native country, I now come at last to my supplication on behalf of the temple. O my

Lord and Master, Caius, this temple has never from the time of its original foundation until now admitted any form made by hands, because it has been the abode of God. Now, pictures and images are only imitations of those gods who are perceptible to the outward senses; but it was not considered by our ancestors to be consistent with the reverence due to God to make any image or representation of the invisible God. Agrippa, when he came to the temple, did honour to it, and he was thy grandfather[1]; and so did Augustus,[2] when by his letters he commanded all first fruits from all quarters to be sent thither; and by the continual sacrifice. And thy great-grandmother[3] had likewise a high veneration for it. On which account no one, whether Greek or barbarian, satrap or king, or implacable enemy; no sedition, no war, no capture, no destruction, no occurrence that has ever taken place, has ever threatened this temple with such innovation as to place in it any image, or statue, or any work of any kind made with hands; for, though enemies have displayed their hostility to the inhabitants of the country, still either reverence or fear has possessed them sufficiently to prevent them from abrogating any of the laws which were established at the beginning, as tending to the honour of the Creator and Father of the Universe; for they knew that it is these and similar actions which bring after them the irremediable calamities of heaven-sent afflictions. On which account they have been careful not to sow an impious seed, fearing lest they should be compelled to reap its natural harvest, in a fruit bearing utter destruction.

But why need I invoke the assistance of foreign witnesses when I have plenty with whom I can furnish you from among your own countrymen and friends? Marcus Agrippa, your own grandfather on the mother's[4] side, the moment that he arrived in Judaea, when Herod, my grandfather, was King of the country, thought fit to go up from the sea coast to the metropolis, which was inland. And when he had beheld the temple, and the decorations of the priests, and the piety and holiness of the people of the country, he marvelled, looking upon the whole matter as one of great solemnity and entitled to great respect, and thinking that he had beheld what was too magnificent to be described. And he could talk of nothing else to his companions but the magnificence of the temple and everything connected with it.

Therefore, every day that he remained in the city, by reason of his friendship for Herod, he went to that sacred place, being delighted with the spectacle of the building, and of the sacrifices, and all the ceremonies connected with the worship of God, and the regularity which was observed, and the dignity and honour paid to the High Priest, and his grandeur when arrayed in his sacred vestments and when about to begin the sacrifices. And after he had adorned the temple with all the offerings in his power to contribute, and had conferred many benefits on the inhabitants, doing them many important services, and having said to Herod many friendly things and having been replied to in corresponding terms, he was conducted back again to the sea coast, and to the harbour, and that not by one city only, but by the whole country, having branches strewed in his road, and being greatly admired and respected for his piety.

What again did your other grandfather, Tiberius Cæsar,[5] do? Does not he appear to have adopted an exactly similar line of conduct? At all events, during the three-and-twenty years that he was emperor, he preserved the form of worship in the temple as it had been handed down from the earliest times, without abrogating or altering the slightest particulars of it. Moreover, I have it in my power to relate one act of grace on his part, though I suffered an infinite number of evils when he was alive; but nevertheless the truth is considered dear, and much to be honoured by you. Pilate[6] was one of the emperor's lieutenants, having been appointed governor of Judaea. He, not more with the object of doing honour to Tiberius than with that of vexing the multitude, dedicated some gilt shields in the palace of Herod in the Holy City; which had no form nor any other forbidden thing represented on them except some necessary inscription, which mentioned these two facts, the name of the person who had placed them there, and the person in whose honour they were placed there. But when the multitude heard what had been done, and when the circumstances became notorious, then the people, putting forward the four sons of the king, who were in no respect inferior to the kings themselves in fortune or in rank, and his other descendants, and those magistrates who were among them at the time, entreated him to alter and rectify the innovation which he had committed in respect of the shields; and not to make any alteration in their national customs, which had hitherto been preserved without any interruption and without being in the least degree changed by any king or emperor.

But when he steadfastly refused this petition (for he was a man of a very inflexible disposition and very merciless as well as very obstinate) they cried out: 'Do not cause a sedition; do not make war on us; do not destroy the peace which exists. The honour of the emperor is not identical with dishonour to the ancient laws; let it not be to you a pretence for heaping insult on our nation. Tiberius is not desirous that any of our laws or customs shall be destroyed. And if you yourself say that he is, show us either some command from him, or some letter, or something of the kind that we, who have been sent to you as ambassadors, may cease to trouble you, and may address our supplications to your master.' But this last sentence exasperated him in the greatest possible degree, as he feared lest they might in reality go on an embassy to the emperor, and might impeach him with respect to other particulars of his government, for his corruption and his acts of insolence, and his rapine, and his habit of insulting people, and his cruelty and his continual murders of people, untried and uncondemned, and his never-ending and gratuitous and most grievous inhumanity. Therefore, being exceedingly angry, and being at all times a man of most ferocious passions, he was in great perplexity, neither venturing to take down what he had once set up, nor wishing to do anything which could be acceptable to his subjects, and at the same time being sufficiently acquainted with the firmness of Tiberius on these points. And those who were in power in our nation, seeing this, and perceiving that he was inclined to change his mind as to what he had done, but that he was not willing to be thought to do so, wrote a most supplicatory letter to Tiberius. And he, when he read it, what did he say of Pilate, and what threats did he utter against him! But it is beside our purpose at present to relate to you how very angry he was, although he was not very liable to sudden anger; since the facts speak for themselves; for immediately, without putting anything off till the next day, he wrote a letter reproaching and reviling him in the most bitter manner for his act of unprecedented audacity and wickedness, and commanding him immediately to take down the shields and to convey them away from the metropolis of Judaea to Caesarea on the sea, which had been named Caesarea Augusta, after his grandfather, in order that they might be set up in the temple of Augustus. And accordingly, they were set up in that edifice. And in this way he provided for two matters: both for the honour of the emperor, and for the preservation of the ancient customs of the city.

Now the things set up on that occasion were shields, on which there was no representation of any living thing whatever engraved. But now the thing proposed to be erected is a colossal statue. Moreover, then the erection was in the dwelling-house of the governor; but they say, that which is now contemplated is to be in the inmost part of the temple, in the very holy of holies itself, into which, once in the year, the High Priest enters, on the day called the great fast, to offer incense, and on no other day, it being then in accordance with our national law also to offer up prayers for a fertile and ample supply of blessings and for peace to all mankind. And if anyone else, I will not say of the Jews, but even of the priests, and not of the lowest order, but even those who are in the rank next to the first, should go in there, either with him or after him, or even if the very High Priest himself should enter in thither on two days of the year, or three or four times on the same day, he is subjected inexorably to inevitable death for his impiety, so great are the precautions taken by the lawgiver with respect to the holy of holies, as he determined to preserve it alone inaccessible to and untouched by any human being.

How many deaths then do you not suppose that the people who have been taught to regard this place with such holy reverence would willingly endure rather than see a statue introduced into it? I verily believe that they would rather slay all their whole families with their wives and children, and themselves last of all, in the ruins of their houses and families.

This was the case in the days of Tiberius. And what did your great-grandfather, the most excellent of all emperors that ever lived upon the earth, he who was the first to have the appellation of Augustus[7] given him, on account of his virtue and good fortune; he who diffused peace in every direction of the earth and sea, to the very furthest extremities of the world? Did not he when he had heard a report of the peculiar characteristics of our temple and that there is in it no image or representation made by hands, no visible likeness of Him who is invisible, no attempt at any imitation of nature, did not he, I say, marvel at and honour it? For as he was imbued with something more than a mere smattering of philosophy, inasmuch as he had deeply feasted on it, and continued to feast on it every day, he partly retraced in his recollection all the precepts of philosophy which his mind had previously learnt, and partly also he kept his learning alive by the conversation of the literary men who were always about him; for at his banquets and entertainments, the greatest part of the time was devoted to learned conversation, in order that not only his friends' bodies but their minds also might be nourished.

And though I may be able to establish this fact and demonstrate to you the feelings of Augustus, your great-grandfather, by an abundance of proofs, I will be content with two; for in the first place he sent commandments to all the governors of the different provinces throughout Asia, because he heard that the sacred first-fruits were neglected, enjoining them to permit the Jews alone of all peoples to assemble together in the synagogues, for that these assemblies were not revels, which from drunkenness and intoxication proceeded to violence so as to disturb the peaceful condition of the country, but were rather schools of temperance and justice, as the men who met in them were studiers of virtue, and contributed the first-fruits every year, sending commissioners to convey the holy things to the temple in Jerusalem.

And in the next place he commanded that no one should hinder the Jews either on their way to the synagogues, or when bringing their contributions, or when proceeding in obedience to their national laws to Jerusalem, for these things were expressly enjoined, if not in so many words, at all events in effect; and I subjoin one letter in order to bring conviction to you who are our master, written by Caius Norbanus Flaccus, in which he records what had been written to him by Cæsar; and the letter with its superscription is as follows:

> 'Gaius Norbanus Flaccus, Proconsul, to the Governors of the Ephesians, Greeting. – Cæsar has written word to me that the Jews, wherever they are, are accustomed to assemble together, in compliance with a peculiar ancient custom of their nation, to contribute money which they send to Jerusalem; and he does not choose that they should have any hindrance offered to them, to prevent them from doing this; therefore I have written to you that you may know that I command that they shall be allowed to do these things.'

Is not this a most convincing proof, O Emperor, of the intention of Cæsar respecting the honours paid to our temple which he had adopted, not considering it right that because of some general rule, with respect to meetings, the assemblies of the Jews in one place should be put down, which they held for the sake of offering the first-fruits and for other pious objects? There is also another piece of evidence, in no respect inferior to this one, and which is the most undeniable proof of the will of Augustus, for he commanded unblemished sacrifices to be offered to the most high God every day, out of his own revenues, which are performed up to the present time, and the victims are two sheep and a bull with which Cæsar honoured the altar of God, well knowing that there is in the temple no image erected, either in open sight or in any part of it. But the great ruler, who was inferior to no one in philosophy, considered within himself, that it is necessary in terrestrial things, that an especial holy place should be set apart for the invisible God who will not permit any visible representation of himself to be made, by which to arrive at a participation in favourable hopes and the enjoyment of perfect blessings.

And your grandmother, Julia Augusta,[8] following the example of so great a guide in the paths of piety, did also adorn the temple with some golden vials and censers, and with a great number of other offerings, of the most costly and magnificent description; and what was her object in doing this, when there is no statue erected within the temple? For the minds of women are, in some degree, weaker than those of men, and are not so well able to comprehend a thing which is appreciable only by the intellect, without any aid of the objects addressed to the outward senses; but she, as she surpassed all her sex in other particulars, so also was she superior to them in this, by reason of the pure learning and wisdom which had been implanted in her, both by nature and by study; so that, having a masculine intellect, she was so sharp-sighted and profound, that she comprehended what is appreciable only by the intellect, even more than those things which are perceptible by the outward senses, and looked upon the latter as only shadows of the former.

Therefore, O Master, having all these examples most nearly connected with yourself and your family, of our purposes and customs, derived from those from whom you are sprung, of whom you are born, and by whom you have been brought up, I implore you to preserve those principles which each of those persons whom I have mentioned did preserve; they who were themselves possessed of imperial power do, by their laws, exhort you, the Emperor; they who were august, speak to you who are also Augustus; your grandfathers and ancestors speak to their descendant; numbers of authorities address one individual, all but saying, in express words: Do not you destroy those things in our councils which remain, and which have been preserved as permanent laws to this very day; for even if no mischief were to ensue from the abrogation of them, still, at all events, the result would be a feeling of uncertainty respecting the future, and such uncertainty is full of fear, even to the most sanguine and confident, if they are not despisers of divine things.

If I were to enumerate the benefits which I myself have received at your hands, the day would be too short for me; besides the fact that it is not proper for one who had undertaken to speak on one subject to branch off to a digression about some other matter. And even if I should be silent, the facts themselves speak and utter a distinct voice. You released me when I was bound in chains and iron. Who is there who is ignorant of this? But do not, after having done so, O Emperor, bind me in bonds of still greater bitterness: for the chains from which you released me surrounded a part of my body,[9] but those which I am now anticipating are the chains of the soul, which are likely to oppress it wholly and in every part; you abated from me a fear of death continually suspended over my head; you received me when I was almost dead through fear; you raised me up as it were from the dead. Continue your favour, O Master, that your Agrippa may not be driven wholly to forsake life; for I shall appear (if you do not do so) to have been released from bondage, not for the purpose of being saved, but for that of being made to perish in a more conspicuous manner.

You have given me the greatest and most glorious inheritance among mankind, the rank and power of a king, at first over one district, then over another and a more important one, adding to my kingdom the districts called Trachonitis and Galilee. Do not then, O Master, after having loaded me with means of superfluity, deprive me of what is actually necessary. Do not, after you have raised me up to the most brilliant light cast me down again from my eminence to the most profound darkness. I am willing to descend from this splendid position in which you have placed me; I do not deprecate a return to the condition in which I was a short time ago: I will give up everything; I look upon everything as of less importance than the one point of preserving the ancient customs and laws of my nation unaltered; for if they are violated, what could I say either to my fellow countrymen or to any other men? It would follow of necessity that I must be looked upon as one of two things, either as a betrayer of my people, or as one who is no longer accounted a friend by you. And what could be a greater misery than either of these two things? For if I am still reckoned among the company of your friends, I shall then receive the imputation of treason against my own nation, if neither my country is preserved free from all misfortune, nor even the temple left inviolate. For you, great man, preserve the property of your companions and those who take refuge in your protection by your imperial splendour and magnificence. And if you have any secret grief of vexation in your mind, do not throw me into prison, like Tiberius, but deliver me from any anticipation of being thrown into prison at any future time; command me at once to be put out of the way. For what advantage would it be to me to live, who place my whole hopes for safety and happiness in your friendship and favour?

This great human document has been preserved to us by the famous philosopher Philo in his 'Legatio ad Gaium'. By a strange coincidence he, too, was present in Rome at the critical time to plead on behalf of the Jews of Alexandria who were alarmed by recent anti-Jewish disturbances. From the style of the letter it would appear that Philo at least participated in the composition of it. Certainly his vivid description of the events which followed the dispatch of the letter seems to emanate from an eye-witness:

Having written this letter and sealed it, he sent it to Gaius, and then shutting himself up he remained in his own house, full of agony, confusion and disorder, and anxiety as to what was the best way of approaching and addressing the Emperor; for he and his people had incurred no slight danger, but they had reason to apprehend expulsion from their country, and slavery, and utter destruction, as impending not only over those who were dwelling in the Holy Land, but over all the Jews in every part of the world. But the Emperor, having taken the letter and read it, and having considered every suggestion which was contained in it, was very angry because his intentions had not been executed, and yet, at the same time, he was moved by the appeals to his justice and by the supplications which were thus addressed to him, and in some respects he was pleased with Agrippa, and in some he blamed him. He blamed him for his excessive desire to please his fellow countrymen, who were the only men who had resisted his orders and shown any unwillingness to submit to his deification; but he praised him for concealing and disguising none of his feelings, which conduct he said was a proof of a noble and liberal disposition. Therefore, being somewhat appeased at least as far as appearance went, he condescended to return a somewhat favourable answer, granting to Agrippa that highest and greatest of all favours, the consent that this erection of his statue should not take place; and he commanded letters to be written to Publius Petronius, the Governor of Syria, enjoining him not to allow any alternations or innovations to be made with respect to the temple of the Jews.

Agrippa's letter was successful in diverting the tyrannical emperor from his purpose for the time being, although soon afterwards he issued new instructions that divine homage should be paid to him in the Temple of Jerusalem. At the beginning of the year 41 C.E., however, he was assassinated. In the same year, Agrippa, confirmed by Claudius, the new emperor, as king, with his rule extended over Samaria, Judaea and Idumaea, returned to his homeland.

Agrippa's past was ended, and a chapter of unrestricted devotion to Judaism and to his people began. Now he presented the golden chain, once received from Caligula, as a votive gift to the Temple, and, like an ordinary worshipper, he carried his basket of first fruits to the altar. The deep affection he inspired in the Jewish people by this conduct, and by his courageous defence of their sanctuary, manifested itself in a striking, spontaneous demonstration. At the Feast of Tabernacles in 41, he recited in the Temple before the assembled worshippers the Book of Deuteronomy, as prescribed in the Torah (Deut. XXXI. 10, 11). When he came to the passage: 'Thou mayest not put a foreigner as a king over thee, who is not thy brother' (XVII. 15), he remembered his Idumaean ancestry and broke into tears, whereupon the assembly cried with one voice: 'Thou art our brother, thou art our brother!'

NOTES

1. Marcus Vipsanius Agrippa (63–12 B.C.E.), Roman general and statesman, victorious commander of Octavian's fleet at Actium (31); husband of Julia, Octavian's daughter; their daughter Agrippina was Caligula's mother.
2. Gaius Julius Cæsar Octavianus Augustus (63 B.C.E.–14 C.E.), first Roman emperor.
3. Apparently Livia, wife of Tiberius Claudius Nero, mother of Tiberius is meant. She later married Augustus.
4. See note 1.
5. Gaius Julius Cæsar Germanicus, Caligula's father (son of Nero Claudius Drusus, and of Antonia, daughter of Mark Antony), was adopted by the Emperor Tiberius, who reigned from 14 to 37 C.E.
6. Pontius Pilatus, Roman Procurator of Judaea and Samaria from 26 to 36 C.E.
7. See note 2.
8. See note 3.
9. When Caligula released Agrippa from prison, he presented him with a golden chain instead of the iron fetters which had bound the prisoner. Afterwards, Agrippa dedicated this golden chain as a votive gift to the Temple.

12

Agrippa II, the last Jewish King, praises the History of the Jewish War by Flavius Josephus

JOSEPH, son of Mathathias, was, before he assumed the Roman name Flavius Josephus, one of the first leaders in the revolt of the Jews against the Romans in 66 C.E. After the fall of the fortress Jodephath, he gave himself up to the Romans, espoused their cause from this moment, gained the favour of Titus and accompanied him on the campaign against Jerusalem. Later he wrote the well-known history of the Jewish War in which he obviously sought to justify his conduct and to put the blame for the national disaster on those who had continued the fight in spite of its hopelessness. He was bitterly attacked by a rival historian, Justin of Tiberias, who belonged to the opposite faction, but whose work has unfortunately not survived. Josephus defended himself with vigour and appealed for confirmation to a man whose character, behaviour and fate resembled in a striking way his own: the ex-King Agrippa II. This son and successor of Agrippa I had from the outset attached himself to the Romans, and even, in a great speech reproduced by Josephus in his history, besought the insurgent people, before the outbreak of the war, to give up the idea of fighting against the invincible power of Rome and so save their country and Temple. Now he, like Josephus, lived in victorious Rome and was in friendly intercourse with the famous author, whose presentation of the events he endorsed wholeheartedly. Josephus states in his autobiography that King Agrippa wrote him no less than sixty-two letters confirming the truth of his narrative. Two of them are reproduced by him verbally.

AGRIPPA II TO FLAVIUS JOSEPHUS

'You seem to me to have written with much greater care and accuracy than any who have dealt with the subject'

[Rome, towards the end of the 1st century C.E.]

(A)

King Agrippa to dearest Josephus, greeting. I have perused the book with the greatest pleasure. You seem to me to have written with much greater care and accuracy than any who have dealt with the subject. Send me the remaining volumes. Farewell.

(B)

King Agrippa to dearest Josephus, greeting. From what you have written you appear to stand in no need of instruction to enable us to learn everything from you from the beginning. But when you meet me, I will myself by word of mouth inform you of much that is not generally known.

These letters, with the bitter but no doubt unintentional irony which they reflect, provide a sombre postcript to the last chapter of ancient Judaea's independence. Even so, we have to be thankful to Josephus for their preservation, for they are the only authentic lines through which the last Jewish king, and incidentally the man with whom the family of the Hasmoneans died out, speaks to posterity.

13

The Byzantine Empress, Eudocia, rouses the Messianic Hopes of the Jews

THE tragic failure of the Bar Kochba revolt in 135 C.E., and the merciless persecution which followed it in the last years of Hadrian's reign, did not destroy in the hearts of the Jews the hope of seeing the recovery of Jerusalem and the rebuilding of the Temple. New rebellions flared up repeatedly in Palestine and had to be suppressed by the Roman emperors up to the middle of the fourth century. Then, however, a strange change seemed to come over the scene. In the year 360 the philosophic Julian ascended the Imperial throne. He was known to history as the Apostate, from his renunciation of Christianity. In his struggle with the Christian hierarchy he saw in the Jews his natural allies and he began to treat them with marked favour. This policy culminated in his solemn promise to restore the Holy City and to rebuild it at his own expense. This proclamation was made in a letter addressed to the Community of the Jews in 363, at the time of Julian's campaign against the Persians.

According to the historian Ammianus Marcellinus, a contemporary of Julian, the Emperor did indeed make preparations for the fulfilment of his promise by appointing Alypius of Antioch to take charge of the rebuilding of the Temple. But although it is stated by a Church historian that the letter had created great joy among the Jews, there is no mention of the subject in Jewish records. This is why some modern scholars deny the authenticity of the letter altogether. It has been, however, plausibly suggested that the Babylonian Rabbis preferred to omit any reference to the Apostate, because in 363 he had already fallen in battle, and any praise of him would have offended his Christian successors, Jovian and Valentinian.

Sixty-five years after the death of Julian, the hopes of Palestine Jewry were again raised, though for a brief instant only, by a strange counterpart of the Apostate: the beautiful Athenais who was the daughter of an Athenian sophist, and who, after having renounced paganism, took the name of Eudocia and married Theodosius II, the Byzantine Emperor. It was a time of great tribulation for the Jewish population in Palestine where, in the years 421 and 422, the masses under the instigation of the fanatics Simeon Stylites and Barsauma committed anti-Jewish outrages and burnt many synagogues. As soon as Eudocia was married to Theodosius on 2 January 423, she exerted her influence on behalf of the Jews. Her uncle, Asclepiodotes, then Consul and Prefect of the East, issued orders that all persecution of the Jews was to cease. In addition, the Empress, on a visit to the East in 438, granted permission to the Jews of Galilee to pray again at the walls of the Temple, which they had not been allowed to do since the reign of Constantine the Great.

All these acts of protection and benevolence were taken by the Jewish population of Palestine to herald the coming of the Messiah. This time the hope that salvation was at hand found open expression. The 'priests and heads of Galilee', a body of dignitaries who, after the extinction of the Patriarchate in 425 C.E., had become the leaders of the Jewish community of Galilee, sent the following brief but enthusiastic letter to the Jews of Persia and the Roman Empire.

THE JEWISH DIGNITARIES OF GALILEE TO THE JEWS OF THE DIASPORA

'The day of the re-union of our tribes is at hand'

[Somewhere in Galilee, 438 C.E.]

To the Great and Mighty People of the Jews from the priests and heads of Galilee, Greeting.

Know that the time of the dispersion of our people has come to an end and that the day of the re-union of our tribes is at hand. For behold, the Kings of the Romans have ordered that our city of Jerusalem should be given to us. Hasten to come to Jerusalem at the Feast of Tabernacles, because the kingdom will be re-established in Jerusalem.

Many Jews followed this extraordinary invitation, and a terrible clash occurred in Jerusalem at the feast of Tabernacles in 438 between the adherents of Barsauma and the Jewish crowds gathered in the Holy City. Many Jews were killed and the riots were suppressed with difficulty. The sequel was tragic both for the Jews and the Empress. In the following year, 439, Theodosius II issued a law which deprived the Jews of the right to hold any public office, and at the same time the noble patroness of the Jews fell into disgrace and was banished from the court. Jerusalem, where the mob had threatened her with death, became the place of her retirement, and here she spent the last years of her life, devoting herself to works of piety.

PART TWO

Letters from the Geonic and Spanish Periods

FROM THE EIGHTH TO THE END OF
THE FIFTEENTH CENTURY

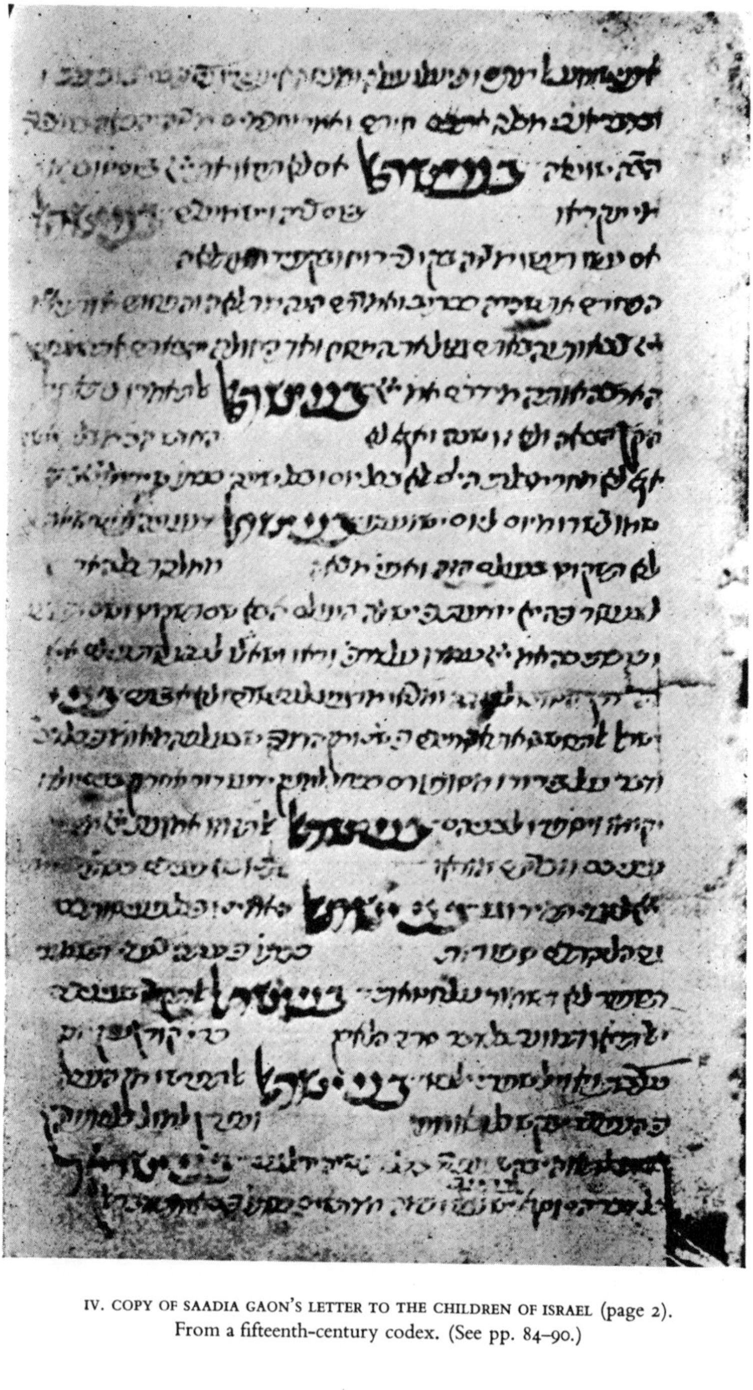

IV. COPY OF SAADIA GAON'S LETTER TO THE CHILDREN OF ISRAEL (page 2).
From a fifteenth-century codex. (See pp. 84–90.)

PART TWO

14

The Rise of the Geonic Responsa

THE generations of scholars who, after the destruction of the Temple, taught and studied in the rabbinic centres of Palestine and Babylonia, the 'Tannaim' (Teachers) and their successors, the 'Amoraim' (Speakers), laid the foundations of a new epoch in Jewish history: the period of the Talmud. From the magnificent compendia of their teaching, the Palestinian and Babylonian Talmuds, an endless stream of inspiration radiated into the life of the Jewish people. This glorious age of Jewish learning left, however, almost no traces in the history of Jewish letter-writing (see Introduction, p. xxxi f.). Only a few letters and fragments of letters have been inserted between the innumerable dialogues and sayings recorded within the many volumes of the Talmud (see *supra*, pp. 44 ff.), while the letter from Galilee (see the preceding chapter, p. 66), which has been preserved merely by its inclusion in the Syriac biography of Barsauma, appears as an isolated example of Jewish letters in the century that witnessed the completion of the Babylonian Talmud.

From the beginning of the eighth century, however, the picture changes completely. The era of the making of the Talmud had by now been succeeded by a new period, called by the name of the 'Geonim' (plural of 'Gaon', i.e. Illustrious One), the heads of the great Talmudical academies in Sura and Pumbedita. From near and distant communities written inquiries (Sheelot) were addressed to them and answered by the Geonim in learned letters called Teshubot (Responsa). It is mainly these letters which distinguish the Geonic period as one of the most creative in the history of Judaism.

A large number of the Geonic Responsa have been preserved, and the following specimens will show the wide range they covered from the outset.

1. *Gaon Natronai pardons the Followers of a Pseudo-Messiah*

About the year 720 an adventurer, Serene (from Shirin, in Syria), proclaimed himself the Messiah and took it upon himself to abolish various Talmudic ordinances. His movement grew rapidly and spread even to

Spain; it was, however, soon suppressed, when the officers of the Caliph Yazid II captured Serene and handed him over to the Jewish authorities. His adherents sought to return to Judaism, but before accepting them some leaders of Syrian Jewry consulted the Gaon of Pumbedita, Natronai ben Nehemia (surnamed Mar Jaupa). Natronai's answer, which reveals, incidentally, the far-reaching powers exercised by the Geonim, was couched in restrained terms, considering the spirit of the age and the gravity of the offence ascribed by the Talmudic law to the apostasy of Serene's followers.

GAON NATRONAI I
TO THE HEADS OF SYRIAN COMMUNITIES

'You are not bound to repulse them'

[Pumbedita, first half of the 8th century]

You have asked about an impostor, called Serene, who arose in our exile, proclaimed himself as the Messiah and misled many who now form a particular sect. They have rejected the prayers, neglect the supervision of the meat, do not guard wine from the touch of pagans, do not celebrate the second holiday and do not execute documents of marriage according to rabbinical ordinances. You ask how to treat such sectarians, who have offended so much, regarding their re-admission. Should they immerse? Or what other formalities have to be performed?

Our opinion is as follows: Although those apostates departed from the right path, although they rejected rabbinical ordinances, neglected feasts and religious customs, and defiled themselves by eating prohibited food, it is nevertheless preferable to readmit than to repulse them. You may let them suffer the legal punishment by flagellation and fines, each of them according to his transgression. They may afterwards declare solemnly in the synagogues that they will never relapse into their evil ways, then you may rehabilitate them and are not bound to repulse them . . .

2. *Advice on Prayers for the Dead*

Paltoi ben Abaye, Gaon of Pumbedita (842–858), was one of the most eminent of the early Geonim. He brought the distant Spanish communities into the sphere of influence of the East and made great efforts to reinstate the Hebrew of the Mishnah as the Jewish literary language in place of the usual Aramaic.

The following example of Paltoi's Responsa shows the charity of the inquirers no less than the mystical disposition of the ancient teacher.

GAON PALTOI TO AN INQUIRER

'The soul receives comfort from the mourning of men'

[Pumbedita, middle of the 9th century]

You ask: If somebody passed away without having left mourning relatives, ten men[1] are obliged according to Rabbi Judah[2] to go to that place where the late person used to dwell – what place is meant? The place of the Synagogue or his lodging? And how many days after his death does this have to be performed? Are these men obliged to say anything on this occasion?

The sages said: The soul of the deceased, said Rabbi Hisdai,[3] mourns for seven days, because it is said: 'But his flesh upon him shall have pain, and his soul with him shall mourn.'[4] If there are no mourners or comforters, the soul gains peace when strangers visit the place where she left the body. Thus our sages told a story about a dead man who had passed away in the neighbourhood of R. Judah without having left mourning relatives or comforters. R. Judah, it is told, assembled ten men and went to the lodging of the deceased. The latter appeared afterwards to R. Judah in his dream and said: 'Mayst thou find satisfaction in the same way as thou hast satisfied my spirit!' Therefore even if no words of comfort are uttered, nevertheless the soul receives comfort from the mourning of the men who went to the dwelling place of the deceased.

3. *The Gaon rejects Discrimination*

Sar Shalom bar Boas was Gaon of Sura between 850 and 860. Toleration and gentleness were the outstanding qualities of this enlightened master who was always reluctant to impose his opinion upon his numerous questioners, but tried rather to persuade them with arguments and illustrations, as the following example shows:

GAON SHALOM BAR BOAS TO AN INQUIRER

'All robbery whatsoever of non-Jewish property is forbidden'

[Sura, second half of the 9th century]

You ask: What is the rule concerning the robbery of non-Jewish property? Is such a robbery prohibited exclusively as a profanation of the Holy Name?[5]

This is our decision: The prohibition of robbery has no reference to the profanation of the Holy Name. For it is a Halakah[6] that all robbery whatsoever (thus also) of non-Jewish property is forbidden. The profanation of the Holy Name is discussed only with respect to lost property.[7] R. Pinhas ben Jair[8] said: It is not permitted to appropriate even the lost property of non-Jews, since it leads to a profanation of the Holy Name. In the story related of R. Ashi[9] that once, when travelling, he sent for a grape grown in the garden of a non-Jew, this is certainly to be understood for payment and in the certain assurance that the grapes were offered for sale. Far be the idea that such a man as Rabbi Ashi committed any falsehood or fraud, he who declared it as a principle that one must not cause an untrue opinion in anybody, Jew or non-Jew.

4. *The Gaon decides a Question of Indemnity in a Case of Brigandage*

The following Responsum appears among a large collection of Geonic decisions preserved in the Cairo Genizah (see Introduction, p. xxxv). Neither the author nor the period of its composition has been established. The Responsum, which decides an unusual legal case, used feigned names though the case may have been a real one. The dramatic account of the events leading to the enquiry is of no less interest than the acute decision of the Gaon.

AN UNKNOWN GAON TO AN INQUIRER

'. . . He did not do wrong because the box with money could not be saved'

[Place and date unknown]

Question: He [i.e. Reuben] went to Egypt. Simeon sent fifteen dinars with him in order to purchase merchandise. He arrived at a place called Agrabia, and from there returned to Egypt. On the journey, brigands attacked them. When he reached Egypt he reported to his companion all that had happened. He wrote him thus: 'When I arrived at Agrabia I hired [Arabs] for my luggage, and sent all the money I possessed through a non-Jew, having regard to the dangers of travelling. I retained only thirteen [qu. fifteen, *vide infra*] dinars of Simeon because I did not want to make it known to him. But brigands came and captured the whole caravan and stole everything I possessed. I was stripped to the skin and they prepared to slaughter me. Although I had you in mind, I thought: I am unable to save anything in my possession from their hands. It is better therefore if I tell them that I have money with me and they spare my life. I told them that I have got money with me, fifteen dinars. They went with me to the place of the caravan. I opened the box, took Simeon's fifteen dinars out of it and saved myself thus. I am ready to pay Simeon half of the money because of my love.' Simeon said: 'This man has saved himself through my money: he is, therefore, obliged to pay me back all, as it is right. The brigands did not know that he had kept fifteen dinars in his hands and nevertheless he delivered the money to them. There is no doubt that he saved his life with the money of another man; he is therefore obliged to pay all.'

Responsum: But if things are as Simeon said, then Reuben was right in saying: Nothing that I possess can be saved from them. If witnesses confirm the narrative he is free. If he has no witness, he shall make an oath that the fifteen dinars were not alienated by him wrongly, that the box was taken by the brigands and could not have been saved from them, and that the dinars would have been seized anyway. If Simeon takes the half of his money offered by Reuben as a compromise, Reuben is free from the oath.

Geonic Responsa such as these opened a new chapter in Jewish letter-writing. They became the models for the Rabbinic letters which followed them in all countries up to modern times (see Introduction pp. xlix f. and lii ff.).

NOTES

1. The number required for prayers in the congregation, the so-called Minyan.
2. R. Judah the Prince, redactor of the Mishnah (135–219), called Rabbi.
3. R. Hisdai of Kaphri, Babylonian Amora of the third century.
4. Job XIV. 22.
5. Every evil act which brings disgrace upon the religion of Israel and the Jewish community is considered a profanation of the Holy Name (Hillul Hashem), according to Lev. XXII. 32. Such acts have to be avoided even if they are not expressly forbidden by the established law. The warning against Hillul Hashem served throughout the ages as a strong deterrent from evil-doing.
6. An ordinance of the established Law.
7. According to Tosef. B.K. X 15, a theft committed against a non-Jew is even more heinous than a theft committed against a Jew, because the sin of Hillul Hashem is added to the transgression of the law.
8. R. Pinhas ben Jair, colleague of Judah the Prince, renowned for his saintliness.
9. R. Ashi ben Shimi (353–427), redactor of the Gemara.

15

Gaon Amram sends the Model of the First Prayer Book to Spain

To Rabbi Amram bar Shechna, Gaon of Sura from 846 to 864, belongs the historic merit of having prepared the first Jewish Prayer Book. There were two main reasons why no Hebrew book of that kind had existed until then. One was a ban on writing down the sacred blessings, the other was that no need for such records was felt in the East, where an uninterrupted liturgical tradition had kept alive the memory of the prayers and their order since ancient times. The lack of such continuous tradition created, however, in the Western countries an urgent desire for liturgical guidance. Thus it came about that the suggestion for the compilation of the Prayer Book came from the Iberian Peninsula. Isaac bar Simeon, the head of a Jewish community in Spain, probably of Barcelona, put to Amram so many questions concerning liturgy that the Gaon made up his mind to compose a written Seder, i.e. order (of prayers), containing a complete sequence of prayers and liturgical rules for the whole year. He sent this manuscript to Rabbi Isaac with the following letter:

GAON AMRAM BAR SHECHNA TO ISAAC BAR SIMEON

'We have composed it according to the preserved traditions . . . as Heaven has enlightened us'

[Sura, between 846 and 864]

Amram bar Shechna, head of the Academy in the city of Sura, to Rabbi Isaac, son of the Master and Rabbi Simeon, who is beloved and esteemed by our whole school.

By God's mercy may there be much peace on you and your children, on all scholars and students, as well as on all our Israelitish brethren living there. Greetings from us and from R. Zemah, the president of the judicial court, from the teachers and sages of the Academy, from its pupils and from the city of Sura! All are well, scholars and students, and all Israelitish inhabitants. We think always of your welfare and keep you in our memory, wishing you well, praying for you and beseeching God to bestow mercy upon you, to keep and guard you from any grief and ruin and from a bad government; may He in His mercy fulfil all wishes of your heart.

R. Jacob, son of R. Isaac, sent us the ten ducats which you have offered to the Academy; five for us, and five for the treasury of the Academy. We have ordered a blessing to be said for you; may it be fulfilled upon you and upon your children and posterity. As regards the arrangement of the prayers and blessings you have asked for, we have composed it according to the extant tradition, on the authority of the Tannaim and Amoraim, as Heaven has enlightened us. For the Talmud says: 'R. Meir[1] declares that we are obliged to utter a hundred blessings daily.' In the Palestinian Gemara the passage reads: 'It has been taught in the name of R. Meir: There is no Israelite who does not utter a hundred blessings daily. Thus it is said in the Scripture: "And now what doth the Lord thy God require of thee"[2] – read instead of מה [what] מאה [a hundred].' David was the first who prescribed them: when he was informed that a hundred people died in Jerusalem daily,[3] he ordered these prayers. It seems, however, that they were forgotten in the course of time and that the Tannaim and Amoraim were obliged to renew them. R. Natronai bar Hilai, head of Sura,[4] sent the following Responsum concerning them to the community of Lucena through R. Joseph: Each of these blessings cannot be said [in the morning when we get up] at the proper moment because our hands are also busy with impure matters. We have, therefore, to wash our face, hands, and feet first, as it is said: 'Prepare to meet thy God, O Israel.'[5] Afterwards every Israelite is bound to recite them simultaneously. In Spain a custom is established for the reader to recite these blessings in order to represent thus the ignorant people at the same time. . . .

Rabbi Amram's Prayer Book, the Siddur Rab Amram, is one of the most important and permanent fruits of the Geonic period. The great builders of modern Judaism, Saadia Gaon and Moses Maimonides, modelled their prayer books on Rabbi Amram's composition. It survived all wanderings and trials of the Jewish people, gave them strength and comfort in their troubles, and became the foundation of the Spanish-Portuguese and German-Polish liturgies.

NOTES

1. R. Meir, disciple of R. Akiba, one of the compilers of the Mishnah.
2. Deut. x. 12.
3. 2 Sam. xxiv. 15.
4. Natronai bar Hilai, Amram's predecessor; his Responsum, 'Mea Barachot', presently mentioned by Amram, was the basis of Amram's Seder.
5. Amos iv. 12.

16

Saadia of Fayum fights for the Rules of the Calendar and for the Ethics of Judaism

IN the long list of Geonim who stood at the head of the Babylonian academies there is none so distinguished as Saadia ben Joseph (892–942), born in the Egyptian province of Fayum, who became head of the Sura Academy in 928. His Arabic translation of the Bible was for the Jews in Mohammedan countries as important as the Septuagint had been for the Jewry of the Hellenistic period. He introduced the principles of deductive logic into all branches of Jewish learning, created an Hebrew philology and became the 'father of the Jewish philosophy of religion'. The values transmitted by Scripture and Jewish tradition were for Saadia, as for all the other Geonim, the unalterable foundations of Judaism, but in examining these values with the methods of Islamic philosophy he succeeded in establishing in his famous philosophical work 'Emunot ve-Deot' (Beliefs and Doctrines), written originally in Arabic, for the first time the mutual relationship between revealed truth and rational thought.

The eminent qualities of Saadia which pervade all his works – his 'wisdom, piety, eloquence, a firm and unbending spirit', for which he was praised already by one of his contemporaries – are reflected also in his letters, of which fortunately some fine specimens have survived.

1. *The Calendar Controversy with Aaron ben Meir*

At the beginning of the tenth century a heated controversy arose in the East over the fixing of the Calendar. As late as 835 the Babylonian Exilarch had recognized that the Palestinian schools were still entitled to fix the days of the new moons and festivals, as they had done for centuries. Soon afterwards, however, with the decay of the Palestinian schools, this privilege was abolished in practice by the authorities in Babylonia. On the other hand, there was a remarkable revival of Jewish learning in Palestine in the first decades of the tenth century, and in 921 Aaron ben Meir, who appears to have been head of a school in Ramlah, proclaimed from the Mount of Olives a revised Calendar according to which the ensuing Passover was to commence on a Sunday, instead of Tuesday as fixed by the Babylonian academies. This announcement gave rise to a controversy which was to be continued for a period of many years and to cause a turmoil in the whole

Jewish world, for nothing less was at stake than the definite shifting of the prerogative in the vital matter of fixing the Calendar.

Saadia was hardly thirty years of age when the controversy started. He had – for unknown reasons – emigrated from Egypt and settled in Aleppo. He at once espoused the Babylonian side and became its protagonist. Two letters addressed to his pupils refer to his activities during the first period of the campaign, while a somewhat defective letter to a group of Rabbis – probably in Fostat (Cairo) – shows the feelings of the master at the climax of the struggle.

S. asserts Babyl. cause

SAADIA TO HIS PUPILS

'Have mercy upon the people of Israel and of the heritage of God'

(A)

[Somewhere in Babylonia, about January 922]

May the Lord grant me a worthy place among his sages. I am unable to praise His glory sufficiently. My love and affection for you, my three dear pupils, has never waned, for educating the young leaves indelible traces in the heart, the more when it has been undertaken for the sake of the fear of God and the glorification of His Name.

As I have been desolate ever since I left my wife and children, so I have grieved over my separation from you. May it be the will of the Almighty that I see you again in health and happiness. It is now six and a half years that no word from you has reached me. I even wrote to you condoling with you over the death of the venerable old man, blessed be his memory, but saw no answer. Only recently I was told by our friend R. David, son of Abraham, that you had written to him and requested him to secure the opinions of the heads of the Academies regarding the fixing of the months Marheshvan and Kislev of the year 1233 [Sel.]. I presume that you wrote to him, and not to me, only because, in accordance with previous reports, you thought that I was still in Palestine. He himself [R. David] suggested that you seem to have thought so. He further requested me to write to you and to inform you [regarding the state of affairs].

Know that when I was still in Aleppo, some pupils came

*w/
29
not
30 days*

*Passover
on
Tuesday*

from Ba'al Gad and brought the news that Ben Meir intended to proclaim Heshvan and Kislev deficient.[1] I did not believe it but as a precaution I wrote to him in the summer [not to do so]. The Exilarch, the heads of the Academies and all the leaders, teachers and scholars, likewise agreed to proclaim Heshvan and Kislev full, and Passover to be celebrated on Tuesday. In conjunction with their letters I, too, wrote to most of the great cities, in order to fulfil my duty.

Persist ye also in this matter and close up this breach, and do not rebel against the command of God. None of the people dare to profane the festivals of God wilfully, to eat leavened bread on Passover, and eat, drink and work on the day of Atonement. May it be the will [of the Lord] that there be no stumbling-block and no pitfall in your place or in any other place of Israel. Pray, answer this letter and tell me of all your affairs and your wellbeing. May your peace grow and increase for ever.

(B)

[Somewhere in Babylonia, about March 922]

During my travels from one city to another, and from one castle to another, I thought always of my sons and daughters as well as of you, my pupils, in my heart and by words. I pray to God that He may help me in order that I see again in great joy their faces and yours.

Concerning the commotion in the country, I was aware of it from the outset, two months ago, and wrote you about this matter enclosing the letters of the Exilarch and one of the heads of the Academies, may God help them!

I informed you that, when I was in Aleppo last summer, I learnt that Ben Meir had made up his mind to proclaim Marheshvan and Kislev deficient. I wrote him some letters entreating him to abstain from this purpose. I tried to make him understand that they [the months mentioned] were full months and to explain to him why this was so. Afterwards I went to Baghdad believing that he would listen to me. But rumour reached Baghdad that he had proclaimed them deficient. All our masters, the sages of the Academies, were afraid of this because no thing similar had ever occurred, namely that the festivals were proclaimed contrary to the Law. That is why they, in their astonishment, wrote to all Jews of all localities announcing to them that all of us agree upon this matter and that there is no difference between us. They also asked him to refrain from his proclamation. He did not obey. . . .

I sent you their letters two months ago, enclosed in my letter. When they arrive, come together and read them. Remain firm, gird your loins like valiant men, like warriors in order to sustain this war of the Lord. Have mercy upon the people of Israel and of the heritage of God, lest they eat leavened bread during Passover, lest they eat, drink and work on the day of Atonement. This great good work will be counted to your benefit afterwards.

Public reading of Responsa [margin note]

Let us be informed about everything you do, about your situation, about your vows and wishes [or questions]. Convey greetings to the masters, to all our friends and brethren.

May your peace increase from the beginning to the end.

SAADIA TO THE RABBIS SHELAMA, EZRA AND ALI

'Be energetic in this matter . . . because it is more important than trade and daily bread'

[Probably Sura or Baghdad, at the beginning of the twenties of the 10th century]

To the Rabbi Shelama, the great Rabbi Ezra, and the Rabbi Ali, may our Rock support and uphold them.[2]

Peace abundant, [divine] mercy and grace and the garment of peace, and understanding your kinswoman,[3] and a good name and . . . shall be unto you.

I did not acknowledge a letter from you for some time, but I trust in God and am firmly convinced that you are well in every respect, especially since your letter reached the Head of the Academy, may God strengthen him, and Abul Fadhl,[4] may

God support him. [I suppose that] you did not send the letter as a private communication, because you are ashamed of what the people of the town did whilst you were with them. . . . I hope, however, that it will be proved that you acted as you did in a moment of perplexity.

. . . Had it been manifest in your eyes that the people of Iraq did not do so, you had not made that mistake in such an important matter. . . . Everyone who hears of it will wonder. I am ashamed to speak about it. Everyone who comes to me to greet me asks my opinion of this affair in Cairo. I cannot give any satisfactory answer but I must write to you as soon as I become aware of the facts of the matter, that it should be considered, that you take counsel and make good what you have mismanaged. . . .

O my brethren, act in this matter on my behalf and on behalf of all the Sages who are in the two Academies. For I know that God has endowed you with intelligence, insight, sagacity, and shrewdness. I do not say this in order to praise you but in order to awaken and admonish you. Fear the God of Israel, guard your souls, be pure and assist others to beso. Be not, contrary to this, the cause of sorrow to us but of pleasure. You should relieve us from this grief and give up that practice. It is known to us that there are people of good sense left in the town, who fear the Merciful and endeavour to be righteous. Be energetic in this matter, day and night, morning and evening, because it is more important than trade and daily bread and every urgent business.

A copy of the letter of the President of the Academy should always be with you and before your eyes, you should read it continually. Every word of it is of fundamental importance. Learn it by heart; let one teach it the other and copy it for him, so that each of you shall read. . . . I have written in it, to the other, until you are all of one mind. May your efforts be fortified and your words united.

Know that we did not lose sight of what is incumbent on us, but everything depends on you, like a chain, as it were, hung around your necks. God expects this of you, and will call you to account for it. Be therefore no longer wayward, as you have been – enough of disgrace. . . . Show zeal for Heaven, since this is the time for zeal – stand in the breach because it is a time of dissoluteness. Trust in God and He will help you.

Let me know in your letter what you intend to do in this affair. . . . Peace upon you for ever.

Saadia contributed greatly to the ultimate victory of the Babylonian party by his work 'The Book of the Seasons', which he was commissioned by the Exilarch, the head of the Jews in Babylonia, to write. In the course of the great struggle he had proved himself to be the greatest religious authority in Israel, and in the year 928 – at the age of thirty-six – he was elevated to the Gaonate of Sura.

great reconciler

2. *Saadia's Exhortation to the Children of Israel*

The newly installed Gaon gave a splendid testimony of his desire to live up to the position of a spiritual leader. Not content merely to answer questions on religious matters sent to him by the public, Saadia determined to take the initiative and address a solemn exhortation to the Jewish people to keep to the path of righteousness. It befits the extraordinary character of this message that it was announced in a prior letter to a community in Egypt, the heads of which had asked the Gaon for an intervention with the authorities in Baghdad.

SAADIA GAON TO THE HEADS OF A JEWISH COMMUNITY IN EGYPT

'Without pupils the sages gain no glory'

[Sura or Baghdad, 22 May 928]

Let us know every wish and every demand made on you by the government in order that we may pass them on to the influential men in Baghdad, the children of the honourable Netira and Aaron, of blessed memory. They will procure a decision from the king that the Lord will help them to obtain. But this you must keep strictly and not deviate from it.

And further we command warnings and admonitions to be written to you in order to awaken your hearts and to keep your

men of status

[83]

ie. "I will liason between you, gov't and Jewish courtiers"

minds vigilant towards the commandments of our Lord, both what you must do in order to live, and what you must refrain from doing in order not to die, for thus we are obliged to fulfil our duty in the great cause we have undertaken to perform.

Let us know your welfare day by day, for it is the welfare of our soul. For without an army there is no king, and without pupils the sages gain no glory. May the Lord be your confidence; may He lead you and us in His great mercy. And may peace, blessing and welfare be upon you for ever.

new type: 'Letter of Admonition'

Shortly after the delivery of his inaugural discourse, Saadia addressed the following letter nominally to the same community, but really, as its contents and the apostrophe 'Children of Israel' before each of the thirty admonitions indicate, to the whole House of Israel. Both in the tone of moral earnestness and in the style of this great Hebrew letter, Saadia follows the sublime example of Jeremiah's letter to the exiles in Babylon and, at the same time, heralds the rise of a new type of Jewish letter-writing: the Letter of Admonition. Some of his injunctions bear considerable resemblance to certain passages of the Sermon on the Mount and early Christian letters. And yet the essence of Judaism has never been restated more emphatically and exactly than by the ingenious selection and interpretation of biblical citations as presented within the framework of Saadia's letter to the Children of Israel. Although there is, in some of the admonitions, an obvious reference to the Karaites, who rejected the Talmud and the Oral Law (see the next chapter) and against whom Saadia had composed several brilliant polemical treatises, the whole conception shows an architectonic unity proceeding from a single original source: Saadia's deep religious mind.

A copy of the letter bound together with other manuscripts was discovered by Dr. Nahum Slouchz in a Moroccan city and published by B. Revel recently; its authenticity is established by the preceding short letter, which had been found independently in the Cairo Genizah.

SAADIA GAON TO A JEWISH COMMUNITY IN EGYPT

Essence of Judaism

'Blessed are the just, blessed are the pious, blessed are those who pay good for good to the Lord, and good for evil to men'

[Sura or Baghdad, in the year 928]

To the holy people that has been warned and to those who are seeking God, to those who listen to the Sages, commandments

31 Doctrines addressed

and authorities; to the noblemen and to the other people; Peace and Welfare! May prosperity, a sincere prayer, the protection of our King and the Glory of the Shekinah be granted to you; may your wishes be fulfilled, and good counsel, success and help be bestowed upon you, safety and assistance; may aid be conferred upon you by the Lord, our mighty God, our strength, our pride. Greetings from us, from our friends and disciples! Know that all are seeking protection in the shadow of God, our Saviour; though we have become a poor people, He will not forsake us, even as He has promised, 'I will also leave in the midst of thee an afflicted and poor people, and they shall take refuge in the name of the Lord.'[5] And we have to thank Him for His promise and to recount His strength and praise His mercy, although not adequately, as it is written, 'He is exalted above all blessing and praise.'[6]

We have previously ordered that a letter be sent to you concerning the gift which God has prepared for His people Israel, and we are sure that you were rejoiced by it, as it is written, 'And Hezekiah rejoiced, and all the people, because of that which God had prepared for the people.'[7] We have also after a thorough study of the tractates [of the Talmud] and interpretation of their motives made a clear discourse and caused more pleasure, because God, our Lord, granted us [the benefit] to teach and explain the Torah to His people, and to reveal all its deeply hidden secrets to them. And they understood the contents of the Mishnah and the Talmud, and also that everything comes from the God of hosts. We have further in all single sections offered a prayer and supplication before the Lord of hosts, our God, for the remnants of the people in order that He may see the sufferings and gather the dispersed people and secure their country and restore their ruins, that He may do and fulfil what He has assured us, 'Sing, O heavens, and be joyful!'[8] 'Shout, ye lowest parts of the earth; break forth in singing, ye mountains . . . ; for the Lord hath redeemed Jacob, and doth glorify himself in Israel.'[9]

We informed you in our previous letter that we ordered

warnings and admonitions to be sent to you later to awaken you to obedience to what has been taught you, 'The Lord God hath given me the tongue of them that are taught. . . . He wakeneth morning by morning.'[10] We are bound to warn you, and you are bound to keep in mind and to fulfil our warnings in order to save your lives.

Children of Israel! When one of you shall be instructed by his neighbour, he must not rebel against it in his heart, saying, 'Does a man, like me, need instruction from that one?' as it is written, 'Hear ye, and give ear, be not proud!'[11]

Children of Israel! You must not make falsehood your refuge and rely upon it, saying, 'All words he spoke to you may be effaced [?],'[12] as it is written about these evil-doers, 'For we have made lies our refuge, and in falsehood have we hid ourselves.'[13]

Children of Israel! When a man commits a sin, it will always be before his eyes; he will be afraid that it will find him out one day, as it is written, 'But if ye will not do so, behold, ye have sinned against the Lord; and know ye your sin will find you out,'[12] and it is also written, 'My sin is ever before me.'[15]

Children of Israel! If your heart aims at achieving a desire, understand it well; perhaps it will taste bitter afterwards, as it is written: 'There is a way which seemeth right unto a man, but the end thereof are the ways of death.'[16]

Children of Israel! If your heart desires to offer a spontaneous fast or an additional prayer, it would be better to avoid a transgression, and this means more than anything else, for of those who do otherwise has been said, 'When they fast, I will not hear their cry; and when they offer burnt-offering and meal-offering, I will not accept them; but I will consume them by the sword and by the famine, and by the pestilence.'[17] And the sages have said, 'The Holy One, blessed be He, hates the good work which is the outcome of an evil work.'[18]

Children of Israel! If you do not look to [or fear] God in good days, to whom will you be able to call in the days of distress, and have him listen?

Children of Israel! When you perform a good work with impatience, irritation and weariness, your reward is already empty, as it is written: 'Behold, what a weariness is it! and ye have snuffed at it, saith the Lord of hosts, and ye have brought that which was taken by violence, and the lame and the sick; thus ye bring the offering: Should I accept this of your hand? saith the Lord.'[19]

Children of Israel! You shall not say that the end which should come and has not come, neither in this year nor in this month, neither on the first nor on the next day nor today, has been delayed: that is of no avail, but on every day and in every hour it can come to pass, as it is written: 'Sing unto the Lord, bless His name; proclaim His salvation from day to day.'[20]

Children of Israel! Know that man's soul will not find rest in this world, even if it finds the kingdoms of the whole world, because it knows that the world-to-come belongs to it; there will it rest and repose, as it is written: 'Thus saith the Lord, Stand ye in the ways and seek and ask for the eternal paths, where is the good way and walk therein, and ye shall find rest for your souls. But they said: "We will not attend." '[21]

Children of Israel! Do not assume that your forefathers have changed anything in the tradition, because every word was understood distinctly, word by word, as it is written: 'That the generation to come might know them, even the children which should be born: who should arise and tell them to their children.'[22]

Children of Israel! Do not push away the faith in God from your eyes, and keep in your minds the fear of God, as it is written: 'I have set the Lord always before me.'[23]

Children of Israel! Believe that all your steps and all your actions are numbered, as it is written: 'For now Thou numberest my steps . . .'[24]

Children of Israel! Wink not with your eyes, nor look for the image of every secret thing. Is it not written: 'He that winketh with the eye causes sorrow, and a prating fool shall fall'?[25]

Children of Israel! Separate not yourselves from the congregation, because he who separates himself from the congregation seeks his own desire and is ready for every opposition, as it is written: 'He that separateth himself seeketh his own desire, and snarleth against all sound wisdom.'[26]

Children of Israel! Every word which is repeated in the Torah has a different meaning, as it is written: 'God speaks in one way, yea, in two, though man perceiveth it not,'[27] and our masters, blessed be their memory, said: 'Every section which has been repeated was repeated only for the reason that it was intended to say something new.'[28]

Children of Israel! You shall not envy one another, because envy kills the wicked men, as it is written: 'For anger killeth the foolish man, and envy slayeth the silly man.'[29]

Children of Israel! You shall not rejoice at the misfortune of your neighbour, as it is written: 'If I rejoiced at the destruction of him that hated me, or exulted when evil found him.'[30]

Children of Israel! You shall not harden yourselves against God, the fear of our fathers. Who hath hardened himself against Him, and has prospered?[31] As it is written: 'And if ye will walk contrary unto Me and will not hearken unto Me; I will bring seven times more plagues upon you according to your sins.'[32]

Children of Israel! All nations trust in chariots or horses[33] but as for you, your chariots and horses are God's Torah and the sages, as it is written: 'My father, my father, the chariot of Israel, and the horsemen thereof.'[34]

Children of Israel! All nations gathered silver and gold in their treasuries, but as for you, your silver and gold is the Torah and the Midrash, as it is written: 'Receive my instruction and not silver, and knowledge rather than gold.'[35]

Children of Israel! If you will forsake God's Torah, He will forsake you in the hands of your enemies, as it is written: 'Israel hath cast off that which is good: the enemy shall pursue him.'[36]

Children of Israel! Make a living for those who learn the Law in order that they may adhere to God's Torah. Is it not written:

'Prepare thy work without and make it fit for thyself in the field; and afterwards build thy house'?[37]

Children of Israel! When a man gathers a fortune gained by robbery and violence, and brings it into safety, will he be able to increase the days of his life by the use of his whole fortune? As it is written: 'He that getteth riches and not by right, in the midst of his days he shall leave them, and at his end he shall be a fool.'[38]

Children of Israel! Teach your tongue to say: 'In Thee we trust, God our God,' because this helps even the wicked, as it is written: 'Many are the sorrows of the wicked, but he that trusteth in the Lord, mercy compasseth him about.'[39]

Children of Israel! When you give a voluntary gift to God, you shall give from the best things you have, because thus it is written: 'That they may live, and that He may give them of the gold of Sheba . . .'[40]

Children of Israel! Know that you eat in order to live, but that you do not live in order to eat, as it is written: 'Let the humble eat and be satisfied'[41]; about the idolators, however, it is written: 'Let us eat and drink, for tomorrow shall we die.'[42]

Children of Israel! Do not say: 'How lovely are the words of this letter, and how sweet are its sentences!' but you shall carry them out. Is it not written: 'And lo, thou art unto them as a love song of one that hath a pleasant voice [and] can play well on an instrument: for they hear thy words, but they do them not.'[43]

Children of Israel! Remember that God has created you upright and that it is you who soil your souls for wickedness, as it is written: 'Behold, this only have I found that God has made man upright: but they have sought out many inventions,'[44] and this is proved by the fact that little children do not lie until they are taught to do so.

Children of Israel! Put down on sheets of paper all our words, learn them by heart and keep them in your hearts, for by them ye will be helped.

Children of Israel! When you want to know anything, do

not be lazy in asking questions and thus perform dubious actions, for this would not be according to God's will; but forward your questions to us, and we shall be with you and not restrain our lips, as it is written: 'I have reached righteousness in the great congregation: Lo, I did not restrain my lips, o Lord, Thou knowest.'[45]

Children of Israel! Turn to God and keep His commandments, His judgments and His decrees, even if you have turned away from the Lord and are covered by sins, as it is written: 'Turn ye unto Him against whom ye have deeply rebelled, O Children of Israel!'[46]

Blessed are the just, blessed are the pious, blessed are those who pay good for good to the Lord, and good for evil to men, and blessed are those, who trust in the Lord, as it is said: 'And therefore will the Lord wait, that He may be gracious unto you, and therefore will He be exalted, that He may have compassion upon you, for the Lord is a God of Justice. Happy are all they that wait for Him.'[47] And He will do as we have hoped, and your peace, welfare and success will increase for ever.

Closed and signed. Blessed be the Lord for ever. Amen and Amen.

NOTES

1. With only twenty-nine and not thirty days.
2. This address – in the original at the end of the letter – contained also other names which are, however, illegible.
3. Prov. VII. 4: 'Say unto wisdom: thou art my sister, and call understanding thy kinswoman.'
4. Probably the Arabic name of the Exilarch, David b. Zaccai.
5. Zeph. III. 12.
6. Neh. IX. 5.
7. 2 Chron. XXIX. 36.
8. Is. XLIX. 13.
9. Is. XLIV. 23.
10. Is. L. 4.
11. Jer. XIII. 15.
12. The writing of this passage is difficult to decipher.
13. Is. XXVIII. 15. Saadia puts the warning against falsehood almost in the first place; cf. the equal value ascribed to the good and the true in Emunot ve-Deot III: 'Wisdom further suggests, and this is perhaps its first principle, that one should speak the truth and abstain from falsehood' (Saadya Gaon, 'The Book of Doctrines and Beliefs'. Translated by A. Altmann, Oxford, 1946; p. 99).
14. Num. XXXII. 23.
15. Ps. LI. 5.
16. Prov. XIV. 12.
17. Jer. XIV. 12.
18. Talmud Sukkoth, fol. 30, col. 1.
19. Mal. I. 13.
20. Ps. XCVI. 2.
21. Jer. VI. 16; cf. Emunot ve-Deot, IX. 1.
22. Ps. LXXVIII. 6.
23. Ps. XVI. 8.
24. Job XIV. 16.
25. Prov. X. 10.
26. Prov. XVIII. 1; cf. Hillel's admonition in Sayings of the Fathers , II. 5.
27. Job XXXIII. 14.
28. Sota g 25.
29. Job V. 2.
30. Job XXXI. 29.
31. Job IX. 4.
32. Lev. XXVI. 21.
33. Ps. XX. 8.
34. 2 Kings II. 12.
35. Prov. VIII. 10.
36. Hosea VIII. 3.
37. Prov. XXIV. 27.
38. Jer. XVII. 11.
39. Ps. XXXII. 10.
40. Ps. LXXII. 15.
41. Ps. XXII. 27.
42. Is. XXII. 13.
43. Ezek. XXXIII. 32.
44. Eccl. VII. 29. The same quotation with a comment, exactly corresponding to the present admonition, occurs in Emunot ve-Deot, VI: 'As to the soul being exposed to the possibility of sin, which some people make a ground of complaint against God, we must bear in mind that sin is the result of the soul's own evil choice as it acts in opposition to the wishes of the Creator; as it says, "Behold, this only have I found, that God made man upright; but they have sought out many inventions" (Eccles. 7, 29).' See Altmann, *op. cit.*, p. 151.
45. Ps. XL. 10.
46. Is. XXXI. 6. This last exhortation is a postscript summarizing the preceding thirty admonitions. It concludes most appropriately with the apostrophe 'Children of Israel'.
47. Is. XXX. 18.

17

Karaites versus Rabbanites: The Epistle of Sahal ben Mazliah

Towards the end of the eighth century Anan ben Joseph, the author of 'The Book of the Law', boldly proclaimed the right of the individual Jew to disregard the decisions of the Talmud and the Geonim, and to base his conduct directly on the Scripture as interpreted by his own judgment. Anan's followers were called Karaites, i.e. Scripture readers. During the next two centuries many of the ablest writers and scholars among the Jews of the East belonged to this sect. One of them was Sahal ben Mazliah (910–950), a leading philologist, whose 'Sefer Dikduk' (Hebrew Grammar) and 'Leshon Limmudim' (Lexicon) were widely used. The letter addressed by him to Jacob ben Samuel, a disciple of Saadia, and to Jacob's fellow-Rabbanites, is a typical example of the propagandist and polemical activity of the Karaites.

SAHAL BEN MAZLIAH TO JACOB BEN SAMUEL AND THE RABBANITES

'Know that everyone of our brethren is responsible for himself'

[First half of the 10th century]

I come from Jerusalem to warn the people. Who but the Karaites, who study the Torah, could enter upon this task? Why art thou angry, Jacob ben Samuel, that I have arrived with the purpose of learning and teaching, of dwelling among the wise and worthy men of my community and of dissuading the remnants of God's people from forbidden pleasure? . . .

O that I had the strength to wander from town to town in order to awaken and warn the People of God; as it is said: 'Go through, go through the gates: clear ye the way of the people!'[1] . . . 'Cast ye up, clear the way, take up the stumbling block out of the way of My people!'[2] And verily, you should know that there is no bigger stumbling block than that of a bad way. . . . I come in the great name of God in order to awaken the hearts of the people, to bring it back to the teaching of the Lord, to regain its mind and its thoughts for the fear of God, and to make them afraid in the face of the Day of Judgement. . . . How could I be silent in the face of idolatry exercised by a part of the Israelites as they are sitting on the tombs, staying with the dead and invoking Rabbi Jose the Galilean: 'Heal me! Make me pregnant!' They kindle lights on the graves of departed pious men, make vows, pray to the dead, and beg them to fulfil their wishes. Should I remain calm when I see, as the Israelites go on the Sabbath to the Synagogues, men laden with bags, women with jewels – and thus degrading the holy day to a workday?. . .

Know that everyone of our brethren, the Children of Israel, is responsible for himself. Our God does not listen to the words of the defendant who says: 'Thus I have been taught by my teachers,' as He did not listen to the excuses of Adam when he said: 'The woman whom Thou gavest to be with me, she gave me of the tree, and I did eat.'[3] He does not listen to the man who says: 'The sages have advised me to do so,' as He did not accept the word of Eve: 'The serpent beguiled me, and I did eat . . .'[4] Know that it will be of no avail to a man to make apologies, saying: 'I walked on the way of my fathers,' because our Lord calls to us: 'Be ye not as your fathers!'[5], and again: 'And might not be as their fathers, a stubborn and rebellious generation.'[6] This proves that we are not obliged at all to walk in the paths of our fathers, but that we should contemplate their ways, and compare their works and laws with those of the Torah: if they are in accordance with them, we accept them, but if they deviate from them, we have to reject them, and search in the laws of the Torah themselves. For these do not need any evidence of their truth and accuracy. What appears to us true, we have to obey. . . . Do not say: 'How can we do this as the Karaites are divided in their opinions? Whom shall we follow?' The Karaites claim no authority for themselves, for they search in the teaching of Moses and in the writings of the Prophets; they also make use of the ancient writings. They call, therefore, to their brethren, the sons of Jacob: 'Learn, search, investigate, and choose what appears irrefutably true to you! . . .' If, however, somebody would object, 'How can laws depend on our judgment?' we answer, 'Why not? We perceive also by the means of our reason that the world has been created, that it was created by One with whom nothing can be compared, and who is the only one in every respect; reason teaches us also that men need the Prophet, and they believe in him owing to signs and miracles. . . . And when the sages find a law, they perceive if, according to their judgment, it has stability or if it is dependent on something else. . . . If you, however, ask, 'What shall the ignorant one do, who does not understand how to search in Scripture?' I answer, 'It is true that such a man must trust in the results of the scholars and biblical students, and follow them' . . .

Our brethren, men of our heritage! May our words not appear hard to you, for out of pure love are we writing all this: remove the foreskin of your heart, for you know that if the inner foreskin is not circumcised, the circumcision of the external foreskin is of no avail, as it is said, 'Circumcise therefore the foreskin of your heart.'[7] There is no other hope than that the stubborn heart humiliate itself, for it is said, 'Then their uncircumcised hearts be humbled, and they then be paid the punishment of their iniquity. . . .'[8] The Lord purifies thus the hearts of the Children of Israel, His people, for His great and terrible name; He bestows on them a new heart and a new spirit that the good promises of comfort may be fulfilled to us and to you and to the whole of Israel. . . . And may we be allowed to see the grace of the Lord, to dwell in His Temple, and may the promise of comfort be thus fulfilled, 'Behold, how good and pleasant is it for brethren to dwell together in unity!'[9] Amen.

NOTES

1. Is. LXII. 10.
2. Is. LVII. 14.
3. Gen. III. 12.
4. Gen. III. 13.
5. Ezek. XX. 18; Zach. I. 4; 2 Chron. XXX. 7.
6. Ps. LXXVIII. 8.
7. Deut. X. 16.
8. Lev. XXVI. 41.
9. Ps. CXXXIII. 1.

18

An Early Hebrew Poetic Letter of Friendship

AMONG the treasures found in the Cairo Genizah in recent times are some purely secular poems which probably belong to the end of the tenth century and therefore precede the compositions of Ibn Gabirol, which previously were thought to be the earliest secular poems in post-biblical Hebrew. They show great command of form as well as subtlety of thought. Some of them have all the appearance of letters sent to real people, and if so, are the earliest extant specimens of poetic epistles composed in Hebrew.

The subjoined example is a letter of friendship from an unknown poet to a sick friend, one Samuel ben al-Lebdi, of whom nothing is known but his name.

AN UNKNOWN POET TO SAMUEL BEN AL-LEBDI

'My friend, I did not remember thee, for how could I remember him who is always in my memory?'

[Probably a Syrian city, second half of the 10th century]

My eyes are fixed on thee, my darling friend,
Like the eyes of the maids on their mistress.
I always hope to hear from thee, as the earth awaits the rain.
My heart longs for thee, like a woman in birth-pangs.
When nothing is left that has the mark of perfection, when all is bare,
When friend is far, brother distant, sleep vanishing, illness heavy, pains great –
How can a man take courage, surrounded and burdened by sorrows?
My friend, I did not remember thee, for how could I remember him who is always present in my memory?
My soul, my only one, is bound to thee, with thee and over thee.
My illness is caused by thy illness, and my troubles brought about by thee.

I am ill and thou art ill, and between us is a day's journey
and inaccessible wastes.
My heart flies to thee like eagles, but my feet are chained,
so that I cannot visit thee.
Oh, that thy inner life were in me, and that thy pains were
shut up
In my limbs, and thou wouldst regain thy strength. Then
thou wouldst pray for me,
So that the healing of my illness would depend on thy lips.
But thou art as thou art, and I am like the ostrich in the
proverb.[1]

NOTE

1. According to Jacob Mann, to whom we are indebted for the discovery of this gem, the last expression contains an allusion to an Arabian proverb, quoted by Saadia, about the ostrich, denoting its uselessness. The meaning is therefore: 'Thou art as thou art (viz. worthy of all praise), but I am like the ostrich in the proverb, i.e. useless.

19

The Epic of a Letter and of a People – Hasdai ibn Shaprut's Correspondence with Joseph, King of the Khazars

THE dawn of the splendid epoch in the history of the Diaspora called the Spanish Period was illuminated by one of the most distinguished figures of post-Talmudic times: Hasdai ben Isaac ben Ezra ibn Shaprut, of whom H. Graetz has said that from his time on Jewish history bears a European impress. He was the principal minister of Abd al-Rahman III, the Caliph of Cordova (912–961), and of his successor Hakem II (961–976), being in charge of commercial, financial and foreign affairs, and also Court physician. At the same time he was head of the Jewish communities in the Iberian peninsula and a great patron of Jewish learning, besides being himself a Hebrew scholar and writer. Above all, Hasdai was the protector of his brethren in exile, always on the watch to improve their lot and yearning for their restoration to their own land.

The fascinating life of Hasdai ibn Shaprut is, in a striking way, linked with another most romantic episode in Jewish history, which took place on the opposite side of the then known world: the story of the Jewish kingdom of the Khazars, a people of mixed Turkish and Finnish origin living between the Caucasus, the Caspian Sea, the Volga and the Dnieper. Judaism spread among the Khazars gradually, and the seal was set on their conversion when the khakan (king) Bulan formally embraced the religion of Israel about 740. Beginning with the khakan Obadiah, the Khazar kings bore Hebrew names. Although the Khazar kingdom was held in such high esteem in the East that one of the Byzantine emperors married a Khazar princess, the strange kingdom of the Jewish proselytes remained hidden from the greater part of the medieval world. But about the middle of the tenth century certain emissaries from Khorasan and ambassadors of the Byzantine emperor came to Cordova and told Hasdai ibn Shaprut of the Jewish kingdom of Khazaria. This report so excited his curiosity and hopes for a redemption of Israel that he at once took steps to obtain further information about this mysterious empire.

For this purpose Hasdai composed, with the help of his secretary, the distinguished Hebrew grammarian Menahem ibn Saruk, a most notable and impressive letter to Joseph, the king of the Khazars, and, as explained in the letter itself, made all possible efforts to have it conveyed to its distant destination. The letter throws a bright light on the personality of the Jewish statesman, and on the literary skill of his learned secretary. The picturesque form of the poetical introduction, with its double acrostic of the names of Hasdai ibn Shaprut and Menahem ben Saruk, cannot, however, be reproduced in a translation.

HASDAI IBN SHAPRUT TO JOSEPH, KING OF THE KHAZARS

'Blessed be the Lord of Israel who has not left us without a kinsman as defender nor suffered the tribes of Israel to be without an independent kingdom'

[Cordova, about 960]

I Hasdai, son of Isaac, may his memory be blessed, son of Ezra, may his memory be blessed, belonging to the exiled Jews of Jerusalem, in Spain, a servant of my lord the King, bow to the earth before him and prostrate myself towards the abode of your Majesty, from a distant land. I rejoice in your tranquillity and magnificence, and stretch forth my hands to God in heaven that He may prolong your reign in Israel. But who am I? and what is my life[1] that I should dare to indite a letter to my lord the King and to address your Majesty? I rely, however, on the integrity and uprightness of my object. How, indeed, can an idea be expressed in fair words by those who have wandered, after the glory of the kingdom has departed[2]; who have long suffered afflictions and calamities, and see their flags in the land no more? We, indeed, who are of the remnant of the captive Israelites, servants of my lord the King, are dwelling peacefully in the land of our sojourning, for our God has not forsaken us, nor has His shadow departed from us.[3] When we had transgressed He brought us into judgement, cast affliction upon our loins, and stirred up the minds of those who had been set over the Israelites to appoint collectors of tribute over them, who aggravated the yoke of the Israelites,[4] oppressed them cruelly, humbled them grievously and inflicted great calamities upon them. But when God saw their misery and labour, and that they were helpless, He led me to present myself before the King, and has graciously turned his heart to me, not because of mine own righteousness, but for His mercy and His covenant's sake. And by this covenant the poor of the flock were exalted to safety, the hands of the oppressors themselves were relaxed, they refrained from further oppression, and through the mercy of our God the yoke was lightened.

Let it be known, then, to the King, my lord, that the name of our land in which we dwell is called in the sacred tongue Sefarad, but in the language of the Arabs, the indwellers of the land, Alandalus,[5] the name of the capital of the kingdom Cordova. The length of it is 25,000 cubits, the breadth 10,000. It is situated at the left of the sea,[6] which flows between your country and the great sea[7] and compasses the whole of your land. Between this city and the great sea beyond which there is no further habitable territory, are nine astronomical degrees; the sun advances one degree on each day, according to the opinions of the astronomers; each degree contains 66 miles and two parts of a mile, each mile consists of 3,000 cubits; so that those nine degrees make 600 miles. From that great sea the whole distance as far as Constantineh[8] is 3,100 miles; but Cordova is 80 miles distant from the shore of the sea which flows into your country. I have found in the books of the wise men that the land of Khazar is 60 degrees longitude, making 270 miles.[9] Such is the journey from Cordova to Constantineh. Before, however, I set forth an account of it I will also premise the measure of the length of its limits. (Your servant is not ignorant that the least of the servants of my lord the King is greater than the wise men of our country; but I am not teaching, only recording.) According to mathematical principles we have found that the distance of our city from the Equator is 38 degrees, that of Constantineh 44, of your boundaries 47.

I have been induced to state these facts because of my surprise that we have no account of your kingdom, and I think this is only due to the great distance of your kingdom from the realm of my lord the King. But I recently heard that two men, inhabitants of our land, had arrived at the dwelling-place of my lord the King, one of them called Rabbi Judah son of Meir, son of Nathan, a prudent and learned man, the other Rabbi Joseph Haggaris, also a wise man (happy they, and blessed their lot, whose fortune it was to see the glorious majesty and splendour of my lord the King, as well as the state and condition of his servants and ministers). I thought that it was easy in the sight of God in His great mercy to do a wonder to me too, and to make me, too, worthy of seeing the majesty and royal throne of my lord, and to enjoy his gracious presence.

I shall inform my lord the King of the name of the King who reigns over us. His name is Abd al-Rahman,[10] son of Mohammed, son of Abd al-Rahman, son of Hakem, son of Hisham, son of Abd al-Rahman, who all reigned in succession except Mohammed alone, the father of our King, who did not ascend the throne, but died in the lifetime of his father. Abd al-Rahman, eighth of the Ommayads,[11] son of Mu'awija, son of Hisham, son of Abd al-Malik who is universally known as Amir al-Muminim,[12] came into Spain from Shinear when there was an insurrection against the Ommayads by the sons of Al-Abbasi.[13] It was he who liberated Spain, and none of the kings who went before can be compared with him. The extent of Spain which is under the sovereignty of Abd al-Rahman, to whom God be propitious, is 16 degrees, making 1,100 miles. The land is rich, abounding in rivers, springs, and aqueducts; a land of corn, oil and wine, of fruits and all manner of delicacies; it has pleasure-gardens and orchards, fruitful trees of every kind, including the leaves of the tree upon which the silkworm feeds, of which we have great abundance. In the mountains and woods of our country cochineal is gathered in great quantity. There are also found among us mountains covered by crocus and with veins of silver, gold, copper, iron, tin, lead, sulphur, porphyry, marble, and crystal. Merchants congregate in it, and traffickers from the ends of the earth, from Egypt and adjacent countries, bringing spices, precious stones, splendid wares for kings and princes, and all the desirable things of Egypt. Our

King has collected very large treasures of silver, gold, precious things, and valuables such as no king has ever collected. His yearly revenue is about 100,000 gold pieces, the greater part of which is derived from the merchants who come hither from various countries and islands; and all their mercantile transactions are placed under my control.

Praised be the beneficent God for His mercy towards me! Kings of the earth to whom the magnificence and power of my king are known bring gifts to him, seeking to win his favour by costly presents, such as the King of the Germans,[14] the king of the Gebalim who are Al-Zekalab,[15] the King of Constantineh[16] and others. All their gifts pass through my hands, and I am charged with making gifts in return. Let my lips express praise to the God of Heaven who so far extends His loving-kindness towards me without any merit of my own, but in the fullness of His mercies.

I always ask the ambassadors of these monarchs about our brethren, the Israelites, the remnant of the captivity, whether they have heard anything concerning the deliverance of those who have pined in bondage and had found no rest. At length mercantile emissaries of Khorasan[17] told me: 'There is a kingdom of Jews who are called Khazars, and between Constantineh and that country is a sea voyage of 15 days, by land many nations dwell between us and them.' But I did not believe these words, for I thought that they told me such things to procure my goodwill and my favour. I was, therefore, hesitating and doubtful till the ambassadors from Constantineh came with presents and a letter from their king to our king, whom I interrogated concerning this matter. They answered me: 'It is quite true; there is in that place a kingdom Alcusari, distant from Constantineh a fifteen days' journey by sea, but many peoples are scattered through the land; the name of the king now reigning is Joseph; ships sometimes come from their country bringing fish, skins, and wares of every kind; the men are our brethren and are honoured by us; there is frequent communication between us by embassies and mutual gifts; they are very powerful; they maintain numerous armies, which they occasionally engage in expeditions.' This account inspired me with hope, wherefore I bowed down and adored the God of heaven.

I now looked about for a faithful messenger whom I might send into your country in order that I might know the truth of this matter and ascertain the welfare of my lord and his servants, our brethren. The thing seemed impossible to me, owing to the very great distance of the locality, but at length, by the will and the favour of God, a man presented himself to me named Mar Isaac, son of Nathan. He put his life into his hand and willingly offered to take my letter to my lord the King. I gave him a large reward, supplying him with gold and silver for his expenses and those of his servants, and with everything necessary. Moreover, I sent out of my own resources a magnificent present to the King of Constantineh, requesting him to aid this my messenger in every possible way till he should arrive at that place where my lord resides. Accordingly this messenger set out, went to the King and showed him my letter and presents. The King, on his part, treated him honourably, and detained him there for six months, with the ambassadors of my lord the King of Cordova. One day he told them and my messenger to return, giving the latter a letter in which he wrote that the way was dangerous, that the peoples among whom he must pass were engaged in warfare, that the sea was stormy and could not be navigated except at a certain time. When I heard this I was grieved even to death, and took it very ill that he had not acted according to my orders and fulfilled my wishes.

Afterwards I wished to send my letter by way of Jerusalem, because persons there guaranteed that my letter should be dispatched from thence to Nisibis,[18] thence to Armenia, from Armenia to Berdaa,[19] and thence to your country. While I was in this state of suspense, behold, ambassadors of the King of Gebalim [Slavonians] arrived, and with them two Israelites; the name of one was Mar Saul, of the other Mar Joseph. These persons understood my perplexity and comforted me, saying

'Give us your letter, and we will take care that it be carried to the King of the Gebalim, who for your sake will send it to the Israelites dwelling in the land of the Hungarians, they will send it to Russ, thence to Bulgar, till at last it will arrive, according to your wish, at its destination.'

He who tries the heart and searches the reins[20] knows that I did none of these things for the sake of mine own honour, but only to know the truth, whether the Israelitish exiles anywhere form one independent kingdom and are not subject to a foreign ruler. If, indeed, I could learn that this was the case, then, despising all my glory, abandoning my high estate, leaving my family, I would go over mountains and hills, through seas and lands, till I should arrive at the place where my lord the King resides, that I might see not only his glory and magnificence, and that of his servants and ministers, but also the tranquillity of the Israelites. On beholding this my eyes would brighten, my reins would exult, my lips would pour forth praises to God who has not withdrawn His favour from His afflicted ones.

Now therefore, let it please your Majesty, I beseech you, to have regard to the desires of your servant, and to command your scribes who are at hand to send back a reply from your distant land to your servant and to inform me fully concerning the condition of the Israelites, and how they came to dwell there. Our fathers told us that the place in which they originally settled was called Mount Seir[21], but my lord knows that Mount Seir is far from the place where you dwell; our ancestors say that it was indeed through persecution and by one calamity after another, till at length they became fixed in the place where they dwell. The ancients, moreover, inform us that when a decree of fierce persecution was issued against the Jews on account of their transgressions, and the army of the Chaldeans rose furiously, they hid the Book of the Law and the Holy Scripture in a certain cave. For this reason they prayed in a cave and taught their sons to pray there morning and evening. At length, however, through distance of time and days, they forgot and lapsed into ignorance as to the meaning of this cave and why they prayed in it; while they still continued to observe the custom of their fathers, ignorant of the reason of it. After a long time there came a certain Israelite who was desirous of knowing the true meaning of this custom, and he entered the cave. He found it full of books which he brought out. From that time they resolved to study the Law. This was what our fathers have related to us as it was handed down from ancient times. The two men who came from the land of the Gebalim, Mar Saul and Mar Joseph, after pledging themselves to forward my letter to my lord the King, told me: 'About six years ago there came to us a wise and intelligent Israelite afflicted with blindness, his name was Mar Amram, and he said that he was from the land of Khoz, and he dwelt in the King's house, ate at his table, and was held in honour by him.' On hearing this I sent messengers to bring him to me, but they did not find him, yet this very circumstance confirmed my hope.

Wherefore I have written this epistle to your Majesty, in which I submissively entreat you not to refuse my request, but to command your servant to write to me about all the things, namely: what is your state? what is the name of your land? what tribes inhabit it? what is the manner of the government, how kings succeed one another, whether they are chosen from a certain tribe or family, or whether sons succeed their fathers, as was customary among our ancestors when they dwelt in their own land? Would my lord the King also inform me as to the extent of his country, its length and breadth? What walled cities and what open town it has; whether it be watered by artificial or natural means, and how far his dominion extends and also the number of his armies and leaders? Let not my lord take it ill, I pray, that I enquire about the number of his forces. May the Lord add unto them, how many soever they be, an hundredfold.[22]. . . My lord sees that I enquire about this with no other object than that I may rejoice when I hear of the increase of the holy people. I wish too that he would tell me of the number of the provinces over which he rules, the amount of tribute paid to him, if they give him tithes, whether he dwells continually in the royal city or goes about through the whole extent of his dominions, if there are islands in the neighbourhood, and if any of their inhabitants conform to Judaism? If he judges over them? how he goes up to the house of God? with what peoples he wages war? whether he allows war to set aside the observance of the Sabbath? what kingdoms or nations are on his borders? what are their names and those of their territories? what are the cities near to his kingdom called Khorasan, Berdaa, and Bab al Abwab?[23] in what way their caravans proceed to his territory? how many kings ruled before him? what were their names, how many years each of them ruled, and what is the current language of the land? In the time of our fathers there was among us a certain Israelite, an intelligent man, who belonged to the tribe of Dan, who traced his descent back to Dan, the son of Jacob.[24] He spoke elegantly and gave everything its name in the holy language. Nor was he at a loss for any expression. When he expounded the Law he was accustomed to say, 'Thus has Othniel, son of Kenaz, handed down by tradition from the mouth of Joshua, and he from the mouth of Moses, who was inspired by the Almighty."

One thing more I ask of my lord, that he would tell me whether there is among you any computation concerning the final redemption[25] which we have been awaiting so many years, whilst we went from one captivity to another, from one exile to another. How strong is the hope of him who awaits the realization of these events! and oh! how can I hold my peace and be restful in the face of the desolation of the house of our glory and remembering those who, escaping the sword, have passed through fire and water, so that the remnant is but small. We have been cast down from our glory, so that we have nothing to reply when they say daily unto us, 'Every other people has its kingdom, but of yours there is no memorial on the earth.' Hearing, therefore, the fame of my lord the King, as well as the power of his dominions, and the multitude of his forces, we were amazed, we lifted up our head, our spirit revived, and our hands were strengthened, and the kingdom of my lord furnished us with an argument in answer to this taunt. May this report be substantiated, for that would add to our greatness. Blessed be the Lord of Israel who has not left us without a kinsman as defender nor suffered the tribes of Israel to be without an independent kingdom. May my lord prosper for ever!

I would indeed have asked more things had I not feared that I should be troublesome to my lord the King by the multitude of my words, for I confess that I have already been longer than is proper. I ask, however, that my lord find not fault with me on this account, for I have spoken hitherto out of great solicitude and anxiety. It is mine to err, yours to forgive.

Doubtless you know how the kings of Israel formerly used to write letters and dispatched their communications. May it please my lord, therefore, to pardon his servant if he has committed any fault in this. . . . I pray for the health and long life of my lord the King, of his family, his house, and that his throne may be established even for ever. Let his days and his son's days be prolonged in the midst of Israel!

The letter in the end reached its destination. Where the Byzantine emperors failed, success was achieved through the agency of Jews from Slavonia, Hungary, Rumania and Bulgaria, who conveyed the message from one community to another until it was delivered by a German Jew to the king of the Khazars in his capital Itil, at the mouth of the Volga. The King replied. His letter, written also in Hebrew, is from the historical point of view even more significant than Hasdai's epistle because it became one of the chief sources of information about the Khazar kingdom.

JOSEPH, THE KING OF THE KHAZARS, TO HASDAI IBN SHAPRUT

'Our eyes are turned to the Lord our God and to the wise men who dwell in Jerusalem and Babylon'

[Itil, Khazaria, about 965]

Joseph, King of the Togarmi, to Hasdai, the Head of the Captivity, son of Isaac, son of Ezra, the Spaniard, beloved and honoured by us.

Behold, I inform you that your honoured epistle was given me by Rabbi Jacob, son of Eleazar, of the land of Nemez.[26] We were rejoiced by it, and pleased with your discretion and wisdom, which we observed therein. I found in it a description of your land, its length and breadth, the descent of its sovereign, Abd al-Rahman, his magnificence and majesty. . . . You also told us that had it not been for the arrival of those ambassadors from Constantineh, who gave an account of the people of our kingdom, and of our institutions, you would have regarded all as false and would not have believed it.

You also inquired concerning our kingdom and descent, how our fathers embraced the laws and religion of the Israelites, how God enlightened our eyes and scattered our enemies; you also desired to know the length and breadth of our land, the nations that are our neighbours, such as are friendly and hostile; whether our ambassadors can go to your land to salute your eminent and gracious King (who draws the hearts of all men to love him and contract friendship with him by the excellence of his character and the uprightness of his actions) because the nations tell you that the Israelites have no dominion and kingdom. . . . We shall, therefore, delighting in your wisdom, answer you with respect to each of these particulars, concerning which you have asked us in your letter.

We had already heard what you have written concerning your land, and the family of the King. Among our fathers there had been mutual intercourse by letters, a thing which is written in our books and is known to the elders of our country. We shall now inform you of what happened to our fathers before us, and what we shall leave as an inheritance to our children.

You ask, also, in your epistle of what people, of what family, and of what tribe we are? Know that we are descended from Japhal, through his son Togarma.[27] We have found in the etgeneogical books of our father that Togarma had ten sons, whose names are these: Agijoe, Tirus, Ouvar, Ugin, Bisal, Zarna, Cusar, Sanar, Balgad, and Savir. We are of Cusar, of whom they write that in his days our fathers were few in number. But God gave them fortitude and power when they were carrying on wars with many and powerful nations, so that they expelled them from the great River Duna,[28] where the conquerors live to this day, near Constantineh, and thus the Khazars took possession of their territory.

After some ages another king rose up, named Bulan,[29] who was a wise God-fearing man. He expelled wizards and all idolators from the land, and trusted in God alone. An angel appeared to him in a dream, saying to him, 'Bulan, God hath sent me to thee, saying to thee, I have heard thy prayers and entreaties, I will bless thee, I will multiply thee,[30] and establish thy kingdom for ever. I will also deliver all thine enemies into thine hand. Come, rise up early in the morning[31] and pray unto the Lord.' And Bulan did so. The angel of the Lord appeared to him the second time, and said to him, 'I have seen thy ways, thy works are pleasing to Me, and I know that you will walk before Me with all your heart, I will give you precepts, statutes, and judgements. If you observe My precepts, statutes, and judgements, I will bless thee and multiply thee.'[32] He answers and says to the angel, 'Thou, Lord, hast known the thoughts of my heart, Thou hast searched my reins, and knowest that I put all my trust only in Thee. But the people subject to my rule are unbelievers; I know not whether they will trust me. If I have found favour in Thine eyes, and if Thou wilt vouchsafe Thy mercy to me, appear to their prince and leader, so that he may assist me.' God did so, in accordance with his wish, and appeared to that prince in a dream. And that man rose early and narrated to the king what had happened to him. The king having assembled all his princes and ministers, and the whole of his people, told them all these things. They were pleased, accepted the divine rule, and sought protection under the wings of the Almighty. Then the angel appeared to him the third time, saying to him, 'Lo, the heaven and the heaven of heavens do not contain[33] Me, yet build thou a house to My name.' The king answered, 'O Sovereign of the Universe, shame overwhelms me in Thy presence, I have not silver and gold to do this as it is right, and as I should wish.' And this answer was given: 'Be strong and of good courage[34]; take with you all your hosts and arise, go into the land Dariel, and into the land Erdevil, and behold, I will put the fear and the terror of you into their hearts, and I will deliver them into your hand. I have destined for you two treasures, one of silver, the other of gold. I will be with you, I will keep you in all your ways, whithersoever you go, that you shall acquire wealth, and return in safety and build a house to My name.' The king believed, and did as he was commanded.

Returning in peace, he consecrated the wealth he had acquired to God, and out of it constructed a tabernacle, ark, candlestick, table, altar and sacred vessels, which are preserved and remain with me to this day.

When these things were finished, the fame of him went forth into all the land, so that by reason of it the Byzantine and the Mohammedan sovereigns sent envoys to him with great riches and many presents, adding some of their wise men with the object of converting them to their own religion. But the king, being wise, sent for a learned Israelite. He brought the followers of the different religions together, that they might enter into a discussion of their respective doctrines. Each of them refuted, however, the arguments of his opponents, so that they could not agree. When the king saw this, he spake thus to the Christian and Mohammedan priests, 'Go home, and I will send for you again on the third day.'

On the following day he sent to the Christian priest, and said to him, 'I know that the Christian ruler is greater than all others, and that his religion is excellent, nor does your religion displease me, but I ask you to tell me the truth: which of these two is better, that of the Israelites or that of the Mohammedans?'

The priest answered him, 'May my lord the King prosper for ever. Know that there is truly no religion in the whole world to be compared with the religion of the Israelites, for God chose Israel out of all peoples, called them His first-born son, wrought among them great miracles and signs, brought them forth from the slavery of Pharaoh, and made them to pass through the sea on dry land, drowned their enemies in the sea, rained down manna upon them, brought water for them out of the rock, gave them the Law out of the midst of fire, assigned them the possession of the land of Canaan, and built for them a sanctuary that He might dwell among them. But after they sinned against Him, He was angry and cast them away from His face, scattering them throughout all regions of the earth. Were it not for this there would be no religion in the world like the religion of the Israelites.' The king answered him, 'Thus far you have told me your opinion; know that I will honour you.'

On the second day the king sent for the Mohammedan Kadi, whom he also consulted, and to whom he said, 'Tell me the truth, what is the difference between the religion of the Israelites and that of the Edomites,[35] which of them is the better?' The Kadi answered and said to him. 'The religion of the Israelites is the better, and is altogether true. They have the Law of God, just statutes and judgements; but because they sinned and acted perversely towards Him, He was wroth with them, and delivered them into the hands of their enemies. What is the religion of the Christians? They eat all things unclean, and bow themselves to the work of their hands.' The king answered him, 'Thou hast told me the truth, therefore I will honour thee.'

On the following day, having assembled all his princes and ministers, and the whole of his people, he said to them, 'I ask you to choose for me the best and truest religion.' They began to speak, without, however, arriving at any result. Thereupon the king said to the Christian priest, 'Of the religions of the Israelites and Mohammedans, which is to be preferred?' The Christian priest answered, 'The religion of the Israelites.' He then asked the Mohammedan Kadi, 'Is the religion of the Israelites, or that of the Christians the better?' The Kadi answered, 'The religion of the Israelites is preferable.' Upon this the king said, 'You both confess that the religion of the Israelites is the best and truest, wherefore I choose the religion of the Israelites, which is that of Abraham. God Almighty will assist my purpose: the gold and silver which you promised to give me He can give me without labour. Depart now in peace to your land.'

Henceforth Almighty God was his helper, and strengthened him, and he was circumcised, and all his servants. This being done, the king sent and called certain of the wise men of Israel, who explained to him the Law and the precepts. Hence we have this excellent and true religion to the present day, praise be to God for ever. From the time our fathers entered under the wings of the Divine Majesty, He humbled before us all our enemies, subjecting all peoples that are round about us; nor has any been able to stand before us to this day: all are tributary to us by the hands of the kings of the Christians and the Mohammedans.

After these things one of his descendants, Obadiah by name, a pious and good man, ascended the throne. He strengthened the kingdom and firmly established religion, built synagogues and colleges, sent for many of the wise men of Israel and rewarded them with much gold and silver. They explained to him the Bible, Mishnah and Talmud, and the order of divine service. This king feared God and loved the Law and the precepts.

He was succeeded by Hezekiah, his son, next to him was Manasseh, his son; next to him was Hanikah, brother of Obadiah; next, Isaac, his son; afterwards, his son Zebulon; then his son Manasseh, then his son Nissi; then his son Menahem; then his son Benjamin; then his son Aaron; and I, Joseph, am the son of this Aaron. We are all members of the same royal house, nor could any stranger occupy the throne of our ancestors. May it be the gracious will of Him who appoints all kings that our kingly line remain true to His laws and precepts.

As to your question concerning the extent of our land, its length and breadth, know that it is situated by the banks of the river[36] near the sea of Gargal[37] towards the region of the East, a journey of four months. Near that river dwell very many populous tribes; there are hamlets, towns, and fortified cities, all of which pay tribute to me. From thence the boundary turns towards Gargal; and all those who dwell by the sea-shore, a month's journey, pay tribute to me. On the south side are fifteen very populous tribes, as far as Bab al Abwab, who live in the mountains. Likewise the inhabitants of the land of Bassa, and Tagat, as far as the sea of Constantineh, a journey of two months; all these give me tribute.

On the western side are thirteen tribes, also very numerous, dwelling on the shores of the sea of Constantineh, and thence the boundary turns to the north as far as the great river called Jaig.[38] These live in open, unwalled towns and occupy the whole wilderness[39] as far as the boundary of the Jugrians,[40] they are numerous as the sand of the sea, and all are tributary to me. Their land has an extent of four months' journey. I dwell at the mouth of the river and do not permit the Russians who come in ships to enter into their country, nor do I allow their enemies who come by land to penetrate into their territory. I have to wage grievous wars with them, for if I would permit them they would lay waste the whole land of the Mohammedans as far as Baghdad.[41]

Moreover, I notify to you that I dwell by the banks of the river, by the grace of God, and have in my kingdom three royal cities.[42]

In the first the Queen dwells with her maids and attendants. The length and breadth of it is fifty square parasangs together with its suburbs and adjacent hamlets. Israelites, Mohammedans, Christians, and other people of various tongues dwell therein. The second, together with the suburbs, comprehends in length and breadth eight square parasangs. In the third I reside with the princes and my servants and all my officers. This is a small city, in length and breadth three square parasangs; this river flows within its walls. The whole winter we remain within the city, and in the month of Nisan[43] we leave this city and each one goes forth to his fields and gardens to cultivate them. Each family has its own hereditary estate. They enter and dwell in it with joy and song. The voice of an oppressor is not heard among us; there are no enmities nor quarrels. I, with the princes and my ministers, then journey a distance of twenty parasangs to the great river Arsan,[44] thence we make a circuit till we arrive at the extremity of the province. This is the extent of our land and the place of our rest. Our country is not frequently watered by rain; it abounds in rivers and streams, having great abundance of fish; we have many springs; the land is fertile and rich; fields, vineyards, gardens and orchards are watered by rivers; we have fruit-bearing trees of every kind and in great abundance. . . . I dwell in a fertile land and by the grace of God I dwell in tranquillity.

With reference to your question concerning the miraculous end of days, our eyes are turned to the Lord our God and to the wise men of Israel who dwell in Jerusalem and Babylon. Although we are far from Zion, we have heard that because of our iniquities the computations are erroneous; nor do we know aught concerning this. But if it please the Lord, He will do it for the sake of His great name; nor will the desolation of His house, the abolition of His service, and all the troubles which have come upon us be lightly esteemed in His sight. He will fulfil His promise, and 'the Lord whom ye seek shall suddenly come to His temple, even the messenger of the Covenant whom ye delight in: behold, he shall come, saith the Lord of hosts'.[45] Besides this we only have the prophecy of Daniel.

May God hasten the redemption of Israel, gather together the captives and dispersed, you and me and all Israel that love His name, in the lifetime of us all.

Finally, you mention that you desire to see my face. I also long and desire to see your honoured face, to behold your wisdom and magnificence. Would that it were according to your word and that it were granted to me to be united with you, so that you might be my father and I your son. All my people would pay homage to you: according to your word and righteous counsel we should go out and come in. Farewell.

We do not know how and when the letter of the King reached Cordova. The records are silent about the impression made by the message from the Khazar kingdom on Hasdai and the scholars of his residence. We find, however, references to it in the twelfth century, and the great Hebrew poet Judah Halevi drew from its narrative the idea of his 'Kuzari', the famous philosophical dialogue between the king of the Khazars and the representatives of Judaism, Christianity and Mohammedanism. This sublime justification of the Jewish faith may be considered the finest fruit of Hasdai's correspondence with King Joseph, and perhaps the most precious result ever produced by an exchange of letters in literature.

Nevertheless, the genuineness of the correspondence, which was not published until the end of the sixteenth century by Isaac ben Abraham Akrish in Constantinople, has been contested since the seventeenth century until recent days. Although the prevailing opinion accepts the letters, the discussion is not yet closed. A new, surprising contribution to this problem was furnished by Solomon Schechter, who edited a fragment, discovered in the Cairo Genizah, bearing on the Khazar story. The Hebrew manuscript seems to be a part of a letter written by a Khazar Jew and – strangely enough – probably addressed to Hasdai ibn Shaprut, as has been inferred particularly from the following passage of this important document:

Behold, I make it known to my lord that the name of our land as we found it in books is Arkanus, and the name of the royal city is Khazar, and the name of the river is Atel; it is south of the sea that comes from . . . through which thy messengers came to Constantinople, and I believe that it starts from the Great Sea . . .

The story told in the fragment differs, however, in various ways from that of King Joseph's letter. Its author attributes the real and final conversion of the Khazars to the proselytising activity of Jews among the population of Khazaria, in which a Jewess, Jerah, played an outstanding part. Modern critics ascribe to the substance of this narrative a high degree of veracity. Thus another Khazar letter, unearthed almost a thousand years after the adventurous dispatch of Hasdai's epistle to King Joseph, has shed new light on the mystery which still surrounds the former Jewish Commonwealth in ancient Russia.

NOTES

1. I Sam. XVIII. 18.
2. I Sam. IV. 21
3. Neh. IX. 19.
4. Exod. I. 11–13.
5. Andalusia.
6. The Mediterranean.
7. The Atlantic.
8. Constantinople.

9. Viz. from Constantinople.
10. Abd al-Rahman III (see supra, p. 97).
11. Abd al-Rahman I, born in 731, after the overthrow of his own dynasty, the Ommayads, by the Abbasides (see the next note), came from Persia to Spain, captured Cordova in 756 and became the founder of the Ommayad empire, which comprised practically the whole of Spain. He ruled until 788.
12. The Abbasides, the posterity of Abbas (566–652), the uncle of Mohammed. They crushed the rule of the Ommayads in Persia in 750, and reigned as caliphs of Baghdad until 1278.
13. Ruler of the Faithful, Abd al-Malik (646–705), the most outstanding caliph of the Ommayad dynasty, who achieved the unification of the Persian caliphate.
14. Otto the Great (912–973) sent, in 957, ambassadors to Abd al-Rahman III.
15. Slavonians.
16. Constantine VII, called Porphyrogenitus (912–959), sent, in 949, ambassadors to Cordova.
17. Chorasan or Khorasan (Land of the Rising Sun), northern province of Persia; became an independent kingdom in the ninth century and by this secession precipitated the downfall of the Abbaside empire.
18. City on the border of Turkish East Anatolia and Syria.
19. City on the Sea of Azov.
20. Jer. XI. 20.
21. Mount Seir, south of the Dead Sea originally inhabited by the Horites and afterwards by the descendants of Esau.
22. 2 Sam. XXIV. 3.
23. The Iron Gate, a fortified city on the western shore of the Caspian Sea.
24. He was the traveller Eldad the Danite, who lived in the second half of the ninth century and brought to the Jews of Kairuan and Spain news about an alleged abode of the tribes Dan, Naphtali, Gad and Asher in the land of Havilah, beyond the rivers of Ethiopia.
25. Messianic expectations and computations (calculations of Dan. XII. 4, 12), cherished and practised since earliest times, were a special feature of Hasdai's age (see Maximilian Landau, 'Der Brief Chasdai ibn Šapruts an den Chasarenkönig' in *Josef Freimann Festschrift*, pp. 125 ff.)
26. Germany.
27. Togarma was Japhet's grandson, being, along with Ashkenaz and Riphath, one of the sons of Gomer, the son of Japhet (Gen. X. 3).
28. The Danube.
29. Bulan means 'the Wise' in Turkish.
30. Deut. VII. 13.
31. Exod. VIII. 25; IX. 13, etc.
32. Deut. VII. 11–13.
33. 1 Kings VIII. 27; 2 Chron. II. 6; VI. 18.
34. Deut. XXXI. 6, 7; Josh. I. 6, 9, 18, etc.
35. The Christians, Edom, i.e. Esau (Gen. XXV. 30; XXXVI. 1) having become the designation of Rome and the Christian world.
36. Viz. Volga.
37. The Caspian Sea.
38. The Dnieper.
39. Viz. Steppe.
40. Finno-Ugrian tribes lived west of the Ural and migrated westwards.
41. It was at the hands of the Russian prince Svyatoslav I (964–972) that King Joseph was to suffer a disastrous defeat not long after having despatched the letter to Hasdai.
42. The three royal cities were: Semender (towards Caucasia), Sarkal (on the Don) and Itil, the capital (on the mouth of the Volga).
43. March.
44. An Armenian river, a tributary of the Euphrates.
45. Mal. III. 1.

20

The Geonim Sherira and Hai write the last classic Responsa of the Geonic Period

ALTHOUGH after the time of Saadia the Gaonate began to be eclipsed by the distinguished scholars of Spain, who were wresting the primacy from the East, Babylonia remained the centre of Jewish and especially Talmudic learning till well into the eleventh century. Even during this period of incipient decline the glories of the Gaonate were revived by two great scholars, the fathers and teachers of Israel as they were called afterwards, Sherira ben Hananiah and his son Hai, both of whom attained patriarchal age and between them held the office for a long period of years. While nominally Geonim of Pumbedita, they actually functioned in Baghdad. Hither questions came to them from all parts of the Jewish world, from Spain to India, and the Geonim displayed an immense activity in composing answers. There was practically no subject of Jewish interest that was not dealt with in the thousands of Responsa which Sherira and Hai drew up and signed either jointly or separately.

1. *The Letter on the History of Oral Tradition*

The most famous of all Geonic Responsa is linked with the name of Sherira. It was written in answer to a letter from Jacob bar Nissim ben Josiah, the head of the Talmudic school in Kairuan in North Africa, containing the following questions:

> (1) How was the Mishnah written? (2) Is there any reason for the existing arrangement of the tractates in each Order? (3) What is the purpose of the Tosefta (supplement, independent Mishnah collection), and how were the Baraitot (continuation of the Mishnah) written? (4) How was the Talmud written down? (5) What is the sequence of the Saboraim (Ponderers, successors of the Amorain) and Geonim?

These questions were no doubt prompted by the conflict between Karaism and Rabbinism. The attack made by the Karaites on the authenticity of the oral tradition had caused doubts even among the faithful adherents of traditional Judaism. Sherira, in his answer, revealed an intimate acquaintance with the matter and drew up a remarkably precise account of the development of Talmudic tradition from the earliest days. Thus, what was intended as a Responsum to a single community became a message to all future generations. 'Gaon Sherira's Letter', written in the usual mixed Aramaic, has remained until our own times the main source for the history of the oral tradition.

The following is an extract from the answer to the fifth question of Jacob bar Nissim:

SHERIRA GAON TO JACOB BAR NISSIM

'After Ezra and Zerubbabel in company with the exiles had returned to the homeland and rebuilt the Temple, those who remained here continued to cultivate the knowledge of the Torah'

[Baghdad, 986]

. . . And as to your question concerning the sequence of the Saboraim after Rabina[1] and which after them have stood in the forefront, we consider it necessary to give you a thorough scheme, a presentation of the authorities in Israel, from the beginning after the division into two Academies [viz. in Babylonia and in Palestine].

Know then first of all that, when the Israelites went into the exile with Jechoniah, and craftsmen and smiths[2] as well as prophets were among them, they were brought to Nehardea, where Jechoniah and his companions built a synagogue from the very stones and dust that they brought there with them from the place of the Temple in order to fulfil the word of the Scripture: 'For Thy servants take pleasure in her stones and love her dust.'[3] They called the synagogue 'Be-Knishta De-Shaf Ve-Jativ' that is 'The Sanctuary that moved from the spot and went hither'. The spirit of the Lord was with them, as we say in the Talmud, 'Where does the spirit of the Lord rest in Babylonia? Rab[4] says: "In the Synagogue Huzal." Samuel says: "In the Synagogue Shaf-Ve-Jativ."' As a matter of fact, neither here nor there, but partly in both of them. Abaye[5] used to say: 'May it be accounted to me as good work! Even when I am at a distance of a mile, I go there to pray.' That synagogue Huzal was near to the academy of Ezra the lawyer, and behind Nehardae.

Now, after Ezra and Zerubbabel in company with the exiles had returned to the homeland and rebuilt the Temple, those who remained here continued to cultivate the knowledge of the Torah, even when Simeon the Just,[6] Antigonus of Soko,[7] and all those famous couples[8] of scholars who came there mainly from Babylonia as well as Hillel the Elder were in office as heads of the Synhedrion. Princes of the Captivity, of the house of David, were the heads in this country, but no heads of the schools were here at that time, because they have to come only from 'the place that was chosen by the Lord'. Up to the death of Rabbi[9] we had, therefore, leading Exilarchs but no academic heads or princes of learning. Only the Presidents of the Synhedrion in the Land of Israel were recognized as representatives of the schools; they are named in the Tractate Abot one after another up to Hillel and Shammai.[10] After Hillel that office was held by his son Simeon, afterwards by the son of the latter, Gamaliel the Elder[11]; afterwards by Simeon ben Gamaliel the First[12] who was killed before the destruction of the Temple and by the High Priest Ismael ben Elisha. Those four generations filled one hundred years, as we read in the section 'On the Carrying away on the Sabbath': 'Hillel, Simeon, Gamaliel and Simeon held the office during the existence of the Temple for a hundred years.'

Simeon ben Gamaliel, who fell as a martyr during the days of tyranny, was followed by Johanan ben Zaccai,[13] the same who was in office during the destruction of the Temple and who was carried as a corpse to the Emperor Vespasianus and obtained from the emperor privileges for the noble family of Gamaliel and for the Academy of Jabne. When Rabban Johanan ben Zaccai and the other scholars found a resting place at Jabne, they issued ten ordinances about which we read in the Mishnah 'after the destruction Rabban Johanan ordained'. He was followed by Rabban Gamaliel,[14] son of Simeon ben Gamaliel who had become a martyr. He was prince of the Academy in Jabne while R. Joshua[15] was President of the Court. He was, however, dismissed because he had three times offended the latter, and to his place was elevated Eleazar ben Azariah,[16] who was both learned and rich and the tenth after Ezra the Lawgiver.

R. Gamaliel afterwards made his peace with the offended Joshua. R. Eleazar remained, however, in office along with the [restored] R. Gamaliel so that they taught in turn on the Sabbaths, as we are told in the section of the Gemara 'On the Morning Prayer'.

Later on Simeon, son of Gamaliel, and after him Rabbi, his son, who was in Sepphoris and Beth Shearim, took the office. In the days of Rabbi, Huna I was prince of the exile. At the same time Rab came also to Babylonia in the year 530 of the common Greek era.

2. *Sherira Gaon defends the Rights of Animals*

The following Responsum is a fine testimony to the spirit of kindness towards animals that has prevailed in the Jewish teaching since the biblical age. The question submitted to the Gaon shows also the range of the moral problems considered by the medieval Jew, who did not hesitate to ask the highest spiritual authority for advice in a matter concerning the treatment of animals.

The story referred to by the interrogator is told in the Talmud, Baba Mezia 85: Judah I, the Patriarch, called 'Rabbi', once drove back into the hands of the slaughterer a calf which sought refuge with him, exclaiming, 'Go there, thou art created for this!' For this harshness he was punished by God, who visited heavy sufferings on him for many years. On a subsequent occasion Rabbi saw that his housemaid was about to sweep away some newborn kittens. 'Don't do them any harm!' he said to her, 'the Lord is good to all and His tender mercies are over all His works.' After this proof of his changed disposition, the sufferings inflicted upon him ceased.

SHERIRA GAON TO AN INQUIRER

'The animal has not been created in order that evil should be inflicted upon it but in order that good should be done to it'

[Baghdad, second half of the 10th century]

You asked: 'Concerning the story of the sufferings which were inflicted upon Rabbi for one act but were removed from him for another – is it the right thing not to slaughter an animal or not to kill kittens or animals doing harm? Let our Master instruct us.'

Our finding is as follows and this was found by us: Animals that do harm, such as snakes, scorpions, lions and wolves, may be killed in any way. On the other hand living creatures that do not hurt us and that are also not needed for food or healing should not be killed and it is even forbidden to make them suffer. The kittens that Rabbi's housemaid was about to throw aside and that were saved by Rabbi, do not belong to the harmful creatures, and such animals rightly may be saved from destruction. We are, however, not ordered to rescue a calf that is necessary for food. If nevertheless sufferings came upon Rabbi as a consequence of the act mentioned, we have to recognize them not as a retributive punishment for a trespass but as the kind of chastisement that the Lord is wont to send upon great and chosen men, because he treats them in a more rigorous way than other people, who have to learn from them and take example from their deeds.

Rabbi Ahai[17] said in this sense: 'It is said: "And round about Him it stormeth mightily"[18]; this means that God the Holy One is particular to a hair-breadth with those who dwell closest to Him.' Rabbi Hanina[19] explains in this sense the verse of the Scripture: 'O Lord of hosts, who is a mighty one like unto Thee, O Lord? And Thy faithfulness is round about Thee.'[20]

If therefore that calf had fled before the knife of the slaughterer and buried its head between the knees of Rabbi in order to be saved, then the immediate delivery to the slaughterer appeared as a particular cruelty. If he had acted mercifully, he would at least have allowed the calf to stay for a while, and anybody who had seen him act in such a way, would have taken this as an example for his own behaviour, and have learnt to be merciful himself. He, however, who saw that Rabbi delivered the animal immediately, and that no pity was stirred in his heart by the living creature that sought shelter with him, might have become more hard-hearted in his behaviour towards other people and towards animals which are not needed and harmless.

It may perhaps also be that the sufferings came upon Rabbi because he had uttered the words: 'Thou art created for this!'

It is true that animals have been created for this destiny, and that men have been permitted to slaughter them; but the Creator did not deprive the animals of a due reward, and we may believe that all creatures, the killing of which has been permitted, will be rewarded for their pains, for there is no doubt that God the Holy One does not deny just recompense to any of His creatures. In this sense the animal has, therefore, not been created in order that evil should be inflicted upon it but in order that good should be done to it; nor is it by any means created for the purpose of being slaughtered, although this has been permitted to man.

3. *The Geonim establish Rules of Attestation*

The following juridical responsum, a joint composition of Sherira and Hai, contains incidentally an elaborate formula of greetings which was often used in the replies of the Geonim.

THE GEONIM SHERIRA AND HAI TO AN INQUIRER

'We have to be very careful in matters of confirmation of documents'

[Baghdad, at the end of the 10th or beginning of the 11th century]

And you have also asked: May Reuben and the son of his sister confirm the signature of Simeon, the brother of Reuben, as witnesses?

It is taught as follows in the Mishnah: Everybody may be trusted when he declares: 'This is the writing of my teacher, this is the writing of my brother.' In the Gemara it is added to this sentence: Rabbi Huna, son of R. Jona,[21] says: 'But only if another witness joins with them.' If, however, this other witness happens also to be a relative of the second or third degree, is the testimony then sufficient, or must even now at least one totally strange witness be added? – If money is claimed and a decision on the payment of the claim cannot be reached because an official confirmation of the signature in question is not available, we have to be more particular and, besides the evidence of the son and the brother, that of a stranger is required. We have to be very careful in matters of confirmation of documents, although confirmations of this kind are only ordinances of Rabbinic origin.

And thou, who belongest to the Princes of Judah, President of the Assembly of Teachers, son of the master and scholar Joseph, thou who hast addressed these questions to us – may the Lord of Mercy enlighten thy eyes with the light of the Torah, may He gird thee with strength and power that thou mayest be able to unriddle its secrets, may He preserve thy learning in order that through it thou mayest climb on the ladder of wisdom, may He reveal and clear up to thee the treasures that are yet dark and veiled, and may He add them to thy accumulated knowledge, may He lift the ensign of the Torah through thy hand, and strengthen thee that thou mayest fight for her; may He go before thee in order that thou without effort mayest break the brazen doors and blow up the iron bars, that thy springs may spread into all roads, that they may overflow like streams. May the fullness of blessings be bestowed upon thee, may thy stock blossom and flourish, and may its branches be extended all over the surface of the earth.

4. *The Responsum on God's Foreknowledge*

This famous Responsum of Hai Gaon was the answer to an interrogator who had been puzzled by the story told in the thirty-eighth chapter of Isaiah: how King Hezekiah, overcome by a dangerous sickness and warned by the prophet to set his house in order because he was to 'die and not live', prayed and was saved. The inquirer felt that there was an inconsistency between the prediction and the actual event, and asked for an explanation of the obscure passage and its philosophical implications culminating in the problem: how man can be said to have free will, if God knows in advance how His creatures will act.

In his answer, which has been carefully analysed by David Kaufmann, Hai tried with great skill, by using the distinction – already conceived by Saadia – that God's prescience does not mean causation of human acts, to reconcile the belief in that prescience with man's responsibility. This distinction was adopted by some Christian philosophers, and, as late as the seventeenth century, Leibniz paid attention to it in his consideration of the question.

HAI GAON TO AN INQUIRER

'God knows that the wicked will not abandon his wickedness, but this does not mean that He causes it'

[Baghdad, first half of the 11th century]

Know – may the Lord assist thee – that the many obscurities involved in this question can easily be elucidated. When the prophet said: 'Thou shalt die and not live,' he did not indicate when Hezekiah would die. For, as we see that Hezekiah did not die from his sickness and that he was healed, we realize that God by no means predicted that he would die from his sickness; for many announcements, promises and menaces are presented in a conditional form; as God has clearly explained in the passage: 'At one instant I may speak concerning a nation and concerning a kingdom, to pluck up and to break down, and to destroy it; but if that nation turn from their evil because of which I have spoken against it, I will repent of the evil that I thought to do unto it.'[22] Indeed, we consider it a very important article of belief that God knows that an event will occur if something is to take place in this way, or that it will not occur if that thing is to take place in another way. This, however, does not mean that God is in doubt about a thing, but that He knows how an event which did not occur would have occurred. In order to imagine the idea clearly, a spiritual training is needed which enables us to conceive that a thing can be known in this way without being an impossibility.

Statements are to be found in Scripture which, if carefully examined, make this matter easy to grasp. Thus David asked the Lord: 'Will the men of Keilah deliver me up into his [Saul's] hand?'[23] He then put two questions separately, and the Lord answered first: 'He will come down.'[42] And then: 'They will deliver thee up.'[25] Now we know that the inhabitants did not deliver David, and that Saul did not come down. There is no doubt that God knew, in reality, what would occur but the words [of God] signified that He knew that if David were to remain in that place, Saul would come down, and, if Saul were to come down, the men of Keilah would deliver him. Thus nothing contradicts the assumption that God knew that, if Hezekiah did not pray or shed tears, he would have to die at that moment, although God knew that it would not be so but that he would pray and that He would add fifteen years to his life, according to the principle we have established: that what is not to be constitutes one part of the things known to God about which He knows Himself how it would have been possible. This is the most subtle point of this question when it is examined. And all conditional promises follow this principle, that God knows that, if the conditions on which God made a promise dependent have been fulfilled, the promise comes true, and that, if they have not been fulfilled, the promise does not come true. It is in the same way that the promises and threats concerning the World-to-Come are fulfilled: if man obeys, he is rewarded, if he does not obey, he is punished, but God knows exactly what will happen; this is the meaning of the verse: 'The fear of the Lord prolongeth days, but the years of the wicked shall be shortened.'[26] This promise is not being fulfilled concerning all those who fear the Lord, but sometimes the fear of the Lord increases the days, and sometimes the years of the wicked are shortened, and sometimes this does not happen.

As to the *adjal*,[27] which thou hast mentioned in the question in order to know whether one increases or diminishes by it, we do not know about which fixed termination thou desirest to speak. If thou intendest to speak about that which God knows, [then it must be said] that it is not His knowledge that causes a thing to happen. Thou seest that He knows that the wicked will not abandon his wickedness, but this does not mean that He causes it.

The theologians of the Moslems say: 'In Arabic the word *adjal* indicates a fixed moment, and the moment when a living being dies is called the *adjal* of his death; and the whole time during which he lives is the time of his life.' But in our language Scripture does not present us with any corresponding expression.

But a question arises about a person whom an enemy attacks

and kills. Shall we say that if the murderer had not killed, the man would nevertheless have died, or would he have continued to live? The answer is that we do not know it, but the Lord knows it. But we consider it possible that he would have died in that moment, even if he had not been killed, and it is also possible that the Lord knows that if he had not been killed he would have continued to live until a later time according to the principle explained above.

There is also another question: Does it not often happen that a large number of people are killed at the same moment? We answer: Yes, it is possible; dost thou not see that the plague breaks out in certain places, and that many people die in a short time? And also that many persons gather in a building which collapses on them so that they perish, or also that they embark on a ship and the tempest blows and drowns all of them? The principle upon which this problem can be solved is as follows: What we find in Scripture, particularly what God said concerning Phinehas: '[He] hath turned My wrath away from the children of Israel'[28] proves that, if Phinehas had not done what he was obliged to do, the others would have had to die. So, too, the verse 'And he [namely Aaron] stood between the dead and living'[29] proves that the plague appeared from one side and was arrested by the effect of the incense. This proves, therefore, that those who died after the arrival of the plague might have lived another space of time just like those who succumb to a violent death; or also that they can die at the same time.

One may perhaps ask: 'If you hold that the man who has been killed would have died through the hand of God if the murderer had not killed him, why has the latter to be condemned to death? We shall answer: Even if the murderer had not found the occasion to meet his victim, and even if he had died without having been killed, the murderer has nevertheless done what he should not do, and he does not deserve to be saved from his condemnation.

What we have explained is all that can be said about this question.

5. *Sherira's Appeals to the West and the centenarian Hai's Farewell*

In the treasury of the Cairo Genizah several personal letters of Sherira and Hai have also been found. They are very different from the Responsa and show the Geonim rather from within, their personalities and activities, especially their desperate efforts to avert the collapse of the Babylonian Academies which was impending for many reasons, above all because of their dwindling resources. In one of these epistles to the Jews in the West, Sherira stated that he was able to convene the regular meetings (Kallah) only with the greatest difficulty and that the critical situation which forced the scholars to earn their living by another occupation embittered him against the notables of Jewry in other countries, the 'Mountains of Israel'. Just as in Talmudic times, he declared, the individual scholars, although each of them possessed his own school, resorted to the centre of Talmudic teaching, so now in the same way should the Academy be regarded as the focus whence answers to questions should radiate. 'You will perhaps say,' the Gaon continued, 'that it is sufficient that you remain in your comfortable state. Your schools will not perish, let therefore the Academy collapse. Know then that her leaders are your heads; the body, however, is directed by the head, and how can it, when the latter is destroyed, remain healthy?' In another letter, the Gaon, writing to Egypt, declared that Babylon was the dwelling place of the Shekinah and that there, in the Synagogue sanctified by the memory of Ezekiel, Daniel and Ezra, prayers were being offered for the welfare of the co-religionists. He implored the people he addressed to impress upon each other the duty of supporting the Academy and to have mercy upon the Glory of Israel and the four cubits of the Halakah.

In striking contrast to the laments of Sherira, the three decades following his death witnessed a continued flourishing of the Babylonian centre under the leadership of Sherira's illustrious son. These years of Hai's office are commonly regarded as the final stage of the Gaonate. Although this view cannot be maintained in the light of other Genizah discoveries, which offer ample evidence that the Geonim exerted a considerable influence upon the Jews of the Orient up to the middle of the thirteenth century, Hai's death in the year 1038, at the age of nearly a hundred years, marks indeed the end of the historic part played by the Babylonian Academies in the development of Judaism. By a most fortunate chance a letter written by Hai only shortly before his death has been preserved, showing that the intellectual powers of the centenarian remained unimpaired up to the very last, and that he took a vivid interest in communal affairs. With his approaching end before his eyes, suffering from extreme physical weakness, he hastens to assist a friend, Sahlan ben Abraham, the spiritual leader of the Babylonian community in Fostat (Cairo), who has been assailed in his position by a party from within his congregation. Thus this letter reads like a farewell of the last great Gaon of Pumbedita.

HAI GAON TO SAHLAN BEN ABRAHAM

'Continue to do good to the little as well as to the great people, whenever thou hast the means to do it'

[Baghdad, Tebet 1038]

In Thy name, O gracious Lord!

My letter – may the Lord prolong the life of our Master, the favourite of the Nasi, the Haber, the Rosh Kallah, the President of the Academy – is being dispatched from Baghdad on the . . . month Tebet of the year 1349 Sel., the soul being in peace, thanks to the Lord!

If I wanted to describe the point to which I have been brought by a great weakness which does not abandon me and makes life unbearable for me because of the vicissitudes of a long existence – this would lead me too far. . . . Bless the Lord, all ye His works![30] I ask Him that He may grant a happy time for this and a prosperous issue because I deserve it well. . . .

I have to tell thee that some days ago I received a letter from Alvan, of the Babylonian community, in which he informs me that some people have risen up against thee. This news has afflicted me and I do not know how this could happen. I received likewise a letter which has been addressed to me by Sliman el Mubarek. The latter spoke to me when he was with us in Baghdad in company of the venerable Sheikh Ephraim known under the name of El Oni – may the Lord prolong his might! He was very much upset by the events and told me that it is the people of Abu Nasr who have roused them against thee and insisted on the signing of the pamphlets which has caused me great sorrow. He added that this did not advance them in the eyes of the Elders of the synagogue – may the Lord fortify them! – and that the majority of the assembly are on thy side, which made me rejoice – may the Lord in His mercy make thee victorious! . . . It will, therefore, be necessary for thee to write me to explain what is true in all this, and to indicate the names of thy followers so that I may offer them thanks, and those of thy adversaries so that I may reconcile thee with them – if it should please the Lord. . . .

As to myself, I am writing to my master the Sheikh, the illustrious Abu Nasr Fadl, son of R. Sahl,[31] may the Lord assist him always, that he may instruct me exactly on what has happened, and that he may bestow all care upon thee. May the Lord grant thee his support, and spare thee all pains and conceive thoughts of peace[32] toward thee. Know that this matter worries me exceedingly. Thou wilt do well to write the explanatory letter in many copies which thou shalt send together.

Before ending this letter I received thine – may the Lord assist thee always! – and we have understood the truth about the seventeen persons of whom thou speakest and who have brandished the weapons against thee. We have also understood what was their trap to which thou makest an allusion, and what were the contents of those pamphlets, namely a letter of curses and excommunication against anyone who would change the tradition established by the ancients. If their letters ever reach us we shall not permit any calumny of a rival against thee nor any jealous attack. On the contrary. . . . And thou, too, continue according to thy habits to do good to the little as well as to the great people, whenever thou hast the means to do it. Tell us to whom it would be convenient to write about this subject. I shall ask the honourable Sheikh Abu Nasr – may the Lord assist him always! – to inform me about this matter impartially and to pay attention to it. We pray the Lord that He may help thee and make thee victorious. May thine enemies dwindle away before thee, and thou shalt tread upon their high places.[33] . . .

We received a letter from R. Solomon ben Yehuda[34] – may the Lord prolong his might! – a native of Fez, which has also rejoiced me. I beg thee to inform me about his position and the rank he occupies. We have also received a letter from R. Hassan el Akuli – may the Lord fortify him! – which has caused me great pleasure, but I was doubly pleased to learn that he is on thy side and that he belongs to the number of those who offer thee their support. In short, of all that thy adversaries will write me I shall take into consideration nothing else than what is compatible with thy friendship and with the constancy of my heart. But assistance rests upon the Lord. Inform me surely about all happenings.

I have told thee already that I am actually in a condition of a very pronounced weakness – may the Lord help me! It is His support which I invoke. . . .

Accept greetings.

To the Haber Sahlan, son of Abraham, – may the Lord prolong his life and make his power and fortune last.

from Hai Gaon – from the Gaon

NOTES

1. Rabina, son of Huna (died 499), Babylonian Amora, who completed the Babylonian Talmud.
2. 2 Kings XXIV. 14.
3. Ps. CII. 15.
4. Rab (i.e. the Master), a name conferred upon Abba Areka (175–247), Babylonian Amora, who in company with Samuel (180–254) laid the foundations of the Gemara.
5. Abaye, nickname for Nahmani (280–338), Amora of the fourth generation.
6. Simon the Just, High Priest, fl. in the third century B.C.E.
7. Antigonus of Soko, disciple and successor of Simon the Just.
8. The spiritual leaders who came after Antigonus up to Hillel, the great teacher at the beginning of the Christian era, are enumerated in the Sayings of the Fathers, in pairs.
9. Judah the Prince (see note 1 to Chapter 15).
10. Shammai, rival of Hillel.
11. R. Gamaliel (see Chapter 10, pp. 46f.).
12. Simon, son of the latter, a leader of the Pharisees during the siege of Jerusalem.
13. Johanan ben Zaccai, the founder of the new centre of learning in Jabne.
14. Gamaliel II, head of the Sanhedrin.
15. Joshua, son of Hananiah, like Gamaliel II a disciple of Johanan ben Zaccai.
16. Eleazar ben Azariah, head of the Sanhedrin about 90 C.E.
17. R. Ahai, leading scholar in the Academy of Pumbedita in the middle of the eighth century, author of the code 'Sheiltot' (Problems).
18. Ps. L. 3.
19. Hanina, son of Hama, Palestinian Amora of the first generation.
20. Ps. LXXXIX. 9.
21. R. Huna (212–292), President of the Academy of Sura.
22. Jer. XVIII. 7.
23. 1 Sam. XXIII. 11.
24. *Ibidem.*
25. 1 Sam. XXIII. 12.
26. Prov. X. 27.
27. Arabic: Termination of life; see explanation in the next paragraph of the Responsum.
28. Num. XXV. 11.
29. Num. XXVII. 13.
30. Ps. CIII. 22.
31. A favourite of the Caliph.
32. Jer. XXIX. 11.
33. Deut. XXXIII. 29.
34. See the next chapter, pp. 130ff.

21

Solomon ben Yehuda, Gaon of Palestine, describes an Earthquake

THE Gaonate which was established in Palestine in the beginning of the tenth century (see *supra*, p. 78) survived into the eleventh century and became, as has been shown by Jacob Mann from numerous references in the Genizah fragments, an important centre of Jewish learning, though much inferior to the Gaonate of Babylonia. An intensive correspondence was maintained by the Geonim from Jerusalem with the heads of the Babylonian schools and with the communities in Egypt, in Sicily, and elsewhere. One of the most prolific correspondents among the Palestinian Geonim was Solomon ben Yehuda, of whose letters numerous specimens and fragments have been found in the Cairo Genizah. These are concerned for the most part with political and internal affairs, quarrels of dignitaries and conflicts between the Karaites and Rabbanites. One of them, however, deals exceptionally not with any communal matter, but with an extraordinary physical event, the great earthquake that occurred in Ramlah and other places in the Holy Land towards the end of the year 1033, a date verified from other, non-Jewish, sources. While in accord with the religious outlook of the pious writer the event is regarded as a visitation from Heaven, his observations of the natural features are remarkably accurate.

The beginning and signature of the letter, which undoubtedly was written by the Gaon himself, are missing.

SOLOMON BEN YEHUDA TO AN UNKNOWN CORRESPONDENT

'All were alike, like people like priest, like servant like his master, when they sought refuge for their lives'

[Jerusalem (?), probably December 1033]

. . . They went out from their houses into the streets because they saw the walls bending though yet intact, and the beams becoming separated from the walls and then reverting to their former position. The strongest buildings collapsed and new houses were pulled down. Many were buried under the ruins, for they could not escape. All went out from their dwellings leaving everything behind. Wherever they turned they beheld God's powerful deeds. The walls shrunk together and collapsed. Those that remained were shaky and rent. Nobody resided in them, for their owners feared they would tumble down over them yet before daybreak.

To describe even a part of the happenings, the hand would weary. Also the mind is distraught by what the eye saw and the ear heard. The verse has been fulfilled, 'Behold, the Lord maketh the earth empty and maketh it waste, and turneth it upside down, and scattereth abroad the inhabitants thereof.'[1] He that is discerning will understand. For all were alike, like people like priest, like servant like his master, when they left their places and sought refuge for their lives. Many resigned themselves to the [Divine] judgement, reciting several verses such as: 'But the Lord God is the true God, He is the living God, and the everlasting King, [at his wrath the earth trembleth and the nations are not able to abide His indignation]'[2]; 'Who looketh on the earth, and it trembleth, [He toucheth the mountains, and they smoke]'[3]; 'Who shaketh the earth out of her place, [and the pillars thereof tremble]'[4]; 'Therefore the land mourns,'[5] ['For the Lord, the God of hosts is He that toucheth the land and it melteth], and they that dwell therein mourn'[6]; 'Who can stand before His indignation? [And who can abide in the fierceness of His anger? His fury is poured out like fire, and the rocks are broken asunder before Him]'[7]

This event took place on Thursday, Tebet 12th, suddenly before sunset, alike in Ramlah, in the whole of Filastin, from fortified city to open village, in all fortresses of Egypt, from the sea to Fort Dan, in all cities of the Negeb and the Mount to Jerusalem [and surrounding places], to Shechem and her villages, Tiberias and her villages, the Galilean mountains and the whole of Palestine.

Those that travelled on the high roads relate the mighty deeds of the living God. They say: 'We have seen the mountains shake, leap like stags, their stones broken into pieces, the hillocks swaying to and fro, and the trees bending down.' In some places the waters in the cisterns reached the brim. The tongue is inadequate to tell the tale. Were it not for God's mercy that it happened before the day was gone, when people could see and warn each other, and had it been in the night when everybody was asleep, only a few would have been saved. But His mercies are many and His kindnesses numerous. Though He decreed, He will not utterly destroy. He, moreover, in His goodness brought out thick clouds and heavy rain-drops fell. Two great rainbows appeared. One of them split up into halves and fire was visible from the south-west. Thereupon the earthquake took place, the like of which was not since early times. On that night [the earth] shook again. All were in the streets, men, women, and children, imploring God, the Lord of the spirits, to quieten the earth and set it at rest and save both man and beast. On Friday, as well as on the following night, the quakes recurred. All were terrified and terror-stricken. Earth and its inhabitants were molten [for fear].[8] They all wept and cried with a loud voice: 'O merciful One, have mercy and refrain from the intended punishment. Do not execute judgement. In anger remember to be merciful[9] and pay no heed to [our] former sins.'[10] All are trembling, sitting on the ground, startled every moment, shaking and swaying to and fro. For eight days the mind has known no peace and the soul has not been at rest.

What could the writer [of this letter] do [but] call on the people to declare a fast, summon a solemn assembly, go out to the field, the cemetery, in fasting, weeping and lamentation, and recite: 'Rend your heart, and not your garments, and turn unto the Lord your God,' etc.[11] 'Come and let us return unto the Lord,' etc.[12] And let us ask for mercy. 'Who knows whether God will not turn and repent.'[13] 'Perhaps He will turn away from His fierce anger, that we perish not.' By a miracle of God, all the days which the people spent in the streets and in the open, no rain fell. The governor of the city, also, and the men in the Caliph's employ, pitched tents for themselves outside the town, and are still there.

May the Lord, the God of the universe, look down mercifully upon this world, have pity on [His] creatures, save man and beast, and have compassion on babes and sucklings and those that know not [to distinguish] between right and left,[14] so that we perish not. May He deliver you from this and the like, guard you from all harsh decrees, hide you in His tabernacle on the day of evil, and shelter you in the protection of His wings. May He exalt you and may your good acts, kindnesses, and righteous deeds stand you in good stead. May He make you dwell securely and at ease from evil fear.[15] And be you at peace, your houses and all that belong to you at peace.[16] Receive peace from the Lord of Peace.

NOTES

1. Is. XXIV. 1.
2. Jer. X. 10.
3. Ps. CIV. 32.
4. Job IX. 6.
5. Hos. IV. 3.
6. Amos IX. 5.
7. Nahum I. 6.
8. Ps. LXXV. 4.
9. Hab. III. 2.
10. Ps. LXXIX. 8.
11. Joel II. 13.
12. Hos. VI. 1.
13. Jonah III. 9.
14. Jonah IV. 11.
15. Prov. I. 33.
16. 1 Sam. XXV. 6.

22

Samuel ha-Nagid's Consolatory Letter on the death of Rabbi Hushiel, the great Talmudist of Kairuan

SAMUEL HA-LEVI BEN JOSEPH IBN NAGDELA (993–1055) was the chief ornament of Spanish Jewry in the generation after Hasdai. His rise to fame reads like a story from the Arabian Nights. Originally a small shopkeeper in Malaga, his skill in calligraphy and his command of Arabic procured him employment with the vizier of Habbus, King of Granada. In this position he displayed such ability that on the vizier's death the King made him his first minister. Like Hasdai, Samuel combined political activity with a keen interest in Jewish learning, of which he was himself a distinguished representative. He composed Talmudic works, and a dictionary of biblical Hebrew, he collected the works of the Geonim and, above all, he excelled as a poet. Some of his hymns were incorporated into the liturgy of the Synagogue, and his 'Ben Mishle' (Son of the Proverbs) became an inspiration for many generations. In virtue of his position and attainments, his fellow-Jews always referred to him as Ha-Nagid or the Leader.

The letter reproduced below was one of condolence written to Rabbi Hananel of Kairuan on the occasion of the death of his father, Rabbi Hushiel ben Elhanan. According to the report of the historian Abraham ibn Daud, Hushiel was one of the four Babylonian Rabbis who had been sent to the West, but were captured by Abd el-Rahman's admiral, Ibn Rumahis, and, after being sold into slavery, were ransomed by the Jews of various Mediterranean communities. Thus Hushiel had become head of the Talmudical academy at Kairuan at the same time that another of the ransomed Babylonians, Moses ben Enoch, founded the Talmudical academy in Cordova. The historical truth of this story has been questioned; there is, however, no doubt that the rise of the Spanish Talmudic school coincided with Hushiel's activity. He was the great authority on Jewish law in North Africa, and his son Hananel became a worthy successor of his father.

SAMUEL HA-NAGID TO RABBI HANANEL BEN HUSHIEL

'Who passes away, and has left a son like himself, has not passed away'

[Granada, first half of the 11th century]

To him who is surrounded by a halo of rays like Moses, for whose sake his people is distinguished, to our friend R. Hananel, the humblest of all sages, peace and consolation!

It is known to my master that, although his fortune is in ruins . . . and his sorrow as great as the sea because his father was called to the assembly of the heavenly hosts, it is not for him alone that the light has been taken away and the torch extinguished, the table shattered and pulled down, but for all inhabitants of the earth under the heaven, as they are aware that a misfortune has befallen the whole world, for all men become kin when a sage has passed away. And particularly from us, the teachers of the Torah – from us has the garment of honour been stolen, the pearl hidden away; the crown has fallen from our head, our beauty has vanished from our midst: we have lost a *man:* he has been turned into dust for our sins. O that I were able to ransom my defunct master with my life! I would offer scores of precious stones in order to acquire a merit for many. I would make rich the physician, abandon my fortune, and distribute it among the people, according to the verse of Scripture, 'Since thou art precious in My sight, thou hast been honourable, and I have loved thee: therefore will I give men for thee, and people for thy life.'[1] What, however, can I do against the decision of the highest master, as it is said: 'No man can by any means redeem his brother, nor give to God a ransom for him'?[2]

When I received the message of his passing, my heart melted, my spirit vanished, my knees trembled, my head burst into sweat, my eyes poured out tears. We tore our garments, and I assembled my friends and addressed them. I made every man who had not known his worth acquainted with it, and proclaimed his fame to all people who were not aware of it, and repeated the well-known lament: 'Our master would have been worthy that the glory of the Lord should rest upon him, but Babylon has prevented this!' And I raised my voice and exclaimed: 'O, our master Hushiel, thou hadst to die on unclean soil! All of us know and feel acutely that the covenant of our friendship has been dissolved, and the people of Israel has been deprived of a man.'

Afterwards I called a meeting, appointed a day of fasting, held the memorial service . . . and arranged the celebration of mourning, all of us standing by with bare shoulders, while the mourners spoke first, according to the dictum of R. Yehuda in the name of Rab: 'The comforters are not allowed to speak before the mourner has spoken, as it is said, "And none spake a word unto him: for they saw that his grief was very great. After this opened Job his mouth . . ."'[3] I also used the formula: 'Woe for the humble man, woe for the pious, woe for him who is great in Kairuan and whose fame reaches Palestine!' And as in Granada, I arranged a mourning celebration also at Lucena, and dispatched letters and messengers with them to Cordova and to most of the Spanish cities where the same has been done as I have done. Surely the shepherd grudges his flock, and the King is angry with his people, as it is said, 'The righteous perisheth, and no man layeth it to heart: and merciful men are taken away, none considering that the righteous is taken away from the evil to come.'[4] In these speeches of mourning we used therefore the words: The Ruler of heaven is angry with His world, He robs the souls, and shouts in delight like a young bride, He rejoices and exults when a soul of an innocent and pious man comes to Him.

In conclusion I should like to say about him what the pious and the hosts of angels have said: 'He entereth into peace; they rest in their beds, each one that walketh in his uprightness.'[5] Our master Hananel, however, is bound to renounce mourning and accept comfort, for the end of all men is death, and all of them must be ready to die, and that man is to be praised who devoted himself to the Torah, who pleases his creator, who gains a good name in his lifetime, and with a good name leaves the world. Hail to thee, our master Hushiel, who has died, and left a memorial in a learned son, the crown of the Torah, the master of the Talmud, the Arioch and King of the epoch,[6] who resembles the King Shabur[7] and the Sinai,[8] and the 'Mountain Raiser and Grinder,'[9] who can be compared with the first seer who outweighed the sixty myriads.[10] May a man like him be born always, for to be born otherwise means not being born at all. He who passes away, and has left a son like himself, has not passed away, all the more pious men like him, who penetrate to the precincts of the Future World, where the gate opens wide before them; and likewise the father has not passed away before the son has risen to heaven, as it was remarked that the sun of Eli did not set until the sun of Samuel radiated from Rama.[11] . . . And when I picture the likeness of the son to his father I realize also my two-fold relation to him. First I am related to him through the Torah, which is our patroness and the aim of our efforts. As she is our sister, we are certainly her brothers, as it is said, 'Say unto wisdom, "Thou art my sister," and call understanding thy kinswoman.'[12]

I raised my voice at the mourning ceremony, and delivered the speech for his sake with deep emotion, and I am sure that all who were present at this ceremony will have a share in the eternal life. Thus, for both these reasons, I entreat my master not to postpone his letter nor delay his answer. May it be a message of his own welfare as well as of his teaching, of the prosperity of his learned friends and the understanding of pupils. And because I have written this letter from the depth of my disturbed soul, with a weakened spirit and a mourning heart, on account of all the sufferings which surround us . . . I approach my master with humble words only and poor praise.[13] As it is, however, known to my master that the prayer of the pious has a mightier effect before the Lord, it is for him to pray for mercy on our behalf, as it is said of him who has suffered an accident, as Scripture saith, 'Abraham prayed unto God; and

God healed Abimelech.'[14] Be blessed and blessed for ever! Samuel ha-Levi bar Joseph, his memory be praised.

NOTES

1. Is. XLIII. 4.
2. Ps. XLIX. 7.
3. Job. II. 13, and III. 1.
4. Is. LVII. 1.
5. Is. LVII. 2.
6. Gen. XIV. 1.
7. The nickname of R. Samuel, one of the most prominent Amoraim, who laid the foundations of the Gemara.
8. The nickname of R. Joseph, son of Hiya (270–334), one of the leading Amoraim of the third generation.
9. Title given to Rabbah, the son of Nahmani (270–332), because of his skill in solving difficulties of interpretation.
10. Namely of Israel: Moses.
11. I Sam. II and III.
12. Prov. VII. 4.
13. Gen. XX. 17.
14. The letter was accompanied by a laudatory poem composed by Samuel, which follows here in a prose translation:

Whenever thou spakest, thy word was like a sweet fruit,
And thy speeches like a mild rain.
All wisdom, all knowledge, all values –
Thou hast kept them like a forsaken bird's nest.
And when thou sattest down to judge men,
Thou wast always the father of the oppressed orphan,
And thy judgment fell like the spray of the rain,
And extinguished the blazing flame of strife.
To every man who approached thee with a question
From the far West thou gavest answer,
As the light of the sun streams down to the surface of the earth,
While he himself is enthroned on the high firmament.
Thou torest thyself from thine own birthplace,
And establishedst thy house of learning at Kairuan.
And while my eyes wander to the distant place,
And never can find his lovely image there,
I would fain offer my heart and soul and spirit,
In company of all hearts as a prize for him.

23

A Jewish Diplomat of the Moslem King of Sicily passes through Alexandria

When Samsam ad-Daula, the Moslem king of Sicily, sent an embassy to Egypt, probably to secure assistance in the civil war which had raged in his island since 1033, a Jew, Moses son of Joseph the Spaniard, was a member of the diplomatic mission. In Alexandria, where he arrived before the New Year, a prominent member of the Jewish community invited him to be his guest during the holy day. The letter of introduction handed to the Jewish diplomat by his host before his departure from Alexandria – also a find from the Cairo Genizah – is our only source of knowledge of this interesting personality. The addressee, Ali ben Amram, was the spiritual head of the Palestinian community in Fostat.

AN UNKNOWN WRITER TO ALI BEN AMRAM IN FOSTAT (CAIRO)

'I have searched his mind, and found it full of knowledge, learning, and wisdom like a pomegranate'

[Alexandria, between 1033 and 1061]

To the companion of my peace, the noble and great Ali, the Haber of the community, may the Lord of heaven, in His mercy, bestow favour and grace upon him, the son of Amram, blessed be his memory! Praised be the most High, may he dwell under the shadow of His shield! Much help!

I approach my great master, the Haber, with two lines in order to inform his Excellency that a Spaniard called Moses son of Joseph, may the Lord protect him, arrived in our country, in company of the ambassador of the Sicilian king Samsam ad-Daula. He stayed on board ship and waited until the news of his arrival reached me. Then I went to him, and asked him to disembark from the ship and to spend the feast with us. He acceded to my request, went with me and remained with us for five days. I have searched his mind, and found it full of knowledge, learning and wisdom like a pomegranate. But what astonished me most was his piety and great modesty. Whenever I consulted him in Bible, Mishnah, Talmud, and secular knowledge, he was ready with proper answers.

May the Lord increase the number of men like him. A very great love and sympathy grew in my heart towards him, and therefore I have described him in these two lines for my master, the excellent Haber, in order to let you know his splendid qualities, knowledge and piety, and to induce you to pay him due honour. He requires no monetary support, as he is of those that give and do not take. May the Lord satisfy him from His goodness, and quench his thirst from the stream of His benevolence.

I have thus informed you and told you all I know of him because I consider it a duty for me and for you to appreciate scholars in order that other people, too, may learn to honour the sons of Torah.

Now peace to my master and noble friend, the Haber of the community, may his peace grow for ever.

24

An Appeal for the Ransom of Captives

ACCORDING to Jewish law, Jews are obliged to ransom their brethren from captivity. In the eleventh century those of Fostat, the ancient Cairo, and Alexandria, were frequently called upon to fulfil this obligation. For various reasons Jews were great seafarers, and the Mediterranean was infested with pirates in those days. The capture of Jews was, therefore, a daily occurrence. They were largely taken prisoners for the express purpose of blackmailing Jewish communities. Great sacrifices were made in order to provide the sums demanded by the brigands, but in many cases single communities were quite unable to cover the expenses from their own resources, and appeals were made to others. The letters written for this purpose are not only moving testimonies to the solidarity of the Jewish people and their pious obedience to the Law, but are also the first documentary traces of that organized relief and rescue work which grew into an invariable concomitant of all the persecutions the Jews have had to suffer in subsequent ages.

The Cairo Genizah contained many such letters, of which the following somewhat incomplete specimen is a good example:

THE JEWS OF ALEXANDRIA TO EPHRAIM BEN SHEMARYA AND THE ELDERS OF THE PALESTINIAN COMMUNITY OF FOSTAT

'When we saw them in the hands of the pirates . . . we had pity on them'

[Alexandria, first half of the 11th century]

To the highly respected Rabbi Ephraim, member of the great assembly,[1] son of the R. Shemarya, of blessed memory, and the Elders, the noble and highly honoured men, may the Lord protect them, from your friends, the community of Alexandria, best greetings! . . . You are the supporters of the poor and the aid of the men in need, you study diligently, you rouse the good against the evil impulse. You walk in the right way and practise justice. We let you know that we always pray for you. May God grant you peace and security!

We turn to you today on behalf of a captive woman who has been brought from Byzantium. We ransomed her for 24 denares[2] besides the governmental tax. You sent us 12 denares; we have paid the remainder and the tax. Soon afterwards sailors brought two other prisoners, one of them a fine young man possessing knowledge of the Torah, the other a boy of about ten. When we saw them in the hands of the pirates, and how they beat and frightened them before our own eyes, we had pity on them and guaranteed their ransom. We had hardly settled this, when another ship arrived carrying many prisoners. Among them were a physician and his wife. Thus we are again in difficulties and distress. And our strength is overstrained, as the taxes are heavy and the times critical. . . .

It may be assumed that these appeals were answered in the most generous manner. We know from other letters that such epistles were read before the congregation in order to 'impress upon them the highly deserving case of the captives, who are respected people in their native country'. This ensured a liberal response in a community like Fostat, of which Jacob Mann says that 'its record as regards fraternal feeling for a Jew, from whatever country he might hail, and for generosity and loving-kindness, is one that any modern congregation might well engrave in golden letters'.

NOTES

1. Ephraim ben Shemarya, head of the community, was a noted scholar and a leading figure of Egyptian Jewry.
2. The normal fixed ransom for a captive was 33 denares, about £16 in gold.

25

A Letter of Introduction for a medieval Jew who travelled from Russia to Jerusalem

THIS letter introduces us to a particular Jewish type of travellers – a member of the great family of Jewish pilgrims to the Holy Land. The magnetic power which has attracted Jews in all countries and during all ages to their sacred homeland is well illustrated by the irresistible desire of this unknown Russian Jew, neither Rabbi nor scholar, but a most simple, unsophisticated soul, to set out on the long and dangerous journey to Palestine. The letter, given to him by the community of Salonica as a kind of passport (once again a gem from the Cairo Genizah), also shows the readiness of the Jews to assist the pilgrims.

THE COMMUNITY OF SALONICA TO THE COMMUNITIES ON THE ROUTE TO PALESTINE

'For he knows only Russian'

[Salonica, probably 11th century]

. . . We send greetings to you and feel it our duty to inform you about the request of Mr. N. N. He is a Jew from Russia and stayed with us here in Salonica, where he met his relative, Mr. X. Y., who returned recently from the holy city of Jerusalem, may it be restored by the Lord for ever. When he was told about the splendour of Palestine, Mr. N. N., too, became very desirous of going there and prostrating himself on the sacred spot. He asked us to give him these few lines in order to use them as means of introduction.

Please help him to reach his goal by the proper route, with the support of reliable men, from town to town, from island to island. For he knows neither Hebrew nor Greek nor Arabic but only Russian, the language of his homeland.

At all times the house of Israel, our brethren . . . excelled in the strength of righteousness and the power of charity, and you know their reward. For it is told first in the Torah, then by the prophets, further in the hagiographa, fourthly in the Mishnah and fifthly in the Talmud, and also indicated in the sequence of the letters Gimel and Daleth.[1] . . .

NOTE

1. See T. B. Shab. 104a, where *gimel daleth* is interpreted as 'gemol dalim' (help the poor).

26

A Family Letter written in Hebrew by a Jewess

LETTERS from Jewish women which have survived from the Middle Ages are few and far between, and this one (also from the Cairo Genizah) is one of the earliest. It is written in elegant paitanic Hebrew, and there is no reason to doubt that it was the composition of Maliha herself. This lady, originally from Egypt, had apparently gone to settle in Byzantium on being married, and after some years of absence she was longing once more to see her family in her native land. That she was afraid of the voyage is not surprising, considering the dangers to which one of the preceding letters (pp. 141 f.) bears forceful testimony. The feminine delicacy with which the writer's longing and anxiety are conveyed makes this document a notable contribution to Jewish letter-writing.

LADY MALIHA TO HER BROTHERS ABU-SAID AND SOLOMON

'Oh for the wings of a dove that I could fly and join my brothers!'

[Byzantium, 11th or 12th century]

May this letter be delivered in gladness to my excellent brothers, Abu Said and Solomon, from your sister Maliha. May peace from Heaven like the drops of water from above [and abundant] like the fishes in the depths [of the sea] be bestowed upon you and strength, vigour, favour, mercy and pity and a long life like his who became father of the people,[1] or his who was bound as a victim on a high mountain,[2] or of Jacob, the plain man[3], or of him who dreamed,[4] or of him who sprinkled the blood on the altar seven times.[5] May all blessings come and be gathered and accumulated upon the heads of my brothers, Solomon and Abu Said, gentle and most beloved brothers, from your sister Maliha. And heartiest greetings from my little daughter Zoe.

We are in good health, and trust in the Rock of your welfare that you, too, are well and safe, prosperous and free, in good heart without trouble and sorrows. But I, while wishing you all good, am not myself in good humour, for when I think of you, my heart sinks, my knees quiver, my limbs tremble, my strength dwindles, because I have been separated from you for many years and am desirous of seeing your faces. I should like to run to you like a lion, nay, to fly! Oh for the wings of a dove, that I could fly and join my brothers, and also our Master, the fourth. I am, however, not able to come, as the hour is not favourable. I was ready to go with this man,[6] but I consulted a Torah scroll[7] and obtained a disappointing answer which boded no good for myself. Thus I could not join them.

And for Heaven's sake do you not see that many Jews are being fetched from Byzantium by their relatives? Why does not one of you make up his mind to come over here in order to bring me back? You will understand that I am reluctant to engage strange people. If I should go alone, may God not deprive me of luck, but if anything evil should befall me during the voyage, it might be fatal to me, and I should die. For I have been devoted to you since your infancy. . . .

NOTES

1. Abraham.
2. Isaac.
3. Gen. xxv. 27.
4. Joseph.
5. Aaron: Lev. xvi. 14.
6. Viz. the bearer of the letter.
7. Viz. by opening the scroll and using as an omen the passage turned up.

27

Medieval Jewish Family Tragedies related in Letters of Introduction

THE two letters (also from the Cairo Genizah) reproduced below belong to a type which must have been common enough in the Middle Ages. They have a poignant human interest (of a kind with which we have become familiar in our own day), and illustrate the insecurity of the Jewish existence among the nations as well as the strong feeling of fraternity which has always pervaded the Jewish community throughout the ages. There is a sad affinity between the broken lives of Reuben ben Isaac of Rhodez, in France, and of the woman proselyte, widow of the Rabbi David Todros of Narbonne: nothing has been left to them except the hope of finding consolation among 'the mourners of Zion' or in the life of a new generation.

(A)

A COMMUNITY, PROBABLY IN SPAIN, TO THE COMMUNITIES ON THE ROAD TO PALESTINE

'I intend to go to Eretz Israel and to Jerusalem to die there. For I have reached the days that do not please me'

[Probably somewhere in Spain, 11th century]

To our brethren in the holy communities of the Diaspora, many greetings from us, your younger brethren, inhabitants of the city. . . .

We wish to inform our brethren about Mr. Reuben, son of Isaac, who came to us from the city of Rhodez in France. This man Reuben was once a very wealthy man; he possessed silver, gold and landed property more than all [his countrymen]. But he fell into the traps of the evil men of his country and became their victim.

One day he sent his only son with his servants to work in the field. Suddenly they were attacked in a forest by rude Christian bandits, bent on destruction. They killed the son and the servants beside him. This became known to the father, and he found the dead son in the forest and there was nobody who could help him. Overwhelmed by this catastrophe, the father broke down and fell into despair. He appealed to the governor of the district, but the latter did not reply because they were . . . Gentiles, and even became his enemy himself when he saw his misfortune. He robbed him and deprived him of all his property and threw him aside like an empty vessel, stripped of everything. He said to him: 'You are an old man and have no son. I shall therefore take possession of your whole fortune.' The father, isolated and in despair, left the place and came to us. He turned to us with this supplication: 'I have been cast away and forced to wander from my place to you, scoffed at for my language. You have heard my story and I have not needed a letter so far. But now I must ask you, my brethren, for the favour of writing a letter about all that has happened to me, in order that it should be my mouthpiece in all the holy communities on the other side of the sea, because I am ignorant of their language. In the name of Him on high who directs the steps of man, I intend to go to Eretz Israel and to Jerusalem to die there, for I have reached the days that do not please me.'

When we, the writers of this letter, saw his suffering and the depression of his soul . . . we wrote these lines. And you, our brethren, esteemed brethren, our pride, haste and be merciful to him, help him, strengthen him. . . .

(B)

A COMMUNITY, PROBABLY ANJOU, TO OTHER COMMUNITIES

'Dear Sirs, lift your eyes to heaven and have pity on her poverty'

[Probably Anjou, France, 11th century]

From us, the community of Anjou[?], the little flock, who are afflicted and troubled, for lions and wolves of the deserts have devoured us with their open mouths,[1] so that only a few of us are left. We are as a beacon upon the top of a mountain, and an ensign on an hill, in the wind during the day, in the frost by night.[2] The name of the Lord be praised for ever, and with the utmost importunity and in the greatness of our affliction we will prepare prayers and supplications before the Lord our refuge to hasten the redemption, to assemble and gather together the dispersed in the land of His glory, on high from the beginning,[3] as it is said, 'He will set up an ensign for the nations, and will assemble the dispersed.'[4]

We beg to inform you, esteemed Sirs, about the case of this widow, a proselyte whose husband was Rabbi David, blessed be his memory, of the community of Narbonne, of the family of Rabbi Todros, blessed be his memory, in Narbonne. He left that place six years ago on account of his wife, the proselyte....

She forsook the very rich house of her parents and her distant country and came in the name of our God to find cover under the wings of the Shekinah, leaving her brothers and sisters and the noble members of her family. She stayed in Narbonne and there the late Rabbi David married her. After six months, on hearing that she was sought by her relatives he escaped with her to our place. Here they lived until the Lord (He is just in all that came upon us[5]) brought this persecution upon us. Her husband was killed in the synagogue, and two of his children, a boy by the name of Jacob, and a girl by the name of Justa, three years old, were taken captive, and all his possessions despoiled. Thus the widow remained in tears, and lamenting over her losses and poverty. Nobody cared for her and for a child a few months old that remained to her. She was thirsty, stripped of everything, and possessed no means to buy anything for herself and the orphan. . . .

And now, dear Sirs, lift your eyes to Heaven and have pity on her poverty for [her own] sake [and] for the sake of her children who have been taken captive.[6] May it be that the Lord of the hosts will be merciful. . . . Receive her with kindness, and treat her in accordance with your character as you treat every traveller. . . .

NOTES

1. Jer. v. 6; Is. IX. 11.
2. Is. XXX. 17; Gen. XXXI. 40.
3. Jer. XVII. 12.
4. Is. XI. 12.
5. Neh. IX. 33.
6. This passage indicates that the main purpose of the letter was to assist the widow in her endeavour to obtain the ransom for the captive children.

28

Two Episodes in the Life of Judah Halevi

TWO memorable moments in the life of Judah ben Samuel Halevi (*c.* 1085–1140), the unsurpassed genius of medieval Hebrew poetry, are illustrated by the following poetical letters. They differ in extent, contents and style, and yet a mysterious unity originating in the character and fate of their inspired author seems to link them together.

1. *An exchange of poems between Judah Halevi and Abraham ibn Ezra*

Judah Halevi and Abraham ibn Ezra (1092–1167), both natives of Toledo, were contemporaries and friends. As creative spirits they stand on the same level, but their personalities belong to different spheres. Two poetical epistles, found in a manuscript of the Bodleian Library, are highly characteristic of this contrast, one of them displaying admirably the tenderness and idealism of Judah Halevi, the other the wit and realism of Ibn Ezra. Whether Judah Halevi's invitation to Ibn Ezra referred to his intended pilgrimage to Eretz Israel or to some other kind of withdrawal from worldly life is an open question, but the sense of Ibn Ezra's exuberant reply is unmistakable.

There is no need to accept the opinion of Geiger and Graetz that both poems were the work of Ibn Ezra, composed by him after Judah Halevi's death, still less a statement elsewhere that the first poem was composed by Judah al-Harizi. We may rather consider as well founded David Kahana's assumption that we have before us a genuine correspondence of the two classical Hebrew poets.

In the absence of any indication where and when the poems were composed, no place and only an approximate time – the first half of the twelfth century – can be assigned to the epistles.

JUDAH HALEVI TO ABRAHAM IBN EZRA

'Come then, and let us sing and rest together'

A deep sleep was upon me, but the desire
To see thee, my beloved friend, awakened me,
The heavenly choirs had chosen just thy songs,

They, yea they, sent me to call thy name.
Come then, and let us sing and rest together.
For what is yet here left to do for thee?

ABRAHAM IBN EZRA TO JUDAH HALEVI

'I shall still beget children, and enjoy good meals'

My brother Judah, lie down again, for God
Does not permit me to come to thee.
I shall still beget children, and enjoy good meals,
And do not want to taste thy delightful manna.
I am very sad because of thy departure,
But I am not prepared to deprive me of this mourning.

2. *Judah Halevi, on the way to the Land of Israel, pays tribute to the Head of the Academy in Egypt*

In 1140 Judah Halevi carried out the design he had long cherished of satisfying his longing for Zion, and set sail for his pilgrimage to the Holy Land. The scholars and poets of Spain gave a magnificent farewell to their great countryman, and he was greeted in the same manner on his arrival in Egypt. After staying in Alexandria for three months as the guest of Aaron Benzion ibn Alemanni, Chief Rabbi, physician and poet, Judah proceeded to Damietta. There he received an invitation from Nathan, son of Samuel, the head of the Academy, to visit him in Fostat. Judah accepted by writing the subjoined letter, and an accompanying poem, both containing an exuberant eulogy of Nathan. The letter, composed in rhymed Hebrew prose, became a famous example of the flowery style which, though of Arabic origin, was adopted and used by Hebrew writers with superb virtuosity.

JUDAH BEN SAMUEL HALEVI TO NATHAN BEN SAMUEL

'Who am I, what is my life, and what is my desire and wish? Worthless dust, crushed and faint'

[Damietta, 1140]

To the store-house of understanding and stronghold of faith, the crown of scholars and chief of the speakers, the pride of the Torah and the bowl of the candlestick,[1] our master and teacher

Rabbi Nathan the scholar, son of our great, honoured and holy master and teacher Rabbi Samuel the scholar, of blessed memory, from one who bows himself down before him and longs to behold his countenance, Judah the Levite, son of Rabbi Samuel, may his soul be in paradise!

... My heart is in a ferment, and my thoughts impel me to write. Thou didst humble me, yet didst thou delight me, for thou didst treat me with honour, though this weighed upon me, and put upon me the crown and the testimony. ... But who can don thy crowns, and who can put on thy wreaths? Gates of justice are thy gates, lofty mountains are thy mountains, and exquisite dawns are thy daybreaks. When thou decidest a law, thou annullest the opinions of others, when thou counsellest, thou breakest every rod, every mouth becomes dumb, even the eloquent feels ashamed, and they who compose songs have mouths, but speak not: their fountains are stopped, and they themselves are still as a stone in the presence of a fountain whose waters fail not. ... The manna descends upon him that hearkens to thy words. Wonderful are thy words, and thy compositions are awe-inspiring; they fly to the west and to the south, and speak from on high. Shall Egypt detain such a man, while Jerusalem as well as the land of Merathaim[2] longs for thee? ...

Yea, thy name is greater than all: our master and teacher, Nathan the scholar, the crown of scholars, the son of our honoured master and teacher Samuel the scholar, the righteous, of blessed memory! From one who is a fragment of thy light and a tributary of thy rivers, Judah the Levite, thy disciple, the gleaning of thy harvest, and the fallen fruit of thy vintage; who sends his heart ahead of his writings; who is fearful and faint-hearted to think on his affairs. ... Who am I, what is my life,[3] and what is my desire and wish? Worthless dust, crushed and faint; fearful on account of my iniquity and the sins of my youth[4] and old age. Yet I venture to stand upon thy threshold with my supplications, though I am but a wayfarer that turns aside to tarry for a night,[5] a Levite who sojourns there. Wherewith shall I draw nigh, and how shall

I keep up with the ruler and potentate? I summoned counsels from afar, took up my weapons, came in, and went out; but I found nothing better than silence. I was humiliated, and put to shame, and despaired of an answer; I lost heart to come out to meet thee; I groped for the wall in the dark, and felt my way like the blind, and sought hiding-places, until I met taskmasters, who were urgent, persistent, and pressing; they came from the wonderful sage, the lord, the exalted nobleman, our master and teacher Halfon the Levite,[6] who speaks in thy name, and endeavours to cleave to thee. O my lord and my pride, may he be exalted and lifted up, and may he be very high! He stands between us to join our hearts with the exchange of our writings and the purity of our love. He importuned me, pressed me, urged me, roused me, and brought me out hastily from the dungeon of slothfulness. He coaxed me unceasingly, saying: 'Come now, I will prove thee; finish thy work, and give the best thereof which is full of understanding; perform in thy old age the deeds of youth. Know before whom thou art about to render the account, near whom thou writest, and near whom thou signest!' Thy enchanters hurried, and thy magicians did great things, until they annulled my vows, and made my bonds void. Then my bands dropped off, my youth was renewed, my songs thronged tumultuously, my lyres were sounded, and forgotten were my fears and the years of my life of sojournings. I remembered not that the day had declined towards evening, that the eternal resting-place was nigh while there was yet abundant work. I mingled with the throng, summoned up my youth, eagerly sought the dawn of life, and dissembled hoariness, as one dissembles a stolen thing, though my leanness testified against me. Then I took some of thy words, and wrestled manfully with the lion, and prevailed; I rescued a piece of an ear,[7] and made merry with myself, for I was likened to the scribes of the King and to them that have ability to stand in the King's palace.[8]

My lord, in thy kindness pardon thy servant, and be not too exacting with me, and weigh not my words; judge me in the scale of merit, and bring me not into the judgement of thy wisdom. Behold, here is the fruit of my intellect, the choicest of my musing, and the best of my meditations, according to the ability of my hand and tongue, until I come unto my lord to watch at thy doors, to gather thy pearls, and to sing thy praises. Lo, these are but the outskirts of thy paths, and a little of the splendour of thy moons.

He that makes peace in His high places shall increase thy peace, shall make thy friends perfect, shall fight against thine enemies, and establish thy plans, that thou mayest spend thy days in prosperity. I conclude with peace. Amen.

Like a wayfarer who tarries for a night, Judah Halevi made indeed only a fleeting stay with the scholars of Fostat. Then he hurried away to fulfil his vow and satisfy his deepest desire. The legend which made him die soon afterwards under the heel of an Arab brigand while reciting the verses of his 'Zionide', may have been founded on the sentiment expressed in the poem that he would count even such a fate happy if he met it in the Holy Land: 'I yearn for my soul to be poured forth in the place where God's spirit was poured out on the chosen ones.' There is a similar feeling in the lines of his 'Pilgrimage to Zion':

No love but God's is great,
  Thy holy gates in love approached, I wait
For death; my heart to Thee I sanctify
  Upon Thine altar, love to testify.

NOTES

1. Zech. IV. 2.
2. I.e. Babylon; cf. Jer. L. 21.
3. 2 Sam. VII. 18; 1 Chron. XVII. 16.
4. Job XX. 11.
5. Jer. XIV. 8.
6. The invitation was delivered through the son of Halfon ha-Levi, 'the generous one of the congregation'.
7. Amos III. 12.
8. Dan. I. 4.

29

Judah ibn Tibbon's Letter of Admonition to his Son

JUDAH, son of Saul ibn Tibbon, was born about 1120 in Granada, but the persecutions of the fanatical sect of the Almohades forced him to leave Spain and to settle in the Provençal city of Lunel. Here, while active as a physician, he gained fame as one of the outstanding Hebrew scholars of his time. Besides producing various original works, he translated several epoch-making books, such as Saadia's 'Emunot ve-Deot', Judah Halevi's 'Cusari' and the poems of Solomon ibn Gabirol from the Arabic into Hebrew, and for these activities became known as 'Father of Translators'. He was a great stylist and calligrapher, and an enthusiastic collector of precious books, in fact, a precursor of the type which later was called humanist.

Judah's character is clearly revealed in the 'Ethical Will' which he addressed to his son Samuel. In this celebrated Letter of Admonition Judah's rich experiences, his own spiritual ardour and erudition, his moral zeal and his passion for education found ample expression. The sharp reproaches of the father to his son and the many autobiographical details inserted into the admonitions add a piquant personal note to the letter and heighten the interest of the reader.

The following reproduction of the letter is somewhat shortened; the poetical version of the admonitions, composed by Judah ibn Tibbon himself, has been entirely omitted.

JUDAH IBN TIBBON TO HIS SON SAMUEL

'All the honour I ask of thee is to attain a higher degree in the pursuit of wisdom, to excel in right conduct and exemplary character, to behave in friendly spirit to all and to gain a good name, that greatest of crowns'

[Lunel, second half of the 12th century]

In the name of God, whose mention be exalted and praised for ever! . . .

My son, listen to my precepts,[1] neglect none of my injunctions. Set my admonition before thine eyes, thus shalt thou prosper and prolong thy days in pleasantness. . . .

Thou knowest, my son, how I swaddled thee and brought thee up, how I led thee in the paths of wisdom and virtue. I fed and clothed thee; I spent myself in educating and protecting thee, I sacrificed my sleep to make thee wise beyond thy fellows, and to raise thee to the highest degree of science and morals. These twelve years I have denied myself the usual pleasures and relaxations of men for thy sake, and I still toil for thine inheritance.

I have assisted thee by providing an extensive library for thy use and have thus relieved thee of the necessity of borrowing books. Most students must wander about to seek books, often without finding them. But thou, thanks be to God, lendest and borrowest not. Of many books, indeed, thou ownest two or three copies. I have besides procured for thee books on all sciences, hoping that thy hand might 'find them all as a nest'. Seeing that thy Creator had graced thee with a wise and understanding heart, I journeyed to the ends of the earth and fetched for thee a teacher in secular sciences. I neither heeded the expense nor the danger of the ways. Untold evil might have befallen me and thee on those travels, had not the Lord been with us!

But thou, my son, didst deceive my hopes! Thou didst not choose to employ thine abilities, hiding thyself from all the books, not caring to know them or even their titles. Hadst thou seen thine own books in the hand of others, thou wouldst not have recognized them; hadst thou needed one of them, thou wouldst not have known whether it was with thee or not, without asking me; thou didst not even consult the catalogue of the library . . .

All this thou hast done. Thus far thou hast relied on me to rouse thee from the sleep of indolence, thinking that I would live with thee for ever! Thou didst not bear in mind that death must divide us, and that there are daily vicissitudes in life. But who will be as tender to thee as I have been, who will take my place – to teach thee out of love and goodwill? Even if thou couldst find such a one, lo! thou seest how the greatest scholars, coming from the corners of the earth, seek to profit by my society and instruction, how eager they are to see me and my books. But thou, though all this was thine without silver and price, thou wert unwilling; and the Lord hath not given thee a heart to know, eyes to see, or ears to hearken unto this day. May thy God endow thee with a new heart and spirit, and instil into thee a desire to retrieve the past, and to follow the true path henceforward!

Seven years and more have passed since thou didst begin to learn Arabic writing but, despite my entreaties, thou hast refused to obey. Yet thou art well aware how our foremost men only attained high distinction through their proficiency in Arabic writing. Thou hast already seen what the Nagid[2] of blessed memory has recorded as to his rise to power being solely due to this cause, when he sang: 'O Pen, I tell of thy kindness!' Similarly with his son. In this country, too, as well as in the kingdom of Ishmael the Nasi R. Shesheth[3] acquired wealth and honour through his Arabic. By means of it, he paid his debts, met all his expenses, and made splendid gifts.

Nor hast thou acquired sufficient skill in Hebrew writing, though I paid, as thou must remember, thirty golden pieces annually to thy master, the clever R. Jacob, son of the generous R. Obadiah. And when I persuaded him to teach thee to write the letters, he answered: 'It will be enough for him to learn one letter a year.' If thou hadst paid attention to this remark of his, thou wouldst have striven to become a better scribe than he or his sons.

Thou art still young, and improvement is possible, if Heaven but grant thee a helping gift of desire and resolution, for ability is of no avail without inclination . . .

If the Lord please to bring me back to thee,[4] I will take upon me all thy wants. For whom indeed do I toil but for thee and thy children? May the Lord let me see their faces again in joy!

Therefore, my son! stay not thy hand when I have left thee, but devote thyself to the study of the Torah and to the science of medicine. But chiefly occupy thyself with the Torah, for thou hast a wise and understanding heart, and all that is needful on thy part is ambition and application. I know that thou wilt repent of the past, as many have repented before thee of their youthful indolence . . .

Therefore, my son! exert thyself whilst still young, the more so as thou even now complainest of weak memory. What, then, wilt thou do in old age, the mother of forgetfulness? Awake, my son! from thy sleep; devote thyself to science and religion; habituate thyself to moral living, for 'habit is master over all things'. As the Arabian philosopher holds, there are two sciences, ethics and physics. Strive to excel in both! . . .

Contend not with men, and meddle not 'with strife not thine own'.[5] Enter into no dispute with the obstinate, not even on matters of Torah. On thy side, too, refrain from subterfuges in argument to maintain thy case even when thou art convinced that thou art in the right. Submit to the majority and do not reject their decision. Risk not thy life by taking the road and leaving thy city in times of disquiet and danger. Even where large sums are involved travel only on the advice of men of mature judgement who are well-disposed to thee; trust not the counsel of the young in preference to that of the old. Let not the prospect of great gain blind thee to make light of thy life; be not as a bird that sees the grain but not the net. Remember what the Sage of blessed memory said: 'A wise man feareth, and departeth from evil, but the fool behaveth overbearingly and is confident.'[6]

Show respect to thyself, thy household, and thy children, by providing decent clothing, as far as thy means allow; for it is unbecoming for any one, when not at work, to go shabbily dressed. Spare from thy belly and put it on thy back!

Thou knowest, my son! the trouble and expense I incurred for the marriage of thy elder and younger sisters. Never in my life had I undergone such dangers, thrice crossing the sea at great cost though my means were scanty. I pledged my books, I borrowed from my friends, though I was never wont to do so, and all this so as not to reduce thy share. Also, at thine own marriage, thou art aware that I did not sell thee for silver, as others richer than I have done with their sons. None of thy companions made a more honourable union. I took for thee the daughter of a cultured and distinguished lineage,[7] all of them the 'seed of truth', learned and of high standing. The community showed its consideration by imposing on thee no tax or due. Thou wast honoured at the wedding by princes and priests, men of the highest distinction, for my sake.

And now, my son! if the Creator has mightily displayed His love to thee and me, so that Jew and Gentile have thus far honoured thee for my sake, endeavour henceforth so to add to thine honour that they may respect thee for thine own self. This thou canst effect by good morals and by courteous behaviour; by steady devotion to thy studies and thy profession, as thou wast wont to do before thy marriage. . . .

My son! Let thy countenance shine upon the sons of men: tend their sick, and may thine advice cure them. Though thou takest fees from the rich, heal the poor gratuitously; the Lord will requite thee. Thereby shalt thou find favour and good understanding in the sight of God and man. Thus wilt thou win the respect of high and low among Jews and non-Jews, and thy good name will go forth far and wide. Thou wilt rejoice thy friends and make thy foes envious. . . .

My son! Examine regularly once a week thy drugs and medicinal herbs, and do not employ an ingredient whose properties are unknown to thee. I have often impressed this on thee in vain when we were together.

My son! If thou writest aught, read it through a second time, for no man can avoid slips. Let not any consideration of hurry prevent thee from revising a short epistle. Be punctilious in regard to grammatical accuracy, in conjugations and genders, for the constant use of the vernacular sometimes leads to error in this matter. A man's mistakes in writing bring him into disrepute; they are remembered against him all his days. As our Sages say: 'Who is it that uncovers his nakedness here and exposes it everywhere? It is he who writes a document and makes mistakes therein.' . . . Endeavour to cultivate conciseness and elegance, do not attempt to write verse unless thou canst do it perfectly. Avoid heaviness, which spoils a composition, making it disagreeable alike to reader and audience. . . .

See to it that thy penmanship and handwriting are as beautiful as thy style. Keep thy pen in fine working order, use ink of good colour. Make thy script as perfect as possible, unless forced to write without proper materials, or in a pressing emergency. The beauty of a composition depends on the writing, and the beauty of the writing, on pen, paper and ink; and all these excellencies are an index to the author's worth. Do not get into the habit of contracting the letters or of running them together, but make each one long, broad, and straight. . . . Be particular, too, in the alignment; the lines must be straight, and the spacing uniform, so that one does not go up and another down. And may thy God prosper thee, and make thee straight in all thy ways!

And now, my son! in many of these matters, wherein thou didst not obey me when I was with thee, obey me at this time, when I am far off. In all thy business, thy buying and selling, thou didst not do me the honour to ask my advice, nor didst thou even keep me informed. . . .

Worse still, when thou didst write thy letters or compose thine odes to send abroad, thou wast unwilling to show a word to me and didst prevent me from seeing. When I said to thee, 'Show me!' thou wouldst answer: 'Why dost thou want to see?' as if thinking that my help was unnecessary. And this was from thy folly, in that thou wast wise in thine own eyes. . . .

Even R. Zerahiah,[8] of blessed memory, who stood alone in his generation, and was more learned than I, never, from the day he knew me, wrote a letter or a poem to send to anyone without showing it to me before it left his hand. Even of his letters to his brother he showed many to me before he sent them off. On my part, when I wrote letters, I said to thee: 'Look at them, perhaps there is something in them to alter or to correct!'

. . . If, my son, thou desirest to undo the past, the Creator will grant His pardon, and I shall forgive all without reserve or reluctance. Reject not my word in all that I have written for thee in this, my Testament, and wherein thou hast not honoured me heretofore, honour me for the rest of my days and after my death! All the honour I ask of thee is to attain a higher degree in the pursuit of wisdom, to excel in right conduct and exemplary character, to behave in friendly spirit to all and to gain a good name, that greatest of crowns, to deserve applause for thy dealings and association with thy fellows, to cleave to the fear of God and the performance of His commandments – thus wilt thou honour me in life and in death! . . .

Thanks to my Creator, I know of thee that thou fearest Heaven in all thy ways, excepts as regards honouring thy father. Thou hast transgressed my commandments and refused me obedience. Great, however, is this thing in the sight of God and man. Acquire the virtue of obedience and prosper! I trust to God that this, my separation, will be for thy good, and that thou wilt take it to thy heart to receive instruction, for thou hast none beside me, except thine own soul, mind and understanding. The Nagid of blessed memory has said:

> What good is there in life if my work
> To-day remains as 'twas yesterday? . . .

And now, O my son! by the God of heaven, by the obedience to me imposed by His law, by the gratitude due for my rearing and educating thee, I adjure thee to abstain, with all thy resolution, from noxious food! Experience has taught thee how much thou hast suffered from carelessness in this regard. Be content with little and good, and beware of hurtful sweets. . . .

Take heed to thyself! Preserve thy life, be not thine own destroyer! And if thou hast no pity on me and on thyself, have compassion on the child of thy delight, the object of thy yearning! For I shall be but a little while with you. . . .

My son! I command thee to honour thy wife to thine utmost capacity. She is intelligent and modest, a daughter of a distinguished and educated family. She is a good housewife and mother, and no spendthrift. Her tastes are simple, whether in food or dress. Remember her assiduous attendance on thee in thine illness, though she had been brought up in elegance and luxury. Remember how she afterwards reared thy son without man or woman to help her. . . .

If thou wouldst acquire my love, honour her with all thy might; do not exercise too strict an authority over her; our Sages have expressly warned men against this. If thou givest orders or reprovest let thy words be gentle. Enough is it if thy displeasure is visible in thy look, let it not be vented in actual rage. . . .

My son! Devote thy mind to thy children as I did to thee; be tender to them as I was tender; instruct them as I instructed thee; keep them as I kept thee, try to teach them Torah as I have tried, and as I did unto thee do thou unto them! Be not indifferent to any slight ailment in them, or in thyself (may God deliver thee and them from all sickness and plague), but if thou dost notice any suspicion of disease in thee or in one of thy limbs, do forthwith what is necessary in the case. As Hippocrates[19] has said: 'Time is short, and experiment is dangerous.' Therefore be prompt, but apply a sure remedy, avoiding doubtful treatment.

Examine thy Hebrew books at every new moon, the Arabic volumes once in two months, and the bound codices once every quarter. Arrange thy library in fair order, so as to avoid wearying thyself in searching for the book thou needest. Always know the case and chest where the book should be. A good plan would be to set in each compartment a written list of the books therein contained. If, then, thou art looking for a book, thou canst see from the list the exact shelf it occupies without disarranging all the books in the search for one. Examine the loose leaves in the volumes and bundles, and preserve them. These fragments contain very important matters which I have collected and copied out. Do not destroy any writing or letter of all that I have left. And cast thine eye frequently over the catalogue so as to remember what books are in thy library.

Never refuse to lend books to anyone who has not means to

purchase books for himself, but only act thus to those who can be trusted to return the volumes. . . . Cover the bookcases with rugs of fine quality; and preserve them from damp and mice, and from all manner of injury, for thy books are thy good treasure. If thou lendest a volume make a note of it before it leaves thy house, and when it is returned, draw thy pen over the entry. Every Passover and Tabernacles call in all books out on loan.

Make it a fixed rule in thy home to read the Scriptures and to peruse grammatical works on Sabbaths and festivals, also to read Proverbs and the Ben Mishle. Also I beg of thee, look at the chapter concerning Jonadab son of Rechab[10] every Sabbath, to instil in thee diligence to fulfil my commands.

My son! If thou hearest abuse of me from the lips of fools, be silent and make no reply. Take no notice of aught that they may say against me. Remember what Ben Mishle says:

> The good will of others is the fruit of meekness,
> And the fruit of contentment is tranquillity;
>
> The fruit of hearing others in silence
> Is peace of mind, confidence, and joy!

Show eagerness in honouring thy teachers and doing them service. Attach thyself to their friends, make their foes thine. Treat them with respect in all places and under all circumstances, even though thou hast no need of them while they have need of thee, a thousand and a thousand times more if thou needest them. . . .

But, my son, honour thy comrades, and seek opportunities to benefit them by thy wisdom, in counsel and deed. . . .

My son! Communicate with thy sisters constantly in thy letters,[11] and inquire after their welfare. Show honour to thy relatives, for they will appreciate courtesies.

I enjoin on thee, my son, to read this, my Testament, once daily, at morn or at eve. Apply thy heart to the fulfilment of its behests, and to the performance of all therein written. Then wilt thou make thy ways prosperous, then shalt thou have good success.[12] . . .

. . . May He who gives prudence to the simple, and to young men knowledge and discretion, bestow on thee a willing heart and a listening ear! Then shall our soul be glad in the Lord and rejoice in His salvation!

Countless Letters of Admonition have been written by Jewish fathers since the days of Judah ibn Tibbon, many containing deeper religious thoughts or a more elaborate ethical doctrine. But in the directness of its appeal and the warmth of its cultural aspirations Judah ibn Tibbon's letter remains unsurpassed. And measured by the subsequent career of the son to whom it was addressed, this letter could claim to have achieved an outstanding success, since its recipient was to become the translator of the 'Guide of the Perplexed' by Moses Maimonides.

NOTES

1. Prov. I. 8.
2. Samuel ha-Nagid (see *supra*, p. 134ff); Judah ibn Tibbon quotes his 'Ben Mishle' copiously (see examples below).
3. R. Shesheth the Prince, a noted physician of Barcelona and author of a Hebrew treatise on purifying medicines.
4. This passage indicates that the letter or at least a part of it had been written before a journey.
5. Prov. XXVI. 17.
6. Prov. XIV. 16.
7. She seems to have been the sister of the well-known scholar, Jacob Anatoli.
8. R. Zerahiah ha-Levi (1125–1186), commentator and codifier, a recognized authority, settled at Lunel, the residence of the Tibbons. The reference to R. Zerahiah, and other remarks, indicate that the letter, or this part of it, was written a few years before Judah's death (about 1190).
9. Hippocrates (460–377 or 359 B.C.E.), the celebrated Greek physician, the Father of Medicine.
10. Jer. XXXV.
11. The daughters of Judah removed from Lunel after their marriage.
12. Josh. I. 8.

30

Maimon ben Joseph's Letter of Consolation

ABOUT the year 1158 Rabbi Maimon ben Joseph, member of the Rabbinical Court of Cordova, an eminent talmudist, astronomer and mathematician, accompanied by his daughter and two sons, Moses and David, arrived in Fez, the capital of Morocco. He and the members of his family were refugees from the bitter persecution to which in the middle of the twelfth century the Jews of Spain along with the Christians and dissident Moslems were subjected at the hands of the Almohades (Moslem Unitarians), the followers of Abdallah ibn Tumart. The whole peninsula having fallen under their sway, no other choice was left to those who did not leave the country but martyrdom or acceptance of Islam. Many Jews embraced Islam, at least in public, salving their consciences with the reflection that the strict monotheism of Ibn Tumart was after all not so far removed from Judaism. Maimon had tried to save himself and his family from this desperate alternative by wandering from Cordova hither and thither, and sailing at length to North Africa. The reason why he chose Fez, the centre of the power of the Almohades, as his abode is unknown, but it was just on this dangerous spot that he even raised his voice in order to strengthen the spirit of the afflicted Jews.

In 1160 he composed a letter in Arabic which, as he says in the introduction, he 'sent to one of his brethren that it might be a source of consolation for himself, and of delight for many souls which were perplexed on account of the sorrows of captivity . . . for day succeeded night, and night day, and still men were slain for their obedience to God and for their adherence to His law'. Maimon's 'Letter of Consolation' tries to heal the wounds of his people, to bring them comfort and confidence. Its language is subtly adopted to the perplexed spiritual outlook of those to whom it was addressed; the author did not hesitate to use Moslem terms, as for instance calling Abraham the Mahdi of God (an expression indicating the leader whose coming is expected by the Mohammedans), or speaking of Moses as the apostle. What Yellin and Abrahams have said about a special passage of the letter we may apply to the whole work: it is 'one of the finest expressions of tolerance which medieval literature can show'.

The following reproduction of the letter is a considerably abridged version of the original.

MAIMON BEN JOSEPH TO ONE OF HIS BRETHREN

'The cord of the ordinances of God and His Law is suspended from heaven to earth, and whoever lays hold of it is relieved from sinking to the pit. . . . He who clings to it with all his hand has, doubtless, more hope than he who clings to it with a part of it, and he who clings to it with the tips of his fingers has more hope than he who lets it go altogether'

[Fez, 1160]

May God lead thee in the way He desires, and remove thee from that which He abhors. May He direct thee in the straight path, and may He make the angels of His people an assistance for thee, assisting thee to do that which He desires, and which the Law demands of thee, in accordance with that which He has promised His saints by the hands of his prophets. 'The Lord is good and upright, and therefore He shows sinners the way!'[1]

Know then that it is clearly and distinctly laid down in the writings of the prophets and the comments of the rabbis that God is true, that the messages He has sent to us are true, and that which generation after generation has handed down to us is true. In these there is no doubt, no defect, no lie, no deception. God knew that which exists before it came into existence and all events pre-exist in His knowledge. He does not desire a thing and then contemn it; He does not favour and then reject. It is only man, from whom the knowledge of the future is hidden, who desires a thing, and then when something happens which he did not anticipate, contemns it. But how can He, whose knowledge of every event preceded the happening of that event, and who brings to pass every event in accordance with His will, how can He wish a thing and then hate it? How can He first distinguish a people and then reject them? This is an impossibility for God, and so God spake to one who declared it to be possible: 'God is not a man that He should lie.'[2] And Samuel also said, 'The strength of Israel will not lie.'[2a] And now that we have seen that God chose a people, and distinguished them and inclined to them His favour, and drew near to them as He had drawn near to none of His creatures before or afterwards, we know that God's knowledge of His people preceded His choice, and that He knew that they would have faith, and adhere to His commandments in the beginning and at the end.

And it is necessary that we should rely upon God, and believe in Him, and not doubt His promises, just as we do not doubt His existence, nor should we fear that He will cast us off when He has promised to draw us near unto Him, nor should the great prosperity of the nations terrify us, or what they assert, or what they hope for, because we confide in God, and put faith in His promises. And in spite of their victory over us, and their anger against us, and our subjection to them, and the renewal of our calamities with the renewal of day and night . . . we must still reflect upon that which He has promised us, and upon that which we hope, and then the weary souls will have rest, and their fears be allayed, for there must needs be repose and healing after this unhappiness, there must needs be enlargement after this straitness.

And a man must strive his best secretly and publicly in whatever he has to perform of the Law and obey of the commandments, whether those commands refer to the duties of the heart or to the external duties, to lay hold of the cord of the Law and not loosen his hand from it, for one in captivity is like one who is drowning. We are almost totally immersed, but we remain grasping something. Overwhelmed with humiliation and contumely and contempt, the sea of captivity surrounds us, and we are submerged in its depth, and the waters reach our faces, and we are left in dire extremities, such as David, peace with him, describes when he says, 'Save me, O God; for the waters are come in unto my soul.'[3] The waters are overwhelming us, but the cord of the ordinances of God and His Law is suspended from heaven to earth, and whoever lays hold of it has hope, for in laying hold of this cord the heart is strengthened, and is relieved from the fear of sinking to the pit and to destruction. But he who loosens his hand from the cord has no union with God, and God allows the flood of waters to prevail over him, and he dies. And according to the manner of his taking hold of the cord is his relief from the fear of drowning. He who clings to it with all his hand has certainly more hope than he who clings to it with part of it, and he who clings to it with the tips of his fingers has more hope than he who lets it go altogether. So none are saved from the toils of captivity except by occupying themselves with the Law and its commentaries, by obeying it, and cleaving to it, and by meditating thereon continually, and by persevering therein day and night in accordance with the words of David, 'Unless Thy law had been my delight, I should then have perished in my affliction . . .'[4]

One who is devout does not set too much store by the events of this world. If all goes well with him he is not elated, and if things do not go well with him he is not depressed, for he is without understanding who desires this world with a desire which draws him away from God. What health can there be for him who is not whole with his Master? What pleasure for him who is not warned by punishment? And what rest for him who has no continued existence in the world? And how can man hope for the attainment of his desires in a thing in which lies his own death; and how can he hope to attain them by pursuing ends which cause a separation between himself and his Master?

But he who is prudent looks to his Master, and strives by means of union with God to be happy, cleaving to God, being contented in this world with little when it is difficult to attain much, nay, being contented with a mere trifle. Should we however wish for plenty we should seek for it in the manner God has enjoined upon us, although the attaining of its limit is to our own hurt. Therefore reflection and firmness are necessary, for man ever toils and strives for himself and for naught else.

And one of the strongest means of union between man and his Creator is to carry out faithfully the obligation imposed upon him of praying three times every day, in the morning out of gratitude to God for sending the dawn, in the midday, the time of the declining of the sun from the east to the west, and also at the end of the day. And of this we find traces since the existence of day and night. Our Rabbis have handed down traditions[5] concerning the first fathers. Abraham, peace be with him, was particular with the morning prayer. He watched for the coming out of the sun, and then placed himself before God, as it is said, 'And Abraham got up early in the morning.'[6] And Isaac was particular with the afternoon prayer. He used to watch for the beginning of the seventh hour of the day in order to pray, as it is said, 'And Isaac went out to meditate in the field at the eventide,'[7] and Jacob was particular with the evening prayer when the stars appeared, as it is said, 'And he lighted on a certain place, and tarried there all night.'[8] But still all of them offered up all three prayers, for although every good man performs all commandments of God, there is still one upon which he lays special stress; Abraham laid special stress on the morning prayer because he was the first of the true believers, and because it was he who, as giver of light to the world and Mahdi, was the means of bringing the dawn. And Isaac, the second of God's messengers, laid stress on the second prayer, and Jacob the third, on the third; and the pious of our faith never neglect the three prayers, and he who is good prays the three, or two, or one at least as it happens to him, but no one ever desists altogether from uttering prescribed prayer, and when David knew the excellence of prayer he described himself and those who like him were diligent in prayer, seldom neglecting it, as follows: 'Evening and morning, and at noon-day will I complain.'[9] And Daniel, peace be with him, describes how particular he was with these three prayers, when he says, 'And he kneeled upon his knees three times a day, and prayed,'[10] and he risked his life by praying when the Persians and the Medes prohibited all prayers on his account, hoping that he would fall, and he did fall, but God did not allow any harm to come to him.

And when the form of prayer was not yet fixed, the three later prophets, Haggai, Zechariah and Malachi, peace be with them, with a hundred and twenty elders, arranged for us a prayer in which the learned and the ignorant might be equal, the learned adding nothing to it, the unlearned omitting nothing from it, and this prayer is the 'Eighteen Blessings'; but this prayer is arranged for those who are in a condition of safety, but for times and places of danger they also arranged a short prayer, that men might not be left without prayer entirely.... And he who does not know the whole prayer should pray the abridged one at the appointed time, and not remain without prayer altogether, for those who do not join the practice of prayer and those who separate themselves from religion altogether are alike....

And he who is able should utter the abridged prayer in Hebrew, as follows: the whole first part 'O Lord, open Thou my lips', till the end of 'And Thou art holy', and the last three blessings in full, but the middle blessings abridged, after the following version of our Rabbis.[11] 'Give us understanding, O Lord, to know Thy ways, and mould our hearts to fear Thee; pardon us, that we may be redeemed. Keep us far from disease, and grant us the bounteous fruits of the earth; gather our outcasts from the four corners of the earth; they that stray from Thy wishes shall be judged, and over the wicked wilt Thou stretch Thy hand; the righteous shall rejoice in the building of the city, and the establishing of Thy Temple in the springing up of the house of David Thy servant, and the rekindling of the lamp of the son of Jesse, Thine anointed; and Thou wilt hearken to our prayers; blessed [art Thou] who hearest.'

This is sufficient in time of necessity as a substitute for 'And Thou graciously bestowest knowledge', and the following blessings, and it may be uttered by the worshipper whether standing or sitting, if there be an excuse to sit, but there is a still more abridged prayer for times of pressing danger in the well-known words of our Rabbis.[12] If we utter this prayer, we need not repeat either the first three or the last three blessings, and he who does not know it in Hebrew may say it in Arabic, and such prayer is sufficient for him, because prayer is permissible in any language, especially if the contents of the prayer are those prescribed by our Rabbis, though translated into Arabic....

In the sight of God there is nought more powerful than prayer, for when the intention of a man is sincere, the heart pure, believing in God and His apostle, then his faith is sound, his belief correct, and he finds favour in the sight of God, and God averts from him misfortune, and he obtains mercy from God, and consolation, and his end is assured him, and he escapes from the fire, and he is worthy of resurrection and the reward of the righteous and the divinely promised bliss. And this is true even if he is one who cannot read and is ignorant. But for those who know and read the law, and occupy themselves with understanding its lessons, there are higher degrees and higher rewards. As he increases in goodness, his reward increases if, in addition to knowledge, he has religion and true faith in God. Dost thou know the dignity of him who was sent to thee, and of the message with which he was sent, for it is indeed great? For if thou know but a portion of the majesty which God bestowed on him, and how He favoured him above all mankind, thy faith in him would be unshakable, and through thy faith in him thou wouldest be firm in God.

Moses was a prophet in whose creation there was the evidence of the strength of God, for God created him in the most beautiful form, as the Scriptures bear testimony. . . .

Moses was a prophet whose body was purified till it became as the body of Michael and Gabriel, but stronger, for those were of light, not of flesh or blood, nor of sinew or matter; but this mortal man entered among thousands of angels of fire, one of whom could have put the earth in flames, how much more all of them! He clave his way amongst them, and ascended above them, and beheld the light of God in ways which, if I were to describe them even approximately, no intellect could grasp. And to this God himself bears testimony in the words 'And Moses drew near unto the thick darkness where God was . . .'[13]

Contemplate the prophet who was sent to thee, and that with which he was sent, and his position. And what was the aim of his message? That he might be an apostle to thee, and urge thee to obedience. And if the Law which he promulgated had to be believed merely on account of his own greatness, which we have already described, it would still have been necessary to believe it; how much more must we believe it when that Law contains the commands of the Creator and His ordinances. Gratitude and cleaving to God are necessary, on account both of Him who sent and him who was sent. And how great is the glory both of the sender and the apostle! So let not him whom God brings near put himself afar off, and let not him to whom Moses is the apostle neglect himself; and in the greatness of the apostle thou mayest understand the dignity of Him from whom he was sent. . . . But in spite of his position before God and his nearness to him, he was the gentlest and most humble of mankind, as Scripture bears testimony when it says of him in the name of God, 'Now the man Moses was very meek, above all the men who were upon the face of the earth . . .'[14]

And when the approach of death was announced to him, this did not terrify him, nor did he consider it a great calamity, but he devoted himself to his people and said to God, 'Let me not die till Thou appointest over them those who shall lead them, for I am jealous on their account, lest I should die and not know who shall be their leader to superintend their affairs.' Then God said to him, 'Appoint Joshua,' and Moses appointed him, and he rejoiced thereat, for he knew his character, and he strengthened him and he presented him to the people, and began to charge him concerning them.

And when the Song[15] was revealed to him, and in it there was made known all that would happen to Israel in the long captivity . . . he was deeply moved, and when he saw that at that time there would be no one to intercede, no one to pray, no one who would be fit to pray, and that no man of learning would be left among them, and that all would be equal in their wickedness, he was troubled. . . . And when Moses knew their degraded condition, and it was said to him when he had recited his prophecy concerning Israel, 'Go up into Mount Abarim and die there,'[16] then Moses (peace be with him) arose and prayed for all Israel who should be driven into captivity, and when he saw that there was no good man fit to bear the name 'the man of God', he uttered 'The prayer of Moses the man of God' . . .[17] He included in it a prayer for all the vicissitudes which should befall Israel from the beginning of the captivity till its end, and a hope that God would deal gently with them, and cause their punishment to descend in gentleness and not in wrath, and that He would not root us out, nor let us pass away from Him, but that He would forgive us, and return to us even as He was in times gone by, and that He would gladden our hearts and give us patience to bear our calamities during the length of the captivity, and that He would repel from us the evil the nations would inflict upon us, and the evils of every persecutor, and that He would still the waves of the seas which surround us, for the nations among whom we are dispersed encompass us about. And he included in this prayer a reference to all which had been, and all which was to be during the existence of the world. . . . If we consider attentively every verse of this prayer we shall find that all God's promises to us and all His prophecies are contained in it. And after God had accepted his intercession on our behalf He made every prophet who came after him utter the same prophecies, showing thereby that God had accepted his request, and He sent prophets to us telling us of those favours that Moses desired, and He promised that He would grant them. This prayer foretells all our calamities, and it has been for us a help, a support and a refuge, a bulwark upon which we could rely, a perfect protection, an impregnable fortress to which we could escape in the hour of sorrow, for we are like a lamb which wandered astray, amongst the thickets, or which forgot the place of its pasture, or was lost in the forests. . . .

And I have for many years taken upon myself the duty of reading every day 'The Prayer of Moses the man of God' before the reading of the Hundred Blessings . . . thereby drawing near to God in the very words used by the best of mankind. . . . And I used to wonder why this prayer came to be handed down from generation to generation, even to the days of David, who gave it a place in the Psalms. . . . Then I considered the whole of the Psalm, and its secret was made clear to me, that Moses had uttered it with reference to the time of captivity, and that David had placed it in the Book of Psalms that it might be a source of comfort and consolation to the followers of our faith. . . . And the following is a commentary on the carefully chosen words of the prayer.

[Only the opening and one central passage are quoted here from this extensive commentary.]

'O Lord, Thou hast been our refuge[18]. . .' O God, our God, Thou art our refuge to which we fly, generation after generation, when we are conquered and dispersed amongst our enemies, when misfortune overtakes us, and there is no king to order our affairs, and no adviser to guide us, and no place of safety whither we can flee, and no army wherewith we may be protected, and no power even to speak, when we are deprived of every resource, then the victories of our enemies and our inability to answer make us dumb as if we were speechless, as if we were unable to open our mouths. . . . And when all resources are cut off and all our hopes are frustrated, there is no escape but to Thee. We call and Thou assistest, we cry and Thou answerest, for Thou art our refuge, as it is said, 'O Lord, Thou hast been our refuge . . .'

. . . And when the best of mankind saw by means of the wonderful inspiration which was granted to him, and by means of his superb intellect, the innermost meaning of things, but still was unable to comprehend the captivity, he exclaimed, 'Who knoweth what will be the power of Thine anger, and just in proportion as man should fear Thee, so is Thy anger?'[19] And when we shall be sunk in the deep mire, do not cut us off entirely. . . . Do not deprive us of the light of Thy Law, and give us wisdom as a substitute for a prophet, who shall prophesy unto us, and supply us with a wise heart, whereby we may understand Thy Law, and be at rest in it. . . .

And this is what our great prophet prayed for on our behalf

before his death. And when we say his 'death' we must not liken it to the death of other mortal men. His corpse remained pure even in death. His eye did not grow dim, and its moisture did not abate. He was as if he were in a sleep, for God appeared to him as usual. The light of God kissed the pure mouth with which He had so often been addressed and caressed its pure words which He made binding even upon Himself. . . .

And after he presented his intercession on our behalf he recited his blessings, and when he finished them, he said farewell to Israel and ascended heavenwards, and his Creator hid him till a time shall come when He shall be pleased with this world, and then He will send him back to it, to assist the king who is to reign in the strength of God, that beloved one of God to whom testimony is borne in the verse 'Thou art my son, this day have I begotten thee.'[20] And this intercession has smoothed for us all the rugged ways of captivity, and it is the strong fortress in which we can take refuge in the time of misfortune until the time shall come which God has appointed for our deliverance, for the fulfilment of His promises to us.

Therefore reflect upon our letter, and what it teaches. May thy faith be perfected. May thy knowledge be freed from error. The fundamental truths which we have placed before thee are sufficient for thee to rely upon. Reflect, then, upon what they demand of thee so that thou mayest become righteous in the sight of thy Creator. It is necessary that this prayer, which I have commented upon, should be treasured up by thee, and that thou shouldest read it every morning and seek a blessing for thyself in its pure words, thus uniting thyself to God by means of the prayer offered up by the best of men and the greatest of prophets, for there is no prayer better than this. And if men had only known its contents, and the fundamental truths which God has established in it for the strengthening of our religion and the purifying of our faith, they would have made it obligatory upon themselves every day, just as they did the reading of the Shema. I have therefore briefly made clear to thee its contents, so that thou mayest be guided in what I have pointed out to thee, and that thou mayest follow the course I have outlined, and may God guide all of us to understand its contents and to know His wishes; and may He cause His redemption to draw near in our days, and establish in our time that which He has promised us, and may He enlighten our darkness as He has assured us, 'And His glory shall be seen upon thee.'[21] And so may it be God's will.

The unshakable confidence of the Jew in the divine promises, his firm belief in the unique greatness of Moses, the consolatory power of the traditional prayers – all the emotional elements of Judaism have rarely been expressed in so sincere and moving a manner. And yet the historic significance of this extraordinary document rests not more on its own merits than on the fact that its author was the father of the man through whom the name Maimon became immortal. The appearance of Moses Maimonides was indeed the perfect fulfilment of the desire which Maimon ben Joseph had expressed in his letter when he complained that the people of Israel were without an adviser to guide them, that they were speechless and unable to open their mouths, and when he asked for 'wisdom as a substitute for a prophet who shall prophesy unto us, and, for a wise heart, whereby we may understand the Law, and be at rest in it'.

NOTES

1. Ps. xxv. 8.
2. Num. xxiii. 19.
2a 1 Sam. xv. 29.
3. Ps. lxix. 2.
4. Ps. cxix. 92.
5. Berakoth 26b.
6. Gen. xxix. 27.
7. Gen. xxiv. 63.
8. Gen. xxviii. 11.
9. Ps. lv. 18.
10. Daniel vi. 11.
11. Berakoth 29a.
12. Berakoth 29b.
13. Exod. xx. 21.
14. Num. xii. 3.
15. Deut. xxxii.
16. Deut. xxxii. 49, 50.
17. Ps. xc.
18. Ps. xc. 1.
19. Ps. xc. 11.
20. Ps. ii. 7.
21. Is. lx. 2.

31

Letters of Maimonides

No spiritual leader of the Jewish people in the post-Talmudic period has exercised such an influence on his own generation and on posterity as Moses son of Maimon, usually called Maimonides or Maimuni, born in Cordova in 1135. In his monumental work, 'Mishneh Torah', he created a new codification of Jewish law which gained general recognition among the dispersed people. His thirteen articles of faith, both in the original wording and in the poetic form, the popular hymn Yigdal, have outlived all later attempts to enlarge or to restrict the foundations of Judaism. And it was Maimonides whose great philosophical treatise 'Moreh Nebukim' ('The Guide of the Perplexed') established a lasting link between faith and reason, and safeguarded the Jewish notion of God against any danger of anthropomorphism.

Maimonides also marks an epoch in Jewish letter-writing. He made the most intensive use of correspondence and considered the exchange of letters as a part of his life work. His influence on the Jews of his days was due, perhaps, to an even greater degree to the extensive correspondence which he carried on with all parts of the Jewish world than to his strictly literary activity. It was above all by his letters that, as a contemporary said of him, Maimonides 'made Israel again one people and brought one to the other so that they became one flesh'. (See also Introduction, pp. lx. f.) Fortunately, a considerable part of this correspondence has been preserved. A cross-section only of these glorious records can be offered by the following selection.

1. *Maimonides defends the Pseudo-Apostates*

This letter, in which Maimonides first introduced himself to the reading public, owed its origin, like that of his father already quoted (pp. 166ff), to the persecution of the professing Jews by the Almohades. In a Responsum circulating among the North-West African Jews in those days, an anonymous rabbinical authority had declared that a Jew who uttered the formula of Mohammedan confession could no longer be regarded as a member of the Jewish community, even if he was strictly and faithfully carrying out the duties of a Jew and offering Jewish prayers in secret. The young Maimonides, then living in Fez, felt himself touched to the quick by this pronouncement, possibly because he himself had belonged to the pseudo-Moslems ('Anusim'), at least for a short period, though this is still an unsettled question. He realized the harm which the dictum of the zealot might do to his co-religionists by plunging them into despair and complete apostasy, and to save them from this danger he wrote his great Arabic epistle 'Maamar Kiddush ha-Shem', known to subsequent generations as the 'Iggeret Hashemad' (Letter concerning Apostasy). The central part of it, somewhat condensed, runs as follows.

MAIMONIDES TO THE JEWS OF MOROCCO

'Any Jew who, after uttering the Moslem formula, wishes to observe the whole 613 precepts in the privacy of his home may do so without hindrance'

[Fez, about 1160]

Thus says Moses son of Maimon the Judge, the Sephardi:

God is a witness that if he who uttered these reproaches [viz. those made in the Responsum of the anonymous Rabbi referred to by Maimonides in the opening passages of the letter] against us had confined them solely to us, yea, if he had uttered more, we should not have sought help for ourselves; we should have said: 'Let us lie in our shame, and let our confusion cover us, for we have sinned against the Lord our God.'[1] 'We know, O God, that we have done wickedly . . .'[2] But as disgrace has been brought on whole communities, and as it has been asserted that those who pray in these times are committing a transgression, I am not allowed to remain silent. For what once has been stated in writing spreads among people and gains followers. Many false opinions have been caused by nothing else but the mere fact of their having been put down somewhere. Thus I became apprehensive lest many who live under the present oppression might become perplexed if confronted with that condemnation. Will they not, in the belief that they are apostates, that to pray is a sin for them and that even if they perform good works it is not pleasing in the sight of God – will they not leave off praying altogether and neglect even those religious duties which they can perform in spite of oppression? That is why I feel obliged to point out the errors of that learned man. . . .

He does not distinguish between those who sin under compulsion and those who do so from sheer wickedness. Such a harsh judgement is untenable. It contradicts Scripture and the testimonies of the past. The children of Israel, before they left Egypt, were, with the exception of the tribe of Levi, submerged in sin. And yet Moses himself was punished because he suspected the faithfulness of the people.[3] Elijah the prophet, too, was blamed by the Lord when he inveighed against the apostasy of Israel.[4] In the days of Isaiah many people became idolaters and evildoers who despised God and religion, but Isaiah's accusation was atoned for only by his death at the hand of Manasseh.[5] If thus Israel's great men have been punished because they maligned Israel, how can an ordinary man dare to assail whole communities and their scholars? They have not strayed from the law because of their evil passions, but because they were threatened by swords and bows, while they in their heart revere God and keep his ordinances.

The statement that all good works performed by the Anusim are without merit and hope of reward is even worse than the previous mistake. It is erroneous to maintain that one who has entered a mosque, without praying there, and later went home and prayed to God, would not find his prayers answered. Ahab, King of Israel, who had denied God and worshipped idols, but afterwards fasted two hours and a half and prayed to God, was rewarded for this single act. The Talmud says that his prayers were accepted and that God had mercy upon him.[6] Even Nebuchadnezzar, who was guilty of the massacre of numberless Jews and the destruction of the Temple, was allowed to reign as long as King Solomon, because he honoured the Lord on one occasion. If God recompensed those evildoers, will He not take into account the good works performed by Israel in a forced pseudo-apostasy?

For all these reasons I made up my mind to confute those false opinions by arguments gathered from Scripture and ancient writings. I shall lay down five main principles:

First: the capital offences – idolatry, unchastity and murder –

have to be avoided everywhere and under all conditions, even at the cost of martyrdom. . . .

Second: we have to avoid Hillul ha-Shem,[6a] the desecration of the Holy Name; this means a sin committed not through mere sensuality but out of a deliberate rejection of religion, or by such a neglect of our duties towards our neighbours that we cast dishonour on our name.

Third: whoever in these cases has yielded to coercion instead of suffering death has acted badly, but no punishment has been imposed upon such deeds and no Jewish court can intervene against him. . . .

Fourth: the present persecution differs from previous experiences. In former cases, Israelites have been called upon to transgress the Law in action. Now we are not asked to render active homage to heathenism but only to recite an empty formula which the Moslems themselves know we utter insincerely in order to circumvent the bigot. . . . Indeed, any Jew who, after uttering the Moslem formula, wishes to observe the whole 613 precepts in the privacy of his home, may do so without hindrance. Nevertheless, if, even under these circumstances, a Jew surrenders his life for the sanctification of the Name of God before men, he has done nobly and well, and his reward is great before the Lord. But if a man asks me, 'Shall I be slain or utter the formula of Islam?'[7] I answer, 'Utter the formula and live! . . .'

The advice I give to myself, to those I love, and to those who ask my opinion, is that we should go forth from these places, and go to a place where we can fulfil the Law without compulsion and without fear, and that we should even forsake our homes and our children, and all possessions. Divine Torah means more for the prudent than all ephemeral possessions; these will vanish, but she will remain. . . .

I have no patience with people who console themselves with the thought that the Messiah will soon appear and lead them to Jerusalem. They who remain in the country, expecting the Messiah, are causing others to transgress the Law. Besides, there is no definite time for which the appearance of the Messiah is foretold. It is not known whether his coming will be in the near future or at some remote period. A sincere wish to observe the Jewish law has no relation to the appearance of the Messiah. If God would grant us the privilege of witnessing that great event it would be well. If not, we should not lose faith but should continue in the observance of the Jewish tradition.

Fifth: although he who yields to coercion and continues to live in such a state has to consider himself as one guilty of having shown contempt for religion, he should nevertheless not abandon the hope that God will reward the good works performed in this state, and even double his reward because he exposed himself to danger. . . .

'Like a skilful physician,' say Yellin and Abrahams in their classical biography of Maimonides, 'who accurately diagnoses his patient's symptoms, he at first soothed the sufferer, then roused him to a sense of his condition. He saved Judaism from absorption into Maghreb (the West) by persuading the pseudo-Moslems that they had not lost their inheritance in the God of Israel.' It may perhaps even be said that Maimonides has written in the 'Iggeret Hashemad' a great confession for many generations to come and the prologue to the long and tragic history of the Marranos.

2. *Maimonides comforts the Jews of Southern Arabia*

Twelve years after writing the 'Iggereth Hashemad' for the Jews of Morocco, Maimonides was called upon to perform a similar service for the Jews of Yemen, on the Red Sea. He had, in the meantime, after a short stay in the Holy Land, settled in Egypt, where the Jews, under the rule of the Fatimids and, soon afterwards, under that of the great Saladin, enjoyed religious freedom and prosperity. At first Alexandria, then – from 1167 – Cairo was the residence of Maimonides. Here alarming news reached him from Yemen, where, after the downfall of the Fatimids in Egypt, a régime had been instituted by the Shiite sectarians resembling in its fanaticism that of the Almohades. The Jews were again the chief victims of these changes within the Mohammedan sphere, and, like their brethren in Western Africa, had to face the tragic choice between apostasy and martyrdom. Internal dissensions aggravated their plight. While a learned Jewish convert tried to prove that the coming of Mohammed was foretold in the Bible, a Jewish enthusiast proclaimed himself as the forerunner of the Messiah. In their perplexity the Yemenite Jews, through their representative Jacob al Fayumi, turned for advice to Maimonides, whose fame had spread to Arabia. The letter which Maimonides wrote in reply has become celebrated under the title of 'Iggeret Teman' (Letter to the South) or 'Petach Tikvah' (Gate of Hope). It is of considerable length, and only a portion can be reproduced here.

MAIMONIDES TO JACOB AL FAYUMI AND TO THE JEWS OF YEMEN

'My brethren, it behoves us to keep ever present before our minds the great day of Sinai, that stupendous occurrence which stands in very deed alone in the annals of mankind. From this lasting memory we must draw our power to strengthen our faith even in a period of persecution and affliction.'

[Cairo, 1172]

'Strengthen ye the hands which are weak, and the knees that stumble make ye firm.'[8]

Moses son of Maimon sends greetings to the wise-hearted and much esteemed R. Jacob son of Nathaniel al Fayumi, and to the faithful brethren of South Arabia, whom may God take under His protection now and evermore. . . . May the Lord sustain you in your righteous endeavours, that ye may always be distinguished as adherents of His covenant. Amen.

As to your letter, respected Rabbi, which was sent to me while in Egypt, and which has afforded me exceeding pleasure, the whole purport attests your fidelity to the mission you were called to perform. You evidently serve God with alacrity, keeping watch over His Law. May the Heavenly Giver of the Torah unfold before your eyes its sacred treasures, and may the light emanating therefrom guide you aright.

What you remark in the same letter, that some of our brethren hold me in high esteem, I consider a token of kind feelings on their part. But you, please, listen to me, and heed not what others say. I am among the least of the scholars that Spain has produced. Overwhelmed with cares, and exposed to frequent setbacks through our sore dispersion, I endeavoured nevertheless to gather knowledge, like the gleaner working slowly behind the reapers. Had it not been for the help obtained from on high, even the little I possess would not have been acquired. But my pupil, R. Solomon Cohen, exaggerates when he alludes to my learning. The affection he bears me – and which I reciprocate – has warped his judgement. Still, I pray that the Lord may gladden him as he seeks to do me honour.

And now let me deal with the rest of the contents of your epistle. I reply to it in the Arabic language, in order that all may easily understand, for all are concerned in what I shall communicate. The news that the government under which you live ordered all Jews in South Arabia to apostatize, in the same manner as the ruling Powers in Western countries have acted towards us, made us turn pale with terror. The whole community shares your grief, for the report is truly one at which 'the ears of him that hears it must tingle'.[9] Our minds are bewildered; we feel unable to think calmly, so terrible is the alternative in which Israel has been placed on all sides, from the East and from the West. . . .

Now, my Brethren! You must lend your attention, and hearken to what I am about to set forth, so that you may impart it to women and children, and they be confirmed in their belief. Let all doubts vanish, and confidence in the unchangeable word of the Lord take deep root in the hearts of all of us, through celestial assistance.

Know for certain, that what we believe in is the Law of God given through the father of the prophets. That by its teaching the heavenly Legislator intended to constitute us an entirely distinct people. The selection was not due to our inherent worth. Indeed we have been distinctly told so in the Scriptures. But because our progenitors acted righteously through their knowledge of the Supreme Being, therefore we, their descendants, reap the benefit of their meritorious deeds.

Be assured, my Brethren, that our three opponents, namely, the system of coercion, that of sophistry, and that which seeks to impress by claiming a high origin to which it is not entitled, will vanish. They may continue to prosper for a certain period, but their glory will be evanescent. We have the infallible promise of the Almighty, that decrees aiming at our apostasy or destruction will be brought to naught. . . . In fact, the Divine declaration to Jacob may be said to prefigure our chequered national life. He was told, 'Thy seed shall be like the *dust* of the earth.'[10] Now, dust is trodden upon by all, and still increases in volume; dust is stamped upon at will, but it rises above him that treads it. Even so would it be with Israel. They would be levelled with the ground, yet augment in numbers. They would be pressed down, and still be uplifted beyond the reach of their oppressors. . . .

Our Brethren of the house of Israel, scattered to the remote regions of the globe, it is your duty to strengthen one another, the older the younger, the few the many. Raise your joint voices ever again in faithfulness which shall never fail, proclaiming that God is a Unity, that Moses is His prophet, who spoke with Him; that he is the master and most perfect of all prophets, that to him was given to attain a knowledge of the Supreme which none can ever reach; that the Torah is from beginning to end the communication of the Almighty to His faithful servant, as proved by the sentence, 'Mouth to mouth do I speak with him'[11]; that nothing was to be changed, nothing to be added to or diminished from it, and that no other Law than this will ever come from the Creator.

My Brethren, it behoves us to keep ever present before our minds the great day of Sinai, for the Lord has forbidden us ever to forget it. Rear your offspring in a thorough understanding of that all-important event. Explain before large assemblies the principles it involves, show that it is a lucid mirror reflecting the truth: aye, the very pivot on which our religion turns. . . . Know, moreover, you who are born in this covenant and raised in this belief, that the stupendous occurrence, the truth of which is testified by the most trusty of witnesses, stands in very deed alone in the annals of mankind. For a whole people heard the word of God and saw the glory of Divinity. From this lasting memory we must draw our power to strengthen our faith even in a period of persecution and affliction such as the present one.

My Brethren! Hold fast to the covenant, be immovable in your convictions, fulfil the statutes of your religion. . . . Rejoice ye that suffer trials, confiscation, contumely, all for the love of God, all to magnify His glorious name. It is the sweetest offering you can make. . . . Should ever the necessity of fleeing for your lives to a wilderness and inhospitable regions arise – painful as it may be to sever oneself from dear associations, or to relinquish one's property – you should still endure all, and be supported by the consoling thought that the Omnipotent Lord who reigns supreme, can recompense you commensurately to your deserts, in this world and in the World-to-Come. Verily, some of our predecessors acted so while merely in search of truth. They would leave their dwelling places and move far away where they conceived that a greater light might irradiate their minds; that they might gain a deeper insight into the character of our legislation, and be drawn thereby closer to its heavenly Giver. If so, why should we hesitate to abandon country and kindred for the sake of upholding the whole Torah? It often happens that a man will part from kindred and friends and travel abroad, because he finds his earnings inadequate to his wants. How much more readily ought we to follow the same course, when we stand in danger of being denied the means to supply our *spiritual* necessities! . . .

With regard to what you reported, that the adversary seeking your apostasy seduces people by trying to show that several words in the Torah can be explained as alluding to the rise of Mohammed, and that in the same book even his name is mentioned, you may rest assured that this theory is not only untenable and preposterous, but supremely ridiculous. . . . The apostates themselves laugh at the idea, but they wish to deceive the Gentiles by pretending to believe. . . . They know that proofs of such a character cannot stand the test of investigation. . . .

Now, what you mention in your letter, in reference to the final restoration, and respecting what Rab Saadia wrote on the subject[11a], needs some remarks, which I submit.

First of all, I will candidly say that the precise time in which the outcasts will be gathered none can possibly find out. For Daniel told us, 'The things are closed up and sealed till the time of the end.'[12] Nevertheless, several of our wise men have searched and imagined that they have discovered what is hidden; thus confirming what the Holy Writ predicts. 'Many will run [mentally] to and fro, and knowledge shall increase,'[13] meaning that opinions will be advanced, according to the diversity of minds, and the depth of learning. But the Almighty has explained by means of His prophets that some may set a period for the advent of the Messiah, and the period will pass away frustrating all expectations, and therefore He cautioned us against despairing on that account – nay, He desired that the further the realization of our ultimate gathering seemed, the stronger should be our hope. It is written: 'For, the vision is yet for the appointed time, but at the end it shall speak, and not lie; though it tarry, wait for it, because it will surely come, it will not delay.'[14]. . . However, we must judge Rab Saadia favourably, for perhaps he indulged in such speculations, despite the prohibition, only to oppose harmful views entertained by his contemporaries, and leading to the entire desertion of the Law. For had it not been for him who undertook in writing, as well as by speaking, to expound the tenets of our faith, Judaism might have been cast into the pit of oblivion. . . .

Concerning your expectations based on what the Arabic School terms 'the science of the stars and their conjunctions', let me advise you that you dismiss them altogether. Cleanse your mind of that impurity, cast it off as you would remove filthy garments. It is a mental hallucination, and in that light it has been regarded by men of intelligence, not of our belief, and more so, of course, by the recipients of the Divine Law. . . . What you say touching our future restoration, that in the opinion of some it will happen when the seven planets[15] come together in the same sign of the Zodiac, is totally false. Such a phenomenon cannot take place.

So much for the science of astrology! But our sufferings have been prolonged, doubtless, for a purpose known unto the Lord. On Him, O my Brethren, your reliance must be placed. Let your hearts be filled with glowing hope, and strengthen one another in the belief that the redeemer *will* come and not delay. . . . The Almighty has announced through Isaiah, the herald of our national felicity, that because of the lengthy and sore captivity many will imagine that Providence has cast us away altogether, but he immediately endeavoured to correct that error, and to show that we shall never be rejected by our God. . . . And by the first prophet of our people, the Most High foretold us the same: 'The Lord thy God will restore thy captivity, and have mercy on thee, and gather thee again from all the peoples whither the Lord thy God has scattered thee.'[16] This, my Brethren, is a cardinal point in our religion; I mean that there will rise a man of the direct descent of David, who will gather our outcasts, roll away our shame, and put an end to our exile. He will make the law of truth triumphant. He will cause those to perish who oppose it. . . .

As to the period at which the expected occurrence will happen, we may infer from the words of Daniel, of Isaiah and other prophets and Sages, that it will be when Christianity and Mohammedanism will grow exceedingly powerful and spread their dominions, as at present, into distant countries. Such will, no doubt, be the case. . . . Respecting the precise period of our restoration we have been kept in ignorance.

. . . About certain signs of which you speak, they are unworthy of the attention of the learned. Do not direct your thoughts to what is irrelevant, and do not waste your words concerning it.

I am not at all surprised to hear of the transactions in South Arabia of the man who proclaims himself the Messiah, nor of the credulity of his adherents. The man is beyond doubt demented. His actions are therefore the effect of his disease, over which he has no control, and those who put faith in him are benighted and cannot form a right idea of the character of the Messiah. . . . But I am surprised at you, who possess learning, and who must have read what the Rabbis have taught. Are you not aware that the personage who is to redeem Israel from their suffering must prove himself greater than all prophets, with the exception of Moses? . . . Besides, the indispensable qualities laid down by the Rabbis for the character of the redeemer of the outcasts are wisdom, vigour and riches, which have further been defined as follows. He must be wise in forecasting the course of events, strong in holding his passions under proper control, and rich in mental resources. . . . Now the signs of the man's poverty of intellect are at once discernible in his conduct of his assumed Messiahship. For he ordered all money to be distributed for charity, thus unwittingly committing a sin, by contradicting the Bible, and leading the stupid people who follow his advice in the path of error. For the Law commands that we bestow only a portion of our substance on the needy. The Sages commenting on the passage 'Any thing that a man devotes to the Lord of what he has . . . is most holy to the Lord',[17] say, *of* what he has he may give, but he must not give *all* he has. Our ancient teachers have moreover set a limit to our freewill offerings by laying it down as a rule that none is called upon to devote to beneficent purposes more than the fifth part of his property. I feel satisfied in my mind that the same folly which led the man to declare himself the Messiah moved him likewise to counsel that the wealthy should enrich the poor, and thus impoverish the rich, a condition of things which would necessitate, of course, a constant exchange, the recipients returning the money to the donors to prevent being made opulent at the expense of the others. The whole plan is the height of nonsense.

Regarding the manner in which the Messiah will present himself, and the place where his operations will begin, let me offer some information. It would seem that the land of the patriarchs is destined to be first trodden by his steps. . . . But touching his presentation to our notice, it will not happen until events shall prove him worthy of our confidence. I mean, that he will not commend himself to our allegiance by reason of his distinguished descent, but the marvellous deeds he shall perform will show him to be the expected Messiah. . . . And after having revealed himself in the Holy Land, having gathered the dispersed in Jerusalem and received recognition from countries nearer to Palestine, the fame of our nation through him will spread eastward and westward, reaching at length you of South Arabia, and those still further in India, who will acknowledge the mission of our leader. . . .

The prophets intimated that when the auspicious period of our redemption was nigh, some would attempt to pass off as true Messiahs, but their projects would be abortive, and productive of evils to themselves and Israel. Because Solomon foresaw that our nation, weary with a long captivity, would try to anticipate the time of its deliverance, and suffer trials through doing so, he figuratively wrote this passage: 'I adjure you, O daughters of Jerusalem, that you will not awaken, that you will not stir up the [Divine] love, until it pleases [to arouse itself].'[18]

Now, beloved Brethren! accept his adjuration, and act accordingly. And let me pray that the beneficent Creator may remember us and you, and gather His heritage and His portion to Himself; that suffering Israel may be drawn up out of the depth of misery, be restored from utter darkness to refulgent light, and again behold the splendour of Divinity and visit His temple. . . .

May peace be with you, dear and esteemed friend, who are noted for your learning and talents, and peace be with all our brethren, both learned and unlearned, for ever and ever. Amen.

And now I beg that you will send a copy of this letter to every congregation, to those who are possessed of knowledge in Israel and to others, so that they may be strengthened in their faith, and may remain unwaveringly steadfast. Read it publicly, and become one of those who bring many to righteousness.

Only be exceedingly careful that the Gentiles do not hear a word of it, lest they use it as an opportunity for renewing their violent attacks from which may God always save us. Indeed, after having written it, I became afraid that perhaps it might be attended with ill results. Yet the thought of confirming my co-religionists in their faith prevailed, and I overcame my apprehension. Nevertheless, I confide the letter to you as a secret; and I trust that, as our Rabbis, who received instruction from the prophets, said, even so will it happen in the present instance, namely that 'Those who go on a meritorious errand, will not meet with harm.' And surely there can be no greater merit than that attached to what you are about to undertake.

Peace to all Israel. Amen.

This letter fully accomplished its object. The people of Yemen were inspired by it to remain true to their religion, and the opinion of Maimonides on the false Messiah also came true when the unhappy man challenged the king to decapitate him, and the promised miracle that he would survive the stroke did not occur. A change of government in the year 1174 finally brought relief to the Yemenite Jews. They expressed their gratitude to Maimonides in a unique manner – by inserting a complimentary reference to him in the daily Kaddish.

3. *A Private Letter to Palestine*

During the first years of his stay in Egypt, Maimonides suffered one misfortune after another. First his father died. Then his beloved brother David too perished tragically. Perfidious denunciations and material losses aggravated these ordeals. But Maimonides emerged from them victoriously. After being left, through the death of his brother David, without any income, Maimonides, true to the principle of the Fathers that one should not use the Torah as a means of livelihood, took up the practice of medicine in order to earn a living for himself and the family of his brother. He acquired such fame in this profession that eventually he was appointed physician to Alfadhel, the Vizir of Saladin, while at the same time being recognized by the Jews of Egypt as the head of their community.

The following letter gives an admirable summary of these events. It shows Maimonides in his purely personal relations, and reveals a deep sensitiveness which one would hardly have expected in a man so absorbed in intellectual pursuits. The addressee, Rabbi Japhet ben Eliahu of Akko, had been the host of Maimonides and his family when they visited Palestine.

MAIMONIDES TO JAPHET BEN ELIAHU

'Were not the study of the Torah my delight . . . I would have succumbed in my affliction'

[Cairo, 1176]

I received your dear letter, but its contents surprised me. You complain that I have not written to you and have not asked about your welfare since I left the country of Glory. You, who want to admonish me, deserve, indeed, admonition yourself; you were untrue to other people, and not other people to you. A few months after our separation, my father and teacher died, and I received letters of consolation from the remotest corners of Spain and North Africa; you, however, took no notice at all of this event.

In Egypt I met with great and severe misfortunes. Illness and material losses came upon me. In addition, various informers plotted against my life. But the most terrible blow which befell me, a blow which caused me more grief than anything I have experienced in my life, was the death of the most perfect and righteous man[19] who was drowned while travelling in the Indian Ocean. Many goods that belonged to me, to him and to other people, were lost with him. He left with me his widow and a little daughter.

For nearly a year after I received the sad news, I lay ill on my bed struggling with fever and despair. Eight years have since passed, and still I mourn, for there is no consolation. What can console me? He grew up on my knees; he was my brother, my pupil. He was engaged in business[20] and earned money that I might stay at home and continue my studies. He was learned in the Talmud and in the Bible and an accomplished grammarian. My one joy was to see him. Now my joy has been changed into darkness: he has gone to his eternal home, and has left me prostrated in a strange land. Whenever I come across his handwriting or one of his books, my heart grows faint within me, and my grief reawakens. In short: 'I will go down into the grave unto my son mourning.'[21] Were not the study of the Torah my delight, and did not the study of philosophy divert me from my grief, 'I should have succumbed in my affliction.'[22]

Nevertheless I complain of no one, neither scholar nor pupil, nor of any acquaintance or friend, and not even of you, who would have deserved more reproaches than all of them. It is long since we four, my father, my brother, you and myself, wandered to the holy places. In the meantime you have not asked one word about us. I would, therefore, certainly be justified in failing to answer you. But I have kept my love for you in my heart, and shall never forget those days when we walked together through the wilderness seeking God. . . .

4. *Maimonides answers Questions*

The Jewish world had suddenly found a new centre: the home of Rabbi Moses ben Maimon in Fostat, the Old City of Cairo. Letters from all corners of the Diaspora arrived in the study of the famous sage, letters filled with praise and admiration, but also with questions and requests for advice. Maimonides never failed to answer. Some of his Responsa assumed the character of complete treatises, like the epistle to the scholars of Marseilles on the study of astrology, wherein Maimonides makes a remarkable distinction between astrology and astronomy, ascribing to the latter only true scientific value. There were, however, other Responsa, which combine great scholarship with the charm and intimacy of personal letters, as the following examples may testify.

(A)

The Responsa on the equality of the proselytes with Jews by birth

The Jewish law of the stranger, placing as it does the 'Ger' on the same footing as the native, is one of the most admirable features of Judaism. It found in Maimonides a congenial commentator. The letters in which he deals with this subject are striking examples of his humanity and breadth of mind. The passage castigating a Jewish scholar for his intolerance towards the Moslems has been called by Yellin and Abrahams 'Maimuni's perhaps most remarkable utterance'.

MAIMONIDES TO OBADIAH THE PROSELYTE

'While we are the descendants of Abraham, Isaac and Jacob, you derive from Him, through whose word the world was created'

[Cairo, last quarter of the 12th century]

Thus says Moses the son of Rabbi Maimon, one of the exiles from Jerusalem, who lived in Spain:

I received the question of the master Obadiah, the wise and learned proselyte, may the Lord reward him for his work, may a perfect recompense be bestowed upon him by the Lord of Israel, under whose wings he has sought cover.

You ask me if you, too, are allowed to say in the blessings and prayers you offer alone or in the congregation: '*Our* God' and 'God of *our* Fathers,' 'Thou who hast sanctified *us* through Thy commandments,' 'Thou who hast separated *us*,' 'Thou who hast chosen *us*,' 'Thou who hast inherited *us*,' 'Thou who hast brought *us* out of the land of Egypt,' 'Thou who hast worked miracles to *our* fathers,' and more of this kind.

Yes, you may say all this in the prescribed order and not change it in the least. In the same way as every Jew by birth says his blessing and prayer, you, too, shall bless and pray alike, whether you are alone or pray in the congregation. The reason for this is, that Abraham, our father, taught the people, opened their minds, and revealed to them the true faith and the unity of God; he rejected the idols and abolished their adoration; he brought many children under the wings of the Divine Presence; he gave them counsel and advice, and ordered his sons and the members of his household after him to keep the ways of the Lord forever, as it is written, 'For I have known him to the end that he may command his children and his household after him, that they may keep the way of the Lord, to do righteousness and justice.'[23] Ever since then whoever adopts Judaism and confesses the unity of the Divine Name, as it is prescribed in the Torah, is counted among the disciples of Abraham, our father, peace be with him. These men are Abraham's household, and he it is who converted them to righteousness.

In the same way as he converted his contemporaries through his words and teaching, he converts future generations through the testament he left to his children and household after him. Thus Abraham, our father, peace be with him, is the father of his pious posterity who keep his ways, and the father of his disciples and of all proselytes who adopt Judaism.

Therefore you shall pray, 'Our God' and 'God of our fathers', because Abraham, peace be with him, is *your* father. And you shall pray, 'Thou who hast taken for his own our fathers,' for the land has been given to Abraham, as it is said, 'Arise, walk through the land in the length of it and in the breadth of it; for I will give it unto thee.'[24] As to the words, 'Thou who hast brought us out of the land of Egypt' or 'Thou who hast done miracles to our fathers' – these you may change, if you will, and say, 'Thou who hast brought Israel out of the land of Egypt' and 'Thou who hast done miracles to Israel.' If, however, you do not change them, it is no transgression, because since you have come under the wings of the Divine Presence and confessed the Lord, no difference exists between you and us, and all miracles done to us have been done as it were to us and to you. Thus it is said in the book of Isaiah, 'Neither let the son of the stranger, that hath joined himself to the Lord, speak, saying, "The Lord hath utterly separated me from His people." '[25] There is no difference whatever between you and us. You shall certainly say the blessing, 'Who hast chosen us,' 'Who hast given us,' 'Who hast taken us for Thine own' and 'Who hast separated us': for the Creator, may He be extolled, has indeed chosen you and separated you from the nations and given you the Torah. For the Torah has been given to us *and* to the proselytes, as it is said, 'One ordinance shall be both for you of the congregation, and also for the stranger that sojourneth with you, an ordinance for ever in your generations; as you are, so shall the stranger be before the Lord.'[26] Know that our fathers, when they came out of Egypt, were mostly idolators; they had mingled with the pagans in Egypt and imitated their way of life, until the Holy One, may He be blessed, sent Moses, our teacher, the master of all prophets, who separated us from the nations and brought us under the wings of the Divine Presence, us and all proselytes, and gave to all of us one Law.

Do not consider your origin as inferior. While we are the descendants of Abraham, Isaac and Jacob, you derive from Him through whose word the world was created. As is said by Isaiah: 'One shall say, I am the Lord's, and another shall call himself by the name of Jacob.'[27]...

MAIMONIDES TO AN INQUIRER

'In the case of "strangers" we are bidden to love with the whole force of our heart's affection'

[Date as above]

... When your teacher called you a fool for denying that Moslems are idolaters he sinned grievously, and it is fitting that he ask your pardon, though he be your master. Then let him fast and weep and pray; perhaps he will find forgiveness. Was he intoxicated that he forgot the thirty-three passages in which the Law admonishes concerning 'strangers'? For even if he had been in the right and you in error, it was his duty to be gentle; how much more, when the truth is with you and he was in error! And when he was discussing whether a Moslem is an idolater, he should have been cautious not to lose his temper with a proselyte of righteousness and put him to shame, for our sages have said, 'He who gives way to his anger shall be esteemed in thine eyes as an idolater.' And how great is the duty which the Law imposes on us with regard to proselytes. Our parents we are commanded to honour and fear; to the prophets we are ordered to hearken. A man may honour and fear and obey without loving. But in the case of 'strangers' we are bidden to love with the whole force of our heart's affection. And he called you fool! Astounding! A man who left father and mother, forsook his birthplace, his country and its power, and attached himself to this lowly, despised, and enslaved race; who recognized the truth and righteousness of this people's Law, and cast the things of this world from his heart – shall such a one be called fool? God forbid! Not witless but wise has God called your name, you disciple of our father Abraham, who also left his father and his kindred and inclined Godwards. And He who blessed Abraham will bless you, and will make you worthy to behold all the consolations destined for Israel; and in all the good that God shall do unto us He will do good unto you, for the Lord hath promised good unto Israel. . . .

(B)

The Responsum on the share of the Gentiles in the World-to-Come

The following passage, an excerpt from a lengthy responsum, in which Maimonides answered various philosophical questions of Hasdai ha-Levi, a Spaniard of European reputation, shows another facet of the tolerance of Maimonides, who demolishes here the prejudice which would deny to the Gentiles ability to achieve the state of blessedness.

MAIMONIDES TO HASDAI HA-LEVI

'. . . every man who ennobles his soul with excellent morals and wisdom based on the faith in God certainly belongs to the men of the World-to-Come'

[Date as above]

. . . As to your question about the nations, know that the Lord desires the heart, and that the intention of the heart is the measure of all things. That is why our sages say, 'The pious men among the Gentiles have a share in the World-to-Come,'[27a] namely, if they have acquired what can be acquired of the knowledge of God, and if they ennoble their souls with worthy qualities. There is no doubt that every man who ennobles his soul with excellent morals and wisdom based on the faith in God, certainly belongs to the men of the World-to-Come.[28] That is why our sages said, 'Even a non-Jew who studies the Torah of our master Moses resembles a High Priest.'[28a] What is essential is nothing else than that one tries to elevate his soul towards God through the Torah. Thus said David, 'I put the

Lord always before me; because He is on my right hand I do not waver.'[29] And Moses is praised for this reason: 'This man was very humble'[30] because this is the height of perfection. Our sages said also, 'Be exceedingly humble.'[31]. . . And the philosophers declared that it is very difficult to find a man who is completely perfect in morality and wisdom. He in whom this perfection is found is called a Saint, and surely such a man is on the steps which lead to the higher world. . . . Besides, there is no doubt that the Patriarchs as well as Noah and Adam, who obviously did not observe the Torah, by no means became denizens of Gehinnom.[32] On the contrary: as they achieved what pertains to the ennoblement of man they are raised aloft. All this cannot be secured by fasting, praying and lamentation if knowledge and true faith are absent, because in such behaviour God can be near to the mouth but far from the heart. The basis of all things is [knowledge] that nothing is eternal save God alone. . . .

(c)

Maimonides instructs a correspondent who intends to study the 'Mishneh Torah'

Like every epoch-making work, the 'Mishneh Torah', Maimuni's code, aroused not only enthusiasm but also opposition. Among its most bitter critics was Samuel ben Ali, head of the Talmudic College of Baghdad, who tried to revive the lost authority of the Gaonate by decrying Maimonides' talmudical learning and in particular by charging him with disbelief in Resurrection.

Maimonides found a staunch supporter in a comparatively unlettered resident of Baghdad, to whom he gives some advice in the following letter.

MAIMONIDES TO JOSEPH IBN GABIR

'It makes no difference whether you study in the holy language, or in Arabic or Aramaic'

[Cairo, 1191]

I gather from the letter of the esteemed Mar Joseph called Ibn Gabir that he regrets being an am-ha-aretz [ignoramus],[33] because he knows Arabic only but not Hebrew and that he, therefore, while studying our Commentary to the Mishnah[34] with great zeal, is unable to read our code 'Mishneh Torah'. He reports further in that letter that some scholars in Baghdad reject some of my decisions. I have been asked for the benefit of learning to give my opinion in my own handwriting. I am going to fulfil these requests herein.

First of all I must tell you, may the Lord keep and increase your welfare, that you are not justified in regarding yourself as an 'am-ha-aretz'. You are our beloved pupil; so is everybody who is desirous of studying even one verse or a single Halakah.[35] It makes also no difference whether you study in the holy language, or in Arabic or Aramaic; it matters only whether it is done with understanding. This is the important thing whichever language may be used in the commentaries or in the summaries. But of the man who neglects the development of his spirit it is said: '. . . he has despised the word of the Lord'[36]; this applies also to a man who fails to continue his studies even if he has become a great scholar, for the advancement of learning is the highest commandment. I say, therefore, in general, that you must not belittle yourself nor give up the intention of improving. There are great scholars who did not begin their studies until an advanced age, and who became scholars of distinction in spite of this.

If you want to study my work you will have to learn Hebrew little by little. It is not so difficult, as the book is written in an easy style, and if you master one part you will soon be able to understand the whole work. I do not intend, however, to produce an Arabic edition, as you suggest; the work would lose its specific colour. How could I do this, when I should like to translate my Arabic writings into the holy language! In any case, you are our brother; may the Lord guard you, lead you to perfection and grant you the happiness of both worlds. . . .

The statement you have heard, namely that I deny in my work the resurrection of the dead, is nothing more than a malicious calumny. He who asserted this is either a wicked man who misrepresents my words, or an ignorant one who does not understand my views on *Olam Haba*[36a]. In order to make impossible any further mistake or doubt, I have composed in the meantime a special treatise on this subject.

You mention also an objection made against me concerning the sign of the covenant which by some is considered not as a Mosaic law but as a tradition dating from the time of Abraham. My opponents rely in this regard upon a Talmudic sentence according to which the Lord, on the occasion of that commandment, made a thirteen-fold covenant with Abraham. This objection is futile, and the pretended evidence shows that those people do not understand the foundations of our religion in the least. My explanation is right. That commandment as well as, for example, the prohibition of the sinew[37] belongs also to those 613 Sinaitic commandments which, although they existed in earlier times, were transmitted by Moses; they have been in force as religious prescriptions since the time of Moses. Ask those people who cite in evidence against me the 'Thirteen-fold covenant' made with Abraham, those blind men who pretend to be seers, ask them if Abraham himself had perhaps written that commandment together with all the verses of Scripture referring to this matter, in such a way that Moses had nothing more to do than to copy them as we are wont to copy an ancient work of another author, or if the verses concerned belong to the Torah through having been composed by Moses for the first time under inspiration? Whoever does not believe the latter alternative denies that the Torah is of divine origin. – The matter is clear, but unknown to people who have never reflected and who, instead of considering the roots of religion, look upon its branches. The Torah in its totality has been given to us by the Lord through Moses; if ancient laws are comprised in it, as, for instance the Noahide laws[38] and the above-mentioned prescriptions, we are not bound by them because they were observed in former times, but because they have become obligatory for us since the general legislation. . . .

I have been informed – although I do not know whether it is true – that there is, in your city, somebody who speaks evil against me, and tries to gain honour by misrepresentation of my teaching. I have heard also that you protested against this, and reprimanded the slanderer. Do not act in this way! I forgive everybody who is opposed to me because of his lack of intelligence, even when he, by opposing, seeks his personal advantage. He does no harm to me. . . . While he is pleased, I do not lose anything. . . . You trouble yourself with useless quarrels, as I do not need the help of other men, and leave it to the people to follow their own will.

May the Lord help you to serve Him in all sincerity, may He lead all your doings and words to His name. May your peace and the peace of the Elders and disciples be great. May our God bless them.

Moses son of Maimon may his memory be blessed.

The Responsum on listening to Music

After the destruction of the Temple the Rabbis placed a ban on secular music – save on Purim and for weddings – which lasted into the Middle Ages. In the time of Maimonides, however, the public was already chafing at the restriction, as is shown by an inquiry submitted to him by an unknown questioner: 'Is it lawful to listen to the singing of the ballads of the Arabs, and to the reed-pipe?' The answer of Maimonides is an important supplement to his views expressed in other writings. It shows that, as a sound psychologist, he appreciated music as a means for the elevation of the soul: what he disapproved of was not listening to music but indulging in frivolity.

(D)

MAIMONIDES TO AN INQUIRER

'. . . that which is aimed at in us is that we should indulge neither . . . in the stirring up of the sensuous faculties to the neglect of all that is good, nor in letting them loose in diversion and play'

[Cairo, between 1190 and 1204]

It is well known that the reed-pipe and the rhythmus, all of them, are forbidden, even apart from such *dicta* as that 'The ear that listens to the reed-pipe shall be cut off.'[39] And the Talmud has explained[40] that there is no difference between listening to the reed-pipe and hearing stringed instruments chanting of melodies apart from prayer, and it is proper to mortify the soul and unlawful to soothe it.

And they [the Rabbis] base themselves on the prohibition of the Prophet who said: 'Rejoice not, O Israel, for joy, as other people!'[41] And we have explained the cause of that thoroughly; namely because it behoves us to tame the sensuous faculty, to repress it, and tighten its rein; not that it should be stimulated and excited. And one should not judge by an individual who is exceptional and rarely to be found, whose mind music renders more subtle and apprehensive and impressionable for the perception of a *noumenon* or submission to religious duties. Legal wisdom prescribes only for the majority and the ordinary because 'the wise have spoken concerning what ordinarily happens'.[42] The prophets have, therefore, prohibited the use of instrumental music even for devotional purposes, saying: 'They that chant to the sound of the viol, and invent to themselves instruments of music like David [shall go into captivity].'[43]

And we have already explained in the Commentary on Abot that there is no difference between Hebrew and Arabic words: both are prohibited or permitted in accordance with the meaning intended in the words. And in reality it is the hearing of folly that is prohibited, even if uttered by stringed instruments. And if such are sung with accompaniment there would be three prohibitions: (1) the prohibition of listening to folly; (2) the prohibition of listening to singing, I mean making music with the mouth; and (3) the prohibition of listening to stringed instruments. And if it were that the listening occurred in a wine shop there would be a fourth prohibition, as in the saying of the Most High: '[Woe unto them that rise early in the morning, that they may follow strong drink: that continue until night, till wine inflame them!] And the harp, and the viol, the tabret, and pipe and wine are in their feasts.'[44] And if the singer be a woman, then there is a fifth prohibition according to the saying of the Rabbis, 'The voice of a woman excites sensual desire.'[45] Then how much [greater the prohibition] if she is singing.

And the undisputed truth is that that which is aimed at in us is that we should be a 'holy nation', and that we should indulge neither in work nor word except in the pursuit of perfection, or what leads to perfection; not in the stirring up of the sensuous faculties to the neglect of all that is good, nor in letting them run loose in diversion and play.

And we have explained this sufficiently in the 'Dalalat',[46] in the last part of it, with words that will carry conviction to the worthy. And that which the blessed Geonim permitted is the setting of melody to songs and praises, as the blessed author of the 'Halakoth'[47] said. As for improper subjects in them – God forbid! This was not heard in Israel, either from Gaon or illiterate person. And the wonder is at your saying, 'in the presence of pious persons', for, in my opinion, they are not pious so long as they attend wine bouts. And we have explained enough regarding that also in the 'Dalalat'.

That is what seems right to us regarding instruments of music. And peace.

Thus wrote Moses [son of Maimon]

5. *Maimonides dedicates 'The Guide of the Perplexed' to Joseph ben Judah ibn Aknin*

In his later years Maimonides formed a friendship of extraordinary strength and intimacy with Joseph, son of Judah ibn Aknin, a native of Ceuta (Morocco) – poet, philosopher and physician – who, like Maimonides, was a fugitive from the persecution of the Almohades. He had chosen Egypt as his place of refuge, among other reasons, in order to associate with Maimonides. Arriving in Alexandria when he was about thirty years of age, Aknin introduced himself to the master in a letter accompanied by some poems. 'Maimonides recognized in his correspondent a kindred mind and welcomed Aknin with a cordiality that soon ripened into love. "If I had none but thee in the world, my world would be full," said Maimonides. Master poured out his heart to pupil, and when Aknin was forced to leave Cairo for Aleppo, the bond between "father" and "son" was so firmly tied that their friendship endured unto death' (Yellin-Abrahams).

Aknin stayed in Cairo less than two years, devoting himself to philosophical and mathematical studies under the guidance of Maimonides. In Aleppo he established a highly successful medical practice, but continued to devote himself to science, philosophy and poetry. He kept in close touch with Maimonides, and frequently consulted him on his religious difficulties, notably on the burning question of the day, whether reason could be overridden by revelation, or whether both were of equal authority. These questionings prompted Maimonides to write, in Arabic, his famous philosophical work 'The Guide of the Perplexed' ('Moreh Nebukim', originally, in Arabic, 'Dalalat al-hairin') as is explained in the following dedicatory letter.

MAIMONIDES TO JOSEPH BEN JUDAH IBN AKNIN

'Your absence has prompted me to compose this treatise for you and for those who are like you'

[Cairo, about 1189]

In the name of God, Lord of Universe!

To R. Joseph, may God protect him, son of R. Judah may his repose be in Paradise!

My dear pupil, from the moment that you resolved to come to me from a distant country, and to study under my direction, I formed a high opinion of your thirst for knowledge and your fondness for speculative pursuits, which found expression in your poems. I refer to the time when I received your writings in prose and verse from Alexandria. I was then not yet able to test your powers of apprehension, and I thought that your desire might possibly exceed your capacity. But when you had gone with me through a course of astronomy, after having completed the [other] elementary studies indispensable for the understanding of that science, I was more than ever gratified by the acuteness and the quickness of your apprehension. Observing your great fondness for mathematics, I let you study them more deeply, for I felt sure of your ultimate success. Afterwards, when I took you through a course of logic, I found that my great expectations of you were confirmed, and I considered you fit to receive from me an exposition of the esoteric ideas contained in the prophetic books, that you might understand them as they are understood by men of insight. When I commenced by way of hints, I noticed that you desired additional explanations and urged me to expound some metaphysical problems; to teach you the system of the Mutakellemim[48], to tell you whether their arguments were based on logical proof; and if not, what their method was. I perceived that you had acquired some knowledge in those matters from others, and that you were perplexed and bewildered; yet you sought to find a solution to your difficulty. I urged you to desist from this pursuit, and enjoined you to continue your studies systematically; for my object was that the truth should present itself by proper stages, and that you should not hit upon it by mere chance. Whilst you studied with me I never refused to explain difficult verses in the Bible or passages in rabbinical literature which we happened to meet.

When, by the will of God, we parted, and you went your way, our discussions aroused in me a resolution which had long been latent. Your absence has prompted me to compose this treatise for you and for those who are like you, however few they may be. I have divided it into chapters, each of which shall be sent to you as soon as it is completed. Farewell!

During the following years Maimonides sent one chapter after another to Joseph (see below, Letter No. 6), so that the 'Guide' is in a way one gigantic philosophical letter. He repeatedly emphasizes the fact that in the first place the 'Guide' was destined for Aknin personally, whom he frequently apostrophizes as 'My son'. It was Aknin to whom Maimonides referred in the emphatic statement of the Introduction:

> 'When I find the road narrow, and can see no other way of teaching a well-established truth except by pleasing one intelligent man and displeasing ten thousand fools, I prefer to address myself to the one man, and to take no notice whatever of the contemplation of the multitude.'

Of the nature of a letter are also some remarks towards the end of the book itself in which Maimonides instructs his pupil how to achieve the highest perfection by 'performing his duty of the permanent and intensive contemplation of God' (Simon Rawidowicz, *Philosophy as Duty*):

The first thing you must do is this: Turn your thoughts away from everything while you read Shema or during the Tefillah, and do not content yourself with being devout when you read the first verse of the Shema, or the first paragraph of the prayer. When you have successfully practised this for many years, try in reading the Law or listening to it to have all your heart and all your thought occupied with understanding what you read or hear. After some time when you have mastered this, accustom yourself to have your mind free from all other thoughts when you read any portion of the other books of the prophets, or when you say any blessing; and to have your attention directed exclusively to the perception and understanding of what you utter. . . .

When you are alone by yourself, when you are awake on your couch, be careful to meditate in such precious moments on nothing but the intellectual worship of God, viz., to approach Him and to minister before Him in the true manner which I have described to you – not in hollow emotions. This I consider the highest perfection wise men can attain by the above training. . . .

6. *Maimonides advises Joseph ibn Aknin not to make his living from the Torah*

About 1190 Aknin proceeded to Baghdad with the intention of establishing there a talmudical school where the views of Maimonides should be accepted as authoritative, and so counteracting the influence of his opponent Samuel ben Ali. Maimonides expressed his attitude to this plan in the following closing passages of a letter in which he refuted the current misrepresentations of his views about resurrection.

MAIMONIDES TO JOSEPH IBN AKNIN

'It is better for you to earn a drachma as wages for the work of a weaver, tailor or carpenter, than to be dependent on the licence of the Exilarch'

[Cairo, autumn 1191]

. . . With regard to your journey to Baghdad which you have mentioned, I do not oppose your intention of founding there a house of learning, delivering lectures and making legal decisions, always provided that they will be based on my Compendium. I am afraid, however, that you will be perpetually involved in troubles with those people, and that you will not be able to achieve any of your aims without great difficulty. Besides, if you devote yourself entirely to teaching, you will reduce your earning to nothing, and I cannot advise you to accept any reward from them. It is better for you to earn a drachma as wages for the work of a weaver, tailor or carpenter, than to be dependent on the licence of the Exilarch. If you quarrel with them, you will lose, and if you accept anything from them, you will humiliate yourself. My opinion is that you should pay full attention to your trade and medical practice, and at the same time continue the study of Torah according to the right method, i.e. by studying the Halakot of the Rab, of blessed memory,[49] and comparing them with my Compendium. If you find any disagreement you must know that it is necessary to go back to the Talmud and try to find the relevant passages there. If, however, you spend your time on commentaries and explanations of obscure passages of the Talmud, I must tell you that these are things which cause much waste of time and little gain. But whatever you may choose as your occupation, let me know of it, and may the Lord guide you to find the right way! . . .

Do not withhold your letters to me, for I have nobody whom I love more than you. . . . All our friends send you greetings. The Sheikh Abu-Ma'ali,[50] his brother, and our son Abul-Rida,[51] in fact all the people of my house, freemen and slaves, look forward with great pleasure to good news from you, and wish most sincerely that your affairs may be settled in the way which would suit you and us most. Convey our best regards to your father-in-law, the venerable, God-fearing, faithful and upright Sheikh, the reverend and holy Rabbi Joshua, the man who stood the test, the fame and pride of the Kohanim, may the Lord protect him, and convey also my best greetings to his son, through whom may the Lord increase his prosperity. May he see descendants and live long! Although one must be mindful of the ancient interdiction, 'never extend greetings to a woman', it is still permitted to offer her good wishes: Welfare to you and to your house, and 'when the time of revival comes, a son to Sarah!'[52]

May your welfare grow and prosper according to your wishes and the wishes of the writer of this letter.

Moses son of Maimon

7. *Maimonides describes his daily work and gives advice to Samuel ibn Tibbon on translating 'The Guide of the Perplexed'*

Although conceived and intended as a piece of private instruction for one individual and like-minded spirits, 'The Guide of the Perplexed' very soon became the most influential book of the Jewish world. Its fame spread to countries where the Jews did not understand Arabic, and a strong demand arose there for a translation of it into Hebrew. This task was undertaken by the Provençal scholar Samuel ben Judah ibn Tibbon (see *supra*, pp. 156–165), who took the precaution of consulting the author on a number of difficulties and at the same time expressed a desire to visit him. Maimonides replied in a letter containing some highly interesting information of a personal nature, revealing to us the physician, grammarian and philosopher, but, above all, Maimonides the man.

MAIMONIDES TO SAMUEL IBN TIBBON

'God knows that, in order to write this to you, I have escaped to a secluded spot, where people would not think to find me . . .'

[Cairo, 30 September 1199]

'A man shall be commended according to his wisdom.'[53]

All the letters of the worthy scholar and excellent sage, R. Samuel son of the learned R. Judah ibn Tibbon, the Sephardi, have duly reached me, Moses the son of Maimon, the Sephardi. Already many years ago the fame of the honoured prince, the wise R. Judah, your father, had reached me; I have heard of his great learning and the elegance of his style, both in Arabic and Hebrew, through well-known and learned men of Granada, the sons of Alfakhar[54], and the aged R. Ibn Mosca. Also one of

V. HEBREW LETTER OF A KHAZAR JEW, probably to Hasdai ibn Shaprut (tenth century), found in the Cairo Genizah, being the concluding part, lines 70–92.
(See p. 114 for the translation of lines 83–88.)

VI. TRADITIONAL PORTRAIT OF MOSES MAIMONIDES.

VII. AUTOGRAPH RESPONSUM OF MAIMONIDES.

VIII. TRADITIONAL PORTRAIT OF ISAAC ABRABANEL.

the learned men of Toledo came here and told me of his reputation. Likewise when the honoured R. Meir, a disciple of R. Abraham, the son of R. David, the great Rabbi of Posquières,[55] who had studied under the learned R. Abraham ibn Ezra, came to me, he [R. Meir] spoke concerning your father, and gave me an account of the works on grammar and other sciences he had translated. I did not, however, know that he had left a son. But when your letters in Hebrew and Arabic reached me, and I learned from them your clearness of mind and elegance of composition; when I read your remarks both on those passages in my *magnum opus*, the Moreh Nebukim, concerning the right signification of which you entertain doubt, and on those in which you have discovered errors made by the transcriber, then I said with the ancient poet[56]:

'Had they known his parentage, they would say,
The father's excellence has passed over to his son.'

Blessed be He who has bestowed His favour on your learned father and granted him such a son; and indeed not to him alone but to all wise men. For, in truth, unto us all a child has been born, unto us all a son has been given. This offspring of the righteous is a tree of life, a delight of our eyes and pleasant to look upon. I have already tasted of his fruit, and lo, it was sweet in my mouth even as honey.[57]

All your questions were just, and all your conjectures with respect to the omission of a word, or words, were correct. At the end of this epistle, I explain everything in Arabic, and give you all the information you desire, and mention the works you should study or neglect. You are thoroughly fitted for the task of translation, because the Creator has given you an intelligent mind to 'understand parables and their interpretation, the words of the wise and their difficult sayings'. I discern from your remarks that you have thoroughly mastered the subject, and that its inmost meaning has become clear to you. I shall explain to you in Hebrew how you shall manage with the entire translation. 'Give instruction to a wise man, and he will be yet wiser; be wise my son, and my heart also will rejoice.'[58]

Be assured that, when I saw the beauty of your style and noted the penetration of your intellect and that your lips utter knowledge clearly, I greatly rejoiced. I was surprised indeed to discover such talents, such a thirst for knowledge, such an acquaintance with Arabic (which I believe to be a partially corrupt dialect of Hebrew) displayed by one who has been born among 'stammerers'. I also admired your familiarity with the niceties of that language in abstruse subjects; this is indeed like a tender plant springing out of a dry ground. May the Lord enlighten your eyes with the light of His law, so that you may be of those that love Him, who are even as the sun when he goes forth in his strength. Amen.

The letters of your esteemed college, which God grant may ever increase in dignity and learning, reached me. I have carefully examined all the passages concerning the translation of which you entertain any doubt, and have looked into all those passages in which the transcriber has made any mistake, and into the various preliminary Propositions and Chapters which were not perfectly clear to you, and of which you sought elucidation.

Let me premise one rule. Whoever wishes to translate, and aims at rendering each word literally, and at the same time adheres slavishly to the order of words and sentences in the original, will meet with much difficulty; his rendering will be faulty and untrustworthy. This is not the right method. The translator should first try to grasp the sense of the passage thoroughly, and then state the author's intention with perfect clearness in the other language. This, however, cannot be done without changing the order of words, putting many words for one, or vice versa, and adding or taking away words, so that the subject may be perfectly intelligible in the language into which he translates. This method was followed by Honein Is'hak with the works of Galen,[59] and by his son Is'hak[60] with the works of Aristotle. It is for this reason that all their versions are so peculiarly lucid, and therefore we should study them to the exclusion of all others. Your distinguished college ought to adopt this rule in all the translations undertaken for those honoured men and the heads of the congregation. And may God grant that the spread of knowledge among the other communities of Israel be promoted by such works.

I now proceed to reply to your questions *seriatim*, to explain all those points which need explanation, to give the correct reading according to which you may amend the faults in your copy, arranged in the order of your epistle and embracing the three books of my work. [Here follow various explanations which refer to the most difficult portion of the 'Guide'].

God knows that, in order to write this to you, I have escaped to a secluded spot, where people would not think to find me, sometimes leaning for support against the wall, sometimes lying down on account of my excessive weakness, for I have grown old and feeble.

But with respect to your wish to come here to me, I cannot but say how greatly your visit would delight me, for I truly long to commune with you, and would anticipate our meeting with even greater joy than you. Yet I must advise you not to expose yourself to the perils of the voyage, for, beyond seeing me, and my doing all I could to honour you, you would not derive any advantage from your visit. Do not expect to be able to confer with me on any scientific subject for even one hour, either by day or by night. For the following is my daily occupation:

I dwell at Mizr [Fostat] and the Sultan[61] resides at Kahira [Cairo]; these two places are two Sabbath days' journey[62] distant from each other. My duties to the Sultan are very heavy. I am obliged to visit him every day, early in the morning; and when he or any of his children, or any of the inmates of his harem, are indisposed, I dare not quit Kahira, but must stay during the greater part of the day in the palace. It also frequently happens that one or two royal officers fall sick, and I must attend to their healing. Hence, as a rule, I repair to Kahira very early in the day, and even if nothing unusual happens. I do not return to Mizr until the afternoon. Then I am almost dying with hunger. . . . I find the antechambers filled with people, both Jews and Gentiles, nobles and common people, judges and bailiffs, friends and foes – a mixed multitude who await the time of my return.

I dismount from my animal, wash my hands, go forth to my patients, and entreat them to bear with me while I partake of some slight refreshment, the only meal I take in the twenty-four hours. Then I go forth to attend to my patients, and write prescriptions and directions for their various ailments. Patients go in and out until nightfall, and sometimes even, I solemnly assure you, until two hours or more in the night. I converse with and prescribe for them while lying down from sheer fatigue; and when night falls, I am so exhausted that I can scarcely speak.

In consequence of this, no Israelite can have any private interview with me, except on the Sabbath. On that day the whole congregation, or at least the majority of the members, come to me after the morning service, when I instruct them as to their proceedings during the whole week; we study together a little until noon, when they depart. Some of them return, and read with me after the afternoon service until evening prayers. In this manner I spend that day. I have here related to you only a part of what you would see if you were to visit me.

Now, when you have completed for our brethren the translation you have commenced, I beg that you will come to me, but not with the hope of deriving any advantage from your visit as regards your studies; for my time is, as I have shown you, excessively occupied.

Be careful not to study the works of Aristotle except with the help of his commentators, the commentary of Alexander,[63] Themistius[64] or Ibn Roshd.[65]

As a general rule I may tell you, study only the works on logic composed by the learned Abunazar Alfarabi,[66] for everything he has written is as fine flour. A man may indeed gain knowledge from his writings because he was a distinguished philosopher. So also Abubekr ben Alsaig[67] was a great philosopher; all his writings are plain to him that understandeth, and right to them that find knowledge.

The writings of Aristotle are the foundations upon which all these philosophical works are based, and, as I have said above, they can only be understood by the help of their commentaries. . . . But other works besides those here enumerated, such as the writings of Empedocles,[68] Pythagoras,[69] Hermes[70] and Porphyrius,[71] all belong to ancient philosophy; it is not right to waste time upon them. He, Aristotle, indeed arrived at the highest summit of knowledge to which man can ascend, unless the emanation of the Divine Spirit be vouchsafed to him, so that he attain the stage of prophecy, above which there is no higher stage.[72] And the works of Ibn Sina,[73] although they contain searching investigations and subtle thoughts, do not come up to the writings of Alfarabi. Still, they are useful, and it is right that you should study them diligently. I have now indicated to you the works you should study, and to which you should devote your mind.

May your happiness, my son and pupil, increase, and salvation be granted to our afflicted people.

Written by Moses, the son of Maimon, the Sephardi, on the 8th of Tishri 1511 according to the Seleucid era.

8. *Maimonides, complimented by the scholars of Lunel, pays tribute to their learning*

The pre-eminent position in the Jewish world gained by Maimonides during his lifetime procured for him many tributes, the most eloquent of which are to be found in letters addressed to him by Rabbi Jonathan, son of David ha-Kohen, the head of the Provençal congregation of Lunel. In one of them his achievement was compared with that of Moses the prophet. This comparison, which later became proverbial in the well-known saying 'From Moses unto Moses there arose none like Moses', was no mere compliment. Rabbi Jonathan showed his sincerity by sending Maimonides twenty-four questions arising out of the 'Mishneh Torah', and also asking that he should forward to Lunel a copy of his great philosophical work, 'The Guide of the Perplexed'. Another letter of the learned men of Lunel contained even a request for a Hebrew translation of the 'Guide'.

More than two years were to pass before the aged sage, whose health had been shattered by overwork, was able to write to Rabbi Jonathan and his friends. He then sent two letters to Lunel, in the second of which – perhaps the most pathetic of all his letters – he painted a gloomy picture of contemporary talmudical study, making a glorious exception of Lunel itself. Written with the presentiment of the approaching end, this letter may well be considered as the master's farewell.

(A)

RABBI JONATHAN OF LUNEL TO MAIMONIDES

'Our souls are linked with thy books in love. If they are here, everything is here'

[Lunel, about 1197]

Now I will arise before him who speaks and acts. . . . His soul is full of fear of God, righteousness and justice is his heart's desire. . . . Where is to be found a man like him? A man so full of divine vision? . . . He is unique – our teacher Rabbi Moses over whose head the sacred ointment is poured out,[74] the son of the venerated saint, Rabbi Maimon. . . . He is indeed entitled to bear the name Moses because he drew his people out of the waters[75] of error. . . . He has sown the seed of holiness, and removed the sway of impurity from his people. . . . With the light of his book, Mishneh Torah, he has illuminated the darkness of the world. . . . May the Lord protect him, and let him rise higher and higher. Amen. Amen.

Thou holy man of the Lord, our teacher and master, thou luminary of the exile, grant the request of thy servants who are eager to draw from thy well, and let us find nourishment in thy 'Guide of the Perplexed'! The energy of thy righteous spirit has not relaxed, and now thou hast surpassed all men. . . . Thou hast gained fame through the treasure of thy learning everywhere; thou hast established law and justice for the sons of Jacob, and pronounced judgement with truth and faithfulness. Thou hast bestowed knowledge, understanding and wisdom on the people of God . . . and placed beyond dispute even the laws of the moon and the stars. . . . The work of thy hands came to us like the dew of heaven.... Thou hast sent gifts to thy people in the days of thy strength, when the hand of the Lord directed thee.... They are desired everywhere, and no other goods can be compared to them. We approach thee, therefore, praying that thou send us also thy other books, in order that our dead may revive again. Our souls are linked with thy books in love. If they are here, everything is here. All is then certain, firm and true, we are not lacking in anything. There is no need for any other elucidation. The fountains of life rise from them.

With thee, illustrious man, and thy school, with the great and the little one, we feel connected in our souls. We bless thee on every Sabbath and in every month. But we are unable to repay truly all the good we have received from thee. Our Creator alone, who has made everything and in whose hands rest the souls of all living men, can reward thee. Let Him in His great mercy cause us to find grace with thy excellency, with thy sages, thy elders, and thy students, that they may satisfy our thirst, not the hunger for bread and the thirst for water, but for the word of the Lord. O Rock, help us! May the King hear us when we cry to Him, and enlighten our eyes in the darkness when we pray to Him, and may He heal the sickness of our hearts when we supplicate Him.

No weapon that is formed against thee shall prosper[76] and every tongue that shall rise against thee in judgement thou shalt split with the arrow of thy answer.... Thou wilt pardon those who ask thee, for thou art full of forgiveness and love to those who invoke thee. Thus may thy wisdom flow like rain....

(B)

MAIMONIDES TO THE RABBIS OF LUNEL

'You, members of the congregation of Lunel, and of the neighbouring towns, stand alone in raising aloft the banner of Moses'

[Cairo, 1199 or 1200]

I received your previous and present letters, signed by men of great distinction, and I send my greetings to all of you and to each of you. Your words and verses as well as your questions reveal your great love of the Torah, your zeal for learning and your desire of knowledge.

I have already apologized for the delay of my answer. I have dealt with your doubts, and am forwarding to you now the third part of the 'Guide of the Perplexed' in the Arabic language. However, with regard to your request that I may translate the text into the holy tongue for you – I myself could wish that I were young enough to be able to fulfil your wish concerning this and the other works which I have composed in the language of Ishmael, and I should be very pleased thus to free their superior from their inferior elements and to give back the stolen goods to the rightful owner. But I must blame the unfavourable times for preventing me from doing so. I have not even time to work out and to improve my commentaries and other works composed in the rabbinic language, which contain various obscurities, in order to arrange new editions – to say nothing of making translations from one language into another.

Yes, my honoured friends, I have no leisure even for writing a little chapter, and only for the sake of showing my respect to your congregation do I undertake to write you with my own hand.

But you have in your midst the learned and well instructed R. Samuel ben Judah [ibn Tibbon], on whom the Lord has bestowed the necessary insight and excellent penmanship for performing the translation you have asked for. I have already written to him about this subject.[77]

To you, my honoured friends, may you remain confident and strong, I have now to tell the truth: You, members of the congregation of Lunel, and of the neighbouring towns, stand alone in raising the banner of Moses. You apply yourselves to the study of the Talmud, and also cherish wisdom. The study of the Torah in our communities has ceased; most of the bigger congregations are dead to spiritual aims, the remaining communities are facing the end. In the whole of Palestine there are three or four places only, and even these are weak, and in the whole of Syria none but a few in Aleppo occupy themselves with the Torah according to the truth, but even they have it not much at heart. In the Babylonian Diaspora there are only two or three groups in Yemen, and in the rest of Arabia they know little of the Talmud and are merely acquainted with Agadic exposition.

Only lately some well-to-do men came forward and purchased three copies of my code which they distributed through messengers, in these countries, one copy for each country. Thus the horizon of these Jews was widened and the religious life in all communities as far as India revived. The Jews of India know nothing of the Torah, and of the laws none save the Sabbath and circumcision. In the towns of Berbery which belong to the realm of Islam, the Jews read the Torah and observe it according to its literal meaning. What was inflicted upon the Jews of Maghreb[78] as punishment for their sins you know. Thus it remains for you alone to be a strong support to our religion.

Therefore be firm and courageous for the sake of our people and our God; make up your minds to remain brave men. Everything depends on you; the decision is in your hands. Do not rely upon my support, because I am an old man with grey hair. And know that for this not my age but my weak body is responsible. . . .

A few years after this correspondence, Maimonides, in the seventieth year of age, died on 13 December 1204. The power of his spirit made itself felt even more strongly after his death than it had during his life. His reputation grew steadily as the centuries advanced, although his philosophical teaching met with sharp opposition from a considerable part of Jewry. For a hundred years an intense struggle raged between the Maimunists and anti-Maimunists (see below, pp. 248–59 and Introduction), but later generations never ceased to turn to Moses Maimonides for enlightenment and stimulation as to no other Jewish teacher of the Middle Ages.

NOTES

1. Jer. III. 25.
2. Ps. CVI. 6.
3. Num. XX. 12.
4. 1 Kings XIX. 15–18.
5. According to a Talmudic legend (Yeb. 49b) Isaiah was doomed to suffer death at the hand of Manasseh, King of Judah, because he had said, 'I dwell in the midst of the people of unclean lips' (Is. VI. 5).
6. Taanit 25b.
6a See above, Chapter 14, Note 5.
7. The formula read as follows: 'La ilaha illa Allah, wa-Muhammed rasul Allah'; i.e. 'There is no God but Allah, and Mohammed is the prophet of Allah.'
8. Is. XXXV. 3.
9. Jer. XIX. 3.
10. Gen. XXVIII. 14.
11. Exod. XXXIII. 11; Num. XII. 8.
11a Maimonides refers to Saadia's reflections on the time of Israel's Redemption in Chapter VIII of Emunot ve-Deot.
12. Dan. XII. 9.
13. Dan. XII. 4.
14. Hab. II. 3.
15. Viz. the Sun, Mercury, Venus, Mars, Jupiter, Saturn and the Moon.
16. Deut. XXX. 3.
17. Lev. XXVII. 28.
18. Song of Songs, II. 7.
19. Namely, his brother David.
20. Viz. with precious stones.
21. Gen. XLII. 38.
22. Ps. CXIX. 92.
23. Gen. XVIII. 19.
24. Gen. XIII. 17.
25. Is. LVI. 3.
26. Num. XV. 15.
27. Is. XLIV. 5.
27a Yalkut Shimoni, Proph., Section 296.
28. Maimonides expounded his own ideas on Olam Haba (The World-to-Come) in his Commentary on the Mishnah.
28a Baba Kamma 38.
29. Ps. XVI. 8.
30. Num. XII. 3.
31. Sayings of the Fathers, IV. 4.
32. The name of a valley south of Jerusalem, the 'valley of slaughter' (Jer. VII. 31–35), which became the synonym of Hell.
33. The word means literally 'people of the land'.
34. The 'Commentary on the Mishnah', called 'Siraj' (Hebrew: 'Maor'), i.e. 'Light', was composed in Arabic; its completion, in 1168, preceded the composition of the Hebrew 'Mishneh Torah', which was completed in 1180.
35. See Note 6 to Chapter 14.
36. Num. XV. 31.
36a See Note 28.
37. Gen. XXXII. 32.
38. Seven basic laws enjoined, according to the Rabbis, by God upon Noah's posterity, i.e. mankind in general.
39. B. Sotah 48a.
40. Gittin 7a.
41. Hosea IX. 1.
42. B. Shabath 68a.
43. Amos VI. 5.
44. Is. V. 12.
45. B. Berakoth 24a.
46. 'Dalalat al-hairin'; in Hebrew: 'Moreh Nebukim ('The Guide of the Perplexed').
47. Isaac Alfasi, great Talmudic scholar (1013–1103).
48. The Arabian philosophers of the Kalam or 'Word', with whom Maimonides had important points in common.
49. Abba Areka, Babylonian Amora (175–247), later called Rab, i.e. The Master, interpreter of the Mishnah and other Halakot, i.e. ordinances.
50. Abu-Ma'ali was the secretary to one of Saladin's wives; Maimonides married his sister.
51. The Hebrew name of the only son of Maimonides was Abraham; he was born in 1186 and became an accomplished scholar who, after his father's

death, defended the spiritual heritage of Maimonides against the anti-Maimunists.

52. Gen. XVIII. 10. The name of Aknin's wife was Sarah.

53. Prov. XII. 8.

54. Probably Abraham ibn Alfakhar (1160–1223), who enjoyed high honour at the Spanish court, and his relative Judah Alfakhar, physician to King Ferdinand III; Judah became one of the fiercest opponents of Maimonides's philosophical teaching.

55. R. Abraham, son of David, Rabbi of Posquières, an outstanding Talmudic scholar; died in 1198

56. Viz. Moses ibn Ezra, died about 1139, in a poem addressed to Meir ben Kamil.

57. Ezek. III. 3.

58. Prov. IX. 9.

59. Claudius Galenus (*c.* 130–201 C.E.), famous Greek physician; he strongly influenced medieval medicine and particularly Maimonides.

60. Celebrated Arabic translators.

61. Maimonides refers evidently to the Vizir Alfadhel who in Saladin's lifetime, and also after his death (1193) jointly with Saladin's brother, Al-Adil, administered Egypt.

62. The distance which a Jew is allowed to walk on the Sabbath from the precincts of his city, namely 2,000 paces; i.e. about one mile and a half.

63. Alexander Aphrodisius lived about 200 C.E.

64. Themistius lived in the fourth century C.E.

65. Ibn Roshd or Averroes (born at Cordova 1126, d. 1198), the most famous of the Arabian philosophers.

66. Abunazar Alfarabi (870–950) flourished at Baghdad.

67. Abubekr ben Alsaig or Ibn Badja (d. 1139).

68. Empedocles, famous Greek philosopher, lived in the fifth century B.C.E.

69. Pythagoras (*c.* 582–500 B.C.E.), born in Samos, celebrated Greek philosopher and founder of a philosophical and religious school.

70. Hermes, Egyptian philosopher.

71. Porphyrius (233–304 C.E.), Neoplatonist.

72. Maimonides was deeply influenced by the arabicized Aristotle. But on the transcendental issue of the creation of the world he rejected the Aristotelian conception of the Eternity of the Universe and maintained the idea of Creation. His philosophy is not 'Judaized Aristotelianism but rather Hellenized Judaism' (A. Steinberg, 'A History of Jewish Religious Thought', in *The Jewish People Past and Present*, Vol. I, New York, 1946; p. 289).

73. Ibn Sina or Avicenna (980–1037), famous Arabian philosopher and physician.

74. I Sam. X. I.

75. Exod. II. 10.

76. Is. LIV. 17.

77. See Letter No. 7.

78. Western North Africa. Maimonides alludes evidently to the persecution by the Almohades (see pp. 178 ff.).

32

Medieval Jewish Business Letters

THE four following letters illustrate the high standard of the correspondence on commercial and financial matters maintained by Jews in the twelfth and thirteenth centuries in all parts of the world, from India to Britain. The first, like the next one from the Genizah, is in rhymed prose, and shows the writer to have been far more interested in cultural achievements than in material gain. This dealer in head-dresses and foxes' furs, who resides in a Syrian town but hankers after Egypt, who longs to shine as a poet, studies talmudical commentaries and sends salutations to 'our master Moses, the teacher of righteousness' – most probably Maimonides – is an attractive example of a medieval Jewish *bel esprit*. The other letters are more matter-of-fact, but give the impression that the writers were men of integrity. The last two offer glimpses of the social position of the Jews in England in the middle of the thirteenth century. They were at that time still financial tools of the kings of England, as they had been since the Norman invasion. The letter from India, written in Judaeo-Arabic, gives a graphic portrait of a seafaring Jewish merchant on a remote corner of the medieval Jewish world.

(A)

AN UNKNOWN MERCHANT TO HIS FRIEND IN CAIRO

'I would dislike this country even if I were to be the owner of whole streets here'

[Kalne (Rakkah) in Syria, 1194 or 1197]

. . . I saw no letter of my master until the 20th of Sivan. Then two letters arrived which were beautiful beyond measure. My heart rejoiced when I saw them, my spirit was elevated when they were before my eyes. I appreciated them, so to say, as riches after poverty, as glory after insignificance, as happiness after misfortune, and as the deliverance from the Galuth. And having read them and understood their contents, I felt abased in my own eyes, and all my affairs appeared to me of no importance!

I said to myself: 'Who am I,[1] and what is my existence worth that my master should in his kindness speak about me so favourably? – I am a simple and ignorant man, like a mere animal in my knowledge! How shall I answer him with fitting language, and how shall I repay all the benefits he has bestowed upon me? I am unable to offer him a gift worthy of him. And if I should make a poem in his praise . . . The best thing I can do is, I think, to serve him as long as I am alive. But for the time being I am not able to do this before I have settled the living of my children and saved the means which are necessary for my journey. This is, however, my firm intention, with the help of God, of this my master may be sure, as his kindness is always before me. I shall never forget him, and greatly appreciate his friendship. I could not, however, fulfil his wish for a month because I had no peace. His letters perplexed my mind. I would dislike this country even if I were to be the owner of whole streets here. . . .

As to his inquiry about the excellent glosses of our Master to the Halakot,[2] I have asked R. Joseph,[3] but he knew nothing of the whole affair. He sent to him[4] a request for the correct text of certain passages. I sent also a courier to Aleppo to R. Samuel and R. Abraham. After the dispatch of the letters, R. Samuel arrived in Kalne by another route and had with him only the Commentary on Berakot.[5] He inquired after the welfare of my master and was very pleased to learn about his marriage, on which he congratulated him and his family.

Concerning the headdress he mentioned in the letter, I do not desire to part with it since I possess in my whole stock none like it. I regret also that I have taken a sum of money from R. Ali for a garment of foxes' fur. If he wishes, let him refund himself from the bearer of the letter. . . . What about the matter with Abu'l-Zahak in Damascus? I have received so far 50 silver pieces of the sum of 7 denar I was authorized to take. From the whole transaction, I assure him, hardly any profit will accrue to me. I shall write again as soon as possible because I like to write to my master. May his peace and that of his house grow!

I salute our Master Moses, the teacher of righteousness,[6] may his name flourish, and his son, may his Rock keep him and let his name shine; and R. Halfon and his son, may he become his joy; and R. Ali and his sons-in-law; and the profound scholar R. Mishael and his sons, may they bear fruit and increase, and his nephew, the Lord keep him and save his life; and all people in the house of the scholar . . . ; and all pupils, headed by Joseph and H . . . and R. Menahem, I am very glad to hear of his and his son's welfare. . . .

(B)

AN UNKNOWN MERCHANT IN INDIA TO ANOTHER MERCHANT IN CAIRO

'I know that my lord is kind to the foreigners'

[Somewhere in India, 12th or 13th century]

. . . And he[6a] prays to God night and day that He may give you health. You have observed his qualities well enough to know that he can be trusted with anything one may wish. And you are his lord and the greatest of men in his eyes.

Neither does he overcharge in his commercial transactions. He makes journeys from Malabar to Ceylon, but his goods are the whole year in Aden.[7] Now it is his intention to make a change, God willing, and to remove. For men cannot avoid misfortune and you are aware of this matter. If, therefore, you will wait until the time of his removal, well and good. But if you require your goods, then send a letter in your own handwriting, and he will hand over the goods to him whomsoever you desire. Wishes . . . sending the account; five thousand bahar,[7a] as little thereof is to be found in India. And he possesses none of it. There is also but little Baspas[8] in the market. And coryphyllum[8a] costs 40 per 10.

I have not sailed to Aden this year. But still I had a little merchandise for you which Sheikh Joseph Ibn Abulmana took with him. I wrote him a letter about it which he was to send you. Should he be in Egypt, I hope my master will support him with the [kindness ?] due to me his slave, for I know that my lord is kind to the foreigners. I know my lord from this point of view.

And I send to your Excellency full greetings of peace as also to those in his circle. Peace, and also to Sheikh Ibrahim.

(C)

ELIAS OF NOTTINGHAM TO THE CUSTODIANS OF THE COFFER

'I solicit you that you will treat her with due consideration'

[about 1250]

May your welfare ever increase, my friend and kinsman, Rabbi Abraham, and my friend Rabbi Eleazar, custodians of the Coffer[9] in the city of Nottingham!

I, the undersigned, hereby request you to do me a service. As you are aware, all the debts of Lady Rica now belong to me, having been handed over to me by the King. I solicit you therefore that should Lady Rica apply for any deed, you will treat her with due consideration and write out the bonds in my name. Kindly inform Citizen William Coroner the same, in my name. Pray do not fail me.

There is no need for me to write more, excepting to hope that your welfare will increase according to the desire of

Elias

(D)

DAVID LUMBARD TO HIS SON

'Give them up to the person bearing this letter without delay, for so I have promised to the Justiciars'

[Nottingham, about 1250]

May thy welfare increase, son Moses, live long!

I am writing to inform thee that Nicholas de Wilton hath settled with all the Jews[10] who shared his debts, and hath paid up the full sum. I desire thee therefore to deliver up to the bearer the three bonds and the corresponding indentures that are in the Coffer – two of my own, and a third from Deulecresse for five marks which thou wilt find among mine. Have thine eyes about thee, then, and give them up to the person bearing this letter without delay, for so I have promised the Justiciars. There is no need for me to write more, excepting to wish thee peace, according to my desire.

Father

Shew the chirographers this acquittance of Deulecresse and his instructions to withdraw the indenture from the Coffer.

NOTES

1. 2 Sam. VII. 18.
2. The writer refers probably to some explanations in the Mishneh Torah.
3. Very probably Joseph ibn Aknin, who lived in Aleppo for several years.
4. Probably Maimonides.
5. According to Jacob Mann, probably the work of either R. Nissim, son of Jacob of Kairuan, or R. Hananel, son of Samuel.
6. See note 4.
6a The writer speaks of himself in the third person.
7. The letter shows the range of voyages undertaken by Jewish merchants of those days; David, the brother of Maimonides, also belonged to these travellers.
7a An East-Indian measure of weight.
8. Baspas is a medical herb (*peganum harmata ruta*).
8a Leaves of the Corypha, one of the Fan Palms growing to 80 feet, a native of Ceylon and the Malabar coast.
9. The financial transactions of the Jews were carried on under the supervision of a special central authority, the Exchequer of the Jews, and in connection with this institution offices for the registration of the records of every business, the so-called Coffer, or Archa, were established.
10. The writer was head of the Jewish community of Nottingham.

33

The Letters of Moses Nahmanides to his sons from the Holy Land

MOSES, son of Nahman, commonly called Nahmanides or Nahmani, born in Gerona about the year 1195, was one of the chief ornaments of Jewish learning in the thirteenth century. In the words of Solomon Schechter, Nahmanides represented Judaism from the side of emotion and feeling, as Maimonides did from the side of reason and logic. His knowledge of early mystical works and his own mystical disposition made him a forerunner of the mystics and cabbalists, who were destined to become a dominating spiritual power in the centuries to come.

Nahmanides spent the greatest part of his life in Christian Spain. In 1263 he distinguished himself by upholding the cause of Judaism in a disputation with the Jewish apostate Pablo Christiani, in the presence of the king and court of Aragon. His victory was almost too complete, as it drew on him the enmity of the Dominicans, through whose machinations he was condemned to exile. He migrated to Palestine, where he arrived after having passed his seventieth year. Here he completed his greatest work, the Commentary on the Pentateuch, and embarked upon an historic enterprise: to revive the nearly extinguished Jewish life in the Holy Land. Here he also wrote the three letters to his children which are quoted below. The first is a moving description of the state of Palestine as it had been left by the Mongolian invasion a few years before (1260). The other two are paternal Letters of Admonition, one apparently to his son Solomon (who seems to have been in the service of the King of Castile), laying particular stress on chastity, and the other to his son Nahman, inculcating the virtue of humility.

(A)

MOSES NAHMANIDES TO HIS SON NAHMAN

'Even in this destruction it is a blessed land'

[Jerusalem, 1267]

May the Lord bless thee, my son Nahman, and mayst thou see the good of Jerusalem. Yea, mayst thou see thy children's children,[1] and may thy table be like that of our father Abraham.

I write this letter in Jerusalem, the Holy City. For, thanks and praise unto the Rock of my Salvation, I was privileged to arrive safely there on the 9th of the month Ellul, and stayed there till the day after the Day of Atonement. Now I intend going to Hebron, to the sepulchre of our ancestors, to prostrate myself, and there to dig my grave.

But what shall I say to you concerning the country? Great is the solitude and great the devastation, and, to put it briefly, the more sacred the places, the greater their desolation. Jerusalem is more desolate than the rest of the country: Judæa more than Galilee. But even in this destruction it is a blessed land. It has about 2,000 inhabitants, about 300 Christians live there who escaped the sword of the Sultan. There are no Jews.[1a] For, after the arrival of the Tartars, some fled while others died by the sword. There are only two brothers, dyers by trade, who have to buy their ingredients from the government. There the Ten Men[1b] meet, and on Sabbaths they hold the service at their home. But we encouraged them, and we succeeded in finding a vacant house, built on pillars of marble with a beautiful arch. That we took for a synagogue. For the town is without a ruler, so that whoever desires to take possession of the ruins can do so. We gave our offering towards the repairs of the house. We have sent already to Shechem to fetch some scrolls of the Law which had been brought thither from Jerusalem on the invasion of the Tartars. Thus they will organize a synagogue and worship there. For continually people crowd into Jerusalem, men and women, from Damascus, Zobah [Aleppo], and from all parts of the country, to see the Sanctuary and to mourn there.

May He who thought us worthy to let us see Jerusalem in her desertion, grant us that we behold her rebuilt and restored, when the glory of the Lord shall return to her. But you, my son, and your brothers and the whole of our family, may you all live to see the salvation of Jerusalem and the comfort of Zion.

These are the words of your father, who is yearning and forgetting, who is seeing and enjoying,

Moses son of Nahman

Give my greeting also to my pupil Moses, the son of Solomon, the nephew of your mother. Tell him . . . that there, before the Holy Temple, I have read his verses, weeping bitterly over them. May He who caused His name to rest in the Holy Temple increase your peace together with the peace of the whole community.

Like an epilogue to this letter, with its strange mixture of sadness and hope, reads an excerpt from the Appendix of Nahmani's Commentary on the Pentateuch:

'Oh, I am the man who saw affliction. I am banished from my table, far removed from friend and kinsman, and too long is the distance to meet again. . . . I left my family, I forsook my house. There with the sweet and beloved children, whom I brought up on my knees, I left also my soul. With them, my heart and my eyes will dwell forever. . . . But the loss of all else which delighted my eyes is compensated by my present joy in a day passed within thy courts, Oh Jerusalem! visiting the ruins of the Temple and crying over the ruined Sanctuary, where it is granted to me to caress thy stones, to fondle thy dust, and to weep over thy ruins. I wept bitterly, but I found joy in my heart. I rent my garments, but I found solace in doing so.'

(B)

NAHMANIDES TO HIS SON SOLOMON

'Let the image of my countenance be never absent from before thine eyes'

[Jerusalem, between 1267 and 1270]

. . . May God bless thee and preserve thee from sin and punishment. Behold, our master, King David, had a son, wise and of an understanding heart, like whom there was never one before or after. Nevertheless he said to him, 'And keep the charge of the Lord thy God, to walk in His ways, to keep His statutes, and His commandments, and His judgements, and His testimonies, as it is written in the law of Moses, that thou mayest prosper in all that thou doest, and whithersoever thou turnest thyself.'[2] He also said unto him, 'And thou, Solomon my son, know thou the God of thy father, and serve Him with a perfect heart and with a willing mind: for the Lord searcheth all hearts, and understandeth all the imaginations of the thoughts: if thou seek Him, He will be found of thee; but if thou forsake Him, He will cast thee off for ever.'[3] Now my son, if thou wilt measure thyself with Solomon, thou wilt find thyself to be a worm – not a man, but merely an insect; nevertheless, if thou wilt seek God He will magnify thee, and if thou wilt forsake Him, thou wilt be cast out and forsaken.

My son, take heed that thou read the Shema morning and evening, and that thou say the daily prayers. Have always with thee an accurate Pentateuch, and read therein the lesson for each Sabbath. . . . 'Cast thy burden upon the Lord,'[4] for the thing which thou believest to be far from thee is often very near unto thee. Know, again, that thou art not master over thy words, nor hast power over thy hand; but everything is in the hands of the Lord, who formeth thy heart. . . . Be especially careful to keep away from the women [of the court]. Know that immorality is an abomination to our God, and that Balaam could by no other means injure Israel than by inciting them to unchastity.[5]. . . My son, remember me always, and let the image of my countenance be never absent from before thine eyes. Love not that which I hate. . . . Let the words of the Psalmist be always upon thy lips, 'I am a stranger upon the earth: hide not Thy commandments from me'[6]; and God, who is good and the dispenser of good, shall increase thy peace and prolong thy life and happiness, and promote thy honour according to thy wish and to the wish of thy father, who begat thee,

Moses son of Nahman

(c)

NAHMANIDES TO HIS SON NAHMAN

'In all thy thoughts, words and deeds, at all times and seasons, regard thyself as though thou stoodest before the supreme King of kings, the Holy One, blessed be He, and as if His Shekinah were upon thee; for His Glory fills the whole earth'

[Jerusalem, between 1267 and 1270]

Hear, my son, the instruction of thy father, and forsake not the law of thy mother.[7] My son, my beloved, accustom thyself always to speak gently to every man, at all times and seasons: and thou shalt thereby avoid anger, which is a very bad and blameworthy disposition, for it leadeth to sin, as our teachers, their memory be blessed, said: 'If a man grows angry, it is regarded as if he worshipped idols.'[8] And all the punishments of Gehinnom[8a] have power over him, as it is written: 'Remove anger from thy heart, and put away evil from thy flesh.'[9] By the word 'evil' Gehinnom is meant, as it is written: 'The Lord hath made all things for himself: yea, even the wicked for the day of evil.'[10]

When thou avoidest anger, thou wilt bring to thy mind the quality of humility, and cleave unto it, for it is the best of all virtues, as it is written: 'The reward of humility is the fear of the Lord.'[11] The Mishnah likewise says: 'Be exceedingly humble of spirit.'[12] Even our teacher Moses, peace be with him, was praised for this quality, as it is written: 'And the man Moses was very meek, above all the men which were upon the face of the earth.'[13] It is also by reason of this virtue that the Torah was given by his hand, and that he was called the teacher of all prophets. He who attains unto this quality is beloved of Heaven, as it is written: 'I dwell in the high and holy place, with him also that is of a contrite and humble spirit.'[14] When thou clingest to the quality of humility, the quality of the fear of God will come to thy mind; for thou wilt continually reflect whence thou camest, and whither thou art going (thou art a worm and maggot in thy life and in thy death), and before whom thou art destined to render account and reckoning – before the supreme King of kings, the Holy One, blessed be He, whose glory fills the earth. It is also written: 'Do not I fill heaven and earth? saith the Lord.'[15] It is also written: 'Behold, heaven and the heaven of heavens cannot contain Thee; how much less the hearts of the children of men!'[16] When thou wilt consider all this, thou wilt fear thy Creator, and guard thyself against sin. By clinging to these qualities thou wilt attain to a perfect and exalted state, and wilt be ever contented with thy lot; this, too, is one of the good qualities, as the Mishnah says: 'Who is rich? he who rejoices in his lot.'[17] If thy conduct is governed by the quality of humility and thou art respectful to every man, and thou fearest thy Creator, who gives thee life, so that thou sinnest not, the Spirit of the Shekinah and the splendour of its glory will dwell upon thee, and thou wilt deserve the life of this world and of the World-to-Come.

My son and my beloved, know assuredly that one who exalts himself above his fellow-men rebels against the kingdom of heaven, for he makes use of God's garment, as it is written: 'The Lord reigneth, he is clothed with majesty.'[18] And God, who is blessed, says concerning the haughty man: 'I and he cannot dwell together in this world.' Accordingly, he who is haughty will be uprooted from the world.

Consider with understanding: Of what should a man be proud? Of his wealth and honour? They surely belong to God, and He, who is blessed, bestows them upon man, as it is written: 'Both riches and honour come of Thee, and Thou reignest over all.'[19] It is also written: 'The Lord maketh poor, and maketh rich.'[20] Of his wisdom? Let him remember the explicit words of Scripture: 'He removeth the speech of men of trust, and taketh away the sense of the elders.'[21] It is thus evident that all comes from Him, blessed be He; in His anger He brings low the haughty, and in His favour He lifts up the lowly. Therefore, my son, make thyself humble, and remove thyself from haughtiness, so that the Lord may raise thee high.

I shall now set forth for thee how thou shouldst conduct thyself according to the quality of humility, to follow it continually. Let all thy words be spoken with gentleness, with respect, with good manners, and with love; thy countenance should be pleasant, and thy head bowed down. Thine eyes should look downwards, and thy heart upwards. Do not gaze too fixedly upon a man when thou addressest him. Let every man be greater than thou in thy sight. If he is rich, thou shalt honour him, as did our saintly teacher, who used to honour the rich. If he is poor and thou art rich, thou shalt have mercy and compassion on him, and honour the Lord with thy substance. If thou art wiser than he, thou shouldst consider that thou art guilty, and he is innocent; for he sins unwittingly, while thou sinnest wilfully, as the Rabbis of blessed memory said: 'The errors of the sages are regarded as wilful sins.'[22]

In all thy thoughts, words, and deeds, at all times and seasons, regard thyself as though thou stoodest before the supreme King of kings, the Holy One, blessed be He, and as if His Shekinah were upon thee; for His glory fills the whole earth. Thy words should be spoken with the deepest reverence and awe, as by a servant addressing his master. Be diligent to study the Law continually, day and night, for thereby thou shalt be able to fulfil the commandments thereof; it is thy life and the length of thy days. When thou hast finished the reading of a book, thou shouldst retain that which thou hast learned, in order to fulfil that which is written in it, as far as thou art able to fulfil. Thou shouldst continually examine thy deeds, every day, morning and evening, in order to depart from evil and to do good. Thus all thy days will be in perfect repentance.

During the prayer of the Eighteen Benedictions thou shouldst remove all the affairs of this world from thy heart; think of no other matter except fixing thy mind on the prayer with perfect devotion. Prepare and purify thy heart and mind before God, blessed be He; thereby thy prayer will be pure, clean, untainted, full of devotion, and acceptable before the Holy One, blessed be His name, as it is written: '[Lord, thou hast heard the desire of the humble]; thou wilt direct their heart, Thou wilt cause Thine ear to attend.'[23] Death and life are in the power of the tongue, and he that keeps his mouth and tongue keeps his soul from troubles. Therefore in every matter think of thy words before thou givest utterance to them, all the days of thy life, so that thou mayest not sin; thereby thy thoughts, words and deeds will be upright and good.

My son, read this epistle once a week with thy friend, and walk continually after God, blessed be He, in order that thou mayest prosper in all thy ways and be worthy of the world to come which is stored up for the righteous. Whenever thou readest it, thou wilt obtain an answer from heaven to all petitions which thou mayest ask from this time forth and for ever.

Not long after he had written this 'Praise of Humility', Nahmanides passed away, in the year 1270. Soon afterwards a faithful Jew, Rabbi Solomon, son of the martyr Isaac, probably a Spaniard, embodied the letter in his own Ethical Will. He advised his son and grandchildren to read it as often as they should read the Will of their own ancestor, which he made incumbent upon them to read weekly, from generation to generation. Since then, Nahmanides's Letter of Advice to his son Nahman has been included in many editions of the Prayer Book and thus transformed into an epistle to the Jewish people.

NOTES

1. Ps. CXXVIII. 5, 6.
1a A Jewish community.
1b Required for public prayer, the so-called Minyan.
2. 1 Kings II. 2.
3. 1 Chron. XXVIII. 9.
4. Ps. LV. 22.
5. Num. XXV. 1–3; XXXI. 16.
6. Ps. CXIX. 19.
7. Prov. I. 8.
8. Midrash le-Olam, Ch. 15.
8a See Note 32 to Chapter 31.
9. Eccles. XI. 10.
10. Prov. XVI. 4.
11. Prov. XXII. 4.
12. Sayings of the Fathers IV. 4.
13. Num. XII. 3.
14. Is. LVII. 15.
15. Jer. XXIII. 24.
16. 1 Kings VIII, 27; Prov. XV. 11.
17. Sayings of the Fathers IV. 1.
18. Ps. XCIII. 1.
19. 1 Chron. XXIX. 12.
20. 1 Sam. II. 7.
21. Job XII. 20.
22. Baba Mezia 33b.
23. Ps. X. 17.

34

Donna Sarah's Plea to her Husband to return to his Family

THIS letter belongs to the private Hebrew letters found in the Genizah. It is addressed to the scribe Solomon who left his home in an Italian town, apparently with the purpose of obtaining release from the taxes, and did not return, for unknown reasons. Whether the letter was composed by his wife, Donna Sarah, herself, or by someone on her behalf, we cannot say. The author certainly displays considerable epistolary skill, which enabled him to plead eloquently the cause of an abandoned wife and mother.

DONNA SARAH TO HER HUSBAND SOLOMON

'We all are longing to see your sweet face, as one longs after the face of God'

[An Italian town, probably 13th century]

May ample peace and welfare be with my master and ruler, the light of my eyes, the crown of my head, my master and husband, the learned R. Solomon, the Scribe, may he live long. May ample peace be bestowed upon you by the Master of peace and from Donna Sarah your wife, your daughters Reina and Rachel, from R. Moses, your son-in-law, and Rebecca.

We are all longing to see your sweet face, as one longs after the face of God,[1] and we are wondering that you have not answered the numerous letters we have sent you. We have written you often begging you to return, but – no answer at all. If you can manage with the help of the esteemed physician, R. Solomon, may he live long, to obtain release from taxes it will be greatly to your profit, and this kindness will exceed all benefits which he has conferred on you. May the Lord grant him a rich reward in this world and the world to come, and may he educate his son for Torah, marriage and good works.

And now let us return to the previous subject. We are all assembled, your wife, your daughters and your son-in-law Moses, to implore you from the bottom of our hearts not to go further, either by sea or by land, because we have heard that you have the intention of leaving for Turkey. I swear to the Lord that, if you do this, you must not speak with us any more; and if you do this, which will make the world despise us and cause a quarrel between your son-in-law and your daughter, who is in certain circumstances, you will inflict pain upon your daughter and perhaps she will suffer a miscarriage. And you will also endanger the happiness of your daughter Rachel, who has grown up and has become a beautiful and modest maiden. People will talk scandal and say: 'Here is a respectable old scribe, who left his wife and daughters and has been missing for many years. Perhaps he is mad. For he went to a distant country and you know what the verse says: "The eyes of a fool are in the ends of the earth." '[2] Beg the physician, R. Solomon, therefore to provide you a confirmation about the release from the taxes; otherwise come home [in the name of] the Blessed one! . . . Do nothing else. And Peace!

NOTES

1. Cf. Gen. xxxiii. 10.
2. Prov. xvii. 24.

35

Joseph Ezobi's Wedding Poem for his Son

THE Provençal family of the Ezobis was a home of Hebrew poetry, which was cultivated both by the father, Hayim ben Nathan, and three sons, Eleazar, Meshullam and Joseph. One poem by Joseph, who lived in Perpignan, most probably in the first half of the thirteenth century, was popular for centuries. It was composed as a wedding poem on the occasion of the marriage of his son, and was called 'Ka'arat Kesef' (The Silver Bowl) because its 130 verses corresponded to the 130 shekels' weight of the priestly bowl. Much of it reads like a poetical version of Judah ibn Tibbon's letter to his son (see *supra*, pp. 156ff.), though the supreme authority of Samuel ha-Nagid is replaced by that of Maimonides, 'the Sage of God's decree'.

The poetic epistle, reproduced here in a shortened version, was presented by Ezobi to his son with the following, likewise abridged, letter.

JOSEPH EZOBI TO HIS SON

'May this song remain like a witness between us'

[Perpignan, France, first half of the 13th century]

. . . I entreat thee, my son and pupil, for the respect thou owest to thy teacher, and for the honour thou owest to thy father, that thy ears may listen to my admonition as if thy eyes would see me in the flesh. May this song remain like a witness between us. Take it and read it in the days of thy youth, do not leave it, and do not deviate from it also in thy old age. Exalt it and it shall promote thee, it shall bring thee to honour when thou dost embrace it. Fix it like nails into thy heart, appoint a special time in order to read it once every week and particularly if New Moon is on Sabbath. And if perhaps a Sabbath shall pass without thy reading it, let not a month pass. . . . The words of the song must not depart from thy mouth and thy heart. For it is a crown for thy head and an ornament for thy neck.[1]

Listen, my son, listen to thy father, who is grieved by his separation from thee, hear me, and the Lord will hear thee. What more can I say or quote? I will finish with the words of our King Solomon, blessed be his memory, who says at the beginning of the Proverbs in his great wisdom: 'My son, forget not my teaching, but let thine heart keep my commandments.'[2] And find grace and good understanding in the sight of God and men.

THE SILVER BOWL

My darling son, thou art my soul's delight,
My hope, my joy, my strength in thee unite!
Peace to thee, peace, my glory and my love,
Thy will is God's, its fruit is Heaven above.
The song I sing is thine, accept the gift,
'Tis offered to thy soul, with heart uplift . . .
My son, a 'Silver Bowl' of poesy,
Thy father's gift, thy father Ezobi . . .
The Silver Bowl is filled with songs of Truth:
Rejoice! but turn it not upon its mouth.

List now, my son, accept this gift divine,
A father's gift, whose soul, whose life is thine.
A wedding gift, to smoothe thy path most fit,
Above all festive song, all clam'rous wit . . .
Its weight is measured as the priestly bowl[3],
When brought to God, to cleanse the erring soul.[4]
From thee with this reward I am content,
An honoured name, a life in virtue spent.
Knowest thou not, hear'st not of thy Grandsire's name,
'Good Samuel the Lion,' first in fame?
Thy name is his, be thou his counterpart,
Upright and pure in thought, in deed, in heart.

Fear thou thy God, yea, more than man fears man,
Was He not God long ere this world began?
Is He not God now that the world is grown?
Eternal Majesty! Yet still unknown.
God bade the heaven o'er the earth be spread;
He is the first, He lives when all is dead.
His glory streams from heaven, it fills the earth,
Beyond the vastest circuit mind can girth!
Take this encirclement, extend it more
And more, to God 'tis small as e'en before.
Because He chose on Zion's hill a shrine,
Wilt thou to Him a finite place assign?
Thou dar'st not God in any form confine,
'He spoke,' 'He saw,' 'He stood,' are but His sign.
He in one week creation's work fulfill'd,
No work of craftsman, but divinely willed.
To nature's Law earth moves obedient,
But God to nature's self her power hath lent.
He can withhold it, as it was withheld
When fountains madly gushed and waters well'd.
And who is he that dares transgress His word?
Not thou, my son, for wisdom thou hast heard.

Seek men of virtue, goodness, knowledge, truth,
Honour their crown of years, waste not thy youth . . .
Seek not youth's counsel, it is worse than guilt.
Its castle totters, as on ruins built.
To teachers, not to books entrust thy mind;
Thy soul to living words, not dead, e'er bind . . .
Put not thy faith in Grecian sophistry:
To climb its vineyard's fence no man is free.
Its draught will make thy footsteps vacillate
From truth; will make thy heart to curse and hate.
But askest thou in what to seek thy lore,
In grammar much, but in the Talmud more. . . .

Alfasi,[5] glory to his memory,
Alone did bring the law to harmony . . .
And after, rose a man of piety,
Maimonides, the Sage of God's decree,
Whose books, that on the world their lustre shed,
In Hebrew and in Arab tongue are read.
Breathe thou the incense of his off'ring soul,
The path of rectitude his words extol.
Accept his laws of life, for he will guide
Thee near to God; in him thy trust confide.
Give ear at times unto the Midrashim;
How oft they brighten words that seem but dim.
And like thy father sing in tunefulness;
Hark thou, a barren soul is profitless. . . .

When thou a letter sendest to thy friend,
If 'tis not neatly writ 'twill sure offend;
For in his penmanship man stands revealed –
Purest intent by chastest style is sealed. . . .
The body's strife against thy soul let cease;
Between the two contrive a bond of peace.
The flesh of man must needs be satiate;
Remember too the soul hath claims as great.
But if the grip of lust seize hold of thee,
Kill lust, lest thou be doomed to slavery. . . .
A little sleep, my son, invigorates;
A sluggard's sleep, my son, his life prostrates. . . .
On festive days, be thine to joy in feast,
But shun debauch on flesh or fatted beast.
Waste not the holy days in wine and meal;
Look more the sickness of thy soul to heal;
Thus make the seventh day, the Day of Rest,
With higher, nobler influences blest.
Seek thou the House of God by night or day,
All humbly open thou thy lips, but pray. . . .

Love thou the poor, for joyless is their lot.
According to thy purse help those who need,
For every gift doth bring an equal meed.
If thou hast nought to give to him who craves,
Yet gently answer him, a word oft saves –
Speak thou the truth, the saving truth instil,
Why should man's word e'er pierce and wound and kill?
Abandon wrath; through anger heroes fell
Ungodly rage made God's own seer rebel. . . .

Do thou, my son, pursue humility
In it behold the grace of dignity.
All friends with kindly cheer to thee enfold,
Acquire their hearts without a gift or gold;
But strive always to honour every man,
The prince and eke the humble artisan. . . .
All gambling games of chance abominate,
Like groves with idol rites contaminate. . . .

My son, on this thy wedding day rejoice,
To song of mirth attune thy heart and voice.
Take thou the graceful doe, the royal bride,
With her thy joy and happiness divide.
A comely form, my darling son, is thine;
Corrupt it not, for 'tis a gift divine.
If thou wouldst see the gates of Paradise,
Refrain! Thy work on earth will thee suffice.
Yea, many rushing heaven's heights to scale
In fruitless quests their life misspent bewail.
Behold reveal'd creation's mystery,
List to the strains of heaven's symphony;
And when the day of good report is nigh
E'en as Elijah thou shalt rise on high.
Three crowns there are, and these the world may love;
A blameless name is more, all crowns above.

Humbly pray God may crown thee with His Light,
To live 'mid men, with heart, with soul, with might.
Rejoice with her, thy graceful tender dove:
God bless you twain, with love as angels love.

NOTES

1. Prov. I. 9.
2. Prov. III. 1.
3. The silver bowl, or dish, which was offered by each of the princes of the tribes at the dedication of the altar and which weighed 130 shekels (*v.* Num. VII. 13 ff.).
4. Cf. Exod. XXX. 12, 15, 16.
5. See Note 47 to Chapter 31.

36

Rabbi Meir ben Baruch of Rothenburg answers questions

MEIR BEN BARUCH of Rothenburg was the glory of German Jewry in the second half of the thirteenth century, and along with Solomon ben Adret of Barcelona the leading rabbinical authority of his time. Questions were addressed to him not only from all parts of Germany but also from Italy and France, and he became one of the most eminent contributors to the Responsa literature. Towards the end of his life he decided to leave the country of his birth and to emigrate to Palestine. His pious intention, however, was not carried out. While in Lombardy, waiting for the arrival of other Jewish emigrants, he was seized and delivered to the authorities. In 1286 he was confined in the fortress of Ensisheim, near Colmar. The Jews offered an enormous sum for his release, but Rabbi Meir refused to be ransomed at such a price lest a dangerous precedent should be established by this procedure. Thus his longing for the Holy Land remained unfulfilled. He died in the German fortress in 1293.

1. *Responsa on Emigration to Palestine*

Many questions arising out of the desire of the Jew for Palestine, which gave such a tragic turn to Rabbi Meir's own life, were addressed to Rothenburg. The following Responsa show what may be regarded as the authoritative opinion about this subject.

MEIR OF ROTHENBURG TO UNKNOWN INQUIRERS

[Rothenburg, second half of the 13th century]

(A)

'If one should commit a sin in the Land of Israel his guilt is greater than elsewhere'

You ask me: What is the chief merit of him who emigrates to the Land of Israel?

I know no more than what is said in Ketubot.[1]

You also ask if sins are forgiven for going to live in the Land of Israel.

So it is said in Ketubot, assuming that one lives there a moral life, is careful not to commit wrong, and is zealous to fulfil the commands which apply there. For if one should commit a sin in the Land of Israel his guilt is greater than elsewhere. For the Land of Israel is 'a land which the Lord thy God careth for; the eyes of the Lord thy God are always upon it'.[2] To rebel against the king in the royal palace itself is a greater offence than to rebel against him outside the palace. This is the meaning of the verse: 'It is a land that eateth up the inhabitants thereof.'[3] Scripture also says: '[Ye shall therefore keep My statutes and My judgements, and shall not commit any of these abominations . . .]: that the land vomit not you out also as it vomited out the nation that was before you.'[4] Even non-Jews meet with ill-fortune there, if they are sinners. For this reason Palestine is desolate now, there is not a single town surrounded by a wall as is the case in other countries. Those who emigrate to Palestine to live a worthless life there and to foment strife are referred to in Scripture in these words: 'But when you entered, you defiled my land.'[5]

He, however, who goes to the Land of Israel for the sake of Heaven, to live there in holiness and purity, obtains reward without limit, assuming that he works there for a livelihood.

(B)

'The honour of the Lord ranks above all'

You ask whether the father is entitled to prevent his son from migrating to the Land of Israel.

Because it is a Mitzwah to go to the Land of Israel, as it is written 'I am the Lord your God,'[6] the son need not obey the father. For the honour of the Lord ranks above all.

(c)

'There is no distinction in this matter between the time when the Temple was still standing and nowadays'

You ask me about one Reuben who has expressed his intention of going to the Land of Israel, while his wife Leah refuses.

You surely are aware of what we are told in the last chapter of the tractate Ketubot, that in such case he has the right to divorce her, and she loses her marriage settlement. I know that there are some persons who draw a distinction in this matter between the time when the Temple was still standing and nowadays, and say that the passage in question refers only to the former time. It is necessary, therefore, for me to explain that there is no distinction. . . . This, however is only if he goes to the Land of Israel and does not return. If, however, he returns to dwell outside Palestine, even after several years, she may claim her settlement from him if she is still alive; and if she has died in the meanwhile, her heirs may do so.

2. *A Responsum on the Candle Lights*

This letter shows the acute interpreter of the law to have been no killjoy and to have been well aware of the emotional value of religious practice.

MEIR OF ROTHENBURG TO AN UNKNOWN INQUIRER

'The light in the synagogue is not idle, as it serves to increase the joy and solemnity'

[Rothenburg, second half of the 13th century]

You wonder that it is permitted to light candles in the synagogues on the holy days even in the morning, although a light in the day is useless, and the lighting of the candles, therefore, a work without any purpose.

To this we have to reply that the light in the synagogue in daylight too is not idle, as it serves to increase the joy and solemnity. The joyful mood is advanced and increased by the lighting, just as it is, on the other hand, banished from places where darkness reigns. Compare these two passages of the holy Scripture: 'Light is sown for the righteous, and gladness for the upright in heart,'[7] and 'Moreover I will cause to cease from among them the voice of mirth and the voice of gladness, the voice of the bridegroom and the voice of the bride, the sound of the millstones, and the light of the lamp.'[8] In the Temple they used to kindle the lights long before the beginning of the night, as they served for the glorification of the Sanctuary, although they were not necessary for lighting during the whole night, and the Lord does not need our light. Also the lights of the Hanukah feast used to be kindled long before the beginning of the night. In short, the lights kindled for religious purposes cannot be regarded as useless. . . .

Besides, the candles burning in the synagogues cannot be considered useless, as even in daylight they add somewhat to the light. Also the brightest light is increased a little by a candle, and this fact alone is sufficient to render the work permissible. Otherwise it would be forbidden to kindle several lights on holy days at night because one only is sufficient to remove darkness, while the others are but adding to the existing light.

Pardon me for not answering your question at once. I had to delay the reply owing to various occupations. And then no traveller could be found who was able to take the letter with him. Health and peace to you and to your learning, to your house and followers.

Your obedient,
Meir son of Baruch

3. *A Letter from Prison*

Even in imprisonment Rabbi Meir continued to teach and to advise his disciples and the people, turning the fortress into a kind of Yeshibah. He also continued to receive and answer letters, though he was hampered by the lack of books. For some time he was buoyed up by the hope of speedy deliverance, but a different mood is revealed in the following passage from a

Responsum to his favourite pupil, Asher ben Yehiel, who became the great teacher of the next generation.

MEIR OF ROTHENBURG TO ASHER BEN YEHIEL

'. . . a trodden threshold which was once called Meir son of Baruch'

[Ensisheim Fortress, about 1290]

. . . In these places of wilderness I do not possess Tosafot[9] to Gittin nor works on ritual, and therefore I am putting down all these words just as I have been inspired by Heaven. If, however, one should find that the Tosafot and ritual codes decide in one or the other respect *against me*, my opinion may be considered null and void. For what can a miserable man know who dwells under the shadow of death, and has lacked all the amenities of life now for three years and six months, who has been forsaken in affliction by all good men, a trodden threshold which was once called Meir son of Baruch?

The end came in 1293, and even then it was some years before Alexander Susskind Wimpfen, a wealthy and noble Jew of Frankfurt, in exchange for a heavy ransom, obtained permission to bury the body of the great teacher at Worms, the city of Rashi.

NOTES

1. Ketubot 110b: True worship of God is possible only in the Land of Israel.
2. Deut. XI. 12.
3. Num. XIII. 32.
4. Lev. XVIII. 26, 28.
5. Jer. II. 7.
6. Lev. XIX. 37.
7. Ps. XCVII. 11.
8. Jer. XXV. 10.
9. Tosafot: supplements to Rashi' commentary to the Talmud.

37

A Jewish Physician seeks a Safe-Conduct from England to Flanders

RABBI ELIJAH MENAHEM, known as Master Elias of London, was the most distinguished figure in English Jewry in the decades before the expulsion. He excelled alike as a Hebrew writer and as a medical practitioner. His reputation in the latter capacity was such that in 1280 he received a call to the court of the Count of Flanders, to attend the Count's nephew. His request to the Chancellor of England for a safe-conduct was written in French, and tells of the great efforts made by the Count to secure the treatment of his relative by the Jewish physician.

ELIAS OF LONDON TO ROBERT BURNELL, BISHOP OF BATH AND WELLS, CHANCELLOR OF ENGLAND

'. . . he hath requested me by express letters and through many high persons of the country that I do go thither in person'

[London, 1280]

To my dear Lord from his liege, salutation!
Sire,

Whereas my name is known much in distant lands at more than its true value (which is naught), I have been requested by the Count of Flanders by many letters and through a special messenger to cure a malady which his nephew hath, which malady is perilous, and to administer thereto a remedy. And whereas by the cure we have sent him he is somewhat eased, more than by any other which hath been administered to him by any other person, he hath requested me by express letters and through many high persons of the country that I do go thither in person or else send him a sure substitute: for a man can work better by sight than by hearsay. He hath written to you that you may procure me safe-conduct from our Lord the

King. For my part, I should fear to go, unless you counsel it and let me have a letter of safe-conduct. I am sending accordingly Abraham Motun fiz Benet, my Jew, to procure this for me. And I pray your Highness, so much as in me lies, that you send courteously to Sir Stephen of Penichester [?], so that he may treat my men gently: for they are bearing with them nothing excepting their expenses only, for fear of slanderers. . . . Dear Lord, please to conceal what I request from Aaron son of Vives. May Our Lord accomplish your desire for your good.

The safe-conduct was granted, and Master Elias was enabled to leave England for Flanders. He died a few years later, in 1284, just escaping the fate and sufferings of his fellow-Jews, who were banished from their homeland in 1290 by the same King Edward I who had permitted the Jewish physician to proceed to the Continent on his mission of mercy.

38

Faith versus Reason
Letters from the Struggle between the Maimunists and Anti-Maimunists

THE dispute between the followers and opponents of Maimonides which broke out with the first appearance of the Hebrew translation of 'The Guide of the Perplexed', engaged the participation of the most famous names in Jewish learning, both in Spain and in France. The last stage of the centennial struggle was reached at the beginning of the fourteenth century. Devotion to secular studies, greatly stimulated by the example of Maimonides, had produced in many Jews an attitude of scepticism even towards some statements of the Bible itself, and made them lax in religious observance. To counteract this tendency, many Rabbis were in favour of placing a general, or at least partial, ban on secular study, especially philosophy and natural science. The leadership of these traditionalists in their conflict with the modernists was assumed by Solomon, son of Abraham ibn Adret, of Barcelona, the outstanding rabbinic authority of the age after the passing of Rabbi Meir of Rothenburg. He was at that time a man of about seventy and was recognized as the spiritual head of the Jewish world on account of his wisdom, his learning and his saintly life. The number of his extant Responsa exceeds three thousand, perhaps the largest number penned by a single respondent. In one of them, his views on the rationalistic approach to the Bible are expressed with great force and precision. This letter can, therefore, well serve to illustrate the spirit of those who fought for the traditional values of Judaism.

SOLOMON IBN ADRET TO AN INQUIRER

'What has been founded on tradition or prophetic inspiration cannot be overthrown by any science in the world'

[Barcelona, second half of the 13th century]

You ask about my attitude to that Agadah according to which the world will come to an end after a certain time; you have found in the writings of R. Moses ben Maimon statements which are opposed to this.

Know that in all these and similar matters, when we try to examine them with the help of pure science, the latter view must prevail; we are then indeed forced to conclude that the world will never cease to exist, since science rests upon perceptions and observations of nature, and we see that all planets as well as the earth move continually without change. He who believes, however, in the end of the world does this not on the ground of any perception but on the ground of the traditions of the sages, his belief in which cannot be shattered. What has been founded on tradition or prophetic inspiration cannot be overthrown by any science in the world, for science ranks far below prophetic inspiration. This is a principle agreed upon by the confessors of all positive religions and most of all by the confessors of our own true faith. We believe in the whole tradition as we believe in the supernatural miracles which have been done to the patriarchs, as we believe in the passing through the Red Sea and the Jordan, in the sun's standing still, etc. To be sure, all this is denied by the philosophers, and Moses as well as the prophets are for them of no avail, but we are not concerned with those who deny the value of tradition on principle. This can, of course, be done only by those who take it as proved that all that is against nature cannot exist and is impossible – as if there were not higher verities than those which can be perceived by them.

. . . What seems to us to be the most curious thing about the adversaries of faith is this, that they themselves are bound to admit that they cannot explain many phenomena and that they are unable to penetrate to the essence of nature. Thus, for example, they cannot say why and how the magnet sets the iron in motion and attracts it to itself; . . . David says rightly against these men, who want to deny miraculous events in nature according to their experience and perceptions, in a Psalm[1]: 'The testimony of the Lord is sure, making wise the simple'; that is: their reason in its foolish doubts perceives through the miraculous facts which reveal themselves before their eyes – the miracles at the Red Sea and on Sinai among them – that there exists an omnipotent God, who is master of nature and alone preserves, or moves, or changes it.

If Jewish scholars accept the point of view maintained by science in general, they are bound to interpret many passages of Scripture in a forced way in order to bring them into agreement with science and to explain many things allegorically because philosophy does not care for any prophets or commandments. If we want, therefore, as true Jewish scholars, to remain in agreement with tradition, we have to explain the words of the Bible without regard to whether they are in agreement with the conclusions of science or not. Thus, for example, one can conceive all passages of the Bible which refer to resurrection allegorically, particularly the narrative of the dry bones[2]; there is no necessity to apply any verse to a real general resurrection, but tradition obliges us to do so, and this is enough to oblige us to interpret the respective verses in a corresponding way, as the divine wisdom is of greater value to us than human wisdom and as we must give unconditional preference to a tradition preserved by our forefathers, which is deeply rooted and takes its origin from the prophets, rather than to the results of our limited human knowledge. . . .

1. *Abba Mari of Montpellier appeals to Solomon ibn Adret to assume the leadership in the struggle against modernism*

In this fight against modernism, Solomon ibn Adret was not at first inclined to go beyond argument and remonstrance. There were others, however, who demanded more positive action. Foremost among them was Abba Mari, son of Moses, of Lunel, a distinguished and cultured resident of Montpellier, known also as Don Astruc de Lunel. Though well trained in philosophical thinking and an admirer of Maimonides, Abba Mari was deeply disturbed by a wave of modernism which seemed to him to threaten religion with complete dissolution, and he felt the urgent need of bringing the assailants of traditional Judaism to a halt. Mistrusting his own powers of leadership, he turned to the one man in his generation who seemed to be marked out for a task of such magnitude: the Sage and Saint of Barcelona. To him he addressed a stirring call full of apostolic fervour.

ABBA MARI OF LUNEL TO SOLOMON IBN ADRET

'And now, our lord and master, how canst thou look on when the sanctuary is being consumed by rotten books?

[Montpellier, 1304]

. . . To whom should belong the distinction . . . of pouring out his wrath according to the ordinances of the Torah? . . . Is there among us a man greater than thou, a man in whom dwelleth the spirit of the Lord, the spirit of counsel and insight, who spreads the fear of God around him daily? Thou art, indeed, a man whose name is distinguished for knowledge of Torah! The sceptre is in thy hands and who would dare to oppose thy majesty with words? Thou who sittest on the bench art bound to pronounce just judgement when people commit sins. And if a man sins against God, thou shalt spread seven ointments over his wounds,[3] to extinguish the sin, and thou art bound to destroy everybody who deviates and detracts from the law. . . . The hour calls for this. For the end is drawing near, the appointed days preceding the coming of the Messiah have come. How proud is the face of this generation which tries her judges and elders, while the lovers of the Torah are without a defender. . . . They have broken the covenant, and debased the Torah to an ordinance of only temporary validity, they please themselves in the children of strangers, waste the riches of the Torah, concoct slanderous legends, and produce many books about them, with their own logic. . . .

And now, our lord and master, prince and great deliverer and lord, to whom there has been no equal since the days of the Judges, since Jerubbaal and Bedan,[4] thou champion and peerless man of these days! How canst thou look on, when the sanctuary is being consumed by rotten books? Gird thy sword round thy loins, lift thy stick and strike at their heads! Give counsel, and say that fences should be built through which the foxes will not be able to break. May the sword of thy wit be swung over the sages of this country. And may thy words fly against the mighty men.

Verily, I know that thy word will be fulfilled, and that we shall honour thee therefore. May all unite with thee, and in their midst I shall see the rising glory of the Lord. May the Lord increase thy welfare and the years of thy life, according to thy wish and the wish of thy servant

Abba Mari

2. *Solomon ibn Adret in Combat*

After some hesitation and further correspondence with some prominent leaders of Provençal Jewry, Solomon ibn Adret took action. In a letter which he signed together with the other Rabbis and dignitaries of Barcelona he urged the community of Montpellier to forbid men under thirty years to take up philosophical studies. This letter created a storm of controversy, in which the leading scholars of France and Spain took part. The correspondence was later collected and published by Abba Mari under the title 'Minhath Kenaoth' (Offering of Zeal). Two letters exchanged between the mathematician and astronomer Jacob, son of Machir ibn Tibbon, and Solomon ibn Adret are of particular interest.

JACOB SON OF MACHIR TO SOLOMON IBN ADRET

'There is nobody among our followers who wants to dissolve all biblical stories into allegories'

[Montpellier, 1304]

... If these studies do damage to faith, why do you allow them at all and ask only that a line should be drawn between youth and maturity? Is a man of advanced years, then, entitled to expose his faith in the verities of religion which he imbibed in his youth to the temptations of philosophical scepticism later on? But I know well your true and secret intention to deny the validity of science altogether, because you have often spoken in a derogatory manner about it and its pioneers, and have even maintained that Maimuni's pronouncements on cosmology are without foundation. Besides, you should not give credit to the accusations of Abba Mari, and attack even that old scholar[5] whose fame and learning are widely known, whose works were already studied with great zeal in Lunel in my youth, and who has dictated the translation into Hebrew of many works which have been praised even by Nahmanides. If therefore the products of a foreign spirit then entered Judaism, why should we ban them now?

I admit that there are some detestable ideas expressed in the philosophical writings, but this does not justify your refusal to make ourselves acquainted with the good ideas they contain. Our scientific efforts provide evidence to the nations that we have an open mind and understanding for everything beautiful and good. We might even take these as an example in this regard, as they honour the scholars of other denominations who translate their writings into the languages spoken by the members of these denominations even if they contradict the notions of the latter sharply. By such a procedure the convictions of a people are by no means weakened, and their faith is nowhere and never undermined, at least not ours, for the truth of which we possess the best proofs. Besides, there is nobody among our followers who wants to dissolve all biblical stories into allegories; I myself know very well the borderline which philosophy must not cross in its criticism of the Bible, and the most ardent zealot cannot censure me for going too far in this respect. I do not over-estimate the value of philosophy, neither do I under-estimate it, and I am thankful to anybody who can give me a satisfactory explanation for one of those wondrous Talmudic legends.

I wonder that you, instead of announcing a decision, try to wash your hands of us with praises which we neither expected nor deserve. As you apparently intend to withdraw from the affair, we have the impression that you wanted to achieve nothing but to make us afraid. But after having kindled the quarrel, it is for you to bring it to an end, and to find a peaceful solution of the conflict.

SOLOMON IBN ADRET TO JACOB BEN MACHIR

'A complete peace between philosophy and revealed religion is inconceivable'

[Barcelona, 1304]

. . . I see that you, my former friend, whom I held in high esteem, do not know any limit to your indignation against me. . . . I thought that you were accustomed to weigh your words, and that you therefore would not direct them against anyone heedlessly. Instead, you trumpet forth words without salt and spice into the world. This bitter remark is suggested to me not by any feeling for my own offended honour, but by quite a different reason: I am sorry for your dignity, which you yourself endanger by stooping to practices unworthy of the height to which you have rightly been elevated by your contemporaries on account of your scholarship, and by joining the boys who are hardly able to cry, My father, and my mother,[5a] who throw themselves into the arms of secular science and make a hobby of astrological reveries and over-hasty syllogisms. It is true that such studies may be of profit to experienced men, whose hair has grown grey while they studied Torah, and that they offer to reasonable people a rather deeper insight into the essence of religion, of which no better evidence can be found than Maimuni himself. Besides, mathematics and medicine do not at all belong to the sciences interdicted by me. But a complete peace between philosophy and revealed religion is inconceivable.

And now, my friend, tell me what great crime we committed when we drew your attention to the excesses of some hotheads in your communities? Was this any detriment to your dignity? . . . May God forgive you for your veiled allusion to my pride. It is not unknown to you that my name is held in honour in France, Germany and other countries. It is, however, certainly also known to you that I was never puffed up with self-esteem because of this, and never made a show of my dignity. From the bottom of my heart I forgive all your colleagues who signed together with you. Most of them have probably been misled more by ignorance of the facts than by the wish to oppose. The friendship maintained between us shall not be altered by this. . . .

About your accusations with regard to my attitude to Maimuni I do not want to waste many words. The man into whose spirit you are able to penetrate as nobody else needs no special defence. Besides, everybody will tell you how devoted I am to Maimuni and his living grandson [David]. The passage in your letter that you yourself disapprove utterly of a complete allegorization of the Bible offers the best comment on your irresponsible behaviour towards me, because I asked for nothing else but the abolition of this evil. . . .

3. *The Ban is proclaimed and refuted*

The struggle reached a climax with the proclamation at Barcelona on the Sabbath of Lamentations, Ab 4th (26 July), 1305, of a Herem (ban) declaring that no member of the Jewish community under the age of twenty-five years should be allowed to study the books of the Greeks on natural science or metaphysics, either in the original or in translation. The study of medicine was, however, expressly, and that of Maimonides and other Jewish philosophers by implication, exempted from the interdict. Solomon ibn Adret defended this procedure in three open letters to the communities of Spain, France and Germany, of which the second, considerably abridged, runs as follows:

SOLOMON IBN ADRET TO THE COMMUNITIES IN SPAIN, FRANCE AND GERMANY

BAN

'Has such a thing ever been heard that men should reduce everything to chaos?'

[Barcelona, 1305]

It is now some time since our attention was drawn by people from the land of Provence, the chosen remnant, who were jealous for the faith of Moses and the Jews, to the fact that there are men there who falsify the Law, and that he is regarded wise who sits down to demolish the walls and who destroys the words of the Law. They hew out for themselves cisterns, broken cisterns,[6] and they impute unto the words of the Law and the words of the sages meanings which are not right. Concerning the two Laws[7] they utter in the synagogues and in the houses of study words by which none can live. Regardless of the glory of all Israel they break down all the fences of the Law and against our holy fathers they put forth their tongue, a thing which even the worshippers of idols have not done. For they say that Abraham and Sarah represent matter and form, and that the twelve tribes of Israel are the twelve constellations. Has a nation ever heard such an evil thing since the world was divided into territories? Or has such a thing ever been heard that men should reduce everything to chaos? The blasphemers of God further say that the holy vessels which were sanctified, the Urim and Thumim,[8] are the instrument known as astrolabe, which men make for themselves. . . . A man who does such things reduces the entire Bible to useless allegories; indeed they trifle with and pervert all the commandments in order to make the yoke of their burden lighter unto themselves. Their reports terrify us, and all who arrive here tell us new things. Truth hath stumbled in the street,[9] for some of them say that all that is written from the section of Bereshit [Genesis] as far as the giving of the Law is nothing more than an allegory. May such men become a proverb and a by-word,[10] and may they have no stay and no staff. Indeed they show that they have no faith in the plain meaning of the commandments. . . . They are more estranged than the Gentiles: for the latter fulfil some of the commandments, while they strongly desire to uproot all.

The chief reason of all this is that they are infatuated with alien sciences, Sidonian and Moabitish,[11] and pay homage to the Greek books. . . . The children that are consecrated unto heaven from their birth and from their mother's womb are drawn away from the breasts and are taught the books and the language of Chaldeans, instead of rising early to study the Jewish faith in the house of their teachers. Now a boy born upon the knees of natural science, who sees Aristotle's seven-fold proofs concerning it, really believes in it, and denies the Chief Cause; if we refute him, he becomes all the more impious. They read the Law with their lips, but their heart is not sound inwardly, and they pervert it in seven ways. . . . They are ashamed when they speak and lecture; they speak with their mouths, but make hints with the finger that it is impossible to change nature, and they thereby declare to all that they do not believe in the creation of the universe, nor in any of the miracles recorded in the Torah.

Now when we saw that the generation had become corrupted and ready to treat religion lightly, we made a fence, and strengthened the wall round our flawless Torah. Had we not made a strong hedge round the vineyard of the Lord of hosts, we should have shared in the blame for their deeds. We have therefore interdicted in the most solemn manner, as ye see recorded with writing of truth in the book of the covenant which we made with God, anyone to teach or to learn these sciences, until the student and the teacher are twenty-five years old, and until they appreciate fully the delicacies of the Law, so that they will not depose it from its queenly rank; for he who espouses it in his youth will not turn away from it even when he grows old. . . .

It is about three years now since we endeavoured to carry out our wish in accordance with our aim; we have made many supplications, asking, requesting, and praying, that the crown of the Torah should be restored to its pristine glory in its place. Our words, however, did not enter into their ears; they made their words, which are directed against us, harsher still, thanks to their ability to write and to speak. Nevertheless we did not cease to write to them. But many strict communities of those provinces inscribed their name to God, and decided to ban and excommunicate them, and they acted wisely in following us, as ye see from the copies of their letters.

Ye mountains of Israel, may ye bear your fruit for ever! Ye people of the God of Abraham, set your eyes upon the palace, lest their folly should destroy the fence of the Law. Let us be

> one band, for we are all the children of one man. With many covenants we and our fathers received truthful laws, written and oral, at the hands of the master of the prophets. How can we deal falsely against our soul and entice our heart to seek the deceptions of Greek philosophy? Those whose eyes look before them, how can they walk with their faces turned backward and ally themselves with Arabic philosophy? Arise, ye princes, anoint the shield, and the Lord shall defend you and your houses, for the Master of your work is faithful to pay the reward of your labour.

The Ban of Barcelona was by no means the last word of the controversy. The modernists of Montpellier reacted vigorously by a counter-ban against those who debarred their children from the study of philosophy, but out of their midst came also the most brilliant defence of philosophy which the whole hundred years' war between tradition and rationalism produced. It was contained in a long letter addressed to Solomon ibn Adret by the poet and scholar Yedaiah ben Abraham ha-Bedersi (of Béziers). Yedaiah defended the use of the allegorical method in dealing with many of the legends and parables woven by the Talmud round biblical characters. He maintained that philosophy was a strong bulwark of religious thought, pointing out that anthropomorphic notions among the Jews had not been finally abolished until Jewish thinkers, above all Maimonides, well versed in Greek and Arabic philosophy, established methodically the truth of God's incorporeality. At the end of the letter Yedaiah appealed to Solomon ibn Adret to restore peace and amity in Israel, and voiced prophetically the ideals of many yet unborn Jewish fighters for the freedom of thought:

> For the heart of this people cannot be turned from the love of science and literature, while their body and soul are kept together. If Joshua himself were to demand it, they would not obey him. For they feel that they wage war in defence of Maimonides and his works; and for his holy teaching they will sacrifice their fortunes, their future generations and their very lives.

Yedaiah's letter turned the scale in favour of liberalism. Solomon ibn Adret himself was so strongly affected by it that he appealed to Abba Mari to desist from his campaign, and though he did not succeed, this peace move itself meant a moral rehabilitation of the banned philosophical party. It is a significant fact that the only extant text of Jedaiah's letter is embodied in one of Ibn Adret's Responsa and so in a way bears the imprimatur of the great Rabbi, the father of his generation, who soon afterwards, in 1310, passed away. Now the great medieval controversy between faith and reason, which had already been halted by the expulsion of French Jewry (1306), faded away, though only to flare up vigorously again and again in modern times.

NOTES

1. Ps. XIX. 7.
2. Ezek. XXXVII.
3. Lev. XIV. 16.
4. 1 Sam. XII. 11.
5. Moses ibn Tibbon, grandson of Judah ibn Tibbon, known as the translator of numerous philosophical, mathematical and astronomical works written in Greek and Arabic.

5a Is. VIII. 4.

6. Jer. II. 13.
7. The written Torah and the Oral Tradition.
8. See Note 8 to Chapter 6.
9. Is. LIX. 14.
10. Ps. XLIV. 14; Job XVII. 6.
11. Judges X. 6.

39

A Correspondence on a Vow of Two Friends to go to the Land of Israel

THE Responsa of the Middle Ages abound with problems arising out of the desire of Jews to go to the Land of Israel, whether on a visit or a pilgrimage or to live and die there (see Chapter 27). Many of the stories revealed in these Responsa are of absorbing interest and show in the most impressive way the strength of the bond which linked the Jews in the Diaspora with the land of their fathers. An excellent example is the following letter written by a Spanish Jew to Rabbi Asher ben Yehiel, the disciple of Rabbi Meir of Rothenburg, who came as an exile from Germany to Toledo and founded there a famous school of learning.

JACOB BEN HANANEL TO ASHER BEN YEHIEL

'May my life and the life of my son be worthy in your eyes, and do you teach me the good and right way'

[Cordova, 1321]

You have already been informed how I and Rabbi Hezekiah swore and vowed to the Mighty One of Jacob to go to the Land of Israel, as you will see from the copy of the oath annexed to this letter. We fixed the time of our journey to be two years from the date of our oath. When the time came, we sold all our property and household goods, bought in their place equipment for exile and provisions for the voyage, and made all preparations to set out. When, however, we desired to hire a boat to take us from Cordova to Seville,[1] we were informed that the ships of the kingdom of Portugal had put to sea to spoil and to seize booty, from every Jew and Moslem they might find at sea, at the bidding of the Pope. Notwithstanding this, we did not rely on the report, and went together to Seville to make inquiries and to find out whether our way was clear. We therefore left our wives and our houses and our daughters and all our property at Cordova. When we arrived at Seville, we could find no boat to take us either to Malaga or to Barcelona, or to any other place whence one may sail towards the Land of Israel. When we saw that we were powerless against the king, Rabbi Hezekiah said to me: 'Return to Cordova, and I will remain here at Seville, and assist you by making all possible inquiries here.' He accordingly brought his household and his books and settled in Seville.

From that day to the present, I have been worrying him to make all efforts to hasten our departure from this land, so as to cancel the ill-fortune which has overtaken me in consequence of my delay in fulfilling my vow; for from that day I have known neither rest nor prosperity nor quiet, but only trouble. . . . For my many sins, in the four years which have passed since I made this vow, I have buried four of my children, some of them already grown up. . . .

When he saw that I had fed on dust as on bread . . . he sent me a letter, shortly before this last Purim, that I should join him, for he was prepared to go together with me to fulfil our vow. I sent bidding him make preparations for the voyage, that we might set out; for with the help of God I would join him after Purim, together with my household. Meanwhile, relations between Cordova and Seville became difficult; the main roads were interrupted, travellers went by devious roads, fully armed, and all the route was highly dangerous. Nevertheless, I did not mind incurring the risk; but those with me would not allow me, my friends and associates preventing me against my will, and not allowing me to act as I pleased. Meanwhile, R. Hezekiah, relying on my letter, hired a boat and put all his property aboard, anticipating that I would join him at the appointed time. When he saw that I did not arrive, as arranged, he would wait no longer but set out with all his property to go overseas; and I, Jacob, was left all alone.

Afterwards he returned to Seville, and sent me a letter, which I attach herewith. I learnt from this that he had not the intention to travel now, but only after having fulfilled another vow, which he had made before our common vow. He told me namely some time after our vow that he had previously made another, according to which he wishes to devote a certain time to the study of the Torah. He declares now that he cannot leave before he has fulfilled this first vow.

The Lord saw my affliction and had mercy upon me in that He left me at least one son of all my many children. If there is now a way to bring me out of this misfortune, I beg you to let me know whether I am obliged to wait until he has fulfilled his vow, as I have been punished already sufficiently for the delay of the vow, or whether I shall leave Cordova in order to go to Mallorca, one of the islands, in order to wait there as he was prepared to do. Perhaps the Lord, in His mercy, will not allow my posterity to be destroyed. . . .

May my life and the life of my son be worthy in your eyes, and do you teach me the good and right way. May the God of Jacob make you great, may He grant your supplication in the time of affliction, and spread the tent of His peace over you in the light of the Torah!

The attached mutual vow reads (in an abridged version) as follows:

. . . We vow unto the Mighty One of Jacob to go to the Land of Israel, to the land of life, to settle in or near Jerusalem, to do the will of God and to serve Him with our whole hearts, because there is the house of our God and the gate of heaven.

We vow each to the other with the scroll of the Torah in our arms, according to the will of God and with the assent of the community, that we shall be associated together as partners for a period of seven years, and that we will not separate from each other during this time. If it be the will of the Creator that we have enough to support ourselves and our families, we shall both devote ourselves wholly to the study of the Torah. If, God forbid, we prove unworthy of this grace and the income does not suffice for both our families, then let one continue his studies and the other engage in worldly occupation to support his associate and his dependants, contenting himself with such time as may be left him for study. . . . If, however, God forbid, the labour of the one does not suffice for both our families, then shall both of us engage in worldly occupations. And all our earnings shall be in common between us.

As part of the oath, we solemnly agree not to resort to legal nullification and not to allow ourselves to be dissuaded jointly or singly from our enterprise. And even if the king should oppose us, we shall strive with all our power to continue to the land of life. . . . The time set for our departure shall be not later than two years from this date in the month of Marheshvan in the year [50]78 *anno mundi* [November 1317].

Rabbi Asher's reply was as follows:

ASHER BEN YEHIEL TO JACOB BEN HANANEL

'If you want to go to the Land of Israel, you do not need the company of Rabbi Hezekiah, because the mutual agreement is dissolved'

[Toledo, 1321]

I share sincerely your pain. May the Lord have mercy upon you, and bring to an end the time of your affliction.

According to your wish, I have carefully studied the vow and the oath which both of you have made together. . . . I cannot agree that any error has occurred. For when he made the previous vow to stay here for the purpose of studying . . . the vow made by him later on to go with you to the Land of Israel could not cancel the vow already made, and, therefore, the second vow was not a vow at all. . . . Now, as his vow is null, and he is not obliged to go, the whole agreement is dissolved. . . . It is clear, therefore, that if R. Hezekiah . . . remains here, no vow rests upon him. If you, however, want to go to the Land of Israel without being bound by a vow, you are free to do so. . . . You do not need the company of R. Hezekiah, because the mutual agreement is dissolved and your vow has become null and void.

I am sorry that you have not told me anything about your community; for I am very anxious to know how they are.

May you prosper, as it is the wish of

R. Asher ben Yehiel may his memory be blessed

The sources are silent about the effect of the Responsum on the unfortunate Rabbi Jacob ben Hananel and about his ultimate fate. But even if he never reached the Land of Israel, his letter to Rabbi Asher ben Yehiel secures to him a glorious place among the lovers of Zion.

NOTE

1. The River Guadalquivir, on which both cities are situated, was at that time navigable up to Cordova; Seville was then, and is still, a port of seafaring vessels.

40

The Admonition of a Philosopher to his Young Son

JOSEPH, son of Abba Mari Caspi, a native of the Provençal city of Argentières (or Caspia, as it is called in Hebrew: from Keseph, i.e. silver) was one of the most prolific Hebrew authors in the first half of the fourteenth century. He wrote a commentary on the entire Bible and also to 'The Guide of the Perplexed', for which he had a profound admiration. His desire to find a teacher or a companion who could help him to resolve the conflict between faith and reason made him a restless wanderer. He visited many places for that purpose but without success. When his son Solomon was twelve years old he determined to try Fez, which he had heard of as a seat of learning. Before setting sail, Caspi, fearing that he might never return, despatched to the boy what he called a 'Guide to Knowledge' in the form of a letter. Though in the introduction he expressed the hope that the Admonition might prove useful for a wider public – an expectation which was fully realized – the intimate character of various passages lends a special epistolary colour to this piece of philosophical instruction, of which an abridged version is given here.

JOSEPH IBN CASPI TO HIS SON SOLOMON

'How can I know that God is One, as is constantly proclaimed in our prayers, unless I know what constitutes unity?

[Valencia, Ellul 1332]

Solomon, my son! Know thou the God of thy father and serve Him. He will cause thee to ride in His 'second chariot'[1] and thine own conduct must raise thee in its chariot, drawing thee as near as thy faculties avail unto Him. . . .

Now, the knowledge of God is the primary precept of all our 613 laws. . . . It is the basis of the precepts enumerated by Maimonides at the beginning of his Code, and which he specifically terms the Foundations of the Torah. These four precepts are (1) to know that there is a First Cause, (2) to recognize that He is One, (3) to love Him, and (4) to fear Him. . . .

Beware, however, lest thou draw from this a wrong inference, arguing: 'Seeing that these four precepts are root and end, what concern have I with the rest of the precepts? Surely it is good for me to disburden myself of the other 609 laws.' God forbid that thou shouldst act thus! As the Lord liveth, all the precepts are of great profit, both in and for themselves, and as reinforcements of the four basic rules. If thou becomest proficient in philosophy, thou wilt understand that man is compounded of body and soul, and that the rational faculty which belongs to the soul is itself partly practical, partly speculative. Neither of these can exist without the other, just as the soul cannot exist without the body. . . .

Hear, my son, the instruction of thy father – and hold firm to my injunction to perform the practical precepts, doing so in the manner befitting them – i.e. by practice. These laws thou must derive from the Bible, from the encyclopedic Compendium of Maimonides, and also from the Compendium of Alfasi.[2] . . .

But 'if there arise a matter too hard for thee in judgement', as regards any of these practical laws, follow the injunction of Scripture: 'Arise and get thee up into the place which the Lord thy God shall choose.'[3] Note the selection of terms. 'Thou shalt come unto the priests the Levites and unto the judge,' 'and thou shalt *do* according to the tenor of the sentence which they shall declare thee.' It is written, 'thou shalt *do*', and not 'thou shalt *know*'. . . . The implication is that we are not all bound to know every detail of the law. . . . That is to say, if I am able to pass my whole life without disputes about the Law, then ignorance of the Law is no defect in my soul. . . .

On the other hand, as God liveth, the case is quite different with regard to the inner, speculative precepts. For their whole substance and being consists in the knowledge of them personally, by every individual, and this knowledge must be a continuous, rational apprehension. . . . This rational apprehension must be fortified by irrefutable proofs. For the knowledge of God, of His existence and His unity, means proven knowledge.

. . . How can I know that God is One, as is constantly proclaimed in our prayers, unless I know what constitutes unity? . . . How can any of us be said to appreciate the meaning of Unity as applied to God unless we have an inner understanding of the declaration so often on our lips that the Lord our God is One; unless we know, and know by demonstration, that this One is not the mover of the diurnal sphere but a power above it? So, too, with the precepts to love and to fear Him. We are not to love God as a man loves his wife and children. But these emotions as applied in our relation to God need definition, of the kind supplied in the works of Maimonides. But to acquire the necessary knowledge a study of the natural sciences and metaphysics is indispensable. . . .

My son, observe my words! To-day thou art twelve years of age. For another two years be a diligent student of the Scriptures and Talmud. When thou art fourteen, fix regular hours for continuing thy previous studies, and give also a good part of thy time to mathematics; first Ibn Ezra's Arithmetic,[4] then Euclid,[5] and the astronomical treatise of Al-Fergani[6] and Abraham b. Hiya.[7] Appoint also set times for reading moral books, which will introduce thee to all good qualities – viz. the Books of Proverbs and Ecclesiastes, the Mishnaic tractate Abot, with the Commentary of Maimonides and his preface thereto, and the same author's Introductory Chapters to the Code. Also read Aristotle's Ethics, of which I have made a digest. There is also available among us the Collection of the Maxims of the Philosophers.

This course should occupy thee for two years. Then, when thou art sixteen, appoint times for the Scriptures, for the writings of Alfasi, Moses of Coucy,[8] and the Code of the perfect teacher.[9] Also give much time to Logic. With the help of God I will make a compendium on this subject, sufficient for thy needs, as I did with the Ethics.

In this way thou shouldst pass another two years, by which time thou wilt be eighteen years old. Then review all thy former work, and study natural science. By that date, being twenty years of age, 'build thy house'.... Marry a wife of good family, beautiful in form and in character. Pay no regard to money, for true wealth consists only of a sufficiency of bread to eat and raiment to wear. Why weary thyself to gain great riches, when neither thou nor any other could equal the vast store accumulated by the great mountain in our native city l'Argentière? . . . Rather occupy thy mind continually with books of morals.... Observe their injunctions faithfully. Above all things be chaste, just as thy father has been before thee. And use thy endeavours to live a virtuous life, and to order well thy home with thy wife and the children whom, God willing, thou shalt beget.... Never fail to read a section of some ethical book daily after every meal, having first blessed the Lord....

There are, my son! two dispositions among contemporary Jews which must be firmly avoided by thee.

The first class consists of sciolists, whose studies have not gone far enough. They are destroyers and rebels, scoff at the words of the Rabbis of blessed memory, treat the practical precepts as of little account, and accept unseemly interpretations of biblical narratives. They betray unmistakably their inadequate acquaintance with the philosophical writings of Aristotle and his disciples. . . . [They] will have to pay the penalty for their offence. They will be called to account, too, for the occasion that they have given to the ignorant to scoff at philosophy, thereby profaning the name of Heaven!

The second class referred to above includes those of our people who hold in contempt genuine philosophy as presented in the works of Aristotle and his like. . . . Now, my son, I do not blame this class because they devote all their time to the Talmudic argumentation, for as Ibn Yanah[10] said: 'Every man deserves praise for his labour, eulogy for his effort.' But I do blame them because they despise science and those engaged in its study.

My son! When thou meetest such men, address them thus: My masters! What sin did your fathers detect in the study of logic and philosophy? . . . Is it a terrible crime to use words with accuracy? . . . And then, what say ye of the work of Aristotle and Maimonides? Have you examined the inside of their books? If ye know more than their covers, ye know of a surety that the books are an exposition and justification of our precious precepts. . . . If you are advanced in years, and have not yet read the words of the philosophers . . . then open your eyes before the sun be darkened! . . . Why, my masters, do ye regard the jibes of women, or of men who play the woman, when they cry: See this grey-beard gone again to school! What have ye in common with such people? Will they go with you, and take you on your way to the Future World, whose duration is eternal? What concern have we with those children of this age who must die tomorrow, and who even now, in their lives, are called dead?

I will confess to thee, my son! that though in my youth I learned a great portion of the Talmud, I did not acquire [for my sins] a knowledge of the Posekim.[11] Now that I am old and grey, I have often to consult Rabbis younger than myself. Why should I be ashamed of this? Can one man be skilled in every craft? If, for instance, I want a golden cup, I go to the goldsmith, and I feel no shame; and so with other products, I turn, in case of need, to those whom God has endowed with the requisite skill. . . .

I have shown thee, my son, the way to wisdom. Yet I will call to thy mind one matter which must never be forgotten, seeing that, whilst still a boy, thou hast read the Talmud, and particularly the opening tractate. There are many Hagadot the literal wording of which posits ideas inadmissible rationally, or attributes to God corporeality, change, or some other affection. . . . Therefore, my son, understand that most of the Hagadot found in the Talmud and other rabbinic books . . . are figures of speech, with an inner meaning, which we can sometimes discern, sometimes not.

Ours is to realize that he who is of the seed of Abraham our father – who risked his life to dissociate himself from all the people and the king of his country, believers in the corporeality of God – is also of Abraham's principles! Whoever believes the contrary, who regards God as corporeal, testifies of himself that he is not of the seed of Abraham, but of the seed of Nimrod or the other Chaldean disputants with Abraham. . . .

But thou mayest be led on to think of similar difficulties in the case of the Scripture where the Law and the Prophets attribute corporeality to God. Such phrases as 'in our image, after our likeness' may occur to thee; or the texts in which face and back, hands and feet are ascribed to God. Understand that there is an explanation for all this, which must not be taken literally. But how canst thou realize it, while thou art a boy of twelve? For thou wilt find the explanation in the 'Guide', and I have already directed thee not to study that work till thou art twenty.

How all this is true, what is its significance, lo, as thou knewest not in the hour of thy entrance into the world, so thou wilt not know it until thou art twenty and over. Then wilt thou rise to this all-important knowledge, then wilt thou enter within the precincts of Pleasure and Delight, the Paradise of all dainty fruits, eating unto satisfaction of the Tree of Life, for as Solomon said of Wisdom: 'She is the tree of life to them that lay hold of her, and happy is everyone that holdeth her fast'.[12]

And as I have bidden thee, my son, to maintain from thy birth this supreme faith – the faith of Abraham thy first father – refusing to attach to God the idea of body, so I command thee to hold through life to the trust that after thy death thou wilt be found worthy of the future life, where nothing bodily is. Thou wilt be as an angel of the Lord of hosts, a brother and comrade of the other Angels there! What good or profit, what happiness or delight, is comparable to this? Yet mayest thou after thy death attain to this level of good, if thou hast in thy earthly life won for thy soul that which I have commanded. . . .

Dost thou ask how this is? Again my son, know that this is beyond thy capacity until thou art twenty, and canst turn thy mind to metaphysical investigations, among them the holy 'Guide'. Then wilt thou see this in a light as clear as the sunshine. But till then trust and lean on me. I am thy surety, my son, that if thou dost fulfil all my behests thou wilt after thy death reach the highest degree of good appointed unto us for the World-to-Come, and the expression 'after death' will be only a figure of speech, and when thy household think thee dead, then wilt thou be truly alive. As our Sages say: 'The righteous in their death are called living.'[13]

May God hold thee worthy of a life of felicity in this world and the next. Amen and Amen!

Ibn Caspi thy father wrote this, in the month Ellul, in the year 92, of the sixth thousand, in the city of Valencia.

NOTES

1. Viz. in the angelic rank.
2. The Compendium of the Talmud by Isaac, son of Jacob Alfasi (1013–1103), was an epoch-making and standard work.
3. Deut. XVII. 8–11.
4. Abraham ibn Ezra (see pp. 151–52) wrote 'Sepher ha-Mispar' (The Book of Numbers) and other mathematical works.
5. Euclid's Elements appeared in several Hebrew versions, one of them by Moses ibn Tibbon.
6. An Arabic astronomer, whose works were translated into Hebrew.
7. Abraham bar Hiya, outstanding scientist and philosopher of the eleventh century.
8. Moses of Coucy, prominent Tosaphist of the thirteenth century.
9. Maimonides.
10. Jonah ibn Yanah, grammarian and exegete of the eleventh century; one of his chief works is the lexicon 'Book of Roots'.
11. Viz. authorities on practical law.
12. Prov. III. 18.
13. T. B. Berakot 19.

41

Rabbi Hasdai Crescas gives an Account of the Spanish Massacres of 1391

IN the summer of 1391 lawless mobs in Seville, Toledo, Valencia, Barcelona, and many other Spanish cities, incited by Ferrand Martinez, the fanatical archdeacon of Seville, attacked and massacred the Jewish population of these cities. Some months later a report of the events and of the Jewish losses was made to the community of Avignon by the celebrated writer and philosopher Hasdai Crescas, Rabbi of Saragossa, who lost his only son in the outrages. The letter records in its brief compass the ghastly prelude to the disaster which befell the whole Spanish Jewry a hundred years later.

HASDAI CRESCAS TO THE COMMUNITY OF AVIGNON

'Among the many who sanctified the name of the Lord was my only son'

[Saragossa, 19 October 1391]

If I were to tell you here all the numerous sufferings we have endured you would be dumbfounded at the thought of them; I will therefore set before you only in brief detail the table of our disaster set with poisonous plant and wormwood, giving you a bare recital of the facts so that you may satiate yourselves on the bitterness of our wormwood and drink from the wine of our grief.[1] As I suppose that you have been told the story already, I will recount it as briefly as possible, commencing as follows:

On the day of the New Moon of the fateful month Tammus in the year 5151 [July 1391] the Lord bent the bow of the enemies against the populous community of Seville where there were between 6,000 – 7,000 heads of families, and they destroyed their gates by fire and killed in that very place a great number of people; the majority, however, changed their faith.

Many of them, children as well as women, were sold tó the Moslems, so that the streets occupied by Jews have become empty. Many of them, sanctifying the Holy Name, endured death, but many also broke the holy Covenant.

From there the fire spread and consumed all the cedars of Lebanon [Jewish scholars, here Jews generally] in the holy community of the city of Cordova. Here, too, many changed their faith, and the community became desolate.

And on the day of misery and punishment, on which the sufferings were intensified, the wrath of the Lord was discharged on the holy city, the source of learning and the word of the Lord, namely the community of Toledo, and in the temple of the Lord the priests and the learned were murdered. In that very place the Rabbis, the descendants of the virtuous and excellent R. Asher of blessed memory,[2] together with their children and pupils, publicly sanctified the Holy Name. However, many who had not the courage to save their souls changed their faith here, too.

The country trembled even on account of these three communities, apart from the others in their neighbourhood to the number of 70. And withal, we were in the greatest danger here, and had to be on the alert day and night. On the 7th of the month Ab the Lord destroyed mercilessly the community of Valencia, in which there were about a thousand heads of families; about 250 men died, sanctifying the name of the Lord; the others fled into the mountain; some of these saved themselves but the majority changed their faith.

From there the plague spread over the communities of glorious Majorca, which is situated on the shore of the sea. On the day of the New Moon of Ellul, the bloodthirsty villains came there, profaned, plundered and robbed them and left them like a net in which there are no fish. There died, sanctifying the Holy Name, about 300 persons, and about 800 took refuge in the royal castle; the others changed their faith.

On the following Sabbath the Lord poured out his fury like fire, destroyed His sanctuary and profaned the crown of His teaching, namely the community of Barcelona, which was destroyed on that day. The number of murdered amounted to 250 souls; the rest fled into the castle, where they were saved. The enemies plundered all streets inhabited by Jews and set fire to some of them. The authorities of the province, however, took no part in this; instead, they endeavoured to protect the Jews with all their might. They offered food and drink to the Jews, and even set about punishing the wrongdoers, when a furious mob rose against the better classes in the country and fought against the Jews who were in the castle, with bows and missiles, and killed them in the castle itself. Amongst the many who sanctified the Name of the Lord was my only son, who was a bridegroom and whom I have offered as a faultless lamb for sacrifice; I submit to God's justice and take comfort in the thought of his excellent portion and his delightful lot. Amongst them were many who slaughtered themselves and others who threw themselves down from the tower and whose limbs were already broken before they had reached half-way down the tower. Many also came forth and sanctified the name of the Lord in the open street. All the others changed their faith, and only few found refuge in the towns of the princes; a child could register the names of these. However, these were precisely the most esteemed. Consequently, because of our many sins, there is none left in Barcelona today who still bears the name of Jew.

In the town of Lerida, too, many died and others changed their faith. There were only a few people who saved their lives.

In the town of Gerona, where knowledge of the Law could be found combined with humility, the Rabbis of that place sanctified the Name of the Lord publicly, and few only changed their faith. The majority of the community escaped to the houses of the citizens and are today in the castle.

In a word, in the state of Valencia not one single Jew remained, with the sole exception of the place called Murviedro. In the province of Catalonia, too, not one single Jew remained except in the towns of the princes and administrators, who nowhere attacked them.

For us, however, who are still in the country of Aragon, there is no more trouble and complaint, because the Lord has taken pity on us and has preserved the remnant of us in all these places after vehement supplication, although nothing but our bodies is left us after the distribution of our belongings. In spite of this, fear fills our hearts, and our eyes are directed towards the Father in heaven, that He may be merciful to us and may heal us of our wounds,[3] and keep our feet from wavering. May this be His will, Amen.

'I am the man that hath seen affliction by the rod of His wrath,'[4] Hasdai ben Abraham ben Hasdai ben Judah Crescas, who writes here in Saragossa, on the 20th day of the month Marheshvan in the year 5152 of the creation.

NOTES

1. Jer. XXIII. 15.
2. Viz. R. Asher ben Yehiel (see *supra*, pp. 260–264); he died in 1328.
3. Jer. XXX. 17.
4. Lament. III. 1.

42

"Be not like unto thy fathers"
Profiat Duran's Polemical Letter on the Conversion of his friend David Bonet Bongoron

AMONG those who had shirked martyrdom and chosen the path of baptism during the Jewish massacres of 1391 in Spain were Isaac, son of Moses Profiat Duran (also called Efodi from the initial letters of his name), an excellent grammarian and philosopher, and his friend David Bonet Bongoron. The forced conversion weighed heavily on their souls. They decided, therefore, to emigrate to Palestine and there return to Judaism. Profiat Duran went to a port in Southern France expecting to meet his friend there, but instead of David a letter arrived from him saying that he had been persuaded by the apostate Paul of Burgos, originally Solomon ha-Levi, to change his mind. Having become unshakably confirmed in his conviction, he was determined to remain a Christian, and he advised his friend to follow his example. Profiat Duran replied with the following piece of bitter sarcasm and brilliant polemics. By arguing ironically like an advocate of the faith accepted by David, he pleaded with fervour for the truth of Judaism. Thus the letter reflects the tragic contradictions raging in the souls of the Jewish converts who tried to justify their apostasy to themselves. This makes the letter of Profiat Duran one of the most original documents of the perennial controversy between Judaism and Christianity.

PROFIAT DURAN TO DAVID BONET BONGORON

'I should like to ask thee one thing, this only thing, please, do for my sake: do not call thyself any longer after the honoured name of thy wise father'

[A port in Southern France, about 1396]

To David, when he changed his mind[1], before the Ruler of the world, and sang of the death of the son who suffered for him and carried the burden for him. He said to his father: 'I do not know thee,' and does not ask after the forefathers any more. I called him once my brother. Maestro Bonet buen Giorno, the new Christian, is his name. In Israel he was called once: David Bonet ben Goron.

I received a letter. . . . I read it with aching head and tired lips, because it was full of hidden meaning, of dark and secret wisdom, as if it were a book sealed with seven seals. I understood little, but *one* thing became clear to me: that the heritage of the ancestors was a deplorable mistake. . . . They missed the light in spite of their learning, they believed they ascended to heaven and went, instead, down to obscure graves. . . . Woe to them for all their labours, for they were in vain! I redoubled my efforts and perceived at last: The holy spirit has awakened thee, blessed be the Messiah who gave thee a willing heart and listening ear! Human Reason will seduce thee never more to dwell with her in dark chambers, thou recognizest her as an enemy, pernicious like vipers. For she was always an adversary of Faith and ever ready to wound Faith time and again. He is a fool who said: 'Reason and Torah are two lights in the heaven of life.' We have nothing to do with Reason, her syllogisms and evidences, any more. . . . Faith alone goes up to heaven. Those who deny this go to hell. Also Scripture says therefore: 'The just shall live by his faith'[1a], if the Hebrew word does mean indeed that which thou and thy teachers wish to understand by it.

Now, my brother, I became aware of thy good intentions, and that all thou dost is for the sake of the Lord. Faith is for thee a girdle round the loins, and Reason with all her lies is unable to entice thee and divert thy paths. Therefore I made up my mind to show thee clearly the ways of the faith which thou hast chosen as thy compass in the light of the Messiah.

Be not like unto thy fathers,[2] who believed in one God from whose unity they removed any plurality. They have erred indeed, when they said, 'Hear Israel, the Lord is One!', when they understood this unity in the purest sense without inclusion of species, kind or number. *Not so thou!* Thou shalt believe that one can become three, and that three united make one. Lips will never tell it, ears never take it in.

Be not like unto thy fathers, who conceived by deep meditations the eternal Ruler beyond change and body, as expressed in the words 'I change not,'[3] and who explained in this sense even those passages which, when interpreted unskilfully, perplex simple souls. *Not so thou!* Heaven forbid that thou shouldst deny His corporeal embodiment, but believe rather that one of His three persons became flesh, when He wanted to shed blood for the atonement of mankind. Offer Him thanks that He suffered death in order to redeem thee. . . . For this was surely the only way which could be found by the wisdom of the Almighty! Believe that He became flesh in the womb of a virgin, of an 'Almah' as the Hebrew word reads;[4] it occurs also in the passage 'the way of the man with a young woman'.[5] This miracle was able to encourage the faint-hearted Ahaz, although he had lived five hundred years earlier.[6]. . .

Be not like unto thy fathers, who by close scrutiny tried to find a deep philosophical meaning in the account of creation, and who had much to disclose about the first human couple, about the four rivers, the tree of knowledge, the serpent, and the coats of skin which the Lord made them for clothing. *Not so thou!* Conceive all this literally! Add, however, yet an inner punishment to Adam's misfortune, increase through it the burden of his bitter fate that he has to carry on his back. He will never get rid of it, and is entirely in the grip of Satan, until the Redeemer comes and purifies him by his death. Now that sin is abolished, although it is not mentioned in our holy Scripture, while the other curses, the punishments of hell, remain for ever. . . . Stick to the mystery of hereditary sin which the head of the Apostles proclaimed, he whose name is identical with that of thy teacher.[7] Thy reward will grow immensely like thy faith.

Be not like unto thy fathers, who were continuously engaged in sciences of all kinds, in mathematics, metaphysics and logic, and tried to penetrate to the foundations of truth. *Not so thou!* Far be it from thee to recognize the first fundamental rule of reasoning in logic. For this would entice thee to deny thy faith by saying: God is Father; the Son, too, is God truly: the Son is therefore the Father. Brother, stick to this belief! It will lead thee to eternal life, and God will be with thee. . . . Alas, thy fathers ate the bread of affliction, suffered thirst and hunger; thou, however, hast saved thy soul, thou eatest and becomest satisfied, thou rejoicest in the Lord and praisest the Holy One of Israel. . . .

But above all believe sincerely in the almighty Redeemer. He is the root . . . of thy faith. . . . But do not believe in the metaphysical principle that affirmation and negation cannot exist at the same time, further that transformation of an accident into essence is impossible, and also that the being of a thing consists in its essence, but that the being of an accident depends on the object which carries it. For the body of the Messiah who sits on the throne in heaven does not move while that on the altar moves in every direction. The wafer is, before the utterance of the priest, nothing else than bread, but by this utterance the essence of the bread becomes an accidental quality or disappears entirely, and the previous accidental qualities become independent and enter the stomach of the priest who eats the wafer. None of the believers denies this. . . . In general, brother, do not accept the principle, 'What is impossible in itself remains impossible', but, on the contrary, accept faithfully all those impossibilities, for the almighty Messiah dominates all things, near or far, possible or impossible. . . .

Be not like unto thy fathers, upon whom the holy Torah of Moses was bestowed as heritage and possession, when they strove after spiritual perfection in thought and deed, when they called that godly doctrine the crown of their head, and kept faithfully the commandments and prohibitions, according to the saying, 'The secret things belong unto the Lord our God; but those things which are revealed belong unto us and to our children for ever.'[8] Every prophet points to this, even the last one declares it through his last word.[9] *Not so thou!* For this would be shameful. If thou beget sons, do not introduce them into the covenant of the fathers! Take no heed of the multitude of those ancient laws of marriage. Neither change thy garb to sanctify the Sabbaths and Festivals. When the great, the only day of the long fast approaches, tell thyself: 'Now, eat and drink, for thou art without any guilt!' Eat leavened bread on the Passover; eat also meat and milk together! Where penalties threaten, believe that it is always better to permit. Eat of pork, of all animals in the water, on the earth and in the air, which have been interdicted thee once.

To be sure, have not the disciples of the Messiah themselves forbidden this to the faithful people, in the book of their teaching called 'The Acts of the Apostles'?[10]. . . Did not those men as descendants of Abraham keep rigidly the Law? Even after the death of their leader? Even after their baptism? But why should I mention them, seeing that the Messiah himself confirmed the permanence of the Law![11]. . .

Behold! I should like to come to thee, my brother, and to thy new teacher, with all these and many other scruples, because I know that the holy spirit speaks through you, elected men! No secret exists for you, thanks to the Lord, who has chosen you. . . . There is one thing, however, which I want to tell thee. . . . Do not care for the shame in thy soul, or the mark on thy forehead, when the enemies will perhaps offend thee in future, for some of them will say 'Apostate' and others 'circumcised Jew': as a reward thy soul will share the eternal pleasures, and thou wilt see the faces of the king and of the queen beside him.

As to the excellence of thy teacher, whom thou praisest so highly for his enormous wisdom, his dignity and ingenuity, that thou considerest him as created in the image of God and wouldst almost elect him Pope – although thou art not sure whether he should go to Rome or remain in Avignon[12] – I am quite aware of the proficiency which this man acquired in astronomy and philosophy. Offer thanks to the Messiah that such a man is in his world. Not without reason our king bestowed upon him rich treasures in recognition of his piety. Thou tellest me also, my brother, that his mighty influence was instrumental for the important decision of the king that 'women and minor children – under fifteen years – are not allowed to pass through the city without escort'. Thus it was published. This is a big thing indeed and very useful for the masses. Now, haste and show it to thy parents! Tell it also to the smart ladies!

There is a rumour that he was about to speak evil things against the Jews in Avignon. But his Excellency the Lord Cardinal of Pampeluna and also other princes protested against this strongly in secret. In addition the Jewish community gave him a lot of money in gold and silver. Then he was silent. The Pope, however, and his friends have the intention of bestowing upon him a bishopric or even appointing him a cardinal. Rejoice then, dear brother: his honour honours thee too. He will certainly not fail to establish many houses of priests and Levites for thy benefit.

I wonder that thou – methinks, just as it is the way of fools – warnest me writing that my friends try to perplex me. For ever and anon I strove seriously after truth, in thought and deed. Thou knowest this very well. I live entirely for my Lord, with all my heart, and with all my soul, today and always. It is my hope and my profound trust that *that* Messiah will come who carries His name. Behold, this is my song and praise, my pleasure, strength and power. To this faith I have clung for many years, without change, without apostasy, and I shall cling for ever.

I should like, however, to ask thee one thing, this thing only, please, do it for my sake: do not call thyself any longer after the honoured name of thy wise father, may his memory be blessed! For his advice does not suit thee any more, and his merit does not shine upon thee. For if he were alive he would say to-day: 'Better no son than such a son!' And his soul in its resting place laments now, too, over thee and thy way. May the Messiah, he to whom thou adherest, he alone and nobody else, give thee light and peace for ever!

He who is writing this loves thee with all his heart. And if thou wilt choose the right way and listen to the voice of the

Lord, He will always be with thee. As it is said, 'In all places where I record my name, I will bless thee.'[13] And then thou wilt again be to me a brother and darling son.

He who wrote this is thy brother

Efodi

We do not know the effect the letter produced on the recipient. But the ingenuity of Profiat Duran's ambiguous expressions is strikingly proved by the fact that the letter was received by Jews and Christians alike as the vindication of their respective faiths. Its circulation was due to Rabbi Meir Alguadez, physician to the King of Castile, to whom Profiat Duran had forwarded a copy. The Christian readers considered the 'Alteca Boteca', as the letter was called from a corruption of the refrain 'Al tehi ka aboteka' (Be not like unto thy fathers!), as an ideal Christian confession. It took some time before they realized their mistake, and before Profiat's epistle was proscribed by the Church authorities and publicly burned. The first printed edition, with a commentary by Joseph ben Shem Tob and an introduction by Isaac Akrish, was published at Constantinople in 1554, and though Profiat Duran wrote other, more scholarly works of note (particularly the philosophical and critical Hebrew Grammar 'Ma'aseh Efod') it is this epistle which has preserved his name through the ages. Nothing is known about his last years except that, not later than 1403, he returned to Spain and there openly embraced Judaism again.

NOTES

1. Ps. XXXIV. 1.
1a Hab. II. 4.
2. Zech. I. 4; 2 Chron. XXX. 7 (see *supra*, pp. 3–4). Cf. also Ezek. XX. 18.
3. Mal. III. 6.
4. Allusion to Is. VII. 14, where the word 'ha-almah', i.e. 'young woman', occurs, which in Christian translations is rendered 'virgin'.
5. Prov. XXX. 19.
6. Is. VII. 1–12; actually, Ahaz lived in the eighth cent. B.C.E. (reigned 735–720).
7. Paul de Burgos.
8. Deut. XXIX. 29.
9. Mal. IV. 4–6.
10. Acts XV.
11. Mat. V. 17.
12. Allusion to the Great Schism; Paul de Burgos was an adherent of Benedict XIII, a Spaniard, the anti-Pope of Avignon (1394–1424).
13. Exod. XX. 24.

43

Isaac Zarfati warns the Jews of Germany to leave their Country and to settle in Turkey

For the Jews of Germany as for those of Spain the fifteenth century was a period of cruel persecution. Utter destruction following the most barbaric treatment came upon the Jews of Austria under the Duke Albert V in the years 1420 and 1421. In other German countries also, trials by the Inquisition, executions, expulsions and excesses committed against the Jews followed in an almost uninterrupted succession. In contrast to this nightmare, a haven of peace and prosperity was opened to the Jews in the Ottoman Empire after the capture of Constantinople by the Turks on 29 May 1453. Two pioneers, Kalmann and David, who almost at once discovered the possibilities of the East, were not slow to bring them to the notice of their oppressed brethren in Germany and to invite them to follow their example. At their request another early settler in Turkey, Isaac Zarfati, of French origin but born and educated in Germany, addressed to the Jews of Germany and Hungary a letter in which he called on them to arrange an exodus to the Ottoman realm. A copy of the letter has been preserved in the Bibliothèque Nationale in Paris. Viewed in the perspective of the ultimate doom of German Jewry, Zarfati's epistle, written in traditional biblical style but full of satire and witty allusions, falls not far short of a prophecy.

The following abridgment of the original document was made by Graetz, who dated the letter at about 1454 on the strength of the reference to the prohibition of assisting Jews to travel to the Holy Land which was issued in the fifteenth century.[1] Some authorities, however, hold that the letter was written in the first half of the sixteenth century.

ISAAC ZARFATI TO THE JEWS OF SUAVIA, THE RHINELAND, STYRIA, MORAVIA AND HUNGARY

'O Israel, wherefore sleepest thou? Arise, and leave this accursed land for ever!'

[Somewhere in Turkey, probably 1454]

I have heard of the afflictions, more bitter than death, that have befallen our brethren in Germany – of the tyrannical laws, the compulsory baptisms and the banishments, which are of daily occurrence. I am told that when they flee from one place a yet harder fate befalls them in another. I hear an insolent people raising its voice in fury against a faithful remnant living among them; I see its hand uplifted to smite my brethren. On all sides I learn of anguish of soul and torment of body; of daily exactions levied by merciless oppressors. The clergy and the monks, false priests that they are, rise up against the unhappy people of God and say: 'Let us pursue them even unto destruction; let the name of Israel be no more known among men.' They imagine that their faith is in danger because the Jews in Jerusalem might, peradventure, buy the Church of the Sepulchre. For this reason they have made a law that every Jew found upon a Christian ship bound for the East shall be flung into the sea.[1] Alas! how evil are the people of God in Germany entreated; how sadly is their strength departed! They are driven hither and thither, and they are pursued even unto death. The sword of the oppressor ever hangs over their heads; they are flung into the devouring flames, into swift-flowing rivers and into foul swamps.

Brothers and teachers, friends and acquaintances! I, Isaac Zarfati, though I spring from a French stock, yet I was born in Germany, and sat there at the feet of my esteemed teachers. I proclaim to you that Turkey is a land wherein nothing is lacking, and where, if you will, all shall yet be well with you. The way to the Holy Land lies open to you through Turkey. Is it not better for you to live under Moslems than under Christians? Here every man may dwell at peace under his own vine and fig-tree.[2] Here you are allowed to wear the most precious garments. In Christendom, on the contrary, ye dare not even venture to clothe your children in red or in blue, according to your taste, without exposing them to the insult of being beaten black and blue, or kicked red and green, and therefore are ye condemned to go about meanly clad in sad-coloured raiment. All your days are full of sorrow, even the Sabbaths and the times appointed for feasting. Strangers enjoy your goods, and, therefore, of what profit is the wealth of your rich men? They hoard it but to their own sorrow, and in a day it is lost to them for ever. Ye call your riches your own – alas, they belong to *them!* They bring false accusations against you. They respect neither age nor wisdom; and though they gave you a pledge sealed sixty-fold, yet would they break it. They continually lay double punishment upon you, a death of torment and confiscation of goods. They prohibit teaching in your schools; they break in upon you during your hours of prayer; and they forbid you to work or conduct your business on Christian feast days. . . .

And now, seeing all these things, O Israel, wherefore sleepest thou? Arise! and leave this accursed land for ever![3]

NOTES

1. Zarfati alludes here to the Bull of Pope Martin V forbidding the seafaring republics of Venice and Ancona to convey Jews to the Holy Land under pain of excommunication.
2. I Kings IV. 25; Is. XXXVI. 16; Mic. IV. 4; Zech. III. 10.
3. Ps. XLIV. 23.

44

Scenes from Medieval anti-Jewish Trials

THE two most dangerous and frequent calumnies levelled at the Jews in the Middle Ages were that they indulged in perpetrating the so-called 'ritual murder' and in desecrating the host. These pitiable superstitions became responsible for countless sufferings of the Jewish people in almost all countries of the Diaspora. By an odd coincidence, two trials took place at the end of the Middle Ages simultaneously in the ancient Bavarian city of Ratisbon, each of which was based on one of those accusations. They gave occasion to two memorable letters.

1. *Rabbi Joseph Colon appeals from Italy to the Jews of Germany for solidarity with their falsely accused brethren*

In 1475 almost all Jews of the Tyrolese city of Trent were burned at the stake as victims of the accusation that in the days before Easter they had crucified a Christian boy. Shortly afterwards, upon the instigation of the Bishop Henry of Ratisbon, seventeen members of the Jewish Ratisbon community were put on trial by the city council under the suspicion of having committed a similar crime eight years before. The danger that after exposure to torture they would have to suffer the same fate as the Jews of Trent was imminent. The only hope remaining was that the Emperor Frederick III would intercede on behalf of the guiltless, imprisoned defendants. The Rabbis of Bavaria, at a special convention held at Nuremberg, decided to make every possible effort to rescue the prisoners and to provide the very considerable funds needed for this purpose through a collection from all Bavarian communities. The Rabbis, however, being unable to impose openly the necessary duties and sanctions, turned to an outsider of undisputed authority for support of their action. They asked one of the most celebrated talmudical scholars of the day, Joseph ben Solomon Colon, Rabbi of Pavia, to give his binding opinion on the obligation of the communities to contribute to the rescue work. Rabbi Colon discharged this duty by the following remarkable pronouncement.

RABBI JOSEPH BEN SOLOMON COLON TO THE COMMUNITIES OF BAVARIA

'I call upon all Jewish inhabitants of Germany, individuals as well as communities, under the threat of excommunication, that they resist not the action of the Rabbis assembled at Nuremberg . . .

[Pavia, 1476]

The news of the danger which threatens the lives of our imprisoned co-religionists at Ratisbon, may their Rock and Redeemer protect them, and which also imperils the neighbouring communities, has spread everywhere. A convention of celebrated Rabbis met, therefore, in the holy community of Nuremberg to take counsel and to consider the means for the deliverance of the guiltless brethren, whose houses are free from any crime and who nevertheless, because of our many sins, have to be submitted to death. It is, however, to be feared that some communities or individuals, even relatives, who are over-confident and believe themselves safe from danger, might deny their assistance to the planned rescue work, although in fact, may the Lord avert it, the fateful cloud could burst even over their heads if the unhappy brethren will not be saved.

I am, therefore, glad to answer the call of those who addressed me and to comply with the request of my teachers for showing the path to the light of salvation.

It is lawful that in the first place the neighbouring communities, which in all probability, too, will have to drain the cup of affliction if the impending misfortune will not be averted from our co-religionists at Ratisbon, should be called on to contribute to the forthcoming expenses. . . . An analogous case is to be found in Baba Mezia.[1] Rabbi Judah says: 'If a stream descending from above dries up, or is impeded by stones, the owners of the fields situated below have to contribute to its restoration because they, too, need the water for the culture of their acres. Likewise house-owners who dwell in the upper part of a city have to contribute to the costs of draining the rainwater if the lower parts of the city are flooded. For although for the present the lower parts only are endangered, the peril for the upper parts of the city is unavoidable if help is not offered in time to the former.' Also in our case the danger for the neighbouring cities, although they seem to be safe for the time being, cannot be avoided if Ratisbon will not be saved. For the thoughts of our enemies are always aimed at assailing and destroying us. – Oh, may the Lord deliver us from their hands! Those neighbouring communities should take to heart the verse, 'Happy is the man that feareth alway: but he that hardeneth his heart shall fall into mischief.'[2]

And even if the communities would object to a request for contributions, saying that the slanderous rumours which have brought so much misfortune to the Jews will not penetrate to them, and that therefore a vague possibility only but not a certainty of the danger is in question, I declare that in such a case, too, it is legitimate to ask them for common contributions. For the pious teachers who protect the possessions of orphans, and are anxious to preserve them from any loss, declare that in situations when the protection against an even not immediate danger is involved, orphans too have to make their contribution, and that it is lawful to ask them for participation in the expenses for the repair of the city walls, for the appointment of a watchman for the arsenal or for the conscription of riders who look out for approaching forces. . . . The inhabitants of a city can also be forced to provide the city with fortifications and gates in order to protect it against a possible danger. And how much more do the neighbouring communities need the protection not only of their bodies but of their souls, and how much more are they obliged to contribute to this protection by paying their contributions, even if to this end they had to give up the last coat or to sell the hair from their heads!

It is for the purpose of providing such a protection that the pious Rabbis assembled at Nuremberg. May it please our Father in heaven to let them succeed in their work! Every community is, therefore, obliged to give as much as they will determine as its duty and it has to accept their decision without complaint if one of the communities is taxed more and the other less. As the Rabbis, however, do not dare to address to the communities formal requests for money for fear of their princes and masters, I call upon all Jewish inhabitants of Germany, individuals as well as communities, under the threat of excommunication, that they resist not the action of the Rabbis assembled at Nuremberg and, instead, make their contributions with readiness according to the prescribed proportions, in order that the brethren who have been thrown into the gaol through deceitful accusations may be liberated. He, however, who defies the call of the Rabbis from Nuremberg, may he be expelled from the community of the Exile, may the curse weigh upon him and penetrate into him and into his bones like oil, and may his name be given up to utter destruction. Those, however, who listen to the voice of the Rabbis will dwell in safety and a rich blessing will be stored up for them.

Thus says the man who is incapable of dominance, thus writes with a humble mind

the lowly Joseph Colon

The co-operation of the German Rabbis with their illustrious Italian colleague led to complete success. With the help of sufficient funds an intervention with the Imperial Court was organized, and in spite of the combined resistance of the city authorities of Ratisbon and of a special papal legate, Frederick III persisted in the release of the guiltless Jews, which took place in 1480.

2. *An early Yiddish letter to an imprisoned woman*

At the time when the seventeen Jews were kept in the gaol of Ratisbon, a certain widow Pelain and her son were accused of having bought, tortured and sold a consecrated wafer. They were imprisoned and their belongings confiscated. A scrap of paper with a brief note in Yiddish, which had been smuggled into the prison cell of the unhappy woman and, strangely enough, has survived, brings home to us the horror of this frightful event.

AN UNKNOWN WRITER TO THE WIDOW PELAIN

'Is it because the tortures prevent you from writing?'

[Ratisbon (?), 1478]

My dear Friend, dear Crown,

I write much to you but you do not answer. Is it because the tortures[3] prevent you from writing? Tomorrow I shall speak to the Mayor; perhaps I can bring your affair to a successful issue. Send out the cap again. Have its hole closed up. Boil pure powder in an apple. You have about five days [to do it in (?)]. Write clearly in German.[4] Sew [it] in.

We do not know who was the author of this moving human document, but we do know that Pelain's brother succeeded in procuring the Emperor Frederick III's intervention to save the two prisoners from being tortured and that, some months later, they were released upon the renewed intervention of the Emperor, who afterwards also ordered the release of the seventeen Jews. That the letter was written by the brother himself is hardly probable in view of his apostrophe 'dear friend' ('libe vründin'). The historical significance of the letter is, however, not exhausted by its contents, for the secret message to Pelain constitutes the earliest extant letter written in Yiddish the date of which has been firmly established, as we know that the trial took place in 1478 (see Introduction).

NOTES

1. Baba Mezia 108.
2. Prov. XXVIII. 14.
3. Pelain was very ill, and therefore spared from torture; this fact was apparently unknown to the writer.
4. Presumably Yiddish.

45

An Offer of Books

THIS letter, composed by an unknown writer and sent to an equally unknown addressee in an Italian community at the end of the fifteenth century, gives a pleasing picture of the mutual help offered by Jewish scholars for the benefit of their learned work in those days. It informs us, too, how even eminent scholars like Johanan Alemanno, the teacher of Pico della Mirandola, pledged their books with more fortunate if less proficient scholars to provide themselves with cash. It further shows the high significance ascribed to letters from Palestine: instead of being regarded as the private possession of their recipients, they were copied and made accessible to a wider circle of friends, who impatiently looked forward to news from the Holy Land.

AN UNKNOWN WRITER TO AN UNKNOWN SCHOLAR

'Why do you implore me so humbly to forward you the books? Is this not the most urgent duty of all of us?'

[An Italian town, about 1490]

I received your letter like a wonderful and precious token when the mail-coach arrived here on Monday morning. We were just in the house of God at that time. My heart was cheered when I saw what your hands had folded, and your strong right hand had written.

I am sending you by this mail the 'Sefer ha-Kavanoth',[1] which you have asked for, as well as the 'Sefer ha-Mishpatim',[2] which you wished to possess. Both of them will come to your residence and will belong to you. But why do you speak to me in such a way? Why do you implore me so humbly to forward you the books? Is this not the most urgent duty of all of us? Am I not ready to hasten from the end of the world upon your call? And if you find that I am too feeble to perform the smallest task for you, you may accept even the will kindly for the sake of the holiness of your name. Then I shall be satisfied and happy for ever. May it cause you no difficulty to give me your orders at any time, because it causes me no difficulty to fulfil them.

As a matter of fact, my dear, R. Johanan Alemanno owes me 10 big florins for the 'Sefer ha-Kavanoth'. . . . You must not, as you have said yourself, deliver to him the book before he has handed you the said 10 florins.

May you increase in the knowledge of the Torah, and also in Philosophy separate the flour from the bran. Be wise, my son; then I and all who love you will be delighted. May the will of the Lord be performed through you.

You must know that the Book on the Ordinances was [lent me (?)] by your honoured father. I have kept it with me ever since in order to study in it, time and again. . . .

You wanted to send us a copy of a letter from the Land of Israel. Please fulfil this promise. Send it by this mail, and we shall hasten to copy it and to forward it to Pisa to your brother, as you have commanded. May the Lord be with you always that you may remain a sage for all your life.

NOTES

1. Literally: The Book on the Devotions; perhaps the commentary written by Moses of Narbonne on the 'Kavanoth-ha Pilusufim' (The Tendencies of the Philosophers) is meant.
2. Literally: The Book on the Ordinances (or Judgements).

46

Letters of Immigrants to Palestine from the Fifteenth Century

We owe to Italian Jews the first comprehensive and the most impressive letters sent from Palestine by early Jewish travellers (see Introduction). The writers of the following somewhat abbreviated letters, Elijah of Ferrara, the celebrated scholar Obadiah Jaré of Bertinoro, author of the well-known commentary on the Mishnah, and an unknown student who was attracted by the fame of the last-named, left Italy in the fifteenth century in order to begin a new life in the Land of Israel devoted to learning and to the welfare of the country. The activities of these pioneers of the 'Italian Alijah' may be regarded as the beginning of the Palestinian revival.

Elijah of Ferrara, who arrived in Palestine as early as 1434, had to pay a high price for the change of his domicile: two sons and a grandson lost their lives on the journey. His letter is an eloquent testimony to the heroism with which he sustained this cruel blow. The interest of the letters of Obadiah da Bertinoro is quite different. When, after a long journey, he reached Palestine in 1488, he found the social and cultural life of the country at a low ebb. But Obadiah's arrival in Jerusalem marked, as has been said, an epoch in the history of the city and the entire land. The letter of the unknown author – a Venetian Jew who arrived in Palestine in 1495 – is largely a tribute to Obadiah's moral eminence and his splendid work in the Holy Land. The particular significance of this letter consists, however, in the various references to the Spanish disaster and to the emigrants from the Iberian Peninsula who, together with the writer, travelled to the homeland of the Jewish people.

All these letters are important contributions to our knowledge of the conditions in Palestine at the close of the Middle Ages. The letters of Elijah and Obadiah also throw light upon a peculiar subject: the great interest in the whereabouts of the lost Ten Tribes, concerning whom many exciting rumours were circulating in Europe – decades before David Reubeni, the ambassador of the Jewish kingdom of Habor, made his appearance in Italy in the 'twenties of the sixteenth century.

The value of the following four letters does not lie, however, merely in the information which they furnish. All of them are personal with a strong human appeal. The insight they offer into the souls of their writers is not less attractive than the recorded picture of countries and peoples.

(A)

ELIJAH OF FERRARA TO HIS SONS

'The Jews ply their trades side by side with the Ishmaelites, and no jealousy between them results such as I have remarked in other places'

[Jerusalem, July 1435]

To the hands of my beloved friends Israel Hayim and Joseph Baruch: May their Creator and Saviour, by whom they have salvation at Jerusalem, grant them His protection! I pray my lords and brethren of the Holy Synagogue of Ferrara to transmit this letter to my sons (may their Creator and Saviour have them in his keeping!) wherever they may be. It shall be counted to them for merit and their reward therefor shall be complete.[1]

Fearing that my previous letters may not have reached your hands, I take up my pen again to acquaint you with the woes we have suffered on our journey – woes that have devoured, have broken me.

In the first place, by the loss of one most near and dear, the desire of my eyes, the joy of my heart. Hardly a breath of life was left in me when, alas, he died – my Jacob, my grandson, whom I mourn in my soul with sighs and secret tears. Woe is me! Oh, my head, my head! Young head so well prepared for the study of the moral sciences, all thy bent and disposition to philosophy. Whatever was perfection in my eyes, he possessed it all.

While still plunged in the depths of this first affliction, fresh sorrows were even then on their way to assail me. On my arrival in Egypt my son Menahem fell ill and died. My soul rejects all consolation for the death of this beloved son, for he was the child of my old age. Alas, I was hoping that he would be a firm rock for my heart, my refuge in troubles; and behold, he has left me, he has departed hence: grief is added to grief.

My well-beloved son Isaac, too, always so faithful to me, he, too, went hence a few days after Menahem.[1a]

Then, through grief for my losses so many and so cruel, I myself fell ill and came nigh to death's door. But thanks be to God, the Physician who exacts no reward, He sent His angel to me and gave me strength to come on here to Jerusalem, the holy city, where I arrived on the 41st of the Sephirah,[2] in the year 5194.[2a] My weakness was still, however, extreme, either because I had not yet entirely recovered from my sickness, or by reason of my afflictions and much grieving. The days of my mourning were not yet over, and my sorrow still lay heavy upon me, when the notables of the community came to visit me and besought me to expound to them, in the synagogue, the Chapters of Maimonides,[3] according to their custom, and from that time they imposed upon me the charge to expound publicly to them three times a day the Ethics of the Fathers in the synagogue, Halakah[4] with Tosafot[5] in the Beth ha-Midrash[6] and again Halakah with Rashi's[7] commentary in the synagogue towards evening. In addition to all this, I am charged with the duties of a religious adviser in this city, and of giving responses upon questions of law from Misr [Cairo], Alexandria, Damascus, and other remote cities. After all this, you will hardly be able to believe it, but, with the help of the Almighty, I have found strength for all. For all this labour and toil, however, I receive but a small reward, yet one which has enabled me so far to live in plenty, because provisions are plentiful and abundant and cheaper to buy (God be thanked!) than in any other place where I lived in the West.

It is not necessary for me to recommend to your care the orphaned children of your brother, your senior in years and in merits (may his soul rest in peace!). The same I say unto you as regards the respect you owe to the wife of your aged father. May the Holy One give you grace to maintain and increase your virtues!

There is a great plague ravaging these countries, in Egypt, in Damascus, and in Jerusalem. Close on ninety victims have perished here, and five hundred at Damascus; but now (praised be the Physician without reward!) the mortality has ceased.

That you may know how fathers of families earn their living here, some engage in business and sell in shops; others work as carpenters and chemists. They have no adept knowledge of the art of preparing drugs and other matters pertaining to pharmacy, they simply buy them and sell them again. I need hardly say that they know nothing of medicine, but are for the most part ignoramuses. Many of them carry on the work of goldsmiths or shoe-makers; some deal in silks, the men doing the buying and selling, the women the actual work.

The Jews ply their trades side by side with the Ishmaelites, and no jealousy between them results such as I have remarked in other places. . . .

An old man informed me that he had been in India, which is in the far East, facing Cush[8] to the West, a sea and a desert separating them. Now in India there is a king, very mighty and powerful, reigning over the Jews only[9]; the rest of the country is governed by peoples rejecting every form of belief: peoples who kill no living creature for food. Their adoration is given principally to the sun, moon and stars.

The children of Moses live upon an island situated near the river Sambation,[10] the tribe of Manasseh live opposite them. Beyond this river are the tribes of Dan, Naphtali, Gad and Asher. The tribe of Issachar live in a province occupied by themselves alone, and hold no communication with anyone else whatsoever. They are marvellously learned in the Law, and their languages are Hebrew, Arabic and Persian, and around them dwell the fire worshippers.

The tribe of Simeon live to the extreme south. They too are governed by their own kings. The tribes of Zebulun and Reuben live on the banks of the Euphrates, the former on this side, the latter on the farther side of the river. They have the Mishnah and the Talmud. Their languages are Hebrew and Arabic. The tribe of Ephraim live to the south of Babylon. They are a fighting race, warriors who live on the booty they capture, and their language is Hebrew. . . .

May God protect you, my beloved sons! Give greetings

from me to my sons-in-law, my daughters and their children. May they all be blessed! I make my prayer to God before His sacred temple, that He may cause you to grow and multiply in the pure fear of Himself: then God in His mercy will bless you as He has promised.

Forget not to recall me to the remembrance of my dear and well-beloved brothers. . . .

Your father and brother
Elijah

In the week 'He shall pour the water out of his buckets'[11] 5195

(B)

OBADIAH JARÉ DA BERTINORO TO HIS FATHER

'In my opinion, an intelligent man versed in political science might easily raise himself to be chief of the Jews as well as of the Arabs'

[Jerusalem, August 1488]

My departure has caused you sorrow and trouble, and I am inconsolable because I have left you at a time when your strength is failing; when I remember, dear father, that I have forsaken your grey hairs I cannot refrain from tears. But since I am denied the happiness of being able to serve you as I ought, for God has decreed our separation, I will at least give you an account of my journey from beginning to end in the way in which you desired me to do in your letters, which I received in Naples about this time last year, by describing the manners and customs of the Jews in all the places I have visited and the nature of their intercourse with the other inhabitants of these cities.

On the first day of the ninth month,[12] having arranged all matters in my place of residence, Citta di Castello, I repaired to Rome, and thence to Naples, where I arrived on the 12th of that month and where I tarried for a long time, not finding any vessel such as I wished. I went to Salerno, where I gave gratuitous instruction for at least four months and then returned to Naples.

In the fourth month, on the fast day[13] 1487, I set out from Naples, in the large and swift ship of Mossen[14] Blanchi, together with nine other Jews; it was five days, however, before we reached Palermo, owing to a calm.

Palermo is the chief town of Sicily, and contains about 850 Jewish families, all living in one street, which is situated in the best part of the town. They are artisans, such as copper-smiths and iron-smiths, porters and peasants, and are despised by the Christians because they wear tattered garments. As a mark of distinction they are obliged to wear a piece of red cloth, about the size of a gold coin, fastened on the breast. The royal tax falls heavily on them, for they are obliged to work for the king at any employment that is given them; they have to draw ships to the shore, to construct dykes, and so on. They are also employed in administering corporal punishment and the sentence of death.

The Synagogue at Palermo has not its equal in the whole world; the stone pillars in the outer court are encircled by vines such as I have never before seen. . . . There are at present five Readers in the community; and on the Sabbath and on Festivals they chant the prayers more sweetly than I ever heard it done in any other congregation. On week-days the number of visitors to the Synagogue is very small, so that a little child might count them. . . .

I remained in Palermo from Tammuz 22nd, 5247, till Sabbath Bereshit, 5248.[15] On my arrival there the chief Jews invited me to deliver lectures on the Sabbath before the Minchah-prayer.[16] I consented, and began on the Sabbath of the New Moon of Ab [5247]. My discourses were very favourably received, so that I was obliged to continue them every Sabbath; but this was no advantage to me, for I had come to Palermo with the object of going on to Syracuse, which is at the extreme end of Sicily, for I had heard that this was the time when Venetian ships going to Beirut, near Jerusalem, would touch there. The Jews of Palermo then got many persons to circulate false rumours to dissuade me from my intention, and succeeded in taking me in their net, so that I missed the good crossing for the ships to Syracuse; I therefore remained in Palermo to give lectures to the people, about three hours before the Minchah. In my discourse I inveighed against informers and other transgressors, so that the elders of the city told me that many refrained from sin, and the number of informers also decreased while I was there; I do not know if they will go back to their old ways. But I cannot spend all my life among them, although they honour and deify me as the Gentiles treat their saints.

The common people said that God had sent me to them, while many wanted a piece of my garment for a remembrance; and a woman who washed my linen was counted happy by the rest. They calculated that I would remain at least a year there, and wanted to assign me an extraordinary salary, which, however, I declined, for my heart longed to reach the Promised Land.

On the eve of Tabernacles, 5248 [1487], a French galley came to Palermo, on its way to Alexandria. The worthy Meshullam of Volterra[17] was in it, with his servant, and I rejoiced to travel in his company. The night after Sabbath Bereshit we embarked, and on Sunday at mid-day we left Palermo. All day and night we had a favourable wind, so that in the morning we were close to the Pharos of Messina; we got safely past this and were in Messina on Monday noon. . . . There are about 400 Jewish families in it, living quietly in a street of their own; they are richer than those of Palermo, and are almost all artisans; there are only a few merchants among them. They have a Synagogue with a porch, open above but enclosed on the four sides, and in the middle of it is a well with spring water. . . .

On the eleventh of Marheshvan [October] we left Messina to go to Rhodes; we were joined in the ship by a Jewish merchant from Sucari[18] with his servant, three Jewish leather-workers from Syracuse, and a Sephardic Jew with his wife, two sons and two daughters, so that together we were fourteen Jewish souls on board . . . and on Sunday, Kislev 3rd, 5248, we arrived joyfully at Rhodes, after 22 days' sail.

Not many Jews have remained in Rhodes: altogether there are twenty-two families, all poor, who subsist with difficulty on vegetables, not eating bread or meat, for they never slaughter nor do they buy any wine, for fear of getting into disputes with the Greeks. . . . The Jews here are all very intelligent and well educated; they speak a pure dialect and are very moral and polite; even the tanners are neatly dressed and speak with propriety. They all allow their hair to grow long and are beautiful in person. Nowhere are there more beautiful Jewesses than in Rhodes; they occupy themselves in doing all kinds of handiwork for the Acomodors [the nobles of the land], and in this way support their husbands. The Acomodors hold the Jews in high esteem, often coming into their houses to chat awhile with the women who work there.

. . . On the 15th of Tebet . . . we left Rhodes, and after six days we were before Alexandria. . . . Here God gave us favour in the eyes of a generous man who was very much beloved even by the Arabs, by name R. Moses Grasso, dragoman to the Venetians. He came to meet us and released us from the hands of the Arabs who sit in the gate and plunder foreign Jews at their pleasure. He took me to his house, and there I had to remain while I stayed in Alexandria. I read with him in a book on the Cabbala, which he had in his possession, for he dearly loved this science. By thus reading with him I found favour in his eyes and we became friends. . . .

I spent seven days in Alexandria, leaving my effects, which were very few, in the large ship, which was still detained in Bukari by the calm. It happened just at this time that there was a man in Alexandria who had made a vow to celebrate the Passover-feast in Jerusalem with his wife and two sons; I joined myself to him, and travelled with him on camels. I commissioned R. Grasso to bring my things from the large ship and send them to Cairo. At Rosetta, on the Nile, we got into a ship. On both sides of the Nile there are towns and villages which are beautiful, large and populous, but all unfortified. We remained two days in Fooah, because the wind was not favourable; it is a beautiful place, and fish and vegetables can be got almost for nothing. We came next to Bulak, which already forms the beginning of Cairo. On the Nile I saw the large species of frog which the natives call El Timsah[19]; it is larger than a bear and spots are visible on the skin. The ship's crew say that there are some twice as big. These are the frogs which remained from the time of Moses, as Nahmanides mentions in his commentary. The Nile is wide and its waters are very sweet but turbid. The part on which we sailed forms merely a branch, for the other runs to Damietta where it flows into the sea.

Before coming to Bulak we observed two very old dome-shaped buildings which lay on the same side of the stream; it is said that they are the magazines which Joseph built. The door is above in the roof. Although they are now only in ruins, it is easy to see that they were once magnificent; the district is uninhabited. Twelve days before Purim, towards evening, we came to Cairo. . . .

I shall not speak of the grandeur of Cairo and of the streams of traffic there, for many before me have described this, and all that has been said of the town is true. . . . The city is very animated, and one hears the different languages of the foreigners who inhabit it. It is situated between the Red Sea and the Mediterranean and all merchants come from India, Ethiopia, and the countries of Prester John[20] through the Red Sea to Cairo both to sell their wares, which consist of spices, pearls, and precious stones, and to purchase commodities which come from France, Germany, Italy and Turkey across the Mediterranean Sea through Alexandria to Cairo. In the Red Sea there are magnets; hence the ships which come through it have no iron in them, not so much as a nail. The place where the sea was divided for our forefathers is said to have been identified, and many priests go to visit it, but I have heard of no Jew who has been there. . . .

In Cairo there are now about seven hundred Jewish families; of these fifty are Samaritans, called also Cutheans, one hundred and fifty are Karaites, and the rest Rabbanites. The Samaritans have only the five books of Moses, and their mode of writing differs from ours – the sacred writing. Maimonides remarks that this writing was customary among the Israelites before the time of the Assyrian exile, as already related in the tractate Sanhedrin; but their Hebrew is like ours. . . .

The Karaites, as you know, do not believe in the words of our sages, but they are familiar with all the Bible. They fix the day of the new moon according to the appearance of the moon; consequently the Karaites in Cairo keep different days for Rosh-ha-Shanah[21] and the Day of Atonement from those in Jerusalem, maintaining that there is nothing wrong in it. . . . They have a synagogue in Cairo; most of their prayers consist of Psalms and other biblical verses. . . .

The Samaritans are the richest of all the Jews in Cairo, and fill most of the higher offices of state; they are cashiers and administrators; one of them is said to have a property of 200,000 pieces of gold. The Karaites are richer than the Rabbanites, but there are opulent men among the latter too. . . . Among the Jews in Cairo there are money-changers and merchants, for the country is large, and some branch of industry is open to everyone. For trade there is no better place in the world than Cairo; it is easy to grow rich; hence one meets there with innumerable foreigners of all nations and languages. You may go out by night as well as by day, for all streets are lighted with torches. . . .

The Jewish Nagid who has his residence in Cairo is appointed over all the Jews who are under the dominion of the King of Egypt; he has all the power of a king and can punish and imprison those who act in opposition to his decrees; he appoints the Dayanim[22] in every community. The present prince lived formerly for a long time in Jerusalem, but was obliged to leave it on account of the Elders, the calumniators, and informers who were there. He is called R. Nathan ha-Kohen; he is rich, wise, pious, and old, and is a native of Barbary. When I came to Cairo he showed me much honour, loved me as a father loves his son, and tried to dissuade me altogether from going to

Jerusalem on account of the informers there; all scholars and Rabbis formerly in Jerusalem left the city in haste in order to preserve their lives from the oppressions of the Elders. The Jews who were in Jerusalem, about three hundred families, disappeared by degrees on account of the heavy taxes and burdens laid upon them by the Elders, so that the poor only remained, and women; and there was scarcely one to whom the name of man could justly be given. . . .

On the 20th of Adar, I left Cairo in company with the Jew who came from Alexandria, and we came to Chanak, which is about two miles distant from Cairo. Before I left Cairo I went to Old Cairo, called Mizraim Atika, which is also inhabited, though not so thickly as Cairo, and both are close together. In Old Cairo there is a very beautiful synagogue built on large and splendid pillars; it is also dedicated to the prophet Elijah, who is said to have appeared there to the pious in the south-east corner, where a light is kept continually burning. . . .

We remained in Chanak two days, and hired there five camels, for two men and two women had joined us in Cairo. It is said that this is Goshen, where the Jews sojourned in Egypt. We then came to Salahia, where we remained over the Sabbath, waiting for a passing caravan, since the way through the wilderness begins here and it is not safe to make the journey with only five camels. Not a Jew lives on the way from here to Gaza.

. . . The wilderness between Egypt and Palestine is not large, for from one day's journey to another there are places of encampment for the camels, erected principally for travellers. . . . The caravans going through the wilderness either encamp at mid-day and journey in the evening till midnight, or travel from midnight into the first third of the day. . . . Generally speaking, they travel by night rather than by day. . . . Gaza is the first town that we found on coming out of the wilderness leading to the land of the Philistines. It is a large and beautiful city of the same size as Jerusalem, but without walls, for among all the places under Egyptian dominion, which now extends over Palestine, the country of the Philistines and Syria[8],

Alexandria and Aleppo alone are surrounded by walls. If the account of the Jews living there be correct, I saw in Gaza the ruins of the building that Samson pulled down on the Philistines. We remained four days in Gaza; there is now a Rabbi from Germany there, by name Rabbi Moses, of Prague, who fled thither from Jerusalem; he insisted on my going to his house, and I was obliged to stay with him all the time I was in Gaza. On the Sabbath all the wardens were invited to dine with us. Cakes of grapes and fruit were brought; we partook of several glasses before eating, and were joyful.

On Sunday, the 11th of Nisan [April], we journeyed from Gaza on asses; we came within two miles of Hebron, and there spent the night. On Monday we reached Hebron, a small town on the slope of the mountain, called by the Turks Khalil.[23]... I was in the Cave of Machpelah, over which the mosque has been built; and the Arabs hold the place in high honour. All the kings of the Arabs come here to repeat their prayers, but neither a Jew nor an Arab may enter the Cave itself, where the real graves of the Patriarchs are. . . . All who come to pray leave money, which they throw into the cave through the window....

On Tuesday morning, the 13th of Nisan, we left Hebron, which is a day's journey distant from Jerusalem, and came on as far as Rachel's tomb, where there is a round, vaulted building in the open road. We got down from our asses and prayed at the grave, each one according to his ability. On the right hand of the traveller to Jerusalem lies the hill on which Bethlehem stands; this is a small village, about half a mile from Rachel's grave, and the Catholic priests have a church there.

From Bethlehem to Jerusalem is a journey of about three miles. The whole way is full of vineyards and orchards. The vineyards are like those in Romagna, the vines being low, but thick. About three-quarters of a mile from Jerusalem, at a place where the mountain is ascended by steps, we beheld the famous city of our delight, and here we rent our garments, as was our duty. A little farther on, the sanctuary, the desolate house of our splendour, became visible, and at the sight of it we again made rents in our garments. We came as far as the gates of Jerusalem, and on the 13th of Nisan, 5248, at noon, our feet stood within the gates of the city. Here we were met by an Ashkenazi who had been educated in Italy, Rabbi Jacob Calmann; he took me into his house, and I remained his guest during the whole time of the Passover.

Jerusalem is for the most part desolate and in ruins. I need not repeat that it is not surrounded by walls. Its inhabitants, I am told, number about 4,000 families. As for Jews, about seventy families of the poorest class have remained; there is scarcely a family that is not in want of the commonest necessaries; one who has bread for a year is called rich. Among the Jewish population there are many aged, forsaken widows from Germany, Spain, Portugal and other countries, so that there are seven women to one man. The land is now quieter and happier than before; for the Elders have repented of the evil they had done, when they saw that only the poorer portion of the inhabitants remained; they are therefore very friendly to every newcomer. They excuse themselves for what has happened, and assert that they never injured anyone who did not try to obtain the mastery over them. As for me, so far I have no complaint to make against them; on the contrary, they have shown me great kindness and have dealt honourably with me, for which I daily give thanks to God.

The Jews are not persecuted by the Arabs in these parts. I have travelled through the country in its length and breadth, and none of them has put an obstacle in my way. They are very kind to strangers, particularly to anyone who does not know the language; and if they see many Jews together they are not annoyed by it. In my opinion, an intelligent man versed in political science might easily raise himself to be chief of the Jews as well as of the Arabs; for among all the inhabitants there is not a wise and sensible man who knows how to deal affably with his fellow men; all are ignorant misanthropes intent only on gain. . . .

The Synagogue here is built on columns; it is long, narrow,

and dark, the light entering only by the door. There is a fountain in the middle of it. In the court of the Synagogue, quite close to it, stands a mosque. The court of the Synagogue is very large, and contains many houses, all of them buildings devoted by the Ashkenazim to charitable purposes and inhabited by Ashkenazi widows. . . . The Jews' street and the houses are very large; some of them dwell also on Zion. At one time they had more houses, but these are now heaps of rubbish and cannot be rebuilt, for the law of the land is that a Jew may not rebuild his ruined house without permission, and the permission often costs more than the whole house is worth. The houses in Jerusalem are of stone, none of wood or plaster.

There are some excellent regulations here. I have nowhere seen the daily service conducted in a better manner. The Jews rise an hour or two before day-break, even on the Sabbath, and recite Psalms and other songs of praise till the day dawns. Then they repeat the Kaddish; after which two of the Readers appointed for the purpose chant the Blessing of the Law, the Chapter on Sacrifices, and all the songs of praise which follow with a suitable melody, the 'Shema'[24] being read on the appearance of the sun's first rays. The Kohanim repeat the priestly benediction daily, on weekdays as well as on the Sabbath; in every service this blessing occurs. At the morning and afternoon service supplications are said with great devotion, together with the Thirteen Attributes of God. . . .

Jerusalem, notwithstanding its destruction, still contains four very beautiful, long bazaars, such as I have never before seen, at the foot of Zion. They all have dome-shaped roofs, and contain wares of every kind. They are divided into different departments, the merchant bazaar, the spice bazaar, the vegetable market, and one in which cooked food and bread are sold. When I came to Jerusalem there was a dreadful famine in the land. . . . Many Jews died of hunger, they had been seen a day or two before asking for bread, which nobody could give them, and the next day they were found dead in their houses. Many lived on grass, going out like stags to look for pasture. At present there is only one German Rabbi here, who was educated in Jerusalem. I have never seen his equal for humility and the fear of God; he weaves night and day when he is not occupied with his studies, and for six months he tasted no bread between Sabbath and Sabbath, his food consisting of raw turnips and the remains of St. John's bread, which is very plentiful here, after the sugar had been taken out of it. . . .

Now, the wheat-harvest being over, the famine is at an end, and there is once more plenty, praise be to God. Here, in Jerusalem, I have seen several kinds of fruit which are not to be found in our country. There is one tree with long leaves, which grows higher than a man's stature, and bears fruit only once; it then withers, and from its roots there rises another similar one, which again bears fruit the next year, and the same thing is continually repeated. The grapes are larger than in our country. . . . All the necessaries of life, such as meat, wine, olives, and sesame-oil, can be had very cheap. The soil is excellent; but it is not possible to gain a living by any branch of industry, unless it be that of a shoe-maker, weaver, or goldsmith. . . .

I made enquiries concerning the Sambation, and I hear from one well-informed person that a man has come from the kingdom of Prester John and has related that there are high mountains and valleys there which can be traversed in a ten days' journey, and which are certainly inhabited by descendants of Israel. They have five princes or kings, and have carried on great wars against the Johannites[25] for more than a century, but, unfortunately, the Johannites prevailed and Ephraim was beaten. The Johannites penetrated into their country and the remembrance of Israel had almost died away in those places. . . .

The Temple enclosure has still twelve gates. Those which are called the gates of mercy are of iron, and are two in number; they look towards the east of the Temple and are always closed. They only reach half-way above the ground, the other half is sunk in the earth. It is said that the Arabs often tried to raise them up but were not able to do so.

The western wall, part of which is still standing, is composed of large, thick stones, such as I have never before seen in an old building, either in Rome or in any other country. At the northeast corner is a tower of very large stones. I entered it and found a vast edifice supported by massive and lofty pillars; there are so many pillars that it wearied me to go to the end of the building. Everything is filled with earth, which has been thrown there from the ruins of the Temple. The Temple building stands on these columns, and in each of them is a hole through which a cord may be drawn. It is said that the bulls and rams for sacrifice were bound here. Throughout the whole region of Jerusalem, in fields as well as in vineyards, there are large caves connected with one another. . . .

The Mount of Olives is lofty and barren; scarcely an olive-tree is to be found on it. From the top, Sodom and Gomorrah may be seen in the distance; they now form a salt sea. I heard from people who had been there that the ground was everywhere covered with salt. Of Lot's wife nobody could tell me anything; for pillars of salt are innumerable, so that it was impossible to distinguish which is Lot's wife.

Mount Abarim, where Moses is buried, is visible from Jerusalem. The district beyond the Jordan, including the lands of Reuben, Gad and Manasseh, and of the sons of Ammon, the Mountain of Moab, and Mount Seir, are now waste places. Not an inhabited city is to be found there, for the Bedouins destroy everything. They come even to the gates of Jerusalem, steal and plunder in the open roads, and no one can interfere with them, they are so numerous. For this reason the district is all waste, without inhabitants; and there is neither ploughing nor sowing. Jericho is a small village, consisting of about twenty to thirty houses. Bethar, formerly a large city, is now a place for cattle and contains about twenty houses; it is half a day's journey from Jerusalem. Nearly all the cities that were formerly great are now waste places. They continue to bear the same names, but are uninhabited. . . .

I have taken a house here close to the Synagogue. The upper chamber of my dwelling is in the wall of the Synagogue. In the court where my house is there are five inhabitants, all of them women. There is only one blind man living here, and his wife attends on me. I must thank God, who has hitherto vouchsafed me His blessing, that I have not been sick, like others who came at the same time with me. Most of those who come to Jerusalem from foreign countries fall ill, owing to climatic changes and sudden variations of the wind, now cold, now warm. All possible winds blow in Jerusalem. It is said that every wind before going where it listeth comes to Jerusalem to prostrate itself before the Lord. Blessed be He that knoweth the truth.

I earnestly entreat that you will not be depressed nor suffer anxiety on account of my having travelled so far away, and that you will not shed tears for my sake. For God in His mercy has brought me to His holy dwelling, which rejoices my heart and should also delight you. God is my witness that I have forgotten all my former sorrows, and all remembrance of my native country has passed away from me. All the memories which I still retain of it are centred in your image, revered father, which is constantly before my eyes. Mine eyes are dimmed when I remember that I have left you in your old age, and I fear lest your tears will recall the sins of my youth.

Now, I beseech you, bestow your blessing upon your servant. Let this letter atone for my absence, for it will show you the disposition of your son and you will no longer be displeased with him. If God will preserve me, I shall send you a letter every year with the galley, which will comfort you. Banish all sorrow from your heart. Rejoice with your dear children and grand-children who sit around your table. They will nourish and sustain your old age. I have prayed for their welfare and continue to do so in the sacred places of Jerusalem, the restoration of which, by means of the Messiah, God grant us to witness, so that you may come joyfully to Zion. Amen.

Finished in haste in Jerusalem, the Holy City. May it soon be rebuilt in our days.

From your son
Obadiah Jaré

On the 8th Ellul, 5248

(c)

OBADIAH JARÉ DA BERTINORO TO HIS BROTHER

'Twice a month I hold discourses in the synagogue in the Hebrew tongue, which most of the people here understand'

[Jerusalem, September 1489]

How precious are your words to me, my brother! They are sweeter than sweet spices.

First of all I praise the Almighty, and thank you for the good news that our aged father, whom I never cease to love tenderly, still lives. May God continue His mercy and preserve him to us in strength and health for a long time to come. But my joy was very much saddened by the death of your eldest daughter, and of your son who was born to you after I had left you. What God determines is ever for the best, however, and there is nothing left for us to do but to pray for those who still remain to us, that God would grant them His blessing, and preserve them.

You ask me about the miracles said to take place on the temple-mountain and graves of the pious. What can I tell you, my brother, about them? I have not seen them. As for the lights on the site of the Temple, of which you have heard that they are always extinguished on the 9th of Ab, I have been told that this is the case, but I cannot speak with certainty respecting it; I need not say that the story about the Sephardi is all deception and falsehood; but intelligent men like you, my brother, must examine such stories, and not trust to false reports. . . .

Jews have come here from Aden; Aden is said to be the site of the garden of Eden: it lies south-east of Ethiopia, but the people keep this a secret. They say that in those provinces there are many and large Jewish communities, that the reigning king is an Arab, and is very kindly disposed to the Jews, and that the country is very large and beautiful, bearing many splendid fruits, of kinds which are not to be found among us. They do not possess the books of the Talmud; all they have are the works of R. Isaac Alfasi, together with commentaries on them, and the works of Maimonides. They are all, from great to small, well versed in the works of Maimonides, for they occupy themselves principally with studying them. The Jews told us also that it is now well known through Arab merchants that the river Sambation is eighty days' journey from them in the wilderness, and surrounds the whole land like a thread, and that the descendants of Jacob dwell there. This river throws up stones and sand, and rests only on the Sabbath, therefore no Jew can cross over it, for otherwise he would violate the Sabbath. It is a tradition among them that the descendants of Moses dwelt there, all pure and innocent as angels, and no evil-doer in their midst. On the other side of the Sambation the Children of Israel are as numerous as the sand of the sea, and there are many kings and princes among them, but they are not so pure and holy as those surrounded by the stream. The Jews of Aden relate all this with a certain confidence, as if it were well known, and no one ever doubted the truth of their assertions.

I live here in Jerusalem, in the house of the Nagid, who has appointed me ruler of his household, and twice a month I hold discourse in the Synagogue in the Hebrew tongue, which most of the people here understand. My sermons sound in their ears like a lovely song, and they praise them and like to listen to them, but they do not act in accordance with them. Yet I cannot say that anybody has done me an injury. . . . And perchance, the Promised Land may now be rebuilt and inhabited, for the king has issued a decree to be permanently in force, that the Jews in Jerusalem shall pay only the poll tax imposed on them. This is a decree such as has not been in Jerusalem for fifty years. Hence many who left Jerusalem are returning. May it please God that the city and the Temple be rebuilt, and that the scattered of Judah and Ephraim may come together here and prostrate themselves before God at the holy mountain. I must now conclude for the present, for I am much occupied.

Sent in haste from Jerusalem, Ellul the 27th, 5249.

From your brother

Obadiah Jarę

(D)

AN UNKNOWN WRITER TO HIS FRIENDS

'All is very cheap here, and I think a man can live here a year on 10 ducats'

[Jerusalem, 1495]

O my soul, praise the Almighty for His mercy, by which we have happily finished the journey over the wide sea; we have not been touched by anyone. I must also thank God that He brought us to our destination. May the Almighty favour you so that you, too, may see the Holy Land, and may you live in peace in your land. I am sending you a letter which contains the description of our journey to Jerusalem.

We left Venice in a joyful mood on August 5, 5255, in order to embark on our journey with the blessing of God; we arrived on Friday at the 22nd hour in Pola, a small but spacious town, where meat, fish and other good food are available at low prices. We remained there for two days in the house of the esteemed R. Jacob Ashkenazi, who received us in a friendly way in his house and provided us with all necessary things. He is the only Jew there and very benevolent.

... We left Pola by a favourable wind and arrived on Monday the 17th of August at Corfu. ... We remained there only for a night ... and arrived at Rhodes on the 27th of August; but nobody left the boat until Friday midday for fear of the corsairs, because Rhodes is their headquarters. ... We left Rhodes on the 29th of August about midday and arrived at Famagusta on the 3rd of September, 5256. ... There are big communities in the towns [of Cyprus] with the exception of Famagusta, where only a few Jews live. While they are nowhere occupied with usury, a certain R. Shabtai of Ashkenaz lives here who is engaged in this business, which according to the laws of the country is nowhere forbidden; the Jews in the other places which I have passed through are artisans or merchants and live in perfect security.

We left this town [Famagusta] on the 6th of September, 5256, and arrived at Beirut on the 8th of September. On Wednesday morning we disembarked in a joyful mood. Altogether the journey from Venice to Beirut took 34 days, although we stayed for some time at all the places mentioned.

Now I want to tell you what I have seen with my own eyes. At all the places we passed, Jews embarked on the ship. Some of them went to Beirut. About 150 Jews also arrived with the merchant galley, all of them poor and needy. Thus we were about 300 altogether. The Arabs behaved very compassionately towards the poor; they distributed money, wheat, bread and fruit among them; while they insult the Christians, often shouting behind them, 'Dog, son of a dog!', they do not offend the Jews; the more had I reason to wonder that no Jews are living there [in Beirut].

We stayed in a house in company with the pious R. Joseph of Saragossa, a Sephardi, and remained with him and his family for seven days until we could make up our minds whether we should go via Damascus or via Sidon, which is only half a day's journey from Beirut and belongs to the Holy Land. R. Joseph decided finally that he would go via Sidon. The old and venerable Jekutiel of Viggasolo with his wife Nobila, R. Daniel of Burgo, and many others joined him. As we heard, however, that corsairs were roving about those places, I decided not to join them but to choose, with my brother Jekutiel, the road via Damascus while the others went via Sidon. The governor as well as the Jewish community of Sidon suggested to R. Joseph that he should stay there, and offered him 50 ducats a year so that he could live there with his family. They urged him very much to stay there because this man was very famous, and the governor even promised him 20 ducats from his own pocket[25a].

Now I must tell you with a sorrowful heart of an accident which occurred soon afterwards. R. Jekutiel of Viggasolo with his wife and the excellent young man Daniel of Burgo, all of blessed memory, in company of other persons went on board of an Arab ship in order to go to Jerusalem. A violent tempest arose as they came just off Acre, and all the Jews, except one Sicilian, were drowned. . . . This misfortune would have been also our lot, because my brother Jekutiel was eager to join their company. But the Lord stopped us from doing so, and I shall praise Him for this as long as I breathe.

. . . We arrived in Damascus in good health on Friday morning, the eve of Rosh-ha-Shanah. . . . Damascus is a big town with broad streets, fine houses, courts, and wells. There are three communities there with 500 Jewish families, which are occupied either with trade in cloth and other objects, as artisans, or as moneylenders.

We left Damascus on Wednesday, the 15th of October, 5256, with our guides . . . and arrived in Safed on Friday morning. We found there a small room at the home of a poor Jew, whom we paid two silver coins for rent and for providing us with bread and food. Safed is a big town on the slope of a mountain; the houses are small and inconsiderable. . . . The community consists of 300 families. Most of the Jews keep shops with spices, cheese, oil, legumes and fruit. I have heard that such a shop with a capital of 25 ducats can provide a living for 5 persons. . . .

Around Safed many caves are to be found where great and pious men are buried. . . . We saw the cave in which Hillel with his 24 disciples was buried. . . . I also saw the tomb of Shammai and his wife.[26] It is hewn out of a stone which is bigger than any I have ever seen. I have been told that under that stone is a cave where the disciples of Shammai are buried. I also saw the synagogue of R. Simeon, son of Johai[27], and the wall of a big building made of stone which has been destroyed. There is a tradition among the people of Safed that when this wall collapses, the coming of the Messiah will be at hand. They told me that lightning struck the wall during the expulsion of the Jews from Spain so that it began to collapse. The inhabitants of Safed therefore proclaimed that day as a day of rejoicing. . . .

I have prayed in the places I mentioned, and at most of them I kindled lights. . . .

We left Safed in the company of several Sicilians who joined other caravans consisting of Jews, Christians and Arabs, on the 12th of Marheshvan, 5256. We paid, like them, 120 silver coins each for the journey to Jerusalem. . . . We arrived on Friday evening, shortly before the beginning of the Sabbath, in the village of Kana, where we stayed until Tuesday, and decided to continue the journey afterwards under the protection of the Lord. You must know, my friends and superiors, that the road from Kana to Jerusalem is dangerous because of the bandits as well as of the toll-gatherers; the latter impose [on the travellers] arbitrary taxes, and, although the guides ought by rights to pay them, the Jews are asked to provide the money if too much is requested from them. If the Jews arrive then in a city and complain of the guides . . . they find no hearing; for in these countries there is no law, and a Jew especially will not win his just cause against an Arab. . . .

We left that place on Tuesday and travelled the whole night without speaking a word; we passed two toll posts without paying. It was on the way to Dothan[28], where I saw the pit into which Joseph was thrown. We remained in the mountains from dawn until the stars became visible. The following night we passed Sichem, which is situated between the mountains Garizim and Ebal; the former is blessed with fruit, the latter, however, looks like a desert. We travelled here always in fear of the custom-houses at night. But the Lord willed that we should meet the custom-collectors even in the same night. They brought us to their camp near Sichem, where we spent the whole night in fear and anxiety. . . . On Thursday morning the Jews and the guides came to an agreement under which 14 ducats had to be paid; I had to pay 14 silver coins for my share. We continued our journey the following night in fear and terror, for we were still threatened by the bloodthirsty men of Sichem, but the Lord led us on the right way.

When morning dawned, we were before Jerusalem. When,

on Friday, the 18th of Marheshvan, I saw from afar the deserted and waste city and the ruins on the mountain of Zion, the dwelling-place of lions and jackals, my heart burst into tears. I sat down and, weeping, I made the two prescribed cuts in my garment; I turned to the square of the Temple and prayed that the Lord might lead the captives of Israel into their land soon in order that we may see the dwelling-place of God. Amen.

After having entered the city I called upon the famous, esteemed and learned R. Obadiah. I poured out my heart to him and told him that I had forsaken my family in my birthplace in order to hide under his wings and to continue my studies with him. He looked like an old, compassionate man, and said to me: 'I shall take care of thee, and shall treat thee as my own son.'... This man is held in great esteem here; nobody dares to do anything without having consulted him. People from all provinces come to him for consultation, and they obey his advice faithfully; his word is recognized even in Egypt, Babylonia, and other countries. The Arabs, too, revere and fear him, because I have heard that he was able to kill an evildoer with his mere breath; he is very humble and self-effacing; his behaviour is gentle so that all people say of him that he is more than an ordinary man.

When I arrived here, I was unable to find a lodging, as the place was so crowded. I was therefore content to rent a room for one month until I could find a definite lodging. I very much wished to live with the scholar Abraham of Messina, may the Lord bless him and his posterity, with the esteemed Moses of Burgo and another cultured and kind-hearted young Sephardi, all of whom stayed in one court and studied day and night. When I revealed this wish to the learned Obadiah, he tried at once with the greatest eagerness to satisfy my desire. He negotiated with the landlady of the court and convinced her that it would be an advantage to me, for the sake of my studies, if I could live together with those persons. And the woman was good enough to let me stay in her house....

In Jerusalem there are about 200 Jewish families, who abstain from every sin and fulfil the commandments of the Lord with great zeal. All people without distinction, old and young, gather together in the evenings for prayers. There are two god-fearing readers here who read with great devotion and pronounce every syllable distinctly. The whole community is eager to listen twice daily to the sermons of the 80-year-old Rabbi Zechariah Sephardi, the Lord bless him and his posterity. . . . The highly learned Rabbi Obadiah delivers sermons only two or three times a year, at Passover, Pentecost and Tabernacles and sometimes also on the penitential days. Only the other day his pleasant voice could be heard as he spoke words of the living God. All people, young and adults, were present, and all were so quiet that no breath could be heard. I shall not dare to utter his praises, for from such an humble and ignorant man as I, it would be by no means an honour for him.

Many remain after the prayer and the sermon in the Synagogue in order to devote themselves to the study of Mishnah and Talmud for three hours. Afterwards they visit the sick and distribute alms according to their means. People here are very benevolent although they are poor themselves and live on alms; may the Lord have mercy upon us and fill our granaries and bless our undertakings.

Here in Jerusalem it is very difficult to earn a living. Even artisans, like workers in gold, smiths, weavers or tailors, get hardly enough for their daily needs. The Jews in Damascus, Cairo, Alexandria, Aleppo and generally in these countries earn as much as they want, particularly those who speak Arabic besides our own language. But here a worker in gold will succeed at best in gaining a bare living. On the other hand all is very cheap here, and I think that a man can live here a year on 10 ducats. We have made an agreement with Aaron Loasi, who lives in this house, according to which he will provide food and laundry for each of us at the price of 40 silver coins a month, but he is not obliged to supply us with wine and oil; he does not pay the rent and provide the bed-clothes either. He is obliged only to provide us with meat, fish or some milky food every night and make our breakfast. We have been told, however, that we are paying too high a price; nevertheless we preferred to make this agreement in order not to be kept away from our studies by having to prepare the food. . . .

The houses of Jerusalem are built with blocks of stone, and they have not several flats like those in your country; they are also built without timber. . . . There are five or six rooms in every house, all made of bricks. No fountains with spring-water are to be found here, but there is a cistern in every house into which water pours when it rains. . . . Near the synagogue, in the middle of the city, there is an empty space where the whole community gathers for another prayer in front of the Temple ruins, which are visible from that place.

The tombs of the Patriarchs in Hebron are a day's journey from here; the tomb of Rachel is on the way to them. I have not gone there so far, as the roads are unsafe because of the Bedouins. Only lately a Jew who came here with his family from Hebron was robbed of everything on the way. I have heard that the Jews of Cairo and Damascus who will arrive here to celebrate the feast of Passover will proceed to Hebron under a safe-conduct; this opportunity I intend to use in order to go there, if the Lord grants me life until then. . . .

NOTES

1. This address was placed at the back of the letter.
1a All these losses were apparently caused by the plague which is mentioned in the letter.
2. Literally: 'Counting', namely of the forty-nine days between Passover and Pentecost; Elijah arrived, therefore, about May.
2a 1434.
3. The 'Eight Chapters' of the Commentary to the Mishnah by Maimonides; they form the introduction to the tractate Abot (Sayings of the Fathers) and contain the ethical teaching of Maimonides.
4. Legal ordinances.
5. See Note 9 to Chapter 36.
6. House of Learning.
7. R. Solomon, son of Isaac, abbr. Rashi (1040–1105), the leading medieval commentator on the Pentateuch and Talmud (see Introduction).
8. Ethiopia.
9. A similar statement occurs in David Reubeni's Diary.
10. The legendary river on the border of the Kingdom of the Ten Tribes; the river runs, according to the legend, during the six working days, but rests on the Sabbath.
11. Num. XXIV. 7.
12. Kislev 1486.
13. The 17th of Tammuz.
14. Monsignor.
15. From about July to October.
16. The afternoon service.
17. Meshullam, son of Menahem of Volterra, composed a description of his voyage to the East, undertaken in 1481.
18. Perhaps Zucco, an island between Palermo and Trapani.
19. The crocodile.
20. Prester (i.e. Presbyter) John, fabulous Christian monarch of Asia, whose seat from the fourteenth century onwards was located in Abyssinia.
21. New Year.
22. The judges.
23. After Abraham, called in Arabic 'Khalil Allah' (The Beloved of God).
24. 'Hear, [O Israel: The Lord our God, the Lord is One'].
25. Abyssinians, followers of St. John Chrysostom.
25a Joseph Saragossi proceeded from Sidon to Safed where he became a pioneer of the community of Cabbalists.
26. Hillel and Shammai, see Notes 8 and 10 to Chapter 20.
27. Simeon ben Johai, Tannaite teacher, disciple of R. Akiba; the composition of the Zohar was ascribed to him.
28. Gen. XXXVII. 17.

47

Two Letters of Don Isaac Abrabanel Before and After the Expulsion of the Jews from Spain

LIKE Hasdai ibn Shaprut at the beginning of the Spanish era of Jewish history, so Isaac ben Judah Abrabanel (1437–1508) at its close combined high political office with Jewish scholarship and leadership of the Jewish community. While many Spanish Jews, in order to keep open the way to influential position, submitted to baptism, Isaac Abrabanel, whose family claimed to be of Davidic origin, remained a professing Jew, and in spite of this was elevated to the dignity of a Minister of Finance by the Christian rulers both of Portugal and Spain. At the same time he maintained a deep attachment to the Jewish people, who justly regarded him as their head and protector.

1. *A piece of diplomatic courtesy and philanthropy*

Abrabanel's dual position is well illustrated in the subjoined letter, written in the following circumstances. King Alfonso V of Portugal had captured in Northern Africa 250 Jews, who were condemned to be sold into slavery. From this fate 220 were saved by a ransom of 10,000 gold doubloons raised by the Portuguese Jews under the leadership of Abrabanel. Money, however, was still required for the feeding and clothing of the liberated Jews, and the ransom of thirty more prisoners. It happened that in 1472 the King sent to the new Pope Sixtus IV an embassy, one member of which was Dr. João Sezira, a friend of Abrabanel and a well-wisher of the Jews. Abrabanel obtained from Sezira a promise to approach the Pope on behalf of the Jews, and also entrusted him with a letter to Yehiel of Pisa, a cultivated Jewish financier and philanthropist. The letter was not merely a request for help. Abrabanel tactfully linked the matter of the prisoners with the misfortune which Yehiel himself had suffered in an anti-Jewish riot in Pisa, and gave the learned friend a brief account of his studies. Thus the letter, accompanied by well-chosen gifts, became a pleasant mixture of private and diplomatic correspondence.

ISAAC ABRABANEL TO YEHIEL OF PISA

'I must ask thee to listen to a story of poor people. . . . Thou wilt certainly share my sorrows, day and night'

[Lisbon, Nisan 1472]

A year ago at this time – O my head, my head, my dear head, may the Lord protect thee! – thy kind letter reached me. I learnt from it about all the troubles caused thee by wicked people. They looked for a pretext for plotting against thee in order to attack thee, to rob and plunder thee, although there is no wrong in thy hands. I was astonished when I saw that fighting and violence were raging in the city which is a place of law, and that the peace has been disturbed and truth suppressed there. When the noblemen rose against thee in fury in order to crush the right of a pious and decent man like thee, and to slander such a man, I was downcast and deeply pained. I lamented that Jews are everywhere in danger of falling into a hell of suffering, that every Jew-baiter can prevail over them and their children, that the wicked should oppress the just and say, 'I will persecute and rob them,' that the law is flouted while our enemies, seizing our money and property, make slaves of us and a prey of Israel. . . . May thy reward be great even if thou must suffer mischief, and may abundance of blessing, happiness and joy be bestowed upon thee in exchange for all they have taken from thee.

In spite of all this I cannot refrain from telling thee about our own troubles and sorrows, which we, the leaders of this community, have to endure. I must ask thee to listen to a story of a poor people, namely the community of Arzilla, which is under the Mohammedan rule. Thou wilt certainly share my sorrows, day and night. They have deprived me of my peace for six months.

Our king, may he live long, rose and conquered many lands. His cavalry, skilled horsemen from distant countries, made a fine show. After having gathered ships and crews, he went over to Africa for conquest and besieged the populous city of Arzilla.

The army captured it and committed wholesale pillage, though the king and his princes did not touch the booty. The population of 10,000 people was either killed or captured. Afterwards he occupied the famous city of Tangier. Although the Lord saved the Jews from the massacre at Arzilla, because they lived dispersed in the city – as a matter of fact no Jew lost his life – yet 250 Jewish prisoners were captured and brought hither exhausted by hunger and deprived of all means. When we saw the children of Zion sold as slaves, the leaders of our community decided to restore their freedom and ransom them with our money.

I, and other leaders who are more just and better than I, chose twelve delegates according to the number of Israel's tribes to carry out the benevolent work and to give back freedom to the prisoners. I and another leader were sent from one city to another with the purpose of liberating the Jews from their wretched plight. Others, too, asked that we might provide money for their ransom and write to the Jews in other countries so that they might give money for this task.

We have made such journeys repeatedly, and have been able with the mercy of the Lord to ransom 150 persons during a short time. In this city there are now 220 people whom we have helped to gain freedom. The amount spent for this purpose was ten thousand doubloons in gold. And as these unhappy people had been robbed of everything, and had neither clothes nor food, and were, in addition, unable to make themselves understood in the language of this country, we had to look for people who were able to unite dispersed members of families and to provide them with all necessities. It will still take some time before they have learnt the language and the habits of this country.

Now, this night has at last brought the hour of success, when they are settled in their dwellings. They offer thanks to the Lord, saying: 'We were slaves for a short time, but the Lord has delivered us from slavery to freedom. Now we are free as all Jews are.' May the Lord now deliver also the remainder of about thirty who are still in captivity. They are not yet ransomed because they have fallen into the hands of hard masters. They have been carried to a distant land, and are not yet here. May the hour of their liberation be near at hand, and may the Lord gather soon the dispersed members of Judah from East and West.

All this was a great burden for me, day and night. The Omniscient knows how little I have told thee about this matter. Nowhere, indeed, have so many Jewish men and women been led into slavery. And, God is my witness, the ears of every Jew who hears this must tingle, and he must "clap his hands and shake his head"[1].

Thou sage and pious man! Our king was pleased to send a mission to the Pope to congratulate him on his coronation. The mission consists of Don Lope de Almeida and of the prudent and kind Doctor João Sezira, who brings this letter to thee. They are favourites of the king. And as the Doctor is always concerned with the welfare of Israel, and loves me very much, I have asked him to speak favourably on behalf of the Jews, when he is received in audience by the Pope. He has promised me solemnly that he will do this and took with him a great store of our wishes and requests. I beg thee, speak very kindly with these gentlemen, and tell them that thou, at the other end of the earth, hast heard so much good about our king, how he exercises law and justice towards his people, and is a friend of the Jews. Therefore all nations will revere him, and it will be said that the Lord is with Israel and that able and pious Jews are working everywhere. Particularly to the Doctor speak kindly, friendly and comforting words, for we are one heart and soul; he is a faithful friend and very much esteemed by the Jews. I beg thee that thou mayest be helpful to him with all kindness. He will tell thee our request faithfully as he knows what happened with us.

Thou, my friend and helper, hast expressed a wish that I might send thee the commentary to the Hagiographa by R. David Kimhi,[1a] and I am forwarding thee also my tract 'Atereth

Zekenim',[2] and the commentary to Deuteronomy[3] on which I am working still. Besides these books I have found only a commentary to the Psalms which thou, however, possessest already. The commentary to Deuteronomy is not finished yet, because I am seldom at home. My voyages involve much labour and detain me from spiritual work. When the Lord grants me peace again, I shall not rest until I have finished that book. And then I will discharge my debt to my Lord. In the meantime I hope that every difficult explanation will be dealt with indulgently by thee. The tract 'Atereth Zekenim' is only a small piece. . . . But what shall I do, since I have no other of my works to send thee as a gift? I am forwarding, therefore, this little treatise to thee as a first sign of affection. May it find favour with thee! Thou wilt also be able to learn from it my way of interpretation of the Torah – whether I tread the straight or the crooked path. Perhaps thou wilt agree with my view, which so far has not been put forward even by the best authors. This book, then, is my gift for thee. May it remain with thee wherever thou wilt dwell. Learning is always the main thing. May it remind thee always of me, who loves thee and sends his words to a distant land.

And now, thou just man, the Lord knows that my children are ready to fulfil thy wishes. But the wife who has been destined by the Lord to thy servant Isaac spoke to me: 'My dear, the Lord has given thee the pleasure of being able to send to my lord something that thou thyself hast made as a kind gift and friendly sign of affection. Why shall I stand back in his house where the scholars assemble, and not offer him a present? As I do not know of a book, I have chosen a young and beautiful Moorish slave-girl, able to work well and also to entertain in our fashion: I want to send her to his wife in order that she may remember me in her presence with feminine love, as he will remember thee.' I obeyed her voice! The Doctor will bring thee the girl. She always served faithfully in his house, too.

Thou hast also an excellent firstborn son, who has the name Isaac in common with me. May the Lord bless his strength.

And I pray the Lord that He may bless thee, and accept thy prayer graciously that thou mayest be able to exercise thy occupation. My heart is glad to dwell in thy house.

[Isaac ben Judah Abrabanel]

[*Postscript*]

Have the goodness to let me know whether this Pope is well disposed towards us, whether there are with him or in the country of Rome Jewish doctors, and whether the Cardinals have doctors.[4]

2. *Isaac Abrabanel invites Saul Hakohen Ashkenazi of Candia to join him in his studies*

When Don Isaac Abrabanel wrote these lines in Lisbon he little dreamt that, twenty years later, he himself would go as a fugitive to Italy. After Alphonso's death a false accusation by King John II forced him to leave Portugal in great haste and to seek refuge in Castile, where Ferdinand and Isabella made him their minister – a remarkable testimony to his gifts and character. When the expulsion decree was issued in 1492 he flatly rejected the offer made to him by the king and queen to stay at his post, preferring to share the plight of his brethren. He settled first in Naples and finally in Venice, where the Senate made use of his financial and diplomatic abilities. A commercial treaty between Portugal and Venice was mainly his work.

In these last years of his life he also composed the most important of his Hebrew works, and conducted an extensive correspondence with Jewish scholars and laymen in almost every part of the Diaspora. One of these correspondents was Rabbi Saul Hakohen Ashkenazi, a distinguished young scholar and philosopher of German origin, then residing in Candia (Crete), who was an ardent follower of Maimonides. In a lengthy letter he asked Abrabanel to answer twelve philosophical questions concerning 'The Guide of the Perplexed'. Abrabanel, then in his seventieth year, not only gave an exhaustive reply but also touched upon his personal life and even appealed to Saul Hakohen to come to Venice in order that both of them together might devote themselves to the study of the 'Guide'. It is this highly emotional part of the letter, reminding one of Moses ben Maimon's relation to Aknin, which follows here.

ISAAC ABRABANEL TO SAUL HAKOHEN ASHKENAZI

'You and I would then in God's name study this book from beginning to end as I should love to do'

[Venice, 1507]

. . . I am now advanced in years, my hands are heavy from old age and the light of my eyes is not with me; my secretary who was with me has gone to Palestine. There is no one to assist me and as a result this reply to you is written [poorly] in Ashkenazic script, to which I am not accustomed. . . .

Would that you were like a brother to me! Become my companion! If you would know my method in the interpretation of this profound book—for it is different from the method of other authorities—I would lead and bring you into the innermost compartments. I would give you drink of the spiced wine of Maimonides' intellect. I would hear you as a father his son. Perhaps you would have done more wisely had you come to me here. You and I would then in God's name study this book from beginning to end as I should love to do. . . . Who is the man who in his youth will not set out on a journey to a distant land for two or three years to engage in business to profit financially? Why will you then be like a horrified or helpless warrior? Behold, this rare wisdom is better merchandise than gold. It is a fact that recently I have planned to interpret this book because of its comparative lack of commentators. The vicissitudes of these days have, however, discouraged me. I would not do it alone. Also my commentary on Scripture and other writings on which I have worked have not given me leisure. . . .

All these commentaries and works I wrote after I had left my country. Before that, all the time that I was in the courts and palaces of the kings, engaged in their service, I had no leisure for study and looked at no book, but spent my days in vanity, and my years in trouble in getting riches and honour; and now those very riches have perished, by evil adventure, and the glory is departed from Israel. It was only after I had become a fugitive, and a wanderer on the earth, from one kingdom to another, and without money, that I sought out the Book of the Lord, according to the words of him who says in the Talmud: 'He is sadly in want, and therefore he studies.'[5]

. . . I confess my guilt that in the vanity of my youth I spent much time on the natural sciences and on philosophy. Now, however, that I have become an old man and am much afflicted, I say to myself, why devote so much attention to Greek literature and other such matters foreign to me. Therefore I have limited myself to the contemplation of the 'Guide of the Perplexed' and to the exposition of the Bible. These are the sources of all knowledge and in their wisdom all doubts and perplexities are dissolved. . . .

The letter to Saul Hakohen was Abrabanel's last work – a worthy postscript to his celebrated commentaries, his philosophical and Messianic treatises. When he died in Venice in the year 1508 the last great figure of the Spanish epoch sank into the grave. But his son Judah, known as Leo Hebraeus, the author of the immortal 'Dialoghi di Amore', was about to add to the name Abrabanel new fame and the splendour of the Italian Renaissance.

NOTES

1. Lam. II. 15
1a David Kimhi (d. 1235), famous grammarian and commentator.
2. 'The Crown of the Aged'; it deals with the problem of Divine Providence.
3. The commentary on Deuteronomy was completed only after the Expulsion, during Abrabanel's stay on the isle of Corfu.
4. I.e. presumably Jewish.
5. The words quoted by Abrabanel are those of a formula which frequently occurs in the Talmud and means properly: 'There is something missing [in a certain statement] and it should read thus.' This is ingeniously twisted by Abrabanel into the meaning given above.